The Funniest One in the Room

The Lives and Legends of Del Close

Kim "Howard" Johnson

CHICAGO
REVIEW
PRESS

Library of Congress Cataloging-in-Publication Data

Johnson, Kim, 1955–
    The funniest one in the room : the lives and legends of Del Close /
Kim "Howard" Johnson.
        p.   cm.
    Includes bibliographical references and index.
    ISBN 978-1-55652-712-8
    1. Close, Del, 1934–   2. Actors—United States—Biography.
I. Title.

    PN2287.C5465J64   2008
    792.02′8092—dc22
    [B]   2007044605

Interior design: Pamela Juárez

© 2008 by Kim "Howard" Johnson
All rights reserved
First edition
Published by Chicago Review Press, Incorporated
814 North Franklin Street
Chicago, Illinois 60610
ISBN 978-1-55652-712-8
Printed in the United States of America
5 4 3 2 1

Contents

Introduction

"**H**ey, you know who's coming to my party? Del Close!"

Every December, my friend Mike Gold hosted a Saturnalia party at his Evanston, Illinois, home, and always invited an eclectic mixture of friends to celebrate the holiday season.

I had always been a comedy aficionado, and in 1983, I moved to Chicago to study improvisation at the Second City. After two levels of training with Don DePollo, I didn't know where else to study. "Del Close is the best," DePollo told me. "If you ever have a chance to work with Del, take it."

Del had achieved his greatest notoriety in recent years for directing the Second City, "discovering" many of the improvisers who had blazed into stardom on *Saturday Night Live* and *SCTV.* He sounded like the best person to teach post–Second City improvisation, and the party would be an opportunity to meet him informally.

The night of the Saturnalia party was a typical mid-December night in Chicagoland—cold, but without the subzero brutality that usually arrives in January and February. Mike had recently founded an independent comics company, so I spent much of the night talking with several comic book writers and artists.

Eventually, a tall, middle-aged man and a younger woman with long, dark hair made their entrance without making an entrance. By now, the guests were all visiting in smaller groups, but each one was aware that someone of importance had arrived.

A consummate actor, he commanded attention from the other guests, if only for a few moments. His deep, commanding voice resonated, and he seemed to dominate the entire apartment just by entering. It was difficult not to be captivated, even transfixed, and I continued watching him from the corner of my eye as the individual conversations resumed. At first glance, he could almost have been mistaken for a homeless person. He was dressed in a flannel shirt and dark trousers, which apparently had not been laundered recently. His dark hair, with only a few hints of gray, was unkempt and stringy. His black horn-rimmed glasses were apparently held together with adhesive tape. But it only took one look into his eyes to see the intelligence, the charisma, the energy behind them. He had lived hard, faced his demons head-on, and was still standing. He had plenty to teach those who could gain his trust.

Mike led him to a few groups of guests. He sounded warm, gregarious, pleased to meet everyone. Finally, Mike led him to me.

"Howard, this is Del Close," said Mike, and we shook hands. "And this is his partner, Charna Halpern."

"Are you a comic book writer?" asked Del.

"Actually, I do most of my writing for *Starlog* magazine," I explained, and when he looked impressed, I added, "I occasionally write a little for *Fangoria* as well."

"*Starlog*? *Fangoria*!" said Del, seizing on what was a relatively small aspect of my freelancing career. Turning to Halpern, he exclaimed, "He writes for *Fangoria* magazine!"

"I've been taking classes at Second City," I offered, "And Don DePollo says you're the best improvisation teacher anywhere."

Del beamed, obviously pleased. "Don DePollo. I used to direct him at Second City with George Wendt and Tim Kazurinsky and Jim Belushi . . ."

Halpern stepped forward. "You should come take classes with Del," she said. "He works with me at the ImprovOlympic."

I had expected a more rigorous audition process, but whether it was mentioning Don DePollo or *Fangoria*, I wasn't complaining.

"We're starting a new session the first Monday in January at Crosscurrents," she said eagerly.

"I'll be there," I promised.

Before my first class, I was determined to learn more about Del Close.

◈

It didn't take long to start collecting Del stories. The picture that began to emerge was confusing and sometimes contradictory, occasionally unflattering yet larger than life in a way that transcended show business hyperbole. If he was not quite a cultural touchstone, he had a finger—or possibly a hand—in much of the great comedy of the latter half of the twentieth century.

Many have called Del Close the most important comedy figure of the last fifty years whom you've never heard of. Just a partial roll call of the talent he either worked with or directed is like a who's who of American comedy: Elaine May, Mike Nichols, Shelley Berman, Joan Rivers, Barbara Harris, Jack Burns, Avery Schreiber, Fred Willard, Peter Boyle, Brian Doyle-Murray, Joe Flaherty, Harold Ramis, John Belushi, John Candy, Bill Murray, Betty Thomas, Dan Aykroyd, Eugene Levy, Gilda Radner, George Wendt, Jim Belushi, Tim Kazurinsky, Mike Myers, Andy Dick, Bonnie Hunt, Chris Farley, Tim Meadows, Joel Murray, Bob Odenkirk, Dave Koechner, Jon Favreau, Vince Vaughn, Rachel Dratch, Tina Fey, Amy Poehler, Stephen Colbert . . . and those are only a few of the ImprovOlympic and Second City–related names.

That alone would be enough to ensure his inclusion in any comedy hall of fame worthy of the name. But his other accomplishments are equally amazing. He was a circus fire-eater billed as Azrad the Incombustible Persian, a confidant of maverick comic legend Lenny Bruce, a stand-up comic of some renown with hit comedy record albums, and a counterculture icon whose prodigious substance abuse was remarkable even among his like-minded peers.

But his true legacy is not in the comedy performers he midwifed, nor in the whispered legends of excess. In fact, Del Close led the movement to revitalize and reinvent improvisation, making it more than a method for developing short sketches, and developing what he would eventually call the Theater of the Heart.

And that is why so many friends and former students flew from across the country to attend his birthday party as he lay dying in a Chicago hospital; why the Goodman Theatre was happy to accept when he willed them his skull; and the reason that there is a Del Close Theater at the ImprovOlympic, where his ashes are perched high on a shelf "where they can affect" his life's work.

The loyalty and cultish devotion he inspires, years after his death, even from those who never knew or worked with the man, only continues to grow.

Yet Del Close, who was so devoted to truth in comedy, was the first to promote legends in the story of his own life, even as the facts were uncovered. His own relationship with the truth was complicated, and he often felt that the only way to tell the truth was with a lie. And as John Ford taught us: when the legend becomes fact, print the legend. So with a view to painting the most complete portrait of the man, the pages ahead are filled with both legend and truth. I leave it to you, the reader, to decide which is stranger.

1

Manhattan, Kansas: Setting the Stage

"I knew there was a great darkness at the heart of America. My hometown of Manhattan, Kansas, was nine miles from the geographical center of the United States. The CENTER—the heart— was in Fort Riley, Kansas—a military base. I always found that ominous."[1]

Del Close arrived in this world six minutes past midnight on March 9, 1934. The night was cold, but it was warm inside Park View Hospital, which overlooked City Park in Manhattan, Kansas, population ten thousand.

Manhattan had been founded seventy-nine years earlier, in the rich agricultural valley where the Blue River and the Kansas River meet and flow eastward into the Missouri River at Kansas City. Ringed by the rolling Flint Hills, the area was often referred to as the Kaw Valley, "Kaw" being a nickname for the Kansas River, named after the Kansas Indians. The residents soon helped to establish the college known in 1934 as Kansas State College of Agricultural and Applied Science (now Kansas State University). Several miles west of Manhattan was Fort Riley, established before Kansas became a territory to protect travelers and settlers from Indians.

1

Del's father, Del Close Sr., was born in Belleville, Kansas, on October 6, 1900, one of four children. After attending Bradley University in Peoria, Illinois, Del Senior lived briefly in Abilene and Salina before moving to Manhattan in 1927, where he found work in a jewelry store. Two years later, he established Del Close Jewelers, located in the 100 block of South Fourth Street in Manhattan. Del Senior's strong work ethic was fueled by the economic problems of the Great Depression. The pressure to remain competitive was continuous. He preferred to be his own boss, which drove him to spend the long hours at work that he believed were necessary to succeed.

To help his business grow, Del Close Sr. became involved in community activities. He was a president of the local Kiwanis Club, a director of the Manhattan Country Club, and for a time served as chairman of the City Planning Commission. He and his family belonged to the First Presbyterian Church.

Mildred Madeline Etheringten Close was born on December 24, 1898. Two years older than her husband, she stayed home, like so many wives at that time, and the family relied on her husband's income. Unlike many, she seemed to hold performers in some regard long before her son joined their ranks.

Many years later, Del Junior claimed that Mildred had been fond of reciting a carnival spiel promoting an acrobatic act that she had first heard at a fair in Abilene in 1914: "Dainty, determined Demona, daily defying death as she takes her own life in her hands and loops the loop in a hollow ball." Her son would often recite this himself in his later years, and speculated that such imagery may have provided the impetus for his own career. "She was the funny one of the family," he would proclaim.

◇

Manhattan was located 125 miles west of Kansas City, but residents knew what was going on in the world. Manhattan had its own daily newspapers, the *Mercury* and the *Nationalist*, where residents got their local news. The *Topeka Capital* and the *Journal* plus the nationally recognized *Kansas City Star* and the *Times* provided broader windows on the nation and world. The only radio station in Manhattan was KSAC, an educational operation at Kansas State College, but residents of the town could easily hear network radio affiliates from the larger cities.

The Close family home
at 1726 Poyntz, little
changed in 2005.
(AUTHOR'S COLLECTION)

Three theaters presented Hollywood's latest offerings, usually weeks after they were first released.

All of these facets of Manhattan appealed to the Closes. They valued respectability, and they appreciated the value of a college education. By all accounts they were typical of the business-oriented residents in town. They were churchgoing, Republican, middle class—not demonstrative in their affections, but that was not unusual for the era. Del Senior devoted his attention to his business, and it was rare to stop by the Close house and discover him at home.

The Closes remained childless until Mildred was thirty-five. As it was apparently her first and only pregnancy, and her son would remain an only child, there were whispers that he might have been unplanned. Of course, with Del Senior spending so much time at work, away from home, Mildred might have wanted a child to fill the empty space. But such is speculation.

Perhaps the most remarkable thing about young Del's childhood is that it was, to all outward appearances, *un*remarkable. But he felt the paternal neglect early in his childhood, and whether it was caused by business worries, alcohol, a chemical imbalance, or simply his own upbringing, didn't matter. How much Mildred compensated for his father's distance is unclear, but Del Junior always felt close to his mother.

There were signs from a very early age that Del was drawn to performing. It may have been an attempt to gain his father's attention, earn his mother's approval, or simply an effort to get attention from *any-*

Del Close Junior
and Senior, June 1934.
(COURTESY OF CHARNA HALPERN)

one, because he quickly learned that people who performed got noticed. He once claimed that his theatrical career began as a lobster in the "Lobster-Quadrille" from *Alice in Wonderland*. Another oft-told story recalled his performance at four years old as the troll under the bridge in *The Three Billy Goats Gruff*, when he refused to die and instead ate all the billy goats. The guilt troubled him even at that young age; he knew he had violated some unspoken principle. Looking back, he realized it taught him that "sometimes it's more heroic to lose."[2]

While his mother may have contributed to his sense of humor, young Del, like so many comics, may have developed or honed his wit as a defense mechanism, a way of staving off ridicule as a child. He was "a chubby kid, hair sticking up, Coke-bottle-thick glasses, ears sticking up," according to grade-school classmate Ron Young, who referred to him by his childhood nickname, Pickle.

Del himself agreed with that assessment.

I was a fat kid with thick glasses, for a while I wore braces on my legs, and I have a potentially funny name—"Del" is very close to "dill pickle"—and also asthma; whatever skin disease was available I had it aplenty, like dermatitis—which is a wonderful disease; it means "skin disease." I suffered from poison ivy, and they gave me

Mildred Close with her son.
(COURTESY OF CHARNA HALPERN)

anti–poison ivy shots and I was, like, immobilized for a long time, watching for flying saucers out of the corner of my window . . . yeah, so, ah, I had to get funny before they did because it hurt less when I got the laughs.[3]

But there is evidence to contradict his own description. Existing photos of Del as a baby reveal no evidence of excessive weight, aside from slightly chubby cheeks. Even photos of his adolescence show little that could be construed as heavy, and his complexion likewise appears normal. Although he claimed he was once tied to a tree while other boys threw firecrackers at him, such pranks were apparently rare.

Whether his health problems made him feel inferior and a worrying responsibility to his parents is a matter of conjecture. Because he was often sick as a child, and his father was emotionally distant, it would be easy for a child to imagine cause and effect. In adulthood, Del would have no use for children, at least in public. Friends felt it stemmed from his own youth, which taught him that children were burdens.

One day in kindergarten, the children were all required to make a train, but young Del could not find it in himself to finish the assignment. Decades later, when he decided to dedicate a notebook to various writings, he recalled:

I have a bad record, completion-wise, with beginnings in kindergarten. I never finished my train. The guilt, the fear! There was the unfinished train at the back of my cubical wooden locker and I dreaded its discovery by the teacher because you weren't allowed on to the next project—what was it? Boring a hole in a piece of plywood?—until you'd *finished your train*! Why I didn't want to finish it, I don't know. Perhaps after I'd built the engine and a passenger car, the caboose held no mysteries for me. No challenge—no revelation. Just more wood, glue, and screw eyes. But I assure you the degree of paranoia my cheating caused me—I *went on*—without finishing!—was, in its childlike excess, equivalent to that experienced by the Rosenbergs before their arrest. I would be found out, denounced, and *sent back*! And I so wanted to *get on*—and I did. I was never discovered—nobody ever gave it a second thought. But me. To me, this was a horrible lesson to learn—"You don't have to finish stuff!"[4]

There were no penalties for failure to finish what you started. The unfinished toy train was a lesson that would cause problems throughout his life.

The modest, white, two-story Cape Cod–style house, with twin gabled dormers overlooking the street, was situated on a small lot at 1726 Poyntz in a quiet residential neighborhood. It was typical for its time, with an unfinished basement, a living room, sitting room, and kitchen on the first floor, and two bedrooms and a bathroom upstairs.

Though he would come to be considered a loner, Del liked to play games like hide-and-seek with the neighborhood children, and was particularly good at hiding. But his favorite game was army. It was more fun to shoot him than anyone else, and Del always wanted to be the one who got shot. Young recalled, "It would take him twenty minutes to die."

Del and the neighborhood kids used the lilac bushes in the yard outside the Close house as their secret clubhouse, where the nine- and ten-year-old boys would play poker and discuss activities more illicit. At one point, Del and two other boys, James Bascom and Billy Harms, formed a club, and Del learned another way to get his father's attention. The three of them would go to Duckwalls, the local five-and-dime, and pocket small items. Then they would gather under the lilac bushes and show off their ill-gotten gains. But their shoplifting club would not last long. Harms's parents found out and alerted the other parents. The

Del as a toddler.
(COURTESY OF CHARNA HALPERN)

reaction of Del Senior to his son's petty larceny is unrecorded, but the activities of the shoplifting club immediately ceased.

Young Del attended Eugene Field Elementary School, viewed at that time as an elite grade school, attended by the children of doctors, professors, and other professionals. Unlike many of his fellow students, Del never skipped a grade, but he grew up feeling the peer pressure of overachieving classmates.

Del was not interested in team sports, and it was his love of performing that occasionally revealed a competitive streak. He put on a play in the basement of his house, while another unnamed friend put on another play in competition. During the other boy's play, Del heckled him mercilessly, ruining the other play.

The Close family was comfortably middle class, and did not want for material possessions. During World War II, Pickle had an allowance of 25¢ per week, an amount unheard of in the neighborhood. One of the more ostentatious displays of his prosperity was the pile of comic books he had amassed. Classmates like Gary Wilson and Young would visit Pickle to trade comic books. His collection included eclectic titles, with war comics, *Classics Illustrated*, and even some horror titles. The other boys would collect soda pop bottles to buy traditional superhero titles like *Batman*, *Green Lantern*, and *Blackhawk*, but they were always happy to trade with Pickle. He had so many that he would often brazenly trade two or three of his comics for one of theirs.

Del was a voracious reader of all manner of literature. Another friend, David Dary, shared with Del a keen interest in magic, and for a time they checked out all of the magic books in the Manhattan Public Library. One book in particular, John Northern Hilliard's *Greater Magic*, was a favorite; because there was only one copy, the two of them attempted to keep it checked out so that no one else could get it. But Del did not have the patience or discipline to learn the subtleties of coin or playing card manipulation. He was much more interested in shocking illusions like cutting off heads or sawing a woman in half.

The neighborhood children considered Mildred Close nervous and fidgety. When they arrived at Del's house to play, she would be waiting in order to inspect their shoes for mud. Only when assured they wouldn't track anything into the house would she show them down to the basement.

Another impressive show of opulence awaited them downstairs. There on the workbench was the largest chemistry set any of them had ever seen. Young Del's interest in magic waned when he received it, and he focused his attention on the Gilbert Chemistry Set, which opened up and telescoped out, then opened again, until it covered the tabletop. In front of it were chemicals, beakers, flasks, and *two* Bunsen burners. His friends assumed that his parents would buy him anything to keep him out of trouble.

Instead, the chemistry set provided new methods of mischief. One day, when several boys were playing with Del in his basement, he showed them the handle of a hammer missing its head. "So what?" asked the others, unimpressed.

Del immediately grabbed a small packet of potassium permanganate and sulfur made with his chemistry set, and ordered the others to the bare concrete stoop just outside his back door. He put the packet at one end of the stoop, and cautioned the others to step back. Del then ducked and hit the package with another hammer. The resulting explosion convinced the other boys. The head of the hammer was never found.

On occasions when Del was caught and talked back, Mildred literally washed his mouth out with soap. One day, Del was leading Young and Wilson into the house, and the other two boys insisted on taking off their muddy shoes. Del scoffed and insisted they keep their shoes on. "The old biddy won't know—" he began, then looked up to see his mother standing directly in front of him. In one motion, and without looking, he automatically extended his right hand to the kitchen counter; he grabbed a half-used bar of Ivory soap, took a bite out of it, and spit it back into the sink. The other boys and even Mildred couldn't resist laughing at Del's mechanical response.

Summers were for vacations. There was a major trip in summer 1946, which saw the family motor to Yellowstone National Park, Salt Lake City, the Grand Canyon, and even as far as Los Angeles. Young Del utilized his new camera to document the trips.

◈

By junior high school, Del had taken an interest in photography, fabricating a makeshift darkroom. It soon became clear that Del had found a way to combine his photographic hobby with his growing curiosity about girls. He surreptitiously showed some of his studies to classmates; they were nude photos of a female classmate, whom Del had somehow managed to talk into posing for him.

Del now found himself in social situations involving the opposite sex. A number of seventh-grade boys, including Del, had signed up for a social dance class, and Del often found himself partnered with Donna Fearing (then known as Donna Joan Morine). Del stuck with the dancing class (which was not affiliated with the school) but when dance recital time came, all of the boys had dropped out but Del. The couple attended dance parties in basement rec rooms and local halls, with Del's father driving them, and Del sitting next to his father in the front seat. While he was not uncomfortable around girls, he could be a bit shy or self-conscious, noted Fearing. When a local newspaper reporter once asked him what it was like to be the only male among a class of leotard-clad females, Del replied that it was a lot of fun.

They were purely platonic, their relationship largely confined to group dances, although Del and Fearing had similar backgrounds and interests (she was also bright and an only child). Their physical relationship was limited to a lone kiss on the cheek. There was no fight or breakup; Del simply quit asking her out during the eighth grade.

Those who consider him a counterculture icon might be shocked to learn that Del was even a Boy Scout. Del's scrapbook includes photographs of and by a fourteen-year-old Del participating in the 1946 Boy Scouts camporee at Leonardville (about eighteen miles northwest of Manhattan) as a member of Troop 74. The troop met regularly at the Presbyterian church on North Eighth Street, where the Close family

Young Del's parents plied him
with expensive gifts and toys,
including a rather extravagant
bicycle, to keep him occupied.
(COURTESY OF CHARNA HALPERN)

were members. But Del rose no higher than the rank of first class scout, and by the time he entered high school, in the tenth grade, he had lost interest in scouting.

But all was not as idyllic as it might seem. A friend in adulthood once claimed that Del alluded to witnessing alcohol and spousal abuse while growing up: "My old man used to knock my old lady around," he allegedly confessed. The account is unreliable, though if true, it would be illuminating. Del never spoke of it to others, even close friends.

Hindsight would suggest that Del Senior may have struggled with depression, and possibly alcoholism, but both conditions were less understood at that time. Whether a modern perspective would have helped the elder Del's uneasy relationship with his son is speculation, but this darker side of family life was kept carefully hidden in that more repressive age.

Del could always escape from any domestic unpleasantness by reading. Even at a young age, his best friends were books, particularly horror, fantasy, and science fiction. But there was no bookstore in Manhattan at that time, and Tal Streeter recalled that Del used to steal books from St. Paul's Episcopal Church at Sixth and Poyntz.

In addition to his comic books, Del would devour the pulp magazines of the 1930s and '40s. He became pen pals with a boy he met in the pages of *Startling Stories*. Joined by a third boy in 1949, they began publishing their own science fiction poetry magazine, called *The Cataclysm*. Robert E. Briney was the editor, while Del served as assistant editor and publisher, and it ran for eight issues. He even recruited Donna Fearing, his junior high girlfriend, to write some poetry for it. During his junior year of high school, an article in the school newspaper announced that he would coauthor *Fantastic Art*, with half of its eighty pages to present science fiction and fantasy artwork, some original and some reprints, but there is no way to confirm whether it was ever actually published.

In the mid-1940s, the Close household welcomed a distinguished visitor. In later years, Del would often mention that General Dwight D. Eisenhower and his wife Mamie stopped by to visit with their cousin's cousin. (It was not a close relationship, nor were they blood relatives. Eisenhower's first cousin, Florence Musser, was the daughter of his aunt, Hannah Eisenhower Musser; Florence married Albert Ray Etherington, who was a cousin of Mildred Etherington Close.)

Del claimed that they came by for Thanksgiving dinner, but the dates do not support this. Historical records show that Ike was in Manhattan for a family reunion the week of January 6, 1944 (his brother Milton had taken over as president of Kansas State the previous year), and could easily have stopped by the Close household for a visit. Additional records show that the general also returned to Abilene on June 21–22, 1945, as a returning war hero; again, on September 12, 1946, for his mother's funeral; and then on October 27, 1947, for a luncheon to present gifts to a museum. Although he could have stopped by the Close house in Manhattan during any one of these visits, the 1944 date seems likeliest. It was apparently an uneventful visit. Del recalled that he was asked to show Eisenhower his room. The youngster showed him the picture of General Douglas MacArthur tacked to his wall, explaining that MacArthur was his hero, which may have left his celebrated relative less than enthused about the boy's taste.

◇

While Del's best friends were books, his first love was performing. His flirtation with the theater had developed at an early age, but when he was nine years old, he began to understand that theater could have a deeper meaning, a more transformative effect than the thrill of performing.

It was in 1943 that young Del discovered *Hamlet*. It would prove to be a touchstone that would surface during pivotal moments in his life. His introduction came by way of Jack Benny in the 1942 film *To Be or Not to Be*. Benny and Carole Lombard star in the Ernst Lubitsch classic about a troupe of Polish actors embroiled in espionage. Benny's performance of the "To be or not to be?" soliloquy struck a chord in the thoughtful youth. He felt it was the first intelligent question he had ever heard a human being ask himself.

For answers, he turned to his grandfather, who operated a round-house (a tavern serving 3.2 beer) in nearby Abilene. His grandfather realized that the boy was keen to unlock the mysteries of Shakespeare and World War II. In response to his grandson's questioning, he led Del to his glassed-in bookcase and presented him with a leatherbound copy of *Hamlet*. The boy devoured it and began memorizing long passages.

Hamlet would change his life. It confirmed that there was more to life than a mundane existence in a quiet Kansas town. He would often repeat to his classes Freud's assertion that "*Hamlet* was the first modern play, because the main conflict was not external, between characters or with nature. It was internal, within the character of Hamlet." Del identified with the title character and it was his attempts at understanding the play that led him intellectually forward. While still in junior high school, he began attending plays at the high school, and displaying the programs on the wall of his bedroom.

Del had also developed an interest in music. He carried a large bass drum, which he played in the marching band throughout his high school years. His selection of the oversized instrument appealed to a love of performing as much as a love of music. Del began playing in the fourth grade, continued through high school, and even played in Manhattan's Municipal Band. His former band teacher, Laurence Norvell, recalled him as "an excellent student" who played well. Del later claimed that his percussion experience served him well one afternoon in high school, when he was helping to construct scenery and hammering on the floor below band practice. "I had the extreme courtesy to hammer in time to the music," he recalled, and said that the band director, apparently impressed, offered him "a bass drum scholarship to the Kansas State College of Agriculture and Applied Science."[5] Many years later, Norvell could not verify Del's account, and while he couldn't substantiate the idea of a bass drum scholarship, neither could he rule it out.

During his high school days, Del became close friends with Tal Streeter, an accomplished alto saxophonist who began playing in dance bands during junior high school. It was a friendship sparked by music— both of them played in the city band, as it was commonly called—but they only became close through their mutual love of science fiction. During the summer of their sophomore year, Del introduced him to *Dianetics*, the book by then–science fiction author L. Ron Hubbard, and Del led them in experiments on prebirth awareness.

Streeter's family had moved nearby, and so Del and his friend would walk to school together each day and back home in the afternoon. It was a pleasant walk down Poyntz Avenue, under the trees that lined the street, past rows of houses, the sprawling City Park, and several churches, before reaching the high school eight blocks away, where they would find classmates sitting along the low concrete retaining wall at the corner.

On weekends, the social life in Manhattan for young people was centered on Teen Town, held in the Community Building a block north of Del Close Jewelers. Although he would occasionally attend Teen Town, Del's social life had not improved since junior high. Even his closest friends could not recall any of Del's dates or relationships with girls, with one exception. Del had a date with a high school classmate who lived nearby, two blocks off Poyntz. Streeter recalled her as a "vapid dullard" who was in his social science class. That weekend, Streeter was walking past the girl's house about ten or eleven at night and noted that her light was on. He started walking toward it, but when he walked into the yard, someone said, "Shhh! Shhh!" Del came out of the bushes. He had dropped off his date, gone around the block, and came back to peek in her window.

Most classmates simply could not remember Del being in any of their classes—only in after-school activities. People rarely sought him out, and he was content to be a loner most of the time. If the attention that he most wanted was denied him, that same desire for attention and a proclivity toward dark humor also drew other boys to him.

Del enjoyed a good practical joke. The musicians dressed in white shirts and white trousers for the weekly band concerts, which triggered Del's imagination. One week when Del was not playing in the band, he and two other musicians went downtown to a local movie theater after a concert. The other two explained at the ticket window that they were taking a patient from the local mental institution for an evening's outing, and would be sitting down in the front, so if there were any problems, the management knew where they were. The three of them sat in the front row, and for the rest of the film, Del would sporadically jump up, yell, or go into a spastic fit.

◆

One stunt during his teen years has taken on legendary stature in Manhattan.

It was a hot, quiet summer night on July 8, 1951. On the east side of Manhattan, a train was pulling away from the station, leaving its passengers to go their separate ways. Home air-conditioning was uncommon, so many Manhattan residents were sitting on their front porches to catch the breeze.

One of the pedestrians took his time as he walked up the 200 block of Pierre Street at 10:17 P.M. The neighbors paid little attention. It was a familiar scene, one that they witnessed whenever a passenger train pulled into the station.

But this night was different. A black Packard turned the corner, and the young man turned to watch it, staring nervously. Then he resumed walking, faster this time, looking over his shoulder as the vehicle approached. A few neighbors began to take notice.

Finally, the large sedan caught up to the young man and pulled over. A shot rang out, then a second, and the young man screamed, staggered, and fell to the ground. Two of the men quickly climbed out of the car. They dragged him away by his feet, threw the body of Del Close into the back seat, and sped away. The car drove through the Union Pacific rail yards, and headed out of town, going east on U.S. 24 and 40.

That might have been the end of it. The perpetrators might have gone unidentified, but a lone car followed them as they drove along a rural road trying to get back into town via the Kearney Street cutoff. After briefly being stuck in the mud, they returned on U.S. 24 and 40. The sedan headed to a service station near the entrance to the stadium to clean off the vehicle at 10:45 P.M.

But an all-points bulletin had alerted authorities as far away as Topeka. Within moments, the gas station was swarming with flashing red lights and armed policemen, all weapons pointing toward the men in the car. Cars from the Kansas Highway Patrol, the Riley County Sheriff's Department, and Manhattan City Police blocked the exits.

Wisely, all of the young men raised their hands, slowly, keeping them in plain sight as they exited the vehicle, one by one. It was loaded with Manhattan High School students: Gene Allen, Robert Fitzgerald, Larry Evans (a local doctor's son), Carl Englehorn, and George Hoover. And there was Del Close.

"The police came with rifles and shotguns at the ready," Englehorn recalled fifty-five years later. "One of us said, 'Those are big guns to be pointing at us.' The reply was, 'How do you think that poor fellow you shot felt?'"

Sheriff Lee Goode opened the trunk. It was empty. Angry but puzzled, he turned to the young men. "Where's the body!" he demanded. "Where's the body!"

Del raised one hand even higher.

"Here," he said quietly. "I'm the body."

This appeared to anger the sheriff even more.

"What?" he barked. "What did you do with the body!"

"I'm right here," said Del, frightened but polite. "I'm the body."

The bewildered sheriff, who was looking for a *dead* body, refused to believe that no one had actually been shot, and that the young man claiming to be the body actually *was* the body. But that was indeed the case.

The next day the *Manhattan Mercury* ran the story on page 1, column 1, under the headline "Shooting Faked by Six Youths Here Sunday Night; Armed Officers Hunt for the Supposed Victim, Killers After Hoax Scene." The whole thing was exposed as a prank. Gene Allen and the other four in the car had reportedly planned it at the Palace Drug Store, Hoover volunteering his father's telephone company car. When they needed a victim, they approached Del, who was happy to oblige, and played his part with aplomb.

The newspaper reported that the six gave written statements to Chief of Police Clinte Bolte:

They were riding around in the Hoover car looking for something exciting to do. Each admitted that he had been thinking of the scheme for some time. They borrowed a .22 caliber pistol belonging to Hoover's father. They obtained blank shots and a raincoat for props. Close acted as the victim. After practicing the shooting three times they said they rode around town looking for an audience. They spotted several persons sitting on a porch in the 100 block on Pierre. [Actually, the 200 block.] Close got out of the car walking down the street, acting suspicious and looking around pretending to see if someone was following him. The car was driven around the block, and as it came up alongside Close, two blank shots were fired at him. He screamed and fell to the ground.

In fact, the teens were lucky. One wrong move, and the officers would have opened fire, a fact the chief impressed upon them. But they had won the admiration of their friends and schoolmates, who praised their timing and their success in frightening the neighbors.

Ultimately, the teens were given probation, and their names were stricken from the record. The most serious punishment was reserved for Gene Allen, after a pregnant friend of his mother's became so frightened that she went into premature labor.

◆

In the midst of his pranks and his unorthodox approach to dating, the teenaged Del availed himself of the opportunities presented by the high school drama department. His most important mentor may have been Harold Loy, who directed him in his first significant role, in the Manhattan High School production of *Cuckoos on the Hearth*, presented in December 1949. The school newspaper, the *Manhattan Mentor*, noted that the cast had time for pranks: "One day they ganged up on Del Close and handcuffed him. This was all right, except someone by mistake lost the keys."[6]

Del didn't mind this sort of prank. The other students admired his talent, and he had their attention. Handcuffs were not enough to deter his interest in the theater, and he began successfully auditioning for other productions, which led to some noteworthy accomplishments while still in high school.

The first was a summer scholarship for a five-week course in drama and theater at Denver University. Del was chosen from applications received across the country, in part because of the letters of recommendation from Loy and principal Herbert Bishop.

The course, which began June 20, 1950, was clearly a formative event. Not only was he on his own, hundred of miles from Manhattan, but he was also immersed in his newfound love for theater.

The High School Group in Drama presented a pair of one-act plays on July 20. Del had a small role as a villager in *The Red Velvet Goat* but a larger role in *Gammer Gurton's Needle*, which also featured Aneta Corsaut, later known for her role as Helen Crump, Andy Taylor's longtime girlfriend on *The Andy Griffith Show*. A high school speech student from Hutchinson, Kansas, she immediately got Del's attention.

> I immediately fell madly in love with [Corsaut], in a totally inept, wasp, Midwestern way, kind of like puppy-dog, tongue hanging out, not knowing precisely what to do about it, just being completely socially inept and everything else, but there was no denying that I was utterly enthralled with this young lady. I used to go down to Wichita—well, that's where the bus went, then you get a bus from Wichita to Hutchinson, which is about 35 miles further on. That's where I met L. Ron Hubbard, was visiting Aneta.[7]

They remained in contact for a time, and he met up with her again years later in New York.

> She had just gone off to New Jersey to make a film called *The Blob* for some religious film company. They weren't making any money doing religious movies, so they thought they had better make a SF-horror movie. This was Aneta's first movie and Steve McQueen's second. So, my high school sweetie was in the first *Blob*.[8]

Denver gave him a taste of acting as a vocation. When he returned, his classmates wanted to hear about his experiences in Denver, and Del was happy to comply. He knew his friends wanted a good story, so he told Tal Streeter and the others about a performance of Shakespearean scenes that included an excerpt from *Hamlet*. Del explained that they had needed a skull and had decided the best place to get one was a graveyard.

They entered, broke into a crypt, and opened a casket, he told his friends. The skeleton was inside, but it wasn't completely skeletal. His companions were queasy, but they pulled the skull off the body and took it with them. But unfortunately, there was still a little flesh and hair stuck to it. So they pulled an old cauldron onto the porch of the house where they were staying, and began boiling the skull to remove the flesh and hair. It was the three witches: "Double, double, toil and trouble."

Someone saw them and called the police, and they were taken into custody, but somehow they were not charged with grave robbing.

His friends were enthralled by his storytelling, and did not question his veracity. Why should they? This was the dead body in the shooting, who had thrown spastic fits in the movie theater. Grave robbing? Del would do it without a second thought, any sort of high jinks and pranks that were more creative than destructive. "The things that happened to him in Denver were more exaggerated than anything that happened to him to that point," Streeter observed.

Although there is no way to completely disprove the story, if Del had been part of a group of theater students who had broken into a crypt, stolen a skull, boiled it clean, and escaped criminal charges, he would undoubtedly have talked about it the rest of his life. But the idea of a real-life skull in *Hamlet* was one that would stay with him in the years to come.

After Denver, his enthusiasm for the theater was greater than ever. Del was cast in the junior class's play that fall, *The Great Big Doorstep*, and also produced, directed, and starred in a language club production of *The Red Velvet Goat*. More important, Del was cast in a college production of *Macbeth*, the first time a high school student had ever been cast by the Kansas State Players. The *Manhattan Mercury* wrote: "When he expressed his desire to play in a college production, Earl G. Hoover, drama director at the college (and no relation to classmate George Hoover), gave him a chance to try out along with the college students."[9] He was cast as Young Siward, doubling as a murderer. The challenges and prestige of appearing in a college production had lured him away from high school theater while still only a junior.

The *Collegian Drama Critic* enjoyed the production, but noted, "Not quite as convincing were the fencing scenes, despite the coaching of Sgt. Al Nazareno of Fort Riley."[10] One of those scenes featured Del showing off his nascent fencing skills. The teenaged Del had become a fencing enthusiast, thanks to Nazareno, and utilized his abilities during a fencing scene between Young Siward and Macbeth.

Del had a knack for fencing, and became an active member of the Wildcat Fencing Club at Kansas State, coached by Nazareno. Seventy-five fencers entered the city's first annual open fencing tournament, and Del emerged as gold medal winner in the intermediate class.

As the end of his junior year drew near, Del was obviously outgrowing Manhattan High School. But he still had more to accomplish during the spring of 1951.

Among the MHS entries to the District Speech and Drama Festival at Clay County Community High School on March 16 was a one-act play, *Balcony Scene*, staged in competition with plays presented by six other schools. Del was top-billed of the cast of eight, playing "Man." Also in the cast, along with Tal Streeter, was a beautiful young student named Inger Stensland who played "Girl." She would later go on to a brief, successful career in Hollywood after changing her name to Inger Stevens. Most notable, she starred in a number of major Hollywood films, including *Hang 'Em High*, and had the title role in *The Farmer's Daughter*, a short-lived TV series on ABC. (A victim of an unhappy home life, Stevens would end her own life at a tragically young age in 1967.)

The *Manhattan Mercury* noted that while Del was classified as a junior in Manhattan High School, he expected to graduate at the end of summer school and go to Kansas State in the fall.[11] Del was certainly bright enough to advance to college. When IQ tests were administered in the tenth grade, the average score was 100. Del scored 160. Del obviously had no plans to return to high school in the fall of 1951, even if it meant going to summer school to gain admission to the local college. Years later, he wrote:

> My last formal brush with math came in 1951, taking a summer high school course in Advanced Algebra so as to amass enough credits to drop out of high school into college.
>
> I was the only student in the class. We'd been in session only five of the scheduled twelve weeks when the school filled up with Kaw River water to a depth of 6'8" (the high water mark is permanently noted on the green-board in ivory institutional furniture enamel: *6'8"—1951*), which allows us to deduce that it was likely to be at least that deep outside, permitting a P8Y2 Flying Boat to dock in the city park, moored to the jungle gym. My private instructor had more pressing problems to attend to than my college entrance requirements, so, in the interests of being fair, yet duty-bound to be accurate, he gave me a projected final grade based on my work prior to the Great Flood.

Del in the high school band,
before becoming the recipient
of a "bass drum scholarship."
(COURTESY OF CHARNA HALPERN)

This netted me an A for the course and an insight into a type
of statistical sleight-of-hand that came in handy many years later in
New York during a slow season when I found it convenient to pose
as an authority on Marketing Trends on the Eastern Seaboard. I
projected some of the niftiest trends of the business, and so secured
a much better paying job than the one held by a guy who could
actually *solve* the equations that followed page 72, and will remain
forever pristine and mysterious to me. Mathematics! Queen of the
Sciences! 'Tis a pity she's a whore.[12]

It is unclear whether this was connected to his "bass drum scholarship to the Kansas State College of Agriculture and Applied Science."
It was, however, a significant step forward for the young man. Del was
cast in a small role as a jury member in a production of Gilbert and Sullivan's *Trial by Jury*, and in a summer production of *The Silver Whistle*,
a three-act comedy, by the Kansas State Players and directed by Earl G.
Hoover.

The production was scheduled to open on Friday, July 20, but the
Great Kaw River Flood thwarted the plan and disrupted the entire town.
When the threatening waters had receded, Del, who apparently did very
little work for his father, was called to the jewelry store to help pick

precious stones out of the mud that covered the floor; how much of a financial loss his father suffered is not recorded.

As the Kaw River settled back into its banks, young Del Close prepared to enter college a year ahead of schedule. Whether he had the same regrets about leaving high school without graduating that he felt about the unfinished toy train in kindergarten is uncertain. But the same forces that lured him out of high school early would pull him away from college and into performing.

He would later wax nostalgic about the Manhattan, Kansas, of his youth.

> I have a theory about why adolescence is so painful and so laden with nostalgia. It's because you know you're saying goodbye to your childhood day-by-day, and it will never come back. When you're an adult, everything comes back. Friends come back. Girlfriends come back (older and fatter). You do the play again. You return to the city. But an adolescent knows that nothing he's been through will come back. Kindergarten is once. Graduation is once. Each grade is once. Each Boy Scout level is once. When you move up, you leave what's gone before forever. There's no nostalgia like adolescent nostalgia. My last day at the University of Denver program, I took a long walk and looked extra-hard at the buildings, knowing I'd never see them again—and I never have.[13]

But sentiment was not enough to keep young Del in his hometown. He could see more exciting opportunities ahead, more things than were dreamt of in the philosophies of Manhattan, Kansas.

2

Dr. Dracula, Dianetics, and Death

When he began his professional career, Del did not prove terribly discriminating. Despite his love for Shakespeare, he was just as drawn to carnivals and burlesque houses.

Del was a carny, a huckster, a barker, and proud of it. How much is literally true is almost immaterial. He embraced the carnival mindset and used it to begin shaping his own legend. If he wasn't really a carny as a teen, he would make himself one.

In the course of an interview with playwright John Guare, Del claimed that he had played "pit drums in the Folly burlesque theater in Kansas City. I had no desire to do it myself, but I did tear the collars when the comedians bent over and split their pants, and I played the slide whistles when they came sliding on the stage. . . . I was 15, and I liked to look at naked ladies, but I realized that wasn't the kind of comedy that I wanted to do."[1]

Years later, his classmates were skeptical of Del's claim. Kansas City was a lengthy commute from Manhattan in the days before the interstate highway system. In addition, they felt, most fifteen-year-old boys who had seen naked ladies while working in a burlesque theater would have told their friends all about it.

The Folly Theater (originally the Standard) stood at the corner of Twelfth and Central in Kansas City, Missouri, and in its heyday it featured such celebrated vaudeville performers as the Marx Brothers, as well as Humphrey Bogart. By the time of the Second World War, it was a burlesque house featuring striptease artists. (The theater was eventually preserved and restored.)

Classmate Inger Stensland had run away from home and began dancing at the Folly in Kansas City. The local story was that her father had remarried, and her stern stepmother made her complete all the housework before she could go to school. She was late to class several times because of this, and friends knew that this troubled her. She finally left home, even though she had not graduated from high school, and made her way to Kansas City and the Folly. Her father learned where she was and retrieved her. When she returned the next day, she told a friend what had happened, and it became the talk of the high school. She understandably became the center of attention, with a reputation as a nonconformist who rebelled against her oppressive stepmother and professor father.

The incident might have provided Del with the underpinnings of his own story. He rarely made up a tale without at least *some* basis in reality. He was undoubtedly envious of her actions. Del thought of himself as a rebel, but the girl had very clearly demonstrated herself to be that to which Del had only aspired.

He told friends that he had run away from home to join a carnival, Mighty Midwest Midway Shows, where he learned to eat fire and served as a human target for the knife-thrower. (Records are notoriously spotty for such traveling shows, so again, there is no evidence to substantiate the experiences Del recounted.) He claimed that this was where he had developed the fire-eating persona of Azrad the Incombustible Persian to display his talents. (According to Hugh Romney, there was an Azrad before Del, but when he failed to live up to his billing by exploding, Del took over the role and held it throughout his life.) Most of the carnival stories Del told in his later years appear to have stemmed from this relatively brief period.

When I was touring with the carnivals in Kansas—you know, the geek show, the freak show, the ten-and-twenty peep show—I used to work with the armless wonder from Tulsa, Oklahoma, ladies and gentlemen, see her dial a telephone, see her comb her hair, hear her play the high-waiian steel guitar with her feet ladies and gentlemen, and—I never thought it was amusing, I used to think it was kind of horrifying, particularly when she was the knife-thrower's target, and it gave rise to all sorts of bad jokes about how she lost her arms— but you sit down there and talk to her about five minutes, with her smoking a cigarette with her feet, and pretty soon the feet turn into arms, and she can shrug with the feet from the hips.[2]

Del shared several tales of his brief carnival career with John Ostrander, a friend and collaborator on Del's *Wasteland* comic book series. At one place where the carnival settled awhile, they shared the space with a troupe that did stunts with cars. Del described being strapped to the hood of an old car and driven through a brick wall, which was carefully constructed to give way so no one would get hurt. Del learned a very memorable rule during the experience: Even if you *were* hurt, if you broke an ankle or a leg, you jumped up, went *"Ta-da!"* to the audience, and then got off before you collapsed. Never let the rubes see you hurt. It might cause a panic and wreck the show. It was a rule that Del took to heart.

He attributed the end of his carnival career to Whitey the Albino Sword Swallower. Del told Ostrander that Whitey had taught him to swallow swords. Before a performance, he would eat a big helping of mashed potatoes; it weighed down his stomach so that the sword could be pulled down further. The biggest problem was fighting the natural gag reaction. Del claimed that the tip of the sword felt very cold in the pit of his stomach.

Del explained that Whitey was obsessed with proving the performance wasn't a fake. He created a sword of thin fluorescent tube, which he would swallow and then light up, and it would glow from within him. One day the act went wrong and the tube broke, and there was broken glass up and down his esophagus. Nothing could be done, and Del and the other carnies didn't want to take Whitey to the hospital. That was for "townies," the people outside the carnival. The carnies stuck together. They gave Whitey an overdose of morphine, which killed him, and then they buried the body quietly. This, Del claimed, was why he decided to leave the carnival.

◆

Following this less prestigious segment of show business, and equipped with his knowledge of fire-eating, Del was ready for another step up on the show business ladder. At one point, possibly during his junior year of high school, Del took time off from school and went on tour with a traveling midnight show. "I used to be able to take time off 'cause fathers would take their kids out of school on these hunting trips—why can't I, y'know, take two weeks to go be with Dr. Dracula and His Tomb of Terror?" Close explained in a *Chicago* magazine interview. Del would enter to music from Ketèlbey's *In a Persian Market* and, dressed in bulbul trousers, would assist Dr. Dracula's magic and perform his fire-eating act.

> This guy had a midnight show—y'know, at the movie theater, bring your date, squeeze her thigh: "Ahhh! Monsters are loose!" Dr. Dracula had this tattered print of *Bride of Frankenstein*, and afterward he used to swallow a pack of razor blades and then put a torch in his mouth and pull them all out strung on a string.
>
> And he would come down to the footlights and say "A plague of worms will descend upon you," and the lights would go out. And my job was to run out in the theatre throwing cooked spaghetti everywhere. And of course, the reaction to this was like, *Eeeyaagh!* . . . This voice came from the back one time: "You call this entertainment? I just shit my pants!" Yes, sir, I do call that entertainment. I want to squeeze you dry, whether it's of laughter or shit.[3]

He considered it a formative experience, and remarked later, "Everything since then has been a striving for that."

Many years later, former high school classmates were dubious that Del would have been allowed to leave school, and certain that if he had, he would have bragged about his adventures. Others felt that given his father's intense interest in his business and his mother's attitude of "Go someplace else and play," Del could have gone and done anything he liked.

David Dary and Del, along with studying books on magic, also attended shows by the traveling magicians who passed through town. One night, they attended a magic and ghost show at the State Theater. When the theater was dark, the magician's assistant tossed handfuls of cooked spaghetti into the audience, implying that the spaghetti was worms. While the theater was dark, glow-in-the-dark cloth on the end of a fishing pole line flew over the audience. The next day in band, Del could barely suppress his excitement. He raved about the show, expressing his fervent desire to put on such a show. "I believe Del's later claim that he joined Dr. Dracula's Magic Horror Show, where similar things happened, is based on his one-night experience," Dary said. His friend felt that Del had embellished the one-night experience and in time believed he actually had toured with such a show. (Dary recalled that Del once told him in high school that he was learning how to eat fire, though he said he never saw a demonstration.)

It is possible that both accounts were accurate. Del could have learned of the show when it performed in Manhattan, and secured employment around that time or later. Indeed, the facts seem to substantiate the Dr. Dracula story. Although Card Mondor—Dr. Dracula—is deceased, his partner Dick Newton, in a 2005 interview, supported Del's memories.

Although Del used to call it Dr. Dracula's Tomb of Terror, it was actually called Dr. Dracula's Den of Living Nightmares. "Del Close was an assistant on the show for not too long a time," confirmed Newton.

Dr. Dracula's Den of Living Nightmares was part of a genre of traveling shows (generically called "spook shows") that sprang up in the days after World War II. They remained popular throughout the 1950s as a way to add one more show to the bill, and attract teenaged audiences.

The Dr. Dracula show was always performed in movie theaters. The group presented an entire magic show with three people: Mondor, Del (the primary assistant), and Mondor's wife (an attractive 5'11" showgirl who was billed as "6 foot 6 inches of hex appeal"). The program featured such illusions as an arm-chopper that would "cut off" the arm of a volunteer. Another illusion involved a man from the audience who would appear to be transformed into a woman, though he would occasionally be turned into a monster instead (the troupe traveled with a spare monster suit). "Card's wife would get into this cabinet—we used to call it Verga's Bath in Blood," explained Newton. "We'd pull down a blind, and she'd have a robe on. She'd turn a light on, and you'd see her silhouette take her robe off, and she'd take her bra off, and her pants—of course, she had another set underneath that was flesh-colored. And then she would scream, and a light would flash, and as the blind went up, this monster would come out."

During the blackout, the troupe would set off flashbulbs on the front of the stage to temporarily blind the audience. As they recovered, they would see "ghosts" floating overhead, ghosts made of balloons and cheesecloth and manipulated by fishing poles. "Then, the magician would say, 'Now bugs are going to drop on you, and you're going to feel 'em, crawling spiders and things.' Then we'd throw raw beans, and people would feel these things hitting them, and their imaginations were working overtime, because being in the dark was scary. Then we'd say, 'You're going to be visited by hundreds of crawling, slimy worms,'" said Newton. They would cut old cotton string mops, soaked in ice water, into three- or four-inch lengths, and throw them out into the audience. "Spaghetti was used sometimes, too—cooked cold spaghetti, not warm, so it would be slimy—that worked great, too," said Newton. After the blackout that ended the show, the group presented a horror movie.

Because his role as the booker required him to travel ahead of the rest of the company, and because Del was with the show for such a short period, Newton never actually met Del. Mondor apparently hired the youth, who was likely in the right place at the right time. "We didn't recruit people," Newton said. "We had Card and his wife and one assistant. The first assistant was a friend of mine who we had done a double act with in college. You'd just know somebody, because there wasn't a big call—you'd just talk to people."

Neither Mondor nor Newton had any experience with fire-eating; if Del had indeed learned to eat fire while traveling with a carnival, it predated his stint with Dr. Dracula. Newton never went more than a couple of months without seeing the company, so Del was likely not with the show for much longer than a month.

◈

Manhattan High School must have seemed dull to the teenaged Del after life on the road, and undoubtedly fueled his taste for more of the same. After finishing high school at the end of summer 1951, Del began his own unique course of studies. He told a reporter in 1969 that he had been planning to go to the University of Denver after high school, but lost his college money as a result of the flood of 1951: "When the flood came there went my money. I didn't know it then, but it was probably a big break."[4]

If he was implying that his father had lost his college money as a result of losses in the flood, it was a puzzling comment. Earlier that spring, months before the flood, Del had already told the newspaper that he would be attending Kansas State in the fall, and there were no indications at that time that he was even considering the University of Denver.

He accepted the "bass drum scholarship" to Kansas State that fall. Little is known of his freshman year of college. Either Kansas State did not meet his expectations or he was becoming restless, because the following summer, he attended the University of South Dakota. After that, he spent the next semester at the University of Iowa's drama and speech program on a fellowship (he claimed on occasion that his roommate had been a young Gene Wilder, who graduated with a degree in communication and theater in 1955).

After that, he apparently dropped out of college altogether, ready to begin his career as a professional actor. The timeline for the next three years is confusing and contradictory. He may have been driving the family's Model A Ford, complete with rumble seat, that he was given by his parents in the years after World War II. Many years later he wrote that "the most erotic non-sexual stimulus I ever got was when I first drove my Model A Ford Coupe (1931) over 35 mph. Big boner. I recall wondering what *that* was all about!"[5]

❖

Del may have done carnival performing during this time. It was also during this period, possibly 1951, that he met L. Ron Hubbard, ostensibly during a visit to Aneta Corsaut in Hutchinson, Kansas (about one hundred miles from Manhattan). Hubbard was a successful science fiction writer long before establishing Scientology, and Del was a fan. When he learned that the writer was located in Wichita, about forty miles from Hutchinson, Del was determined to meet him.

Del cowrote (with John Ostrander) a fanciful version of the incident many years later for the *Wasteland* comic book series. In the story, titled "Del & Elron," Hubbard helps Del analyze his dreams, in this case a dream supposed to represent birth. Hubbard plies him with cigarettes during the "auditing session," and the two of them fence together. Hubbard asks about his asthma; they discuss Gestalt psychology; and Hubbard whacks Del from behind with his foil, telling him, "Lesson for ya. Somebody hits ya, hit 'em back hard!"[6]

As Del packs to go, Elron says, "Damn A.M.A. Damn I.R.S. I got to get out of Wichita and regroup. If I had any sense, I'd turn this whole thing into a religion and they couldn't touch me!" Del then asks Hubbard to autograph a copy of *Death's Deputy*, which the author offers to buy from him because he doesn't have a copy himself.

The comic book story agrees with the accounts Del would give to friends of his time with Hubbard. In his later years, Del would explain that Hubbard cured his asthma in 1951 at the Wichita Dianetics Foundation; however, Del also said that Hubbard taught him to smoke Kools. He claimed that Hubbard was always complaining about the AMA and the IRS, reiterating his desire to start a religion. His retellings of his experiences with Hubbard remained consistent, and there is little doubt he was being truthful; he would often meet and correspond with science fiction authors throughout his life. The significance of the youthful encounter was not fully realized until many years later, when Hubbard apparently followed his own advice, and his fame grew beyond science fiction fans.

◇

By one account, Del was seventeen when he was doing summer stock in Wisconsin (though he was possibly as old as twenty). He and a friend traveled to Chicago to find an agent. While waiting for work, he ran out of money and accepted an offer to paint hotel rooms in exchange for lodging.

A production of *Volpone* marked his first exposure to many of the talents he would work with in the years to come. The Playwrights Theatre Club, formed by a group of University of Chicago students in 1953, included such future luminaries as Edward Asner, Elaine May, Barbara Harris, Byrne Piven, and eventual Second City cofounder Paul Sills. It was the beginning of a theatrical tradition that would give birth to the Compass Players and the St. Louis Compass, which would lead directly to the Second City.

> I thought "this is pretty sleazy, but this kind of rings a bell somewhere. These strike me as the kind of people I'd like to work with." I went backstage, complimenting the actors on their performances, and they all walked right by me. They wouldn't even tell me who their director was. Finally, I got somebody in the corner who told me they were going to be auditioning soon for a production of *The*

Glass Menagerie. But before that, my agent came up with something
in North Carolina. . . . So I missed my first chance to get involved
with Paul Sills.[7]

Del left Chicago to tour North Carolina and the South for nine
months, at least part of that time working with western star Lash Larue.
The experience was turned into another autobiographical story in
Wasteland, "Under the Lash." Larue had been a favorite of his, starring
in westerns shown at the State Theater; Larue had a rebel image, and
unlike other cowboy stars, used a whip instead of a gun. Del appreciated
this aspect of the character. Larue was traveling with a carnival at the

Del's retelling of his encounter with L. Ron Hubbard. (ARTWORK BY DAVID LLOYD. FROM *WASTELAND* #9 © 1988 DC COMICS. ALL RIGHTS RESERVED. USED WITH PERMISSION)

time. (Del later told Ed Greenberg that his stint with the western star was his first experience with a carnival, contradicting other accounts.)

In the *Wasteland* story, Del was emcee for Lash Larue in 1954 in North Carolina. Del would introduce the star of the show, and an off-stage whip would extinguish his cigarette, to great applause, before Lash himself finally appeared. In the *Wasteland* story, on the third attempt, the whip slices the tip of Del's nose, which results in a round of jeers from the audience. Afterward, Lash fires his young emcee for making him look bad. "Damn Lash, anyway! For him I had to learn to smoke!" says the young Del, walking away. (Whether it was Hubbard or Larue who actually taught him to smoke, it was soon rare to see Del without a cigarette in arm's reach.) At the conclusion of the Lash Larue tale, Del climbs on a New York–bound bus, deciding he is ready for anything the Big City can throw at him.[8]

Indeed, when his tour ended, he went to New York, achieving some success in children's theater and working off-Broadway, claiming that he "was very precocious and was able to get every role I ever auditioned for."[9] He was highly dismissive of Lee Strasberg and the Actors Studio, which was all the rage in New York at that time. With three years as a working actor behind him, the twenty-year-old Close was doing well enough on his own.

After establishing himself on the fringes of the New York theater scene, he began drumming again. He took percussion lessons; one of the other five students in his class was Strasberg student James Dean, just before his sudden rise to stardom. While no record exists of his drumming skills, Del later claimed that he had been selected to fill in for John Cage's ailing percussionist for a concert at Julliard.

His acting abilities were being noted as well during this time. According to Janet Coleman, author of *The Compass*, Del "played Lucky in a reading of an obscure translation of an unproduced play by Samuel Beckett called *Waiting for Goodie*," which was presented in the loft apartment of Jasper Johns, an artist Del knew from the University of Iowa.

Despite his wide performing experience, however, Del was not yet a member of Actors' Equity, and took on other opportunities. He signed a contract to perform in Bermuda as a human torch, and then did what he referred to as a "spectacular" audition and won an offer of an Equity contract for the Barter Theatre in Abingdon, Virginia. "I called [my agent] and said 'What's this human torch?' And he said 'No problem. You just set your head on fire and jump into the water.'"[10] Apparently, he was torn between the two opportunities, until he began performing the torch act, which he described as "a high dive into a burning tank. . . . I only did it three times; the wind kept shifting."[11]

Del was on track with a promising acting career at last, with a job offer from the respected Barter Theatre. He had the opportunity to do what he loved. For Del, life was finally working out. Then tragedy struck.

◇

Del Close Senior.
(COURTESY OF CHARNA HALPERN)

Del Close Sr. died in Manhattan, Kansas, on December 16, 1954. His death was ruled a suicide.

People who knew Del in his later years would inevitably hear him relate the details of his father's death. It was a dramatic story, and Del told it in a way to ensure maximum impact from listeners.

He was ten years old, he would claim, when his father called him into his office. "Hand me that glass," he ordered young Del. His son obeyed, and Del Senior took a long drink of the clear liquid. When he began to react, his son realized that he had handed him a glass of Drāno. He was sent to the hospital and died a slow, agonizing death.

But there were differing versions. Details would change. Sometimes his father called him into the kitchen and asked his son to watch as he drank what his son assumed was a glass of water but turned out to be battery acid. It was unsettling to hear Del change the details of such a traumatic incident, details that surely must have been burned into his memory, but the gist of it remained the same: his father drank a powerful acid in front of his son, and died a few days later at a local hospital. No one ever seems to have questioned him about the discrepancies in the story. This was the version Del wanted to present, in public and in private.

The truth of the matter is somewhat different, however, at least in regard to Del's involvement. A page-one story in the December 16, 1954, *Manhattan Mercury* reported that Del Senior had been found unconscious in his jewelry store the previous day, and died twenty-four hours later, at 11 A.M., in the local hospital of "self-inflicted" causes. (Another variation of his son's story, which sounds plausible, is that his father died from drinking cyanide, or prussic acid, which was commonly used to clean jewelry.) The local newspaper reported that his son had been living in New York, but traveled back to Kansas to his father's bedside, arriving shortly before he died.

Those are the details, according to local journalists at that time, and there is no reason to dispute them. The reason for his father's suicide may never be known. Alcohol and depression might have played a role, but were there other factors?

The newspaper reported that at the time of his death, Del Senior had been planning to move his jewelry store to a new location, around the corner on Poyntz. This could have made it less likely that he would have killed himself, or, if he had run into financial difficulties as a result, might have contributed to it. There were also rumors of financial losses as a result of the flood of 1951, but the three-year time lapse makes that seem unlikely.

One widely accepted local theory suggests that pride led him to take his own life. Del Senior was considered an expert on diamonds, emeralds, and other gems, but he sold a rare gem under the mistaken impression that it was genuine. A week before his suicide, the gem was revealed to be a fake, and even though he provided a full refund, he was ashamed that he had sold it in the first place without realizing it was a phony.

The theory was accepted by many townspeople, though there was no way to prove it. If true, it does not explain why he waited a week before killing himself.

If his son ever learned the reason, he never said. Del's relationship with his cold, distant father had never been easy. If some of Del's more outrageous actions as a teenager were intended to provoke a response from his father, it was not often enough to make a difference. And by the time his father died, Del had done his best to stop caring.

"He loved his mother dearly. He wanted to love his father dearly. Other than wanting to love his father, I don't believe he had any regrets about his father's death. But of course, it was his father, and that's about all I would care to say," said Hammond Guthrie, who became friends with Del in the 1960s. "That's what he said to me. There isn't as much mystery to it as some people would like to read in, but it isn't quite as simple as a lot of other people would say, either."

It certainly wasn't the sort of thing discussed in 1950s Kansas, not even with close friends. Tal Streeter recalled talking with Del about it later. His only comment: "You'd expect stuff like that to happen in New York City, not in Manhattan."

There obviously remained issues that Del could never resolve, even with professional help. Why did he invent a story that placed him at his father's side, and even had him contributing to his death by handing him the acid? It may have been a way to wield some control over a deeply personal matter in which he actually had no direct involvement. When the father drank the poison, the son was robbed of any chance of a closer relationship.

It may have been the combination of sorrow, anger, and guilt—sorrow that, despite their distance, he had lost his father; anger that his father had cheated them of a better future together; and guilt that he had somehow contributed to it, even if it was as innocent as periods of illness as a youth.

Like the father of the youthful hero of *Hamlet*, Del's father was dead. But while the Prince of Denmark could seek vengeance on his father's killer, Del was robbed of that satisfaction. His father was his own murderer. How could he avenge his father's death? The answer was right in front of him.

To be, or not to be? His father had answered that question for him.

And so, consciously or not, he would embark on a path to self-destruction, a long, slow suicide. But as it led him down a dark path, he saw another way, seemingly contradictory, the one that would ultimately save him.

When asked about his mother and his sense of humor many years later, Del described her as "a very, very funny woman, unlike my father, who was a coward and killed himself. . . . He drank a quart of sulphuric acid and the fucking monotheists kept him alive for three days. That's two days longer than Christ hung on the cross. He was in a Catholic hospital. [Likely St. Mary's Hospital, a block south of Park View Hospital.] They wouldn't kill him, the swine. With a background like that, you automatically get funny, if you have any brains."[12]

Young Del obviously had the brains. And now, he was ready to get funny.

3

On the Road with the Barter Theatre

The Barter Theatre was a significant achievement for twenty-year-old Del Close. It was a steady job that let him hone his acting skills and obtain his Actors' Equity card. And it was there that he met Severn Darden, who would become one of his closest friends.

The Barter Theatre first opened its doors on June 10, 1933, providing relief and diversions for Depression-era audiences. It was founded by Robert Porterfield, a young actor who suggested that audiences barter homegrown produce for admission. Its motto was "With vegetables you cannot sell, you can buy a good laugh." Crowds were receptive to the idea of "ham for *Hamlet*," and an estimated 80 percent of the audiences paid with fruits, vegetables, livestock, or dairy products. The Barter Theatre toured as far away as Kansas, where Del saw a Barter production of *The Chocolate Soldier* at Manhattan High School.

Del's most colorful stories about the Barter involved life on the road, and became the only two-part autobiographical story in *Wasteland*. "On the Road, or . . . How We Changed the Price of Whiskey at the Butterfly Mine #2 in West Virginia" provides a surprisingly atmospheric re-creation of life on the road for the young theater company. Back in 1955, Del explains, they were "doing a bus and truck tour of West Virginia mining towns of *Dial M for Murder*, *Sabrina Fair*, and *Julius Caesar*, nine guys, two gals, and a gay stage manager." As they perform in front of the rustic crowd, the ingénue actress asks Del if the audience is hissing at them, but Del assures her that it's just the sound of the old geezers spitting tobacco juice on the potbellied stove. Afterward, the locals indicate that they liked the show, but didn't laugh because the performers talked too fast. Del loads a crate of Roman candles onto the bus, and they are off again.[1]

The details are finely drawn. On the bus, one of the actors tells the ingénue, "Diane you've got to stop using that airplane glue to keep your ears back. You came unstuck in the second act tonight. I thought you were going to take off." Del adds, "Besides, it makes the back of your ears real gross, Diane."

Arriving in the next town, he writes, "In one town we played, it looked like all the kids had been interbred from three adults. In other places, they had their heads shaved and wore old nylons to battle ringworm. We came to bring them sophisticated New York entertainment."

In the town of Butterfly #2, West Virginia (where, Del is told, their football team is nicknamed the Crushers), "The miners turned out for us. Many came straight from their shift, embedded with the coal dust they could never completely wash away. With their wives and their children and their hog's legs on their hips, they came to watch Shakespeare and get cultured."

During the evening's performance of *Julius Caesar*, Del, as Brutus, vows to kill Caesar, and an angry miner takes a shot at him. Del tosses a knife through the miner's shoulder. After the local sheriff rules it self-defense, the group is paid in company scrip, which can only be exchanged the next morning at the company store. The actors decide to get drunk, but avoid one place where a sign reads "No Niggers or Show People" ("Redundant. Actors are niggers," quips Del).

The bus is stopped by an angry mob led by the bandaged miner. Noting that "Bill, the actor who doubled as a driver, was the only other one on the tour besides myself who'd been a carny at one time," they send him out to distract the crowd long enough for them to attack with Roman candles. Though it drives the locals away, the troupe is locked up overnight because fireworks are illegal.

In the morning, the actors are released and, forced to spend the scrip at the company store, they buy up the town's supply of whiskey. As they head out of town once again, the sheriff stops them, and offers to buy back their whiskey, because the price has gone sky-high back in town. "Hell, yes, Sheriff! We're all dope fiends anyway!" quips Del. As the bus rolls out of town, each member of the company has made an extra $20, and they still have a few bottles of whiskey left.

The romantic appeal of a traveling troupe of actors in simpler times is evident, and overall, it is consistent with the stories of the Barter that Del told throughout the years.

The only element missing from the story was Severn Darden. Francis Xavier Severn Teakel Darden Jr. was a gentleman of the Old South; his father was district attorney of New Orleans. Del and Darden were "entirely, utterly different sorts of personalities, a New Orleans aristocrat and this 20-year-old hayseed just in from Bermuda, all scorched. So he said 'What's your favorite novel?' And I said '*Titus Groane* by Mervyn Peake.' 'How strange, that's my favorite novel, too.'"[2]

A founding member of the Compass Players and the Second City, and a well-known eccentric, Darden drove a 1926 Rolls-Royce Phantom II, would often wear a cape, and had picked up the habit of chewing on a handkerchief or other piece of cloth. Jeffrey Sweet's *Something Wonderful Right Away* and Sheldon Patinkin's *The Second City* both recount the story of Darden sneaking into Rockefeller Chapel at the University of Chicago to play the organ; when campus police came after him, he threw himself across the spot where the altar would have been and cried, "Sanctuary! Sanctuary!" He then ran across the street and hid in the girls' dormitory.

If Del had not met Severn Darden, there would likely have been no Compass Players for him, no Second City, perhaps even no improvisation. It was through Darden that Del became acquainted with the Compass Players. After acting with the Barter in 1955, Darden drove to New York, where David Shepherd was recruiting people for the fledgling Compass Players. Darden was hired, along with Mike Nichols, and the two of them joined the company in Chicago at the same time.

In the interim, Del was touring with the Barter. After his first season, Del traveled to New Orleans during a hiatus to eat fire in a small club. At Darden's urging, Del took a small, twin-engine plane to Chicago one weekend, where he auditioned for the Compass Players at the Argo Off-Beat Room. He improvised a seduction scene with Elaine May (apparently their first meeting), and ate fire for the polite but somewhat bewildered group.

The audition may have marked his first attempt at improvising. Del was to play a businessman with a flight to catch, and had a limited amount of time to bed a girl before he had to leave. Del claimed that the more experienced Elaine May apparently took a liking to him—or at least sympathized—enough to help guide him through the scene.

"I really didn't know what to do up there, but Elaine brought me through the scene and made me look good. I guess I kind of charmed them. I mean, here was this extremely high intelligence and very high reference level, combined with absolute fucking naivete—Kansas innocence right off the farm."[3]

Although he charmed them enough to obtain a job offer, Del had not realized that he was contractually bound to the Barter Theatre for a second season, and had to decline. He returned to the Barter, where, coincidentally enough, he would obtain his first experience improvising in front of an audience.

> The first actual "improvisation" I took part in was in the style of the commedia dell'arte—a short scenario by Flaminio Scala. Severn played Il Dottore, Jerry Hardin was Pantalone, and I was cast as Arlecchino. When the moment came to begin work on the piece, we looked at each other blankly. "Well, what do we do?" We improvised.
>
> Months later, when a show that included the commedia bit played New York, Theodore J. Flicker, who was casting for the St. Louis version of the Compass theatre, saw it and hired Hardin and myself. (Hardin later dropped out.) Primarily because we improvised in a style obviously not "method." (He'd never seen anyone improvise before, it turned out, or he might not have been so enthusiastic.) Flicker, two young ladies, equally inexperienced, named Nancy Ponder and Jo Henderson, and I were the company. To aid us, we had a page-and-a-half of notes and scene synopses from David Shepherd from the Compass theatre in Chicago—the first "new style" improvisational theatre in America, then recently defunct after two years.
>
> We opened, powered by Flicker's energy and nerve alone. *We did not know what we were doing.* After a few weeks of doing what I didn't know how to, and not very well, at that, I became hysterical, and, with the assistance of Norbert Weiner's *Cybernetics* and an IBM pamphlet on "Game Theory," began to develop a *theory.* (Flicker's strategy: "Let's just keep trying—one of these days it'll work!")

Later, Mike Nichols and Elaine May joined the company, and Theodore went to New York to find backing for a theatre there— somehow we had become successful—and Mike, Elaine, Nancy and I conducted some experimental sessions in which we tried to figure out why what worked, worked, and why what didn't work, didn't. The first workshops. This was in 1956–7.[4]

This was how Del described his introduction to improvisation in typewritten pages kept with his notebooks, scrapbooks, and other writings, probably from around 1980. The extract reveals a concise version of the events in the mid-1950s that is mostly factual.

It was during Del's second season with the Barter Theatre that it put together a presentation for a library theater festival, with little in the way of scenery and costumes. It would include excerpts, from *Antigone* to *Death of a Salesman*, and a commedia dell'arte scenario, which would mean a certain amount of improvisation.

We're going to have to go out and fill this . . . how do you improvise, what is the very first thing you have to do? So I was standing up there, worse than standing up on the fire-dive thing; we were all out there in this barn and *somebody has to say the first thing.* God! I think I said it; I'm not sure. And there began a process that has never stopped.[5]

◆

Mitchell Ryan (in recent years best identified with his role in *Dharma and Greg*) joined the Barter in 1956, just in time to perform *Nine by Six*, as the "history of theater" piece was officially titled. The cast of six included Ryan, Jerry Hardin, Richard McKenzie, Marcie Hubert, Annette Hunt, and Del. *Nine by Six* opened at the Barter in mid-1956, and went over extremely well with audiences. There were nine scenes in the piece, including material from the ancient Greeks, Shakespeare, a Restoration comedy, an early American play, Chekhov, Strindberg, and Arthur Miller. "Del was an excellent, excellent actor," recalled Ryan. "He had an extraordinary feeling for language, which was kind of amazing, because he didn't seem to be that kind of an actor when we first met him."

Del was featured in three of the pieces, including the Restoration comedy scene, where he had no problem garnering laughs from the material. He played Brutus to Hardin's Cassius in the lengthy scene from *Julius Caesar* in which Cassius tells Brutus he should be king instead of Caesar. The third scene, the commedia dell'arte piece, would have the farthest-reaching repercussions.

The exact piece performed is unclear (Del recalled it being by Flaminio Scala, while Ryan remembered it as loosely based on Carlo Goldoni's *Servant of Two Masters*). Del and Hardin used slapstick and masks to improvise on the scenario, using local jokes wherever they were, referring to local football teams, even asking for a topic from the audience and then doing a riff on it. "Del was good at doing that," said Ryan. "He blabbered on about any old thing and put six thousand different things into the same stew—it was unbelievable."

As was typical of Barter productions, *Nine by Six* played at Abingdon through the summer and was taken on tour that fall around the Southeast, roaming as far as Texas, Louisiana, and Missouri, traveling a circuit of schools and community theaters. "You would play a lovely little theater one night, and then the next night you'd play in somebody's garage, or a gym," recalled Ryan.

Life on the road for the troupe of actors could occasionally be grueling, but the group was young, and doing what they loved. The six actors traveled on their own bus; the luggage and sets were in the back. Each morning they would drive from one to two hundred miles to the next town. When they arrived, they would put up the set, then go out for dinner before performing the show. Afterward, they would strike the set and load it in the bus. They would then either go to a local motel or drive to the next town if it was nearby. "Every day was like this, the same thing over and over again," said Ryan. "There was a lot of sitting on the bus, a lot of jokes and carrying on like that. You have to be really young to handle all that, but it was fun."

The group occupied themselves during the bus rides. Marcie Hubert tried to grow a flower from a tulip bulb she had buried in a flowerpot kept at the front of the bus. She watered it for months, but nothing ever came up. Frustrated, she dug it up, only to discover that the bulb was missing. Del was the chief suspect.

Incidents like the Butterfly Mine #2 were not uncommon. In one town, the audience brought their own chairs. There was another memorable performance where there was no audience reaction at all. After the show, they were told, "God it was wonderful, we loved it. We could hardly keep from laughing." Audiences that had never seen Restoration comedy or Shakespeare were afraid that laughing would be deemed impolite.

The men in the company were a diverse group, "four very strange, incredibly difficult, different people," recalled Ryan. He characterized himself as a "bon vivant Irish asshole." Dick McKenzie, older than the others, didn't care for Del or Jerry Hardin and often criticized them both, with Del singled out because McKenzie apparently didn't approve of his acting. Hardin had been to RADA (Royal Academy of Dramatic Art), while Del was a mystery, according to Ryan. "I didn't mind him, I would drink beer with him, but I never really struck up a [friend-ship]. We just didn't warm up [to each other]." Del and Hardin were "thick as thieves," but the others didn't share his growing interest in improvisation.

Though Del was unsophisticated, he wasn't completely innocent. "I wouldn't call him naive, but he wasn't hep," said Ryan. "He and I were equally idealistic, wanting to get ahead, wondering how we were going to get there, should we go to New York, and things like that." While there was sometimes marijuana around, any use was highly guarded. Del would occasionally speak of it in hushed tones around Ryan, which led him to think Del might have been smoking pot by that time. There were undoubtedly opportunities for Del to meet young women, but if he dated any girls at the theater, he kept it quiet. When the group went on tour that fall, opportunities were even fewer.

In January 1957, after their fall tour, *Nine by Six* opened at the Open Stage Theatre in New York City, where they played to good reviews but small audiences. A critic in the January 13, 1957, *Chicago Tribune* noted, "Performing without props or scenery of any kind, they manage to move the audience to wild laughter with their performance of 'Punch and Judy' or bring them close to tears with a scene from 'Death of a Salesman.'"[6]

It was during the New York run that Del was hired by Theodore J. Flicker for a new company of Compass Players, to be based in St. Louis.

The exact circumstances remain unclear. Del thought that Flicker had come to see *Nine by Six* one evening, possibly at the instigation of Severn Darden. According to one story, Flicker offered both Del and Hardin jobs with the incipient St. Louis Compass; however, Flicker quickly discovered that he couldn't afford both of them. The offer to Hardin was rescinded, while Del left the Barter. In an interview fifty years later, Flicker simply could not recall the exact circumstances. "I liked Jerry, and Jerry had been doing commedia dell'arte. He was going around with the troupe towing a wagon, just like it was sixteenth-century Italy. It may be I had a choice between him and Del, and I chose Del."

Del felt guilty at leaving his partner (and then-roommate) Hardin high and dry, but he couldn't turn down the Compass again.

Flicker himself said that his first encounter with Del was at a regular audition held at his apartment on Thirty-fourth Street: "There was no question, before the audition was half over, he was on his way to St. Louis with me." It wasn't Del's improvisational skill that sold him on the young actor, but his madness, his intelligence, and his outrageousness: "All the things that we loved about Del were all there when we were kids."

Mary Jo Henderson and Nancy Ponder were selected to round out the cast; both approached improvisation from a more serious theatrical background, and both had studied acting under Uta Hagen. The four of them would meet in Missouri, ready to make improvisational history with the St. Louis Compass Players.

4

Learning the Rules
with the St. Louis Compass

Theodore J. Flicker, Nancy Ponder, Mary Jo Henderson, and Del Close arrived in St. Louis in early March 1957. They moved into rooms in Fred Landesman's mansion and began rehearsing. Landesman, a member of a well-to-do, artistic St. Louis family, had built the Crystal Palace at 3516 Olive Street and allowed Flicker and his group to take over its ninety-seat theater.

The quartet of performers would have to discover their own approach to improvisation. Del had performed brief scenario plays in *Nine by Six*, and Ponder had studied improvisation in an acting class (it is unclear how much experience Henderson had). In addition, the women had never seen the Chicago Compass, while Del had apparently only seen the Compass once, recalling a long, meandering scene between Elaine May and Shelley Berman that had failed to hold his attention.

The original Chicago Compass was created with the purpose of performing scenario plays, explained Janet Coleman, author of *The Compass*.

Frustrated that nobody was writing plays reflecting contemporary life in Chicago, Compass producer and creator David Shepherd turned to the improvisational methods of Viola Spolin and Paul Sills to create plays quickly by improvising from outlines written by members of the company. Borrowing a term from the commedia dell'arte, Shepherd called these outlines scenarios.

Shepherd asked Roger Bowen to pen a scenario for the Compass to serve as a trial balloon, which was called "Enterprise." Its success led to further scenarios by Sills, Bowen, Shepherd, and eventually Elaine May, who proved her mastery of the form with "Georgina's First Date."

"The Game of Hurt" was the first official Compass scenario, written by Sills, by way of *The Mayor of Casterbridge*. These full-length plays allowed the actors to invent their lines. They aspired to a socialist-leaning realism, but because they were improvised, they couldn't help but turn out funny. They featured scenes from the lives of real people— the minister's daughter, the steelworker, the put-upon high school nerd, the used-car dealer—and the emotional and sociopolitical issues that involved them.

The Compass focused on Shepherd's goal of putting up a new scenario play each week, one that would help the audience examine their lives and move them to social action. But practical considerations arose when the owner of the bar in which they were performing noticed that audiences would leave after the hour-long scenario plays ended. He wanted people to linger and order more drinks, so he requested longer performances. They decided to improvise. "That's where improvising based on audience suggestions came in," explained Jeffrey Sweet. "It was designed just to make the show longer so more booze could be sold. But it became the most popular part of the show." The improvised scenes began to displace the scenario plays, and Shepherd's dream of moving audiences to social action was hijacked by those very audiences in favor of improvisation.

Shortly after the Chicago Compass was on its feet, Paul Sills left town with Barbara Harris, leaving David Shepherd, Andrew Duncan, and Roger Bowen to work on the scenario plays. When Sills returned, he was increasingly interested in making the performances more polished, focusing on acting skills rather than improvisation. They began to involve more professional actors, people who weren't just University of Chicago students and scientists, performers who wanted it to be good every night. They didn't want to fail, and so they started perfect-

ing their scenes in repertory. Nichols and May began creating and per-
fecting some of their classic scenes during this period, including those
of Pirandello and Gertrude Stein, scenes that would later make them
famous. The original Compass Players in Chicago were still improvising, but they were also polishing scenes that they had discovered
improvisationally.

The opposite, however, was about to happen with the St. Louis Compass. Ted Flicker saw it as a more daring enterprise, a circus act in which
they would be working without a net every night. Del quickly became
swept up in his enthusiasm, and Flicker was anxious to harness his obvious exuberance, performing talent, and intellect.

It fell to Flicker to figure out what the St. Louis Compass would ultimately be. He did not want it to be like the Chicago Compass. Flicker
was irritated by their appearance. The Chicago performers wore street
clothes and smoked, which he felt impaired the illusion. He also disliked
the lack of respect among the various players, often perpetrated simply
for the sake of a cheap laugh. The worst offender, he felt, was Shelley
Berman. "Severn would come onstage and be one of his winsome characters, one who just tears your heart out," explained Flicker. "He would
hold out his empty cupped hands and say, 'Look at my bunny rabbit.'
And Shelley would form an alliance with the audience to make fun of
Severn because there was no bunny rabbit in his hands. That would
stop Severn from taking that chance again with Shelley." (Darden held
no grudges, and is effusive in his praise of Berman in Sweet's *Something
Wonderful Right Away*.)

When they began rehearsing in St. Louis, the only guidance they
had was the "page and a half of notes from David Shepherd." To achieve
success, they would have to figure it out by themselves.

The actors soon learned to listen to one another, and they looked
for ways to help the others achieve their goals. But being improvisational, the goal was constantly changing. Flicker maintained, "It
required a wealth of good will, of unselfishness, a rare commodity in
the theater."

Upon his arrival in St. Louis, Del had become what Flicker called a
"brilliant, funny, marvelous performer." He was a confident, outgoing
actor in front of the others. But when that became too much, he would
retreat behind a wall, the wall where he kept the private Del.

Del was terrified at the prospect of improvising an entire show with
three other people, and might have left were it not for Flicker's sup-

port and supreme confidence. But Flicker drilled the group repeatedly in games that had become standard at the Compass in Chicago. Taken from Shepherd's list, they included improvised poems and songs, stories told in a variety of improvisational styles, and such exercises as First Line–Last Line, in which audience members suggested the opening and closing lines of dialogue in a scene.

Del's confidence grew as he looked for patterns and connections, trying to reduce the element of risk in performance. Flicker also wanted to make their shows as foolproof as an improvisation-inspired show could be; he knew there must be rules for this fledgling performance style.

Near the end of the month, David Shepherd came down from the Chicago Compass, intending to create a scenario for the new company and then return to Chicago. However, with opening night fast approaching, he soon was caught up in everything from publicity and promotion to building sets. He unenthusiastically fulfilled his commitments, and returned to Chicago. It was at this point, according to Del, that things finally started to work.

◇

This new Compass seemed to have less interest in longer scenes than the original. The St. Louis Compass followed the "louder, faster, funnier" guidelines Flicker suggested and to which the audience responded so enthusiastically. Noted Del: "Ted's approach to improvisation was that of a mental stunt: Give these folks handicaps and watch them think their way out of the predicament. We became the instant darlings of . . . I mean, we *were* the avant-garde."[1]

The Crystal Palace was a home for the hipper crowd in St. Louis in the late 1950s. St. Louis in those days had a decadent streak running through it, and the Crystal Ballroom attracted the nightclub crowd of Old St. Louis, people whose families hadn't worked in three generations and lived grandly, explained Flicker. "It was the '50s, and so there was serious wife-swapping going on. And we were their pets. They just adopted us. They came every night."

While Flicker, just learning to direct, could be overbearing, he brought a discipline to the group that established frameworks and work habits. Del had trouble dealing with adversity and hostility, and Ponder brought "a wonderful fey quality" to the work, according to the director. But the four of them became real creative allies. Flicker had the two women dress in belted men's shirts and tights, while the men wore dark pants and pale yellow shirts unbuttoned at the collar. It was minimal costuming, but Flicker was content.

The opening night of the St. Louis Compass, on April 2, 1957, was apparently a rollicking success. Fred Landesman's brother Jay wrote excitedly about the premiere in his autobiography, *Rebel Without Applause.*

> No one in the audience for the first night of the Compass at the Palace was likely to forget its impact. The stage was dark. Two of the players were planted at a table in the audience. They began to argue, until the audience was hollering for them to shut up. As the couple made their way to the stage, Flicker, a small volatile man with a Mephistopheles beard, hopped onto the stage and shouted, "Freeze!" The lights went up on the performers. "What happens next?" he asked the audience. "You tell us."[2]

Audiences had never seen anything like it. Flicker presented the shows to the audience with the attitude of a magician presenting a mystifying, never-before-seen trick. These were highly skilled, highly trained performers; don't try this at home, he seemed to be telling them.

Del was not bothered by this approach. In fact, the sideshow performer that still lurked not far beneath his surface may have embraced the idea of their performances as carnival acts.

The group would perform for twenty to twenty-five minutes, take suggestions from the audience, then reconvene backstage for five or ten minutes to discuss the suggestions and plan scenes. (Saturday night shows consisted of the best improvised scenes presented during the week.) It was a point of honor for the group to incorporate each and every suggestion when they returned for another set. Flicker planned this improvisation, as opposed to the spot improvisation that was made up in front of audiences.

They would perform an astonishing four to six sets per night, and with that much practice before a live audience, they rapidly improved. The first act became completely improvised. Just before intermission, they asked the audience for news events, and then retreated backstage to invent the scenes that made up the second act. The company eschewed games. The practice of asking audiences for suggestions was for one purpose, Del would often explain: "It was so the audiences would know that we were really making it all up."

The women of the company became dissatisfied with the more superficial scenes and yearned for a little more substance. But Del told Janet Coleman that when Flicker did allow the women to try "a real improv," he saw "the most conflictual situation: two sisters in love with the same guy. It lasted about twenty minutes. It didn't do any of the things they wanted it to do. The situation didn't really lend itself to disagreement. They forced themselves into red-faced emotion. . . . It was a great lesson: that conflict is boring and agreement is less boring and that we were into a new era of improvisation."[3]

For Del, another breakthrough presented itself in the pages of Norbert Weiner's *The Human Use of Human Beings*, which included a portion dealing with John von Neumann's game theory; Del felt von Neumann's work could be the basis for more ambitious improvisation.

Severn Darden was an occasional visitor. Del had talked him into buying a huge motorcycle, a BMW Double Twin Cylinder 650-CC, and Darden apparently ran a stop sign and was struck by a car. His leg was crushed and doctors held it together with a number of pins. While under a variety of painkillers, Darden began sending his friends at the St. Louis Compass a number of long-winded tapes. The cast used to sit at the bar after hours and listen to Darden, gradually losing interest until only Del was left, listening and sipping aperitifs poured from strange, dusty bottles.

The St. Louis Compass became popular very quickly, but was ultimately frustrating for David Shepherd, who visited again about a month into the show. At the end of the performance, he turned to Flicker and said, "You've turned it into entertainment. You've ruined my dream."[4]

But Shepherd's uneasy business relationship with Flicker continued, fueled by the possibility of a New York Compass. It appeared as though Flicker might have to take a few business trips to New York to iron out the details, which would leave at least a temporary opening in the cast that would have to be filled. (Darden, an obvious choice, was still in an enormous leg brace.)

In late May, Mike Nichols and Elaine May arrived in St. Louis for a visit, and Nichols, May, and Shepherd joined the cast that evening. Afterward, Nichols and May announced that they would be interested in joining the show in July. Flicker and Shepherd were happy, but it also meant that someone else would have to go. In this case, it was Henderson.

Mary Jo Henderson was learning the ropes, but apparently not as quickly as the others. Del would often speak of Elaine May and her effect on him, both intellectually and romantically, but many people who knew him well felt that, at least initially, he had feelings for Henderson, even if she did not respond to them. Flicker said that while Del was very much an innocent in those days, such a romance was certainly possible. "It's not a big stretch for me to think that she may have been his first [romance]. In those days, he was not a man who gave easily of himself to strangers. She was a good-looking kid, and she had talent." If there was a romance, though, the others in the company were unaware of it, and the truth remains a mystery.

Henderson would go on to a successful if more traditional acting career. Appearing in a number of TV movies throughout the 1980s, she became a regular on *Search for Tomorrow* and *All My Children*, and was nominated for a 1984 Tony Award for Best Featured Actress in a Play for her role in *Play Memory*. She died an untimely death in an automobile accident in Arizona in August 1988.

Henderson's death affected Del deeply. The *Chicago Tribune*'s account of her passing was dutifully tacked up on the bulletin board in his kitchen, and remained there long after most of the other clippings had been recycled. Whether it was due to guilt over her firing, or something deeper, may never be known.

◇

The arrival of Mike Nichols and Elaine May had a powerful impact on improvisation in general, on the St. Louis Compass, and on Del personally. The Chicago Compass had disbanded the previous winter. May was interested in improvisation and Nichols was interested in working with May, so the recently married Nichols traveled to St. Louis and did his best to focus on improvisation, though Del always felt that his heart was not in it. But Elaine May seemed to embrace it, injecting new life into the efforts of Flicker, Ponder, and Del.

While Del may have lacked the sophistication of the others, he could hold his own intellectually. Although the psychological, University of

Chicago intellectual approach of Nichols and May initially clashed with Flicker's circus tricks, they managed to meld their styles to advance the work.

Years later, Del would tell the *Chicago Tribune*: "It was an exciting time. I knew I was looking at people who were going to be stars, who were going to be genuine theatrical heavies. We were doing that kind of improvisation that had never been done before."[5]

The company grew close. Everyone lived in the Landesman quarters (Flicker referred to it as a "boardinghouse"), with Del in the guesthouse and the others on the third floor. They were performing together every night, spending their days together rehearsing and eating most of their meals together.

The new group relied heavily on literary references and appealed to Del's penchant for utilizing plots from books. Del felt that Elaine May utilized her experiences at the original Compass to help him enhance his individual work, teaching him generosity as an actor, and self-assurance while offstage. He was highly skilled verbally but was not yet the actor he was capable of becoming. He felt a sense of inferiority around the new Nichols and May, lacking their erudition. Elaine gave him the confidence he was sorely lacking.

Writing in *PerformInk* following Del's death, Flicker claims that before Elaine May arrived in St. Louis, Del was skinny, hiding behind big glasses, with a mechanical, if authentic, smile. While he brought the truly unknown into their improvisations, "he redefined the uptight, and his only pleasure in life was doing the show."

Flicker apologizes in advance for the remainder of the story, hoping it will not cause any embarrassment, and "in tribute to a great lady and in loving memory of Del":

> Elaine and I were in her room working out some new improv theory. I was pacing and she was sitting on the floor. We got stuck on an idea and in silence she looked up at me and changed the subject. "Where does a girl get laid around here?" she asked. And then, God inspired me to an act of supreme unselfishness. An act that would save Del and the future of improvisational theatre.
>
> "Del," I said.
>
> The next night, the show was the best improvisation would ever be. Del the automaton was gone. In its place was Del Diony-

sus. He danced, he flew. He flung joyous madness into the sounds of all present. That night, stunned, and sated, the audience left in a post-coitus daze.[6]

Whatever transpired, the change in Del was startling. He was gaining confidence in his abilities, and he was entering into a relationship like none before. Elaine May was more than a match for him intellectually. She was the most brilliant, talented, creative person he had ever known, and he knew he had to be a worthy partner.

Shortly after her arrival, May began examining the nature of improvisation with Flicker, why it worked, why it failed, and whether there was a way to develop rules that would consistently reduce failures onstage.

Flicker and Elaine May would develop those rules in an astonishing three-week burst of creativity, the foundation of all the significant improvisation that would follow. Called variously the Rules, the Boarding House Rules, and the Westminster Place Kitchen Rules, they formed the basis of modern improvisation. Flicker and May would sit at the table of the third-story kitchen of the Landesman mansion each morning to discuss what had gone wrong the previous night, and then determine how it could be corrected and whether any general principles were being revealed. Then they would attempt to develop an exercise to enhance the cast's understanding of those principles. After reaching their conclusions in the morning, they would bring the cast in for the afternoon rehearsal, and test the new principles in that evening's show. "Over a period of about three weeks, we really came up with a workable set of rules for public improvisation that we were able to teach to anybody, and that really worked," noted Flicker.

These differed from Viola Spolin's rules, which would eventually end up in her first book, *Improvisation for the Theater.* Spolin was not a performer, and wanted to explore improvisation as a teaching system. The St. Louis company was interested in public improvisation, and hoped to learn what worked in front of an audience.

Three basic rules emerged that are still so fundamental that they are taught to virtually every beginning improvisation student.

1. Never deny reality. If another actor establishes something as real, the other actors cannot negate it.

2. Take the active choice. Whenever an actor is faced with a decision during a scene or a game, the actor should always choose the
   one that will lead to more action.
3. It is the actor's business to justify whatever happens onstage.
   An actor cannot invent a character that can deny the reality
   of the scene by claiming it is "out of character." In improvisation, your character is actually you, but with a few additional
   characteristics.

Many corollaries developed from these three basic principles, but
they are still at the core of improvisation today. Years later, Del would
say "they formed a tripod on which I was able to base a much more complex, and probably not much more profound, theory or system aimed
at the professional theatre, which is opposed to the way Viola's book is
aimed at the amateur and personality development."[7] Although he may
not have helped originate the Rules, Del went on to become, arguably,
their greatest proselytizer; for the rest of his teaching days, he would
quote such Elaine May advice as "When in doubt, seduce," or "Take the
unlikely choice."

Soon after Severn Darden's leg healed, he joined the St. Louis Compass, proving a valuable if eccentric addition to the cast. Just before leaving town, Darden told Flicker, "Ted, while you're gone, I thought I might
do the Tristan Tzara piece." Flicker said, "Severn, you will not, under
any circumstances, do anything dada on that stage!" When Flicker came
back early, he found Darden reading a dada poem by Tristan Tzara,
while the rest of the cast was wrapping the audience in toilet paper. At
the end of the poem, Darden said in an angry German accent, "Why are
you people sitting there taking this shit?" And they got up and left.

With the addition of Nichols and May, the range of improvisational
abilities knew no bounds. One evening, the audience wanted to see an
improvisation based on a Mozart opera. "We went into the intermission,
and none of us knew anything about opera, except Mike, who knew
all about it!" recalled Flicker. Nichols gave them the general shape of a
Mozart opera, and they performed it successfully.

Another night, the audience wanted to see *Hamlet* as written by
Paddy Chayefsky. It was set in a delicatessen, and Del was Hamlet/
Marty. Elaine May, who grew up in the Yiddish theater, taught Flicker
how to recite a Yiddish version of the ghost's speech.

According to Flicker, "The Compass Players must have been the real awakening of Del Close, to who Del Close was in the world, and what the world was to him."

◈

It was also in St. Louis that Del began his first serious experimentation with drugs. The St. Louis Compass was in the heart of the Beat Generation. Flicker recalled that there weren't many hard drugs, mostly downers like sleeping pills and uppers like Benzedrine, but there was marijuana everywhere, and everyone seemed to be smoking. But Del soon shifted into the fast lane ahead of his peers; the uptight Kansas boy was rapidly loosening up.

> Every state of consciousness achievable through chemicals was ours to experience, and we were determined to do it. We got our drugs from antique stores in those days, because urban renewal was rife across the land, and many old pharmacies were being torn down and their old bottles were being sold to antique stores—we got opium, we got morphine, you know, bottles half full of the fucking stuff; it's World War One anesthetic; who knows what it is? I encountered marijuana for the first time in St. Louis. Took me three or four times, then I finally got high; took me a month to walk home down the alley, half a block. Boy, this is different, hmmmm.[8]

Del's introduction to drugs began a lifetime of use. He would see them as tools to release his mind, free him, throw open his own doors of perception. He would say he was a better person when he was on drugs, even though in years to come, fewer and fewer of his collaborators and associates shared that viewpoint. Their antiauthoritarian nature also appealed to Del. Drug users were on the fringes of society, where Del had come to see himself, and it was another way of thumbing his nose at the mainstream.

Del was happy. He was part of the hottest show in town and helping to develop a new art form. He and Elaine had become close, he was expanding his mind and losing his small-town inhibitions with pot, and his best friend was working alongside him. Only his ongoing squabbles with Mike Nichols would mar what was, for him, an otherwise perfect situation.

In subsequent years, Del would speak of varying degrees of animosity toward Nichols. Their disagreements centered on their different approaches toward the work they were doing, and their all-too-similar feelings toward Elaine May. Their attitudes toward improvisation and acting could scarcely have been more different. Del thrived on the excitement, the energy of discovery. Nichols did not thrive on improvisation; he thrived on working with May. If this is what May wanted to do, he would put up with it.

Nichols was caught up in the Actors Studio approach that was becoming prevalent in the 1950s, techniques that relied on elements like conflict. But conflict was anathema to improvisation, according to the rules being developed in St. Louis, so perhaps it was inevitable that he and Del would clash. Del had no use for the Method, and was openly disdainful of it. He felt that Nichols wanted a more emotive, Actors Studio–influenced style of improvisation, and Del was strongly opposed to changing the work. They simply had fundamental artistic disagreements.

Their backgrounds were also dissimilar. They were both intellectuals, but the small-town Kansas boy knew he lacked the polish of the New York sophisticate with his psychoanalytic approach to the work. The personal closeness that was developing between Del and Elaine May also served to drive him further apart from Nichols. Although she had been involved with Howard Alk in Chicago, by this point the other cast members considered Del and Elaine a couple.

Romantic entanglements aside, Elaine May remained the biggest single influence on his improvisational work. Nichols saw the two of them drawing closer, and he may have viewed Del as a threat to his own theatrical ambitions, of which Elaine was an indispensable part. Nichols had gotten married a few months earlier, and was literally a newlywed, but he confessed:

> I had nothing but good feelings toward Del until we were in the St. Louis Compass and Elaine was keeping company with him. I was not a very mature person and even though I had been recently married, I was obsessed with Elaine and went a little crazy watching her

with Del. So I persecuted him in the company, something of which I have been ashamed ever since.

Finally, old-fashioned professional jealousy undoubtedly played a role as well in the relationship between Del and Nichols, even if it was one-sided. Long after the St. Louis Compass had dissolved, after Nichols and May became the toast of Broadway, Del saw Nichols become an acclaimed director, producer, and writer, while he was still struggling as an actor and a stand-up comic.

Del performed in one particularly memorable three-person scene with the pair. Bringing their real-life rivalry onstage resulted in a very funny and very telling scene.

Del and Elaine are two lovers carrying on, when Elaine's husband, played by Mike, bursts in on them. Del is overly apologetic, confessing that he is almost glad Mike has discovered them, because he was feeling so guilty about carrying on the affair with his wife, and had planned to break it off that very day. "I'm glad to hear that," Mike responds. "Your friendship has been really important to me. This is a relief, because now I don't have to do that cliched married husband thing."

DEL: Would you like a drink?

MIKE: What have you got?

DEL: I've got a martini.

Mike: A martini?

DEL: Oh, no, I make very good martinis. As a matter of fact, I worked my way through college as a bartender because I make good martinis. Here, I think you'll like this. *(hands Mike the martini)* Isn't that the best goddamn martini you ever tasted?

MIKE: Well, it's a pretty damned good martini.

DEL: Pretty damned good? It's a great martini! It's a wonderful martini!

MIKE: Yeah, well, I've got to tell you, they may have been kind to you back in your college days. This is an adequate martini, but it's nothing to write home about.

Del still stands up for the honor of his martini. Finally, Mike says, "This martini tastes like shit, and if you ever touch my wife again, I'll kill you!"

◇

The facts behind the breakup of the St. Louis Compass have become obscured over the years by conflicting accounts of the participants. Del's own version of the story, as told to Janet Coleman and related in her book *The Compass*, is highly dramatic and accusatory.

When interviewed by Coleman, Del spun a tale of a messy theatrical divorce and betrayal. Nichols, May, Close, and Ponder supposedly seized an opportunity to audition for New York producer Jack Rollins. But instead of all four of them flying to New York, Nichols and May would make an overnight trip to the East Coast and audition for Rollins on the group's behalf, and Del and Ponder would lend them money to pay a portion of their airfare. Del claimed that after their audition, Nichols and May returned the next day and they all resumed their performances in St. Louis. Not long after they returned, Flicker fired Nichols, and Nichols returned to New York.

A few months later, Del, May, and Ponder went to New York, where Flicker had supposedly set up a deal for the Compass. When Flicker's deal fell through, they abandoned him, but soon found that the only work in New York was for Nichols and May as a duo. Del and Ponder were stranded in Manhattan. As Del related to Coleman, it was karma—they were being paid back for betraying Flicker. He described the dramatic situation, in which he felt tremendous guilt for turning on his friend Ted Flicker.

Del's version of events, repeated in various permutations over the years, contained classic elements of drama. There was the young hero's temptation and ultimate betrayal of his friend. There was his love for Elaine May. And there was Mike Nichols, whom he would cast as the villain of the piece, stealing his love, a potential career, and even his money. (Even though the story he told indicated Elaine May was equally culpable in borrowing money, none of the blame was ever shifted to her.)

There was only one problem: the story that Del told to Janet Coleman as reported in *The Compass* is not true.

Somehow over the years, Del transformed the end of the St. Louis Compass into an epic of Shakespearean proportions. But there are logical flaws in the timeline and circumstances described by Del, as pointed out by Nichols (who was not interviewed for the Coleman book), whose recollections reflect a more realistic and accurate account.

There was no financial betrayal. Del and Ponder never lent money to Nichols and May for an overnight trip to New York, because there was no such clandestine trip, recalled Nichols. The sole audition for Jack Rollins came many months later, long after he had left St. Louis, and only involved Nichols and May.

Nichols was ultimately fired from the St. Louis Compass, but the reason for his dismissal is unclear. According to Flicker, the incident began when he was in New York in late August 1957: "I got a call from Elaine saying that . . . if I didn't come back and fire Mike, she would quit. Man, I was on the next plane! And I fired Mike. I really liked Mike, I thought Mike and I were going to be lifetime best friends—shows how much I know!"

Decades later, Nichols explained that he and Elaine May still disagree over the reason he was fired by Flicker. "I remember that she asked him to fire me because I was making Del miserable, but [Elaine] says nonsense," said Nichols. According to Nichols, May believes he was dismissed because he made no secret of his disdain for the St. Louis Compass, regarding it as a mere footnote to Sills's original Compass Players in Chicago, and did not hesitate to tell Flicker that he thought his ideas were seriously flawed.

Whatever the cause, upon his dismissal, Nichols packed his bags and left for New York, where he struggled on his own for several months. Making matters worse was the knowledge that the material he had developed with the Compass continued to be used in the St. Louis show. "I was furious at Flicker for using my material after I was gone," said Nichols. "Sixty bucks a week or whatever it was didn't seem to me to warrant taking my stuff."

Near the end of the year, an opportunity arose to meet with Jack Rollins. Nichols called May, who immediately agreed. May pragmatically gave up improvising with the St. Louis Compass to become half of a comedy team. Thus Nichols and May began their rapid ascent to stardom.

Del claimed that he and Nancy Ponder left St. Louis for New York around this time, but his sequence of events is highly questionable. According to Janet Coleman, Del, May, and Ponder left for New York, Del driving May in his Volkswagen, while Darden stayed behind to direct the replacement company in St. Louis. But Nichols notes that May traveled to New York by herself, immediately auditioned with Nichols for Rollins, and two days later they began performing at the

Village Vanguard, and two weeks after that at the Blue Angel. He was with her from the time she arrived, and if Del was in New York, he could not have seen much of Elaine.

Another version is related by Del in *Something Wonderful Right Away*. He claimed that "after St. Louis, at just about the time Mike and Elaine were making it . . . I got an offer to take a group down to Miami." He decided to call original Compass member Larry Arrick, who eventually declined to participate, and the Miami offer failed to materialize.

Del maintained his relationship with Elaine May for a time. The intensity of his anger toward Nichols apparently rose in direct proportion to his feelings for May. He had lost a professional collaborator and a mentor, and he knew that her career success did not bode well for their personal relationship. He laid the blame at the feet of Nichols, even though he knew deep down that his feelings could not be justified. Elaine was a rising star, and her true relationship was with Nichols.

Nichols and May proved to be a fabulous creative team, with May reaching to the center of a relationship to offer a startling human insight, and Nichols dazzlingly shaping it. Even on Broadway, the pair continued to improvise one scene each night in hopes of developing new material.

Del could only stand to the side and watch their ascent. His bitterness continued through the years. Only later did Del express regret about the way his relationship with Nichols had deteriorated. As he told Jeffrey Sweet in *Something Wonderful Right Away*, "Mike and I just didn't hit it off, which was a pity. . . . We weren't mature enough to treat each other properly." Nichols certainly echoed those sentiments in a 2007 letter: "Del was an artist and a rare and good man. I wish I had known him really. . . . I regret that I seem to have become a symbol to him of . . . what? Ambition maybe? Cruelty? I hope not."

◈

Del held out some hope for another Compass. Two weeks after turning down Del's Miami offer, Larry Arrick called and invited him to join a new Compass in New York. Del was quick to say yes. The new group, which also consisted of Rose Arrick, Paul Mazursky, Barbara "Bobbi" Gordon, and Severn Darden, opened to great houses and terrific reviews, Del would later recall, but it was forced to close after two weeks. "We got into some idiot hassle with the fucking union, AGDA, and they closed us down. We were right on the verge of being a sensation, and poof, we were gone."[9]

The group did receive an offer to become the resident company for Steve Allen's *Tonight* show, a huge opportunity at that time, but when Del refused to show up for rehearsal, the deal for the entire group fell apart. Del claimed that he didn't show up because he was uncomfortable with a scene critical of the United Nations, but years later, Bobbi Gordon explained that the real reason was his increasing use of drugs. Darden sympathized with his friend, but the others were angry.

It was during this period, facing personal and professional disappointments, that Del "went mad." The details are unclear and the specific cause is unknown, though his growing drug use seems to have contributed. It is also easy to speculate that his mental infirmity was related to his father's suicide, but Del did not discuss his battles with mental illness in any detail, often only revealing them through suicide attempts.

It was his first brush with mental illness. He had an aversion to psychoanalysis (which Mike Nichols extolled—another point of contention between the two men), so one can only guess at how serious it must have been if it caused him to seek treatment.

For Del, fatherhood apparently meant so little that he rarely mentioned it. As he explained it, during his hospitalization, a nurse at the mental facility took note of him, and was particularly impressed by his intelligence. She asked him to father a child. He would have no responsibilities whatsoever, economic or familial, with regard to the child's upbringing. She simply wanted his genes.

Del did not have a particular desire to be a father. It would simply be a sexual relationship, and so he agreed. Nine months later, a son, named Christopher, was born. By that time, Del was gone. He never met his son. Although the mother would occasionally send him a letter or a photograph, he professed to have no interest in the boy. He would refer to him among close friends, sometimes speculating on what the child must be like, but always rebuffed suggestions that he establish a relationship, or even contact his son.

His reaction to the child's birth was almost certainly a response on some level to his relationship with his own father. If Del Senior was cold, uncaring, unresponsive to his son, then Del Junior would react the same way to his own son, but even more so.

Were his mental problems the direct result of his father's death? Did Del inherit his father's demons? There seems to be little justification for blaming his instability on his drug use, however, and there is more reason to think that he was self-medicating to cope with his problems.

Though he would be no stranger to what he called "the loony bin" in the coming years, this was apparently his first attempt to seek treatment, undergoing therapy with Theodor Reik. It was successful enough to allow him to function, but it did not guarantee him success. It was a dark period for Del, and he would soon learn to deal with it the only way he knew how. He would turn it into laughter.

5

Broadway, Beatniks, and
The Doors of Perception

During the next two years, Del would struggle to scrape by, while friends like Shelley Berman and Elaine May skyrocketed to fame and fortune. Hip, intelligent comedy was in demand by nightclubs, and comedy albums would soon become huge sellers. But for Del, who had always been an ensemble member, the Compass was history, and the Second City was still in his future.

Although he had never performed stand-up comedy, that seemed his most promising prospect. But he would first have to start taking day jobs, painting houses and typing in offices by day, while working the lower-rung clubs for little or no money at night.

He began putting together a solo act, assembling suitable Compass material, and adding new bits, until he had a serviceable act. But it took him two years to get noticed: "Two years of absolutely humiliating defeat. I don't know how I kept alive. Elaine helped me with money part of the time. . . . I had to buy a tuxedo. The sleazier the joint, the fancier they wanted the comics to dress. Mort Sahl could wear a T-shirt in Mister Kelly's. I had to wear a tux in this toilet in New Jersey."[1]

Del in a publicity still while
"playing toilets in New Jersey."
(COURTESY OF CHARNA HALPERN)

He continued to see Elaine May, but having to borrow money from her was painful. His professional failure juxtaposed with her success alongside Nichols made their relationship difficult.

Del's drug use continued unabated, and among friends, he referred to himself as the chairman of the New York Narcotics Festival. When there was a new drug on the New York scene, he would show up with it, according to Ted Flicker: "The problem with Del was that, in fulfilling his obligations as chairman of the festival, he was never too sure about the dosage."

Del had discovered peyote, dried cactus buttons known for their psychedelic properties, which were still legal at that time, and he would order them by the case. He was determined to experience whatever reality-altering substances he could find, ostensibly with the idea of improving his performances.

I'd read Huxley's *The Doors of Perception* and decided, well, it's necessary I should experience these things, too . . . and right around this period I found these people around town who sold this chemical, mescaline; it's a solvent, a lubricant used in photography. Yeah, a reality lubricant. And we'd take it and play elaborate games. . . . This is where a lot of our ideas about shaping reality came from.[2]

As he hustled to find ways to make money for food, lodging, and drugs, Del signed up for a government experiment in a laboratory in Brooklyn run by the Air Force, which was preparing for the upcoming Mercury Space Program. Scientists were studying REM—rapid eye movement—and conducting experiments on human subjects. As Del explained it, his job was to take LSD, a comparatively new, very pure psychedelic; he was then hooked up to a machine and allowed to sleep. When the REM machine indicated that he was dreaming, the scientists would immediately wake him: "'Are you dreaming?' 'Yes, I am, you motherfucker.' 'What were you dreaming about?' 'I don't know. Bunny rabbits.' I didn't like it. I grew tired of it real fast."[3]

Del related another version of the experience in an interview many years later. He explained that the scientists were curious as to which kind of person would function better strapped into a tiny capsule hurling through space, an introvert or an extrovert. Del gladly answered an ad on the Actors' Equity bulletin board that read, "Wanted: test subject for government program. Must be willing to take drug." LSD was the drug of choice in clinical psychological experimentation, and he always advocated the use of government drugs because of their strength and purity.[4]

He was strapped into a fake capsule and injected with a massive dose of pure LSD-25—and the capsule "took off." All was well with Del's space exploration, until someone opened the hatch and handed him the lunch menu. Del watched as the letters on the menu jumped off the page and began running around the capsule. "One phrase leapt up off the paper at him: 'Tuna Salad Sandwich,' which, at the moment, seemed to be the most uproariously funny words in existence. The door closed, then reopened with the Tuna Salad Sandwich, which he stared at for a long time. He never went back for the second session."[5]

Del later told friends that he didn't return because he had taken acid and they wanted him to report on its effects. But he felt he couldn't truthfully report because his knowledge base regarding drugs was too great. Rather than admit his drug history, he quit the program.

He was still struggling as a performer, and apparently performed (presumably as the fire-eating Azrad) alongside Sealo the Seal Boy at Hubert's Museum and Flea Circus, the storied emporium of freaks and oddities located on Forty-second Street in New York City. Established in the mid-1920s, Hubert's featured a wide assortment of sideshow and variety acts, as well as the last American flea circus. The erratic records indicate that Sealo was performing at Hubert's in mid-November 1958, along with sword-swallower Lady Estelline Pike, Lydia the contortionist, and voodoo man Congo Jungle Creep. If Del's claim of performing at Hubert's is accurate, it was almost certainly during the latter half of 1958. (Another of the many performers who played Hubert's was a singer billed as Larry Love the Human Canary; Del would later come to know him as Tiny Tim.)

◈

In early 1959, help came from a familiar source. Theodore J. Flicker invited him back to St. Louis to take on an "unplayable role" in a new musical comedy, to be called *The Nervous Set*. The lead character was based on Jack Kerouac; Del would portray a character named "Yogi," associate editor of *Nerves*, loosely based on Jay Landesman's own *Neurotica* magazine. It would require Del to sing and dance as well as act. Del filled a suitcase with peyote and strapped it onto his motorcycle, then rode it to St. Louis. After he had arrived, he said, a letter was forwarded to him in St. Louis; it read, "Dear Mr. Close, You still owe the United States Air Force one dream."

The Nervous Set was adapted for the stage and directed by Flicker. St. Louis loved *The Nervous Set*, which opened on March 10, 1959, and after a highly successful run at the new Crystal Palace, which had reopened in a new location, the producers decided it was ready for Broadway.

It should be noted that Del seldom drove ordinary vehicles. The first time he moved to St. Louis, he had driven a Volkswagen with no floor; he burned Sterno to keep from freezing, and the car had to be junked shortly after he arrived. When he decided to replace his motorcycle during this second period in St. Louis, Del bought a flashy Jaguar for just $600.

Del was delighted with the sports car, but his peers were not as happy. When he agreed to come to New York to be in *Nervous Set*, his contract even included a clause that stated that the agreement would be voided if he drove the Jaguar to New York. Disappointed, Del left the Jaguar in St. Louis, but called set designer Dave Moon after he arrived.

Moon agreed to drive the Jaguar to New York for him, but quickly regretted his decision: "I could have gotten there faster walking. The thing broke down every four feet. I blew a tire going 120 miles an hour. I blew a carburetor out, and finding a carburetor at 2 A.M. in Pennsylvania is not easy." The minute he got it into New York, he put it in a parking lot and gave Del the bill.

The total budget for "Broadway's first wholly locally-created musical" was $35,000. The set was minimal, consisting of four large revolving panels. There was no choreographer and no orchestra, with the music provided by a jazz quartet. There were no props, and costumes consisted of jeans and sneakers; Jules Feiffer designed the poster.

When *The Nervous Set* opened on May 12, 1959, the cast featured Richard Hayes, Tani Seitz, Larry Hagman (in his pre–*I Dream of Jeannie* days), Gerald Hiken, and Thomas Aldredge, along with Del, and nine supporting players. The show opens in Washington Square Park, where Brad (Hayes), editor of the avant-garde *Nerves*, author Bummy (Hagman), and poet Danny (Aldredge) musically proclaim their beat credentials. Uptown girl Jan (Seitz) appears and marries Brad, and their apartment is invaded by associate editor Yogi (Close). There is a visit to Jan's square family in Connecticut, and the couple's inevitable fight sends Brad scurrying off with Danny and Yogi to a Sutton Place party prior to a happy ending. Del sang one of the sixteen musical numbers, "How Do You Like Your Love?"

Del had to call on his acting skills rather than improvisation for the show, but it didn't matter, said Flicker: "We had a language between us, we had great fun, him playing a part I wrote, and he loved doing that song." Critical reaction was mixed, some suggesting that it would have worked better off-Broadway, though Del noted that his own performance received "fucking raves."[6] *The Nervous Set* closed after twenty-one performances, just long enough to record and release a cast album.

Afterward, Flicker took the summer off to rest and recover, then went to England for a year. After he returned, he launched the Premise, a hugely successful improvisational company, on November 22, 1960, in Greenwich Village. The Premise included such up-and-comers as George Segal and Buck Henry, and Flicker went on to a successful Hollywood career directing films like *The President's Analyst*.

But Del was not a part of the Premise. His stand-up act was coming together at last. The edgier comedy of Mort Sahl and Lenny Bruce was beginning to find favor among more progressive audiences (though the squares still labeled it "sick comedy"). Del became friends with Bruce when he was appearing with Nichols and May, and May introduced him to Bruce.

> Elaine had talked about him, never mentioned that he was controversial or dirty or weird or anything but real smart. That's what I thought, too. He's just very incisive and doesn't give a fuck.[7]

Bruce recognized Del as a kindred spirit, while Del saw in Bruce someone unafraid to push things even further than he dared. But Del was less impressed by Bruce's outrageous material than by the comedic risks he would take, going for uncomfortably long stretches without a laugh.

> Another comedian, Frank Buxton, and I were watching him, and he'd done like ten funny minutes and suddenly the laughs stopped. He was talking on and on, making sense, building various points, but—Frank and I started sweating, looking at our watches—if you didn't get a laugh every minute and a half, then every minute, then every thirty seconds. . . so Lenny's 15 minutes, no laughs, you know; then suddenly Lenny tied about eight trains of thought together, faz-zooom! And there's this—wham—burst of laughter, like wow, total approval, that multiple collision of energetic through-lines. . . .
>
> Frank and I were in the front row, and he sort of caught our eyes. . . . He realized we were two comics. So we went backstage; we're introduced. He says "Stick around for the next show, Frank and Del. Frank and Del, I got a piece for you. . . ."
>
> In the next set he says "I want to tell you a little story about this comedian who goes to the Palladium in London. His name is Frank Del, king of satire." Me and Buxton sitting down there going, *Ohhh, Christ*, you know?[8]

◆

It was also during this time that Del met the man he came to consider his best friend, beatnik poet John Brent. Late in 1990, he sat down and drafted a letter to Brent's son, who hoped to find out more about his father. Del reveals much about their friendship and his affection for the man, in his own words.

We met in a sub-basement to an Off-Broadway theatre where some young Beats had set up camp, sleeping in coal bins, stealing power from the power company, etc. To enter, you went down to the basement, climbed down a ladder to the sub-basement, crawled under a wooden rack of pipes and wooden shelves, lifted a burlap flap, and Voila! Shangri-La! I forget who first took me there, but I'll never forget whom I met there: your father John. . . .

The only air conditioning in that sweltering hole was an electric fan missing one blade, causing it, when turned on, to leap about the table, on which it sat, in an erratic and amusing manner. Somebody had spilled salt on the table, and the jumping fan appeared to be inscribing inscrutable runes in the salt. John began to interpret the meaning of these marks—"Oh Great Fan! Tell us your wisdom. . . ." This we later referred to as the Great Fan Riff. This was the first time I had ever heard a Stoned Riff, in High Hieratic Mode, and I was dazzled and charmed. John and I became friends; Hey, a Real Beatnik Poet! I was only *playing* one on Broadway! This was the real thing! I introduced him to my Chicago and St. Louis friends (I was going by the nickname of St. Louis at the time—the Broadway show had originated at the Crystal Palace in St. Louis)—and that's how John got hooked up with many people who later shaped his life—Howard Alk in particular. Howard and I were working our way through *Drugs and the Mind* by Robt. S. DeRopp, trying everything at least once. Strenuous. I mean, Black Henbane, camphor (mothballs boiled and inhaled—ugh!), nutmeg, etc. I had a crate of peyote buds I'd ordered from the Pirtle Cactus Gardens in Laredo, Texas—$30 for 100 lbs! (Shipped Railway Express) We were all on the fringes of the drug scene—we'd all read Huxley's *The Doors of Perception* and approached drugs from—basically—a religious perspective. We all said to each other at various times—"I'll *never* put a *needle* in my arm!" Yeah.

Howard [Alk] and John met at a party John threw at his older brother's house. . . . We smoked pot, played music and danced with these things held in front of our faces, making "Stained Glass Masks!" At the party, Howard gave me a lesson in joint rolling— "Two heaps in the crease, Close, all in the thumbs!" Howard was as taken with John as I was, and moved him into *his* circle of friends, which led to John's association with the Second City in Chicago. Howard brought John to Chicago to be in the original Second City company, but rehearsals went on and on, and John wound up selling shirts at Mandel Brothers to pay the rent, and eventually he went back to NY.

The Second City opened on Dec. 16, 1959 while I was appearing in a chi-chi revue at Julius Monk's "Upstairs at the Downstairs" and seeing John occasionally. Christmas 1959 I did a Christmas show with Will Geer—a medieval Mummers play we performed in peoples' apartments on our days off. (I played the Black Prince of Paradise and ate fine.) (Will Geer was Father Christmas.) We performed at the fancy apartment of Gerald Peil, publisher of the *Scientific American*. Dr. Edwin Land was there. Later that evening, we performed in John's new Village pad. There were about 20 people there, lying on the floor, out of their heads on LSD. After the performance (*The Play of St. George*) we passed the hat—John gave us a check for $100. (That was a lot in 1959.) I believe John had come into some money somehow—about this time he became associated with the Fat Black Pussycat Café, a Village music and poetry bistro. He was part owner—junior partner, I believe. Performers at the FBPC included Hugh Romney (now Wavy Gravy), Cassius Clay (now Muhammad Ali), and Bobby Zimmerman (now Bob Dylan). I never performed there—and never changed my name.

Lordy, as I look back, I'm amazed at the amount of *activity* we managed to cram into those years. From 1959 to 1969 it seems we managed to live several lifetimes. Of course time moves more slowly when you're young. . . .

But first: *Bibleland!* (John's most successful and widely known poem.) John claimed that I had a hand in inspiring this poem—that he got the idea for it after a conversation we'd had about the Antichrist. Apparently John wasn't familiar with the notion of the Antichrist—I told him it was the last cruel joke of the Christian God, a false messiah sent to deceive as many Christians as possible into damnation before the Second Coming. Today we'd call it a "sting" operation, no doubt. . . . Neither John nor I—nor Hugh [Romney], for that matter—were beatniks, we were too young. We were the latecoming fellow travelers who picked up on the "beat" Lifestyle, along with the devotion to jazz, poetry and pot. I wasn't aware of the beats until I got in the musical play *The Nervous Set*, and played one. Two phony Beatniks, quite ready to become average hippies later. I think maybe we thought of ourselves as hipsters for a while—well, of course we did—Hence the album *How to Speak Hip* in 1961—the hipster being a kind of transitional form between beatnik and hippie. Perhaps we were extremely late-blooming Bohemians. Hard to tell. At any rate, *Bibleland* was John's most notorious poem—it was considered sacrilegious at the time. It was his best-known—and perhaps his only—published poem. I remember a few fragments from his other poems—not much—one began "I wake up in the morning and strap on my guilt. . . ." Another, to an ex-lover, I think—"You would not know my skull upon a field of skulls."[9]

The undated letter continues, promising to relate how his friend traveled from the Village to Chicago, to Mexico, to London, to Tangiers, to Brasilia, to New York—and back to Chicago. It was never mailed (he explains later that he does not have the younger Brent's phone number or address), so remained tucked away in his notebooks.

◇

Del's stand-up career finally began to blossom. After two years of "playing toilets in New Jersey," he had developed a solid routine that he called Resistentialism: "I was out in New Jersey doing literary material about Gertrude Stein and Hemingway for an audience of Mafia drunks, and the microphone [stand] collapses. So I explained the phenomenon of how the mike stand collapsed as this French idiot school of philosophy about the inherent perversity of objects. The point is to frustrate humans, resist them at every point. Hence the term Resistentialism."[10]

The act led to nine months performing at Julius Monk's trendy Upstairs at the Downstairs, where his career began to take off. A manager began booking him into some of the hottest nightclubs in the country, places like San Francisco's hungry i, the Blue Angel, and the Village Vanguard.

He opened at the Gate of Horn on August 4, 1959, billed as a satirist who is only "mildly ill," as opposed to the "really sick ones." In his *On the Town* column in the August 9, 1959, *Chicago Tribune*, Will Leonard was obviously impressed by the young comic.

Del Close's surname is a misnomer, for he isn't at all close, he's "way out." A low pressure chatter with a semi-beatnik haircut, he explains

His publicity stills did not reveal
Del's struggles to succeed in
stand-up comedy in New York.
(COURTESY OF CHARNA HALPERN)

his theory of Resistentialism (in which inanimate objects gang up against human beings), impersonates a Univac [an early computer], lectures on flying saucers, and enacts the role of a milktoast gent handling the complaint department of a department store. His touch is light and deft, his humor clean and sparkling, and his future bright.

When he returned to the Gate of Horn the following April, this time with guitar duo Bud and Travis, Leonard wrote in the April 24, 1960, *Chicago Tribune*: "Bud and Travis are funny enough, but Del Close, resident satirist who majors in describing humanity's defeat at the hands of inanimate objects, is even funnier."

Del was on the verge of national success, with twenty-eight months of bookings at Playboy Clubs across America. But then, during a three-week run at the Racquet Club outside Dayton, Ohio, he described an epiphany: "I'm here with four Republican drunks, the Crosby brothers, Dennis, Gary, Lindsay, and Phil. Anybody that wants to hear them doesn't want to hear me, and everybody wants to hear them reminiscing about old times with their dad on the front porch. . . . It was like a Lenny Bruce routine: 'Across the street there was a gravel pit; you could go watch it. . . .' I thought 'Oh, God, this is what Lenny's talking about.'"[11]

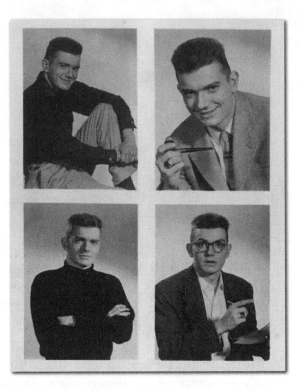

The many faces of Del Close, hoping to show his versatility and build an acting career in New York City.

(COURTESY OF CHARNA HALPERN)

When Del returned to New York, he was arrested for a joint and a half of marijuana. As a result, he lost his cabaret card and the right to perform in New York nightclubs. Del later claimed he had sabotaged his career on purpose, perhaps subconsciously: "I think I set myself up for it, 'cause I didn't have the balls to turn down twenty-eight months at the Playboy Clubs."[12]

It may have been self-destruction, the sort of risky behavior in which he had been dabbling since his father's suicide. He didn't want to invest himself any more deeply in his stand-up career, but couldn't bring himself to turn it down. Like Hamlet, paralyzed into inaction, a pot bust was an easy way to slow his career without making a firm decision. Del wanted to be successful, but may have felt that the only way he could strike back at his father was by harming his health, his relationships, and his career. Hamlet would try to destroy Claudius, his father's killer, but Del had to direct his anger at himself.

Del returned to St. Louis and the new Crystal Palace, where he starred alongside Jay Landesman in the latter's production of *New Direc-*

tions. Del also had other opportunities. In 1960, as comedy albums were becoming popular, he wrote (with help from Elaine May) and recorded his only solo comedy album, *The Do It Yourself Psychoanalysis Kit*. It was an inspired attempt at an interactive album, in which Del was the doctor and the listener was his patient. The conceit was to provide psychoanalysis to people who couldn't afford it. It was comedy with a deeply personal agenda. Del had found an ideal format to explore and parody his therapy with Theodor Reik. It was the best kind of analysis. He looked inward at the same time he was entertaining others.

If there is any doubt about his obsession with the Prince of Denmark, the B-side of *The Do It Yourself Psychoanalysis Kit* dispels it. The record features a dialogue between Hamlet and his analyst, Hamlet spouting his Shakespearean dialogue, as the shrink analyzes him (Del plays both parts). After concluding that Hamlet is in love with Claudius, the doctor is thrilled to discover that Hamlet is responsible for the deaths of most of the people around him, because it means he has finally taken action, and thus his therapy is a success.

The following year, Del expanded on the lessons he learned doing *The Do It Yourself Psychoanalysis Kit* with the even more successful *How to Speak Hip*. Teaming with John Brent, the two friends wrote, riffed, and improvised a parody of albums that promised to teach the listener a foreign language with minimal effort. While some of the jokes are dated, much of it still holds up well. Del plays the Instructor, the square narrator attempting to understand the expressions used on "the hip scene." Brent's character is well versed in all aspects of hip, and translates them for the Instructor.

The success of *How to Speak Hip* helped to solidify Del's reputation among other comedians and gained him tremendous national acclaim. Still, he was unable to capitalize on it further. After *How to Speak Hip*, Del went to see Steve Allen in hopes of garnering a TV appearance, but the host politely brushed him off with "This is great. Come back and see me after you've done your next one."

Despite the loss of his New York cabaret card, Del could tour nationally. In the summer of 1960, he was working at the Club Renaissance in Hollywood when he got a call from Howard Alk, one of the founding members of the new cabaret theater in Chicago.

◆

The Second City had opened the previous December at 1842 North Wells Street, the site of a former Chinese laundry. Alk joined with Paul Sills, who would direct, and Bernie Sahlins, who would serve as producer. The three of them rounded up former Compass players Severn Darden, Andrew Duncan, Eugene Troobnik, Roger Bowen, Barbara Harris, and newcomer Mina Kolb. Alk and Bowen soon left (replaced by Alan Arkin and Paul Sand, with Sheldon Patinkin joining as business manager), though Alk continued in a producer's role.

Many years later, Del recounted to Jeffrey Sweet the message that he received from Alk: "Communications have broken down between Paul Sills and the company. Would you come and be our director for a while?" Although Sahlins disputed the communiqué, he said Sills was becoming disinterested after the second revue, which opened just four weeks after the first one. "Then it was time to do our third show," said Sahlins. "If communications had broken down, it was not because of artistic differences, but because Paul was tired. We asked Del to come in, not so much to have him direct, but to goad Paul—which worked!"

Sills found it a "desperate job" to keep coming up with a new Second City show every two or three months. While Del's presence in Chicago did not necessarily "goad" him, Sills said it did serve to improve the work: "Del could inspire me, and . . . I'd come up with a lot of good ideas." Both Sills and Sahlins had first seen Del performing with the St. Louis Compass, where his sense of humor and his intelligence made him a prime candidate to be a director at the Second City. Even though his only previous directing involved the scenario plays in St. Louis in conjunction with Elaine May, Sahlins noted, "There weren't many people who knew how to do this stuff."

In addition to goading Sills, Del's original role was not as an actor, but "as a director in the wings," and he soon found himself running workshops for the actors. This was a chance to pick up some directing experience, visit friends, and see Chicago.

But there was more going on in town than the Second City. The Republican National Convention was in town the week of July 25–28, 1960, and the normally apolitical Del decided to become involved. He had been an Adlai Stevenson supporter, and both Del and Severn Darden were disappointed when John F. Kennedy got the Democratic nomination. They decided that the Republicans should draft the former Democratic hopeful. They enlisted the support of friends and fellow actors, who called their representatives to obtain credentials for the first day of the convention.

Although it seems incredible in a more security-conscious era, the requests were granted, and they obtained three dozen passes for the main floor of the convention. (Del later speculated that had they attempted this just eight years later, at the Democratic Convention in Chicago, they probably would have been killed.) Shortly before the convention opened, the courtyard at the Second City was full of activity as "Independent Republicans to Draft Stevenson!" signs and placards were being painted. Banners displayed blankets with a picture of a shoe with a hole in it—Stevenson's campaign symbol—draped over Republican elephants.

The opening session began at 2 P.M., and Del and his group walked in, quiet and inconspicuous, until the first speaker began to deliver the keynote address. They unfurled the banners and silently paraded across the room with their "Nominate Stevenson" signs. The only sounds in the hall were from every television camera turning around, sending their message across America for a few moments, until the police threw them out immediately afterward.

Shortly after the convention, on Monday, August 8, 1960, Del teamed with the legendary Lord Buckley and Severn Darden for a one-night-only comedy concert at the Second City, titled "The Suncoast of Bohemia" (an homage to the Second City's fourth, then-current revue, called *The Seacoast of Bohemia*, which featured Darden). By this time, however, Del was about to hit the road for more stand-up.

In the fall of 1960, he was hired to open for the Kingston Trio, who were riding the crest of a wave of hit records at that time. Hugh Romney, a stand-up comic and a friend of Brent and Darden (and later to become famous as Wavy Gravy), called the Kingston Trio booking a "huge gig" that paid Del very good money. Opening for the singers caused Del to dress more nattily than usual. "He was very slick," recalled Romney. Despite his stylish dress, his eyeglasses were still being held together precariously with pieces of tape and paper clips. That, according to Romney, never changed.

Del continued to write to his mother whenever time would allow, but years went by without a visit. A letter postmarked October 23, 1960, on Eastern Air Lines "in flight" stationery and written "En route from Raleigh, N.C. to Washington, D.C.," indicates a good relationship and regular contact.

Well, I'm about to finish my Kingston Trio tour with this last performance in Washington. All in all, we will have performed for about 40,000 people in 5 performances. I did pretty well, all things considered, and now I go back to saloons, opening Oct. 27 at the Racquet Club in Dayton, Ohio. Two weeks there, and then on to points unknown.

It'll be fun playing Washington. I'll get to see some old friends.

Nothing much to report—just that I've been on the road and will probably *be* on the road for the next year or so. Spent a few days in New York, but many of my old friends have disappeared—to the west coast, to Europe, on the road, or just into obscurity.

A few friends have become so famous it's difficult to get near them any more. But there's always Jerry Hardin and Al Manley— although we don't seem to have much in common any more.

This seems to be a somewhat morose letter—guess I'm just resigning myself to another rather lonely year of solo-ing around the country.

Love,
Del

Once again, Del had to confront the threat of success. Opening for the Kingston Trio at that time was tremendous exposure for a young stand-up, yet the $1,500 per night he was earning made him feel unworthy, as he admitted years later: "I felt very guilty about that."[13] Whether it was a propensity for self-destruction, or the loneliness of the road taking its toll, Del had enough of stand-up. He had a choice: keep touring and making good money at a job he disliked, or rejoin the nascent Second City in Chicago.

6

The Second City and the Spider King

The Second City pay was abysmal; Del claimed it was "one-twentieth" of what he earned at the height of his stand-up career.

Nevertheless, the Second City offered a chance to work and play with Howard Alk, Severn Darden, John Brent, and Hamilton Camp, and he knew most of the others in the cast as well from the Compass days. For Del, it was an easy choice. Though he wasn't yet being asked to join the company, Paul Sills had something else in mind.

That spring, the Second City opened a slightly larger theater called Playwrights at Second City next door to the original, intended for more dramatic works presented with the Second City sensibilities. The first show, *The Explainers*, opened in early May 1961, and was written by Jules Feiffer, based on his cartoons. The cast included Bob (Hamilton) Camp, John Brent, and Del. The music was written by the Second City's original music director, Allaudin (Bill) Mathieu, and played by Fred Kaz. This was to be the first of many collaborations between Del and Kaz, a Second City musical icon. The *Chicago Tribune*'s William Leonard was unenthusiastic in his May 10, 1961, review: "A cast of nine . . . plays several dozen roles to the hilt. Paul Sills, who directs the next door Second City players hilariously, seldom gets this show out of the semi-static stage, however."

The follow-up to *The Explainers* was a jazz musical, with a scenario by David Shepherd, based on both *The Beggar's Opera* and *The Three-*

77

penny Opera. The cast featured Alan Arkin as Macheath, and included Del, Avery Schreiber, Ann Raim, Dick Schaal, and Delores Alton.

This new show was called *Big Deal*, subtitled "An Opera for Politicians." After it opened, director Sills recognized that it needed more work, and looked to Del, who had done a satisfactory job in the previous summer's workshops. Sills replaced Del as an actor, and asked him to direct instead. "I've always been a pretty good fixer," said Del. "I mean, that's the job at Second City; it's not being the creator. The actors make the first effort, then you kind of clean it up for them."[1]

Original Second City cast member Barbara Harris recalled Del as "gentle and obviously very shy with women." She was young and somewhat sheltered at the Second City; the theater's drug enthusiasts kept them away from her. While Del respected her (and, perhaps, because she had been married to Sills), being around his friends—and LSD—brought out his mischievous side.

Del and Darden spent one evening doing LSD, according to Harris, and at one point obtained a small plastic toy rocket. They decided to wake Harris at sunrise, and filled the rocket with orange juice. They launched their rocket, which broke her second-floor window and flew into her room. She woke up to find a small plastic rocket with orange juice dribbling out of it. Furious, she ran to the window and looked at the figures below, both dressed in black capes, giggling and turning circles before running off. "They thought it was just the funniest thing that ever happened," recalled Harris.

Even though all outward signs indicated that he was happy, it was not long after he arrived at the Second City that he began attempting suicide. When he didn't show up at the theater one evening, Schaal and Camp were sent to his nearby apartment and found him unconscious. He had waited until shortly before the evening's performance to swallow a handful of pills. When he didn't turn up for the show, he knew someone would come looking for him, and alert the medics in plenty of time. And, of course, everyone at the theater would be talking about him. "Del was never accused of being completely sane!" joked Schaal. It was a classic cry for attention; they knew that anyone with Del's drug knowledge had the capacity to end it all if he wished.

◆

Not long afterward occurred a brief, all-but-forgotten episode in Del's life. On September 9, 1961, Del Close and Doris Holland were married in Chicago. It was a surprise to his friends and coworkers. It may have represented a final attempt at a normal, middle-class Kansas life. It did not end well.

Very little is remembered of his wife and their marriage. Sheldon Patinkin recalled that she was, briefly, a waitress at the Second City; Sills remembered her as an actress who was also a sculptress. By all accounts, she was an attractive brunette who wore large glasses, nice but quiet, not vivid enough to stand out decades later. Patinkin and Bernie Sahlins attended the small ceremony in a Buddhist temple. "I knew his wife vaguely, but I think I probably knew her as well as he did," said Sills. "I don't know what his relationship with her was. They used to make jokes at Second City. I don't know what happened with the marriage. As they say, nothing but jokes were told. Nobody ever seemed to have eaten a meal there [at their apartment]. A normal kind of thing, it wasn't!"

Years later, Del would explain that he had a wife for a couple of weeks, but it didn't work out. They drove each other crazy; they put each other in the mental hospital; they got divorced. It was all a mistake, and he never repeated it.

Although the marriage likely lasted months rather than weeks, Del quickly brushed the episode under the carpet, and his colleagues at the Second City were never made aware of when it ended.

There was a bizarre postscript to the brief, failed marriage. Not long after they split up, Del told a few friends that his former wife had killed herself. The story remains unconfirmed. Sahlins, Patinkin, Sills, and Second City bartender Dennis Cunningham, all of whom were in close contact with him at that time, could not recall Del ever mentioning her suicide. Cunningham was particularly skeptical: if such a thing had happened, it would have been all over the theater.

But according to Alan Myerson, Del did tell all of them occasionally about his ex-wife, who he said had committed suicide. And company member Schaal clearly recalled hearing the news, noting that Del's first suicide attempt preceded his ex-wife's reportedly successful suicide. There were remarks made that she had "followed in his footsteps," albeit more successfully. The records remain elusive.

Coming less than a decade after his own father's suicide, her death, one assumes, would have had a significant effect on Del. Although he never denied that he once had been married, briefly, he never again spoke of her fate, whether the suicide was true or yet another invention.

◇

Although well received, Playwrights at Second City did not draw the same crowds as the original theater, so the two swapped spaces in October 1961. Del joined the main company, where he could improvise with the rest of the cast. "I mostly did interviews and stand-up stuff, gimmicks where I could exercise my wit rather than my improvisational ability, which was really rather slight until I started working with The Committee later. But I did some clever stuff."[2]

Del's return to performing was spurred by the theater's success. In late 1961, Barbara Harris and the rest of the company moved to the Ivar Theatre in Los Angeles with a revue called *From the Second City*, featuring scenes from the first five shows in Chicago. It was an eight-week pre-Broadway run that proved so popular that when the show moved to Broadway, a new cast replaced it and the show continued in L.A.

In Chicago, the Second City launched its seventh revue, titled *Alarums & Excursions*, on October 31, 1961, with a cast made up of Bill Alton, Hamilton (Bob) Camp, Anthony Holland, Joan Rivers, Avery Schreiber, and Del.

The relationship between Rivers and the rest of the cast would be described by Del as contentious (the only exception seemed to be Anthony Holland; the two became close friends and developed a couple of scenes together). To Del, Rivers was ultimately more interested in becoming a stand-up comic than an ensemble member. Though she undoubtedly tried to fit in, she seldom resisted the temptation to go for the quick one-liner.

Del would later point to her in his workshops as an example of what *not* to do in improvisation. If she was in a scene and her partner asked about her husband, Del would claim, she would step downstage center, scene forgotten, and unleash a barrage of one-liners (this was clearly not always true, in light of her scene work with Holland and sometimes Alton). Del also criticized her as a comedian for her lack of a consistent worldview—her honeymoon was so sexy, her honeymoon was so awful—which was something he felt all the best comedians had in common.

Worst of all for Del were the scenes they tried to improvise together. He claimed that she would sacrifice a potentially good scene for a cheap laugh. He would describe a scene that they were improvising about a couple having an intense discussion. He finally implored her: "But what about the children?" To which she responded: "But we don't *have* any children!" Big laugh from the audience, at the expense of the scene's development. It was a textbook example of the importance of agreement in improvisation, and succinctly underscored how denial can destroy a scene. To Del, it was unforgivable.

After *Alarums & Excursions*, Rivers left Chicago and soon began forging her highly successful stand-up career. If her time at the Second City served no other purpose, Del would forever use it to teach the evils of denial in improvisation.

The revue was well received by critic Will Leonard, writing in the November 12, 1961, *Chicago Tribune*:

> *Alarums and Excursions* . . . is remarkable for the number of hilarious blackouts, rather than for the intellectual mood of its more than a dozen skits. The little company across the street from Lincoln Park has had a more bitter bite and a tighter script than in earlier shows, but it seldom has had more laughs. There is a certain preoccupation with megatons and fallout shelters, but the remarkable directorial touch of Paul Sills brings comedy even to such fairly unfunny phenomena, as well as to the East German embarrassment, foreign movies, atonal music, and good old love. If the dialogue lags more than once in mid-scene, it almost invariably springs back to life for a vivid closing line as the lights go out. . . . They're on a histrionic level with the original Second City cast now on Broadway in the First City.

Alarums & Excursions was, contrary to the assurances of the *Chicago Tribune*, directed by Alan Myerson. He had previously directed a group in New York called Stewed Prunes, which had impressed both Del and Sills so much that Sills hired him. But Del was unimpressed, or at least resistant, to Myerson when they actually began working together in Chicago.

"He didn't start off very brilliantly, but in fairness to Alan, we gave him a lot of trouble," noted Del. "His first idea was 'Let's do a commedia piece.' We thought 'Oh God, commedia! If this guy's first thought in improvisation is to do a commedia piece. . . . I mean, we all thought of that years ago, right?' Actually, I must say the first show he put together was quite good. That had the first General Clevis scene."[3]

That didn't prevent Del from rebelling, however. Myerson felt that both Del and Alton were upset because he was given the directing gig. Del denied this, and claimed that he "only wanted to direct Myerson's mistakes."

Del was not the only one who didn't get along with Myerson at that time. Sahlins asserted that they were all unhappy with what he referred to as "simplistic political notions." (Myerson felt that the disagreement with Sahlins over political attitudes stemmed from his suggestion that the theater close for one performance in order to join a national demonstration called the General Strike for Peace; Sahlins rejected the notion, which would have meant the loss of income.)

During this period, Del often portrayed teachers, professors, and fathers, concentrating on intellectual and verbal traits, with little physical humor. He was usually "talking off the top of his head about something, or answering questions from the audience," according to Mina Kolb; while he was often marvelous, even brilliant, he wasn't doing scenes. "Del inherited Severn Darden's role in the company—an expert, sometimes spouting intelligent-sounding nonsense with wit and verve, but usually in a format that showcased his stand-up rather than scenic proclivities," said Myerson.

◇

His most memorable role in the early days of the Second City was undoubtedly General J. C. Clevis. "A clevis is the little ring that you hang up mess kits and things with, like 'Bayonet, M-1, with clevis.' A clevis is the least important piece of military equipment," explained Del.[4]

Clevis appeared in Del's first three shows at the Second City, and the character grew with each subsequent appearance. In the first General Clevis scene, which takes place by the Berlin Wall, he tells the interviewer that the way to resist Communist brainwashing is to teach the soldiers brainwashing techniques. When the interviewer asks how he teaches the men, Clevis tells him that they "pound it into their heads, day after day after day." In his first appearance, Clevis was little more than a caricature.

> I was attempting to . . . make a double joke. . . . This guy was demonstrating how to resist brainwashing, yet it was patently obvious that he had been brainwashed. So the character was subservient to the idea. I don't know anything about the military at all, so I just played somebody with a ramrod up his ass, with his eyes bugging, and not particularly bright.[5]

A Knocking Within, the Second City's eighth show, opened on February 6, 1962. It was also directed by Myerson, with Kolb and Schaal replacing Holland, Rivers, and Camp. General Clevis returned in the new show—unusual for the Second City—as America began testing the waters in Vietnam. According to Del, the cast decided to deal with the situation.

> We started off with an extremely reluctant brigade of Vietnamese soldiers going through these fucked-up maneuvers. Demonstrating not their incompetence but their extreme reluctance at being driven to war. We wanted to show America lending the wrong kind of assistance. And here was Brigadier General Clevis as an "advisor." He was teaching courses again. Preposterous stuff. It was a guerrilla war being fought, and he was teaching tank maintenance in a swamp. The interviewer asks "What happens to tanks in a swamp?" "They sink." Clevis also pointed with pride to the fine audiovisual program which the Vietnamese were very enthusiastic about. They particularly liked a film called "Industrial Canada."[6]

> In the second one, in South Vietnam, the general became a little more human because he was kind of good-intentioned. We were trying to do a job that was very difficult and not doing it particularly well and, of course, operating on all the wrong premises.[7]

Five months after Myerson was hired by the Second City, after the opening of *A Knocking Within*, the situation with the cast erupted. "Alan was directing a scene and he gave some direction to us, and we sort of looked at each other and I said, 'It's all right. Wait till the director gets here,' meaning Paul [Sills] next door," said Del. "What a hostile bastard I was in those days! There was a flare-up, and at this point Paul walked in and I went over to him and said 'Look, it's either me or him. I can't work with this guy.' Which was a ratty thing for me to do."[8]

Both Bernie Sahlins and Sheldon Patinkin have differing recollections of Myerson's departure. "I don't know how much we can say that it was Del's responsibility for getting Alan fired," said Patinkin. "There was a certain amount of animosity, not just from Del, but from other people as well, and at the same time, Del really wanted to direct."

According to Sahlins, Myerson was not sent to New York because of any argument with Del or the cast, but because of his talent. When the original Second City company closed on Broadway after two months, the show was moved to Square East in the Village in January 1962 (where it would run for five years). Sills apparently grew tired of the struggle against incipient stardom for some of the New York company, as well as their demand for autonomy from Sahlins and the Chicago group, led by Howard Alk. Sills needed a home base and Chicago was still the center of his life at that point. At the same time, Myerson wanted to return to New York City, where he had lived before moving to Chicago. "The whole thing was serendipitous," noted Myerson, and he happily swapped theaters—and cities—with Sills. Myerson remained at Square East until he quit to get married and move to California.

And so, Sills once again took over the direction of the Chicago company. Although Sills recalled that Del's desire to direct grew slowly, at that time, he was satisfied that Sahlins had decided to bring back Sills. "Del was *so* happy! He just ran around happily at that thought," recalled Sills.

◇

Sills took over in time to direct the groundbreaking scenario show *My Friend Art Is Dead*, which opened on June 12, 1962, with a cast that included Alton, Darden, Kolb, Schaal, Schreiber, Dennis Cunningham, and Del. The now-promoted Brigadier General John C. Clevis had

Richard Schaal, Severn Darden, and Del Close as General Clevis (handcuffed to Darden's protester) from *My Friend Art Is Dead*. (COURTESY OF CHARNA HALPERN)

become one of the first notable characters at the Second City. Clevis appeared at the end of the first act of *Art*, when a peacenik played by Severn handcuffs himself to the general in protest.

> A bunch of people start pulling Clevis away from this maniac, and a bunch of peace freaks start pulling the maniac the other way, resulting in a great Marx Brothers moment when we were lifted off our feet connected only by handcuffs. Sometimes it was terribly painful. I would often bleed. When we were finally released from the handcuffs, we would be interviewed by the audience. Oh, General Clevis was always willing to be interviewed.[9]

My Friend Art Is Dead experimented with linking scenes together, rare for the Second City. Many years later, Bernie Sahlins downplayed the innovation: "When you tend to link characters in a sketch format, it should have a secondary life, a subtext, and the point of the sketch is to have a beginning, a middle and an end. And also, because whatever doesn't fit, you sort of shove in and lop off the corners. It's not really an organic whole." For Sahlins, the proof was that "it was never done again." But the very next revue, *To the Water Tower*, experimented with an overriding plot that linked the show's sketches. (Though after *Water Tower*, there would not be another such attempt for more than twenty-five years.)

Not everyone agreed with Sahlins's assessment of *Art*. Cast members, including Cunningham, Kolb, and Schaal, agreed with Del's feelings, and Sills remembered it fondly. Even critics were enthusiastic about the innovations in *Art*, including Will Leonard, writing in the June 17, 1962, *Chicago Tribune*:

> They seem to have invented a new kind of show—a revue with a plot. Well, a pretty thin plot, perhaps, but a slightly perceptible one. The sketches, the blackouts, the audience participation, the good old Second City gimmicks all are there, but the same cast of characters appears in every scene. And what a wacky array of roles! There's a militant peace marcher [Severn Darden] who delights in hand-cuffing himself to flagpoles, a Teamsters' Union official [Avery Schreiber] who can see the ghost of Joe Hill, his wife [Mina Kolb] who can see both sides of almost anything, a detective [Dick Schaal] who likes her more than he should, an army general [Del Close] who likes red tape and dislikes Otto Preminger, a radio interviewer [Bill Alton] who doubles as narrator, and several other oddballs [Dennis Cunningham].
>
> They toss off tart remarks about O'Hare field, Cook county jail, the Playboy club, Billy Graham, the Bomb, Loop traffic, love, and other vital issues, all with hilarious irreverence and jaunty good spirits. This is one of the very best of the nine shows that have romped through Second City. . . . Sumup: recommended.

William Leonard stopped by the Second City several weeks later and visited with the cast for a feature in the September 2, 1962, *Chicago Tribune*.

> "Comic or sad, the scenes always change a great deal," says Paul [Sills]. "Usually they get tighter and smoother, but sometimes they go right down hill. The hardest thing is to recapture a scene that was right the first time. It's just never as good again. . . ."
>
> "You're independent," says Del Close, "but you're part of a team, not a member of a cast. If I left here, I guess I might like to be listed in the next place I worked as 'Del Close of Second City.'"
>
> "I went to the Goodman Theatre for years, to learn to act," says Avery [Schreiber], "and then I come here and hear Paul hollering at us 'You're acting again! Stop it! Stop that acting!' . . ."

"The longer you work with the others at Second City," Mina [Kolb] adds, "the longer you know what you can and can't do with them. Sometimes you try to break the other fellow up, and that keeps you on your toes. When Bill [Alton] is the reporter interviewing Del, as the general, he can throw him almost any kind of question because he knows Del can handle any kind of a surprise."

◆

Viola Spolin, the matriarch of improvisation, had come to Chicago in 1960, where she was running compulsory workshops for the actors.

Spolin came from a strong family tradition of game playing. The younger people played charades religiously every week, noted her son, Paul Sills: "My mother was right in the middle of that, and that's where she got it. It was a family that just played all the time. And they were good at it!" Spolin began cataloging the games that would eventually comprise her landmark 1963 book, *Improvisation for the Theater.*

Del saw her as an authority figure, but his instinct to rebel was largely superseded by her confidence and knowledge. Spolin was a fervent advocate of the "discover your where" approach to improvisation, letting the environment strongly affect the scene. Del never managed to find his way through "her space," because he was much more interested in immediate results, and felt the use of her work was "slightly misplaced" in a professional theater company. Even though her work had much to offer, he felt they had slightly different problems that were not solved by "walking through space."

Much of Spolin's work actually involved *sharing* the space. At that time, Del was uncomfortable with the equality of players that her work required. He knew that he could garner enough laughs and acclaim on his own with his one-man turns or favorites like Clevis, and did not have to share. It was one reason that Del had difficulty coming up with scenes, according to Myerson, along with his feeling that "he was so much the smartest guy in the room that the others couldn't keep up with him—which I believe was simply a rationale for his deep distrust of placing his fate (even the fate of a character in a five-minute scene) in the hands of anyone else."

Del liked Spolin as a person, however. She was a surrogate mother in many ways, and she exhibited the same qualities that he loved in his own mother. He was mostly deferential in her workshops and recognized that she was, arguably, the founding figure of modern improvisation. Nevertheless, he would have to experiment and make his own mistakes before he came to realize that Spolin was correct about more than he had initially cared to admit, according to a 1978 interview.

> My major disagreement with Viola may have been based on a misconception. I had the feeling that she wanted to take theatre and reduce it to the level of a game. At the same time, I had independently of Viola cooked up various theories of my own. Since then, I've had to . . . well, not exactly eat my words, but on the other hand, I am using more of Viola's work now than I have in the past.[10]

When her *Improvisation for the Theater* was eventually published, Del would not read it for many years. Until the publication of his own *Truth in Comedy*, the only improvisation book he ever recommended to students was Keith Johnstone's *Impro*. Later in his life, in a more forgiving mood, he announced that he had finally read Viola's book, and that she had come to many of the same conclusions in her book that he had reached over the course of decades. Del had true philosophical differences with Spolin's approach. Spolin's work was predominantly physical, tapping the intuitive, so that expression was spontaneous. Del went through the mind, while the others, like Avery Schreiber and Dick Schaal, were more physical and avid followers of Spolin.

Actor Larry Hankin remembered first meeting Del at Spolin's Second City workshops. Hankin recalled being forced to take classes with Spolin on Saturday afternoons. He recalled the many times she would walk through the room saying "Remember your 'where,'" while Hankin and Del giggled like naughty, if not stoned, schoolboys.

But another workshop made the biggest impression on Hankin. During the Something Just Happened game, in which the class had to guess what had just transpired, based on the reactions of the actors onstage, Del stood with another actor just outside a door. They were quiet and he was smoking a cigarette. The students made a few guesses, but finally gave up, and Del revealed: "My father just died." He explained that his father had called him into the kitchen and said, "Come here, I want to show you something," then drank battery acid in front of him. The embellished story was one of the first public tellings of his father's suicide, and the horrified response it elicited undoubtedly encouraged Del's retellings.

Despite reservations about Spolin, Del was quick to acknowledge Sills as a huge influence as a director. He was the master, "not in any mystical-guru bullshit sense, but as a master craftsman," and Del was his apprentice, emulating his approach: "I would imitate some of Paul's most glaring flaws, such as yelling at the actors, terrifying everybody. What was missing in my imitation was his incisive ability to set things right."[11]

In *Something Wonderful Right Away*, Del recounted an instance where Sills screamed at Schaal while banging his head against the floor, which left the rest of the company with a strong dread of being reprimanded by Sills. In the same interview, Del claimed that while the show was going on, Sills hurried backstage during the middle of a show to confront the actors. Del stood at the top of the stairs, glaring down at him. "Don't you *ever* come backstage and give notes during a performance!" he thundered.[12] He said Sills slunk away meekly (an unbelievable image, according to Myerson).

Del's relationship with Sills was generally good both on- and off-stage. Sills viewed him as "an oddball . . . capable of anything," but they respected each other. Even among his colleagues, Del guarded his privacy. Kolb recalled that he "scared me because he was an intellectual in a beat kind of way. . . . I don't know how many people really got to know Del." Schaal characterized Del as "the intellectual of the company at that time . . . [he was] always reading."

◈

Meanwhile, Del's mental demons had continued to rage unabated, with more suicide attempts, and he was finally sent to a psychiatric facility in late 1961 or early 1962. The last straw came the night after an opening, when he took a number of pills and didn't show up at curtain time. Patinkin walked to his apartment, looked through the window, and saw Del lying on the floor. He called an ambulance, and the medics pumped his stomach. The doctors were going to commit him to Cook County Hospital, but a Second City lawyer knew of a small clinic on the Near South Side, and so Del was taken there.

His stay in the mental hospital was apparently the result of drug overdoses, suicide attempts, and need for a safe haven. Del obviously battled with depressive feelings, and may have been self-medicating. After a few weeks, doctors decided it was OK for him to start doing the show again, and so each night before a show, Patinkin would drive to the mental facility, sign him out, drive him to the show, and then take him back afterward.

Even though the young man was going out of his way for him, Del seemed to be resentful toward Patinkin, who felt that Del "liked to be thought of as evil." The doctor treating Del was using LSD for his psychiatric treatments, which did not seem to be a beneficial drug for Del. One time when he was under its influence, he called Patinkin and told him he was being devoured, inch by inch, by the Spider King.

While many at the Second City eschewed drugs, Del was at the forefront of the theater's drug culture. But the drug use went unnoticed by many, and Del's own usage did not by itself make him irresponsible or cause him to be absent from shows.

Sahlins claimed to be ignorant of the drug scene at that time, only afterward learning that it was "a very drug-ridden group." He was older than the others, and drugs were not a part of his background, so the possibility didn't occur to him, he explained. Although he was close to the original Second City company and others that followed, he rarely socialized with the current company, even though he admired their talent; they represented the spirit of the 1960s, for which Sahlins had little patience.

◆

Still, the members of the company managed to craft some of the theater's finest material. Their individual strengths and weaknesses complemented one another's abilities. Most of the cast were physically creative, whereas Del was mentally adept, which worked to their advantage.

One classic scene (Mina Kolb considers it her favorite) was "The Ex-Urbanites," developed by the company with minimal planning. The premise saw a group of snooty people having a party, crashed by cab driver Harry Mankiewicz (Schaal). That was as much as was planned, but the company turned it into art. Mankiewicz tries to fit in with the stunned intellectuals. He eventually tells the group about his wonderful pet turtle, who has learned to plunge down a slide, while the others listen in disbelief. Del's character performs a long, affected poem by Gerard Manley Hopkins, and injects clever, topical remarks, exhibiting his vast knowledge base.

By this time, John Brent had joined the Chicago company, appearing in the Second City's sixth revue, *Six of One*. Del and Brent took apartments in the same building at 1943 North Hudson Street, not far from the Second City, Del living on the lower floor and his friend directly upstairs. Several stories of legendary excess would spring from that building over the next four years.

Del and Brent had begun to increase their drug intake, and at the same time, Del seemed to be gaining even more confidence with the opposite sex. Whether it was due to his natural charisma, his burgeoning success as a performer, or simply his generosity with his plentiful supply of drugs, women seemed to flock to him. Del reveled in their attentions. He always seemed to have waitresses, students, and female fans over after the shows. He would get high with massive amounts of pot, as well as speed and amphetamines in general. His consumption did not seem to impair his skills as a performer, however. "Del could easily blow your mind, but not vice versa," noted Larry Hankin.

So popular had the Second City and General Clevis become that Del and Bill Alton were invited on to *The Tonight Show* the week of June 11, 1962, while Mort Sahl was guest-hosting, to perform a piece as Clevis, and wound up on the couch next to director Otto Preminger. The tape is apparently lost, but shortly after the performance Del recalled being savaged by Preminger.

> I just wanted to spark a conversation about his interpretation of various movies, and indeed I did have greetings to bring to him from Nelson Algren, because Nelson had said, "Don't forget to say hello to Otto Preminger." I knew they hated each other, but I didn't expect to get this vicious middle-European paranoid response. That was a slashing attack. I was completely stunned.[13]

The Second City was becoming an international phenomenon. Plans were made for an extended visit to England, an exchange program in which the Americans would perform at the Establishment Club in London, while the English cast would come to Chicago and perform at the Second City.

◆

While they were getting ready to leave for London, the twenty-eight-year-old Del sat down to share his thoughts on comedy with *The Aardvark*, which called itself "The Intercollegiate Magazine of Satire and Parody."

> AARDVARK: Bob Newhart said recently, "I've never heard a good reactionary comic. There's no Republican Mort Sahl. Anybody as individual as a comic would naturally tend toward the liberal party." Do you agree with that?
>
> CLOSE: Yes, although I thought that Bob Newhart would probably be a Republican. But I base this on having seen him a long time ago, when he was first starting out. I hear from Lenny Bruce that Newhart's beginning to cook now, but I haven't seen him in a long time. But, yes, I would agree with that. And we've been asked the same thing: Why is satire always left of center? And people say the Second City's socialist or communist oriented, but actually it's even further out than that. It's anarchistic. Anything that's organized has got to be bad, somehow or other. There's got to be something to knock in anything.[14]

The interviewer then asked Del to define "sick humor," a term then coming into vogue to describe the innovative comedy exemplified by Bruce, and unsettling to conservative factions in the country.

> Sick humor is the humor that exploits, rather than exposes. . . . The thing is, you can do sick humor with taste. It may sound like a contradiction in terms, but you can. The general definition of sick comedy is anything that has any intellectual content whatsoever. . . . Mort Sahl was one of the original sick comedians, as far as the Great American Public is concerned. Mike and Elaine were theoretically sick comedians. I was, when I started out. Shelley Berman was. The weird people that we almost consider old-timers like Bob Hope were called sick comics because they were not sticking to the format. They weren't telling mother-in-law jokes. Like the Alan King routines. They were not scatological for their own sake. They were using comedy as a medium, not as an end in itself. I think there's a place for that kind of humor. Sick humor is purely latter-half twentieth-century. I don't think there was a lot of sick humor before the Second World War, a few people to the side, like Edward Lear.

The *Aardvark* writer then asked Del his thoughts on the purpose of comedy.

Well, I'm not going to say that comedy should have a didactic purpose. It just so happens I wouldn't be in comedy unless *I* had a didactic purpose. I would be in another medium.

The conversation next turned to what the interviewer referred to as "snob humor," and the Second City's use of highbrow references.

Now, you get that particular kind of snob-laugh . . . the recognition laugh. They'll laugh, for instance, when you say Vivaldi, just because they want to show that they know who Vivaldi is. . . . I think that most of the people that come to the Second City know who Vivaldi is. Also, in that particular scene—you're talking about the *Ex-Urbanites*—we are playing snobs. We are dealing in every cliché we can think of that snobs can exploit. I get some snob laughs, I suppose, in my act, when I lay out a line like "Neitzche [*sic*] is peachy, but Sartre is smarter." But I suspect that the people that are really breaking up hard are faking it, because it's just not that funny.

Del vigorously rejected an attempt at what he called "the Pagliacci syndrome," to portray comedians as sad and depressed at heart. Despite his suicide attempts and his issues with his father, he refused to consider himself depressive:

I don't think there's anything particularly tragic about any of the breed of modern comedians. I'm happy. In general, I'm not a depressive type. . . . Somebody who feels compelled to be funny all the time and is never off—like we are told that all comedians are great clowns—this is some sort of a pathological symptom.

The interviewer wraps up by asking Del how he responds when someone approaches him and asks him to "say something funny."

Belly button. That's an interesting thing. I'm writing a piece on it. A startling number of people, once they find out you're a comedian, instantly say "Say something funny." It's as if they're challenging the fact that you claim to be funnier than they are. If I had a cookie for every time somebody said "Say something funny," I would have a lot of cookies. That's Orson Bean's reply. Whenever anyone says "Say something funny," he says "Belly button," because there's something funny about belly button under any circumstances. Sometimes I fly into a rage. "What do *you* do for a living? Well, dig me a ditch!"

To the end of his days, whenever anyone asked him to "say something funny," Del unfailingly would respond "belly button."

7

Stonehenge and a Skate
Through the Sewers

In the fall of 1962, the Second City headed to London. There was a theatrical comedy boom in Britain that had begun with *Beyond the Fringe*, written by and starring Peter Cook, Dudley Moore, Jonathan Miller, and Alan Bennett. Its irreverent humor spawned similar university revues, most notably at Cambridge and Oxford, culminating in 1969 with *Monty Python's Flying Circus*.

Cook founded the Establishment Club in Soho, which featured many of Britain's brightest satirical stars, and was arguably the English equivalent of the Second City (although the Brits, including such talents as John Bird, Eleanor Bron, and John Fortune, rarely improvised). It seemed natural for the hottest comedy companies of both countries to perform at each other's theaters for a few weeks.

The Second City had assembled a "greatest hits" revue called *The London Show* in Chicago, and opened in Britain on October 2, 1962. A spokesman for the Establishment told United Press International the following day that the group, made up of Bill Alton, Mina Kolb, Avery Schreiber, Dick Schaal, and Del, performed American material "selected for English audiences. They stress international politics and their choices have proven to be just right."[1] The cast rented a flat in Eton Square; Kolb had a downstairs bedroom, Schaal and Schreiber had tiny cubbyhole bedrooms, and Del and Alton made the dining room into a bedroom.

According to Bernie Sahlins, the Americans quickly found that the Establishment were far ahead of their Chicago counterparts in the use of sexuality and profanity. The first night they were taking audience suggestions, someone yelled "Fuck you!" Second City didn't use profanity onstage in regular sketches, Sahlins said, and it had never even occurred to them to do so. (It was not uncommon for their predecessors at the St. Louis Compass to use "shit," which Mike Nichols noted they did quite regularly.) It was over two years before Del would break the rules at Second City, in a Lenny Bruce–inspired blackout in which he uttered "No shit."

◇

Three weeks into their run, the world was poised on the brink of nuclear war.

On October 22, 1962, President John F. Kennedy reported that the Soviet Union was building secret missile bases in Cuba, ninety miles from U.S. shores. Kennedy demanded that the Soviets remove the missiles and ordered a naval blockade. Russian premier Nikita Khrushchev authorized the Soviets in Cuba to launch their missiles if the Americans invaded. For the next seven days, the world held its breath. "The London audience wanted to kill us," recalled Kolb. "They figured we were about to set the world on fire again." And the Second City had to make people laugh.

Del would later explain that the cast learned of the blockade late one night. They all huddled around the only available radio, located in the kitchen of a restaurant next to the theater. (Bill Alton recalled walking down to a restaurant with Del and David Frost in order to listen to Kennedy's Cuban missile speech.) Like much of America, they were convinced that World War III was imminent.

The five comedians—political satirists in a foreign country, without even a director (Sills had left after opening night)—had to deal with an unthinkable political situation. They decided to consult Del's *I Ching*.

The question was "What stance should we take on this issue?" Was Kennedy a maniac? They tossed the coins. It revealed the Creative and the Taming Power of the Great. The group decided that, as arbitrary as it was, they would take the position that Kennedy was *not* insane, and that there *were* Soviet missile sites in Cuba. Explained Del: "We decided that our stance should be that this is an extraordinarily dangerous situation, and don't attempt to defend the President's actions; they're totally immoral, but they'll work, don't worry."[2]

One particularly tense night, the audience resentment toward America was almost palpable. Del tried to calm the crowd, saying, "Remember, we're all in NATO, so if anything happens, we're all going together."

One of the first pieces in the show was the classic IBM machine (which Avery Schreiber would most prominently perform with his partner Jack Burns). Del was the computer operator, reading questions from the audience to Schreiber's computer. As the IBM machine, Schreiber would go through a series of contortions and sound effects, and then eject the answer on his tongue. This usually gave Del enough time to think of a good answer. Ironically, Del would do his part so well that people would compliment Schreiber afterward on his brilliant answers, completely forgetting that Del was the one making up the witty replies.

The IBM machine was a particular favorite with the crowds, recalled Kolb: "A couple of nights were tough, because the audience was furious about this Cuban missile thing. But Del could handle it. He was amazing. He could handle anything, it was astounding." On one evening, an archetypal British gentleman stood up with the first question. "I say, sir, can you tell me the difference between Suez and Cuba?" Del snapped his fingers, which was the secret signal for an immediate answer. Avery spat it out, and Del "read" the response. "The difference, sir, is that we're strong enough to pull it off!"

There was a moment of silence, then the rumbles began: "I say, what was that?"; "Did he say what I think he said?"; "Hmmm, I say, now!"; "Well, well, good show!" And it became a standing ovation. They had been transformed from American interlopers to conquerors, and their success continued for the rest of their stay in London.

An unnamed reporter, writing in the October 28, 1962, *Sunday Times* ("Almost a Battlefield"), gave his own version of the evening's events.

> Somebody . . . shouted "Cuba" at Mr. Del Close, who was alone on stage at the time. "Cuba," repeated Mr. Del Close, and there was a murmur through the club, not exactly of anger, but of that indeter-

minate but uncomfortable feeling out of which, at a misplaced word or gesture, anger can easily and uglily arise. "We are lucky," said Mr. Del Close, "to know a word which, by itself, can rouse such an animated response." Then he paused and appeared to be thinking, while the challenging murmur continued. "I must remind you," he said, "that you are all members of N.A.T.O."

I must admit that I do not find this remark a masterpiece of logic. Membership of N.A.T.O. implies (or am I wrong?) consultation between allies; and on Cuba, though there had been information, consultation had been lacking. I must also admit that this objection did not occur to me at the time, but only the next morning. Nor did it occur to anyone else so far as I could see. In fact, Mr. Del Close's observation was a complete success. This success must, I think, have been due to his sangfroid. . . . In its way, the Establishment last Tuesday was, or could quickly have become, a battlefield, and in these circumstances, it was Mr. Del Close's calm that turned it all so decisively to sweetness and light.

Nobody after that showed any signs of being ruffled, or of wanting to raise awkward questions of international law, and Turkey was not even mentioned. Cuba did indeed keep coming up during the evening, but the acerbity had gone. Mr. Schreiber's clairvoyant robot, commanded by Mr. Del Close, answered the question from the audience, "Will all those ships get through?" with an ambiguity as brilliant as it was flippant; and Miss Mina Kolb and Mr. Schreiber improvised a guitar song on a Russian freighter to Cuba filled with Volga boatmen. This again was suggested by the audience; turning the song into a lullaby, Miss Kolb and Mr. Schreiber were as calm as Mr. Close had been. . . . I understand that before the performance began, the five players were sick at heart. Well, I do not suppose that America will hear of this evening, but if she did she could be proud of it.

During their stay, Del decided to issue his own personal responses to the Communists, who were affirming the party's accusations each day at the Speakers' Corner in Hyde Park. They claimed that the spy photographs of the Cuban missiles were fake, but each day brought out new information, forcing new denials from the Communists. "I went to Hyde Park, where this Communist speaker would get up on a box and spiel that day's party line," said Del. "Because of what was coming out, the party line changed every day. So I got a box and stood next to him and announced 'Yesterday's party line repeated here,' and while he did his spiel, I did the one he'd done the day before, which bugged the hell out of him."[3]

◇

After the missile crisis ended, the remainder of their British stint was largely anticlimactic. Avery Schreiber, writing in *PerformInk* in March 1999, claimed that one of the longest-running intracompany improvisational games began during the London visit, as a way to reduce the tensions brought about by the Cuban crisis.[4] (Alan Myerson and others claim it began with the Committee; while it may have been created during the Second City London visit, it certainly reached its zenith during the Committee years in San Francisco.)

The game was called, by some accounts, Gotcha! Players would point their index finger with thumb cocked, and the other fingers curled back. They would get three shots per day to shoot fellow players, who had to die in the most elaborate, dramatic manner possible under the circumstances. According to Schreiber, there were only three exceptions to this rule: players could not be shot if they were (1) onstage working, (2) carrying a pot of boiling water, or (3) holding an expensive camera (apparently instituted by Del after he bought an expensive camera). Schreiber further wrote:

> The game became so prevalent that it was adopted by the then imminent Shakespearean Company. Leo McKern was a player and one day as I was coming out of Harrods, McKern, across the street, shouted, "Avery, BANG. Gotcha!" and I reacted as if a bullet had ripped through me and fell face forward off the curb into a huge puddle of water. . . .
>
> [Dick Schaal remembered the Gotcha! game-playing by the Royal Shakespeare Company members, because "they just died beautifully!"]
>
> The most amazing thing I ever saw him do with this game was, when shot in the dressing room of the Establishment Nightclub, he tumbled down eight flights of the circular stairway to the backstage area without stopping—a stuntman if ever there was one. . . .

[Del was apparently no stranger to spectacular deaths; Bill Alton recalled shooting Del in Soho one evening in London, and it took Del four blocks before he finally died.]

Del created a game called Marienbad, which I call The Game Game. There were no rules, and it was loosely based on word association and gestures that were at once challenging and had to be answered immediately. He and John Brent created it together and I was called in to play it when Brent was absent or not interested in playing it. During the first game, which calls for three points scored in order to win, Del and I were tied at two points each and he started the new round with "I win!"

"How do you win?" I challenged.

Del smiled over his glasses as he turned to leave the stage. "I cheat!"[5]

The British visit marked one of the few times that he tried to induce others to get high. He talked the cast into trying some hash brownies at intermission to see what effect they would have on their performances. The effects of the hash were particularly obvious during the performance of the "Ex-Urbanites" scene. Schaal was supposed to make an entrance, but he remained backstage. The onstage cast started saying, "I think I hear someone at the door!" "There's someone at the door there!" Finally, somebody went to the door and said, "A-ha! I thought I heard someone at the door!" and brought him in, and they somehow finished the scene. Schaal recalled feeling embarrassed and helpless as they stood silently on the stage.

Del couldn't resist taking advantage of the trusting Kolb. A cab or minibus would pick up the actors and take them to the theater, and he would approach Kolb, saying, "Carry this for me, would you?" and hand her an old film tin. She always agreed to carry it for him, having no idea that it was filled with hash. Del even enlisted her to carry the film tin back to the States for him.

Shortly after their return to Chicago, the company opened *The London Show* on December 4. Less than two weeks later, the company underwent another major change. Bill Alton did not return from London with the group, and Kolb decided to move to New York. Only Del, Schaal, and Schreiber stayed on from the London trip; they were joined by Tom Erhart and newcomers Dick Libertini and Macintyre Dixon of the Stewed Prunes, Larry Hankin (introduced to the Second City in a workshop run by Myerson in New York City), Ruth Weiss of the University of Chicago, and Jack Burns (formerly partnered with George Carlin, and soon to be partners with Schreiber). Dennis Cunningham had been working as a bartender at the Second City since the early days of the theater, but after taking some of Del's very early workshops, he was put into the cast of *My Friend Art Is Dead.*

◈

The new players, with a few further changes, opened the Second City's eleventh revue in February 1963, *To the Water Tower.* Most of the cast referred to it simply as "Peep Show," a reference to the framing device used to connect sketches. Like *My Friend Art Is Dead* before it, *To the Water Tower* continued early experiments to link sketches, an idea strongly promoted by Sills. Both included scenes about the peace movement and antinuclear protests. Del's General Clevis would make his final appearance here, completing the cycle begun in *A Knocking Within* and *My Friend Art.* By this third appearance, though, Del was becoming more interested in acting and character development, and made the general a more rounded, three-dimensional creation.

In *Something Wonderful Right Away,* Del recounted the sketch, which had General Clevis inspecting a nuclear laboratory.

> Although he devoutly believed in his extremely right-wing military stance, he turned out to be a completely vulnerable human being. Some scientists played a practical joke on him in a radiation laboratory, telling him that something he's handled—actually a child's toy—is a nuclear device he's done something wrong with. They convince him he's got a fatal dose of radiation. His first thought is to save the men. "Get them out of here! Get them away! Stand back! I must be hot."... So there was a progression in the three appearances.[6]

While *Water Tower* did not exactly involve a plot, it had a unified theme. The result was more than the usual collection of scenes. Though the first act of *To the Water Tower* was comprised of traditional sketches, the second act began with two conventioneers who get in a cab, calling out "To the Water Tower." Instead, they are taken to what they believe is a house of ill repute, but it is one in which the customer can get whatever "action" he desires. One of the men decides he wants to be on a CIA hit team that will assassinate Castro (before similar real-life CIA plots were revealed). The rest of the show involves scenes presenting the customers' various fantasies.

The political material went beyond what was presented by most other American theaters at that time (with notable exceptions like New York's Living Theatre, the San Francisco Mime Troupe, and the nascent Committee). There was a large cutout of John F. Kennedy as they played one of his speeches dealing with nuclear weapons, but the record would stick at appropriate moments. "He'd say, 'The multiplication of awesome weapons beyond all rational need—*tik!*—rational need—*tik!*—rational need—' Then we would bang the cutout and the speech would go on," recalled Cunningham. Even the intermission was innovative. Del donated a book of photographs and mock-ups of water tower designs and the company made slides of the various photos—some outlandish, some beautiful, some simply bizarre—which were then projected through the intermission.

Will Leonard wrote another flattering review in the *Chicago Tribune* on February 24, 1963.

> If there's a place for courage in the saloon business, then the Second City players have it. They are not afraid to try something new and different. Sometimes they miss, more often they hit. In *To the Water Tower*, they have a show whose first half consists of their customary blackout and revue material, but whose second part is a single powerful sequence in a serious mood but with a dashing style. A colorful, complicated, somewhat fantastic satire with a dreamlike quality, it's called "A Peep Show for Conventioneers," and Second City should be proud of it.
>
> Two conventioneers, looking for away-from-home thrills, inquire of the man at the door of a mysterious place if this is where the action is. He assures them they can get action here, and they do. But it isn't in the wine, women, and song cliché. The conventioneers get their thrills on a national, international, cosmic scale. They are hurled about the globe, now in dire peril, now with destiny in their hands, on a scale limited only by the onlookers' imagination, and with an insinuation that no man today actually can comprehend how much action there is on this earth. Myself, I imagine that this time, they have hit again.

The eleven skits before intermission are an excellent show in themselves, with a Marina Towers ballet that is a fine example of that Second City rarity, corn.

Shortly after the group's return from London, Del came down with hepatitis, which hampered his performing. His drug intake began to increase around the same time, likely accelerated by the proximity of John Brent.

In [Brent's] apartment above mine on Hudson St., we'd get high after the Second City show—him on junk and me on speed—and he would nod out holding a burning cigarette. I would watch and catch the hand before it burned his chest. A couple of times I experimented with *not* "spotting" him, and he somehow managed not to burn himself. Nor did he set the pad on fire.

We used to do a bit at Second City involving three folksingers—John, me and Avery Schreiber. In those days, a lot of folk singers would stick a cigarette under the strings above the top fret of a guitar—and below the pegs to keep it burning and handy for easy access. I would tuck a cigarette just *below* the top fret under the thickest string, pluck the string with a resounding "boing" and the cigarette would be flipped high into the air. John's hand would flick out and grab it as it descended, four out of five times.[7]

In his 1990 letter to John Brent's son, he wrote that in 1963,

we were aware that every time we stuck a needle in our arm we might end up dead. This fostered a "screw you" attitude towards death. John used to describe his vision of the death experience—as he expected it to be—in typical cartoon fashion: Brightly colored concentric circles close about your field of vision, and you see—written in front of you in *backwards* script, "That's All, Folks!" On his altar—oh, yes, we always had *altars*—was an old-fashioned long-billed Donald Duck with a scythe. He called him Donald Death.[8]

Del's fascination with death was evidenced by increasingly risky drug usage, which resulted in overdoses and trips to the emergency room. He later recounted a game he would play, usually with Darden, that they called the Suicide Game. Each player would describe the most elaborate suicide that he could imagine. Darden's plan was to rent offices on the top floor of the Empire State Building, then bring up his 1930 Rolls-Royce Phantom II, one piece at a time, and assemble it. Then, he would take out the bricks from the inside, and drive out through the wall of the Empire State Building.

But it was hard to top someone who thought about suicide as often as Del. His idea was to hang himself from a weather balloon and fly over the city. As he was strangled, he explained, his sphincter would relax, and he would dribble all over the city. The authorities would be busy trying to figure out whose jurisdiction he fell under, and what they should do about it, noting, "If they shot me down and I landed in a playground, it would really be depressing for the children!"

Another of Del's mythic moments occurred during this period. The exact details are impossible to determine, though it almost certainly took place in Chicago.

> One day I found myself with this .32 automatic and an acetylene lamp taped to my head, and I was skating through the [Chicago] sewers firing at rats.[9]

Del would go on to embellish this in the pages of *Wasteland*, as the first of his autobiographical stories. Titled "Sewer Rat" and written with assistance from John Ostrander, it affirms the date and the city as Chicago, 1964. It begins with him skating in the sewers, shooting rats. There is a hallucinatory quality as he encounters a rapidly changing array of images. After rejecting his own suicide, he discovers a Dixieland band, several duplicate versions of himself, and his mother in her rocking chair. He explains, "At first drugs were a sort of religious experience . . . and then, as you can see, things deteriorated a little bit . . . !" Del finally emerges, skating away as the closing caption is careful to point out "Insofar as I can determine, the events in this story are true."[10]

◇

The twelfth revue, *20,000 Frozen Grenadiers or There's Been a Terrible Accident at the Factory*, was the only one directed in part by Del during the 1960s. Sally Hart, Ann Elder, and Omar Shapli joined Schaal, Cunningham, Burns, and Schreiber in the cast. Sills got the show on its feet, but when he left town immediately after the opening, he left it to Del to direct. While not a bad show, it was far from the Second City's most memorable. Piano player Bill Mathieu helped create an opera spoof; the show also included a pool hall scene by Brent and Schaal about fear of homosexuality.

Del was admittedly not the most evenhanded or well-adjusted director: "I didn't know anything about it, but I was about the only one available. I was very bad at it—imitating the worst things Paul did. I knew all of the external pyrotechnics without any real understanding of what Sills was doing. In fact, my main imitation of Paul consisted in being totally obnoxious to everyone in the cast."[11]

Sills returned to direct the thirteenth revue in midsummer 1963, but would not stay long. During the rehearsals for *13 Minotaurs or Slouching Toward Bethlehem*, Sills left abruptly—this time for good. The confrontation occurred during an early rehearsal of the "Family Reunion" scene, which examines a family returning home from their Aunt Emily's funeral. Del later admitted that he was invoking his own father for the character of the inhibited father who is in denial about everything, from Aunt Emily's drinking to his son Warren's sexuality, and he rebuffs every attempt by his son to discuss the youth's homosexuality. (Del explained that his own father was blankly incapable of understanding anything that he didn't want to understand.)

Unlike most of the earlier family scenes at the Second City, it was about a repressed white Anglo-Saxon Protestant family. As Del would later recall, Sills came into the rehearsal and called to them in the middle of the scene: "'People don't behave like that!' I spun on my heel and said 'Per-fucking-haps and per-fucking-haps not!' And Paul spun on *his* heel and went to New York for four months."[12]

Patinkin, who was Sills's assistant director, was overseeing the rehearsal of the highly emotional piece that day. As Sills stormed out of the theater after shouting at the cast, he walked past Patinkin and muttered, "You can do it then, Sheldon." An hour later, Patinkin called Sahlins and asked where Sills had gone. Sahlins told him, "He's on his way to New York. You're the director now."

With that, Sheldon Patinkin became the new director of the Second City. Until that moment, Del had considered himself Sills's heir apparent. Instead, he saw Sills's upstart assistant appointed to the job that he coveted. He was stunned, furious at being passed over.

Until that surprising development, Del and Patinkin were cordial, if not close. Del never viewed him as any sort of creative threat to his ambitions. All that changed with Sahlins's announcement. "We did not have a good relationship," noted Patinkin. "I got along fine—I didn't care! *I* wasn't jealous of *him*." Unlike Sahlins, however, Patinkin took it personally, and their relationship began a rapid downward spiral.

Even still, the "Family Reunion" scene rehearsal the next day was highly productive. The cast all liked it, though they complained that Sills had kept trying to turn it into a scene about his mother, Viola. They improvised it for Patinkin, and then improvised it again that evening as part of the set, and it barely changed from that point on. It was a brilliant sketch that the audience loved as much as the actors. The company was proud of the result, even though at points it was brutal and uncomfortable.

It was one of the few creative highlights for Del under Patinkin's directorship, however. The professional jealousy and personal animosity caused Del's relationship to deteriorate further during the run of *13 Minotaurs*, which opened in September 1963 with a cast that included Del, Burns, Elder, Hart, Schaal, Schreiber, Shapli, and John Brent.

Although he would continue to perform with them for another six months, Del was effectively finished with the Second City. He would stop restraining himself. But he would not quit. Like Hamlet, he would not take such a firm, decisive action. He would see how long it took them to fire him.

◇

Del was clearly losing control. Patinkin claims that his erratic behavior increased, and he would begin swearing at the audience, usually without provocation. Following the Kennedy assassination, Del became the first person to use the word "fuck" before an audience on the Second City stage, albeit improvised. The Second City closed on Friday, November 22, 1963—the only Friday night it has ever been closed—but reopened the following night. While taking suggestions for the improvisation set, an audience member called out "the assassination." The audience gasped, and Del turned to the man and angrily asked, "Just what the fuck did you want to see, sir?" The audience burst into applause.[13]

But audiences were not responding as enthusiastically to his more gratuitous profanity. Lenny Bruce was in the headlines for his various arrests for obscenity, and Del was using language nearly as strong as

Bruce's in some cases. His drug use increased to the point at which he became incoherent onstage, and it became impossible to let him continue with the show. Del was asking to be fired, expected it, and even admitted as much. But it took Sahlins and Patinkin a long time to decide that it was necessary.

The 1963 holiday season was not a pleasant time for the company, and everyone knew the boom was about to be lowered on Del. At that point, *13 Minotaurs* was ending its run, and Patinkin had begun to direct Del in the Second City's fourteenth revue, *New York City Is Missing*, which was to open January 1964.

The cumulative effect of his behavior forced their hand, however. After several meetings, Sahlins and Patinkin decided to fire Del shortly before opening night. His replacement would be a rising young comedian named David Steinberg. Del had seen his act and recommended that Patinkin and Sahlins go see him and hire him. Ironically, he would become Del's replacement.

It fell to Patinkin to deliver the news. "I lost that one. I'd won the one before it. I fired a waiter, [Sahlins] had to fire an actor," said Patinkin, noting it went well. By his own admission, Del was "too stoned" to continue performing. He even defended the Second City's decision. "I was too high too often and it was affecting my work," he explained. "Some people told me that some Loyola students were thinking of demonstrating in protest in front of the theater, so I went and found the people who were talking about it and told them not to. The management was absolutely correct in firing me."[14]

A notice appeared in Will Leonard's column in the January 12, 1964, *Chicago Tribune*, announcing the title and cast, minus Del, for the upcoming revue: "That means the capable Del Close will be absent and we shall miss him." There were other repercussions a month later, when John Brent decided to quit the Second City. Although he was as deeply into drugs as Del, he wasn't fired. He simply couldn't stay there any longer without his best friend.

Del stayed around Chicago for the next year. He attempted to develop a nightclub act incorporating his newfound interest in optics and light effects, but it was less successful than his earlier comedy. The Centaur, a new coffee shop located in the basement of a grocery store, opened on January 8, 1965, with folksinger Jo Mapes and Del introducing "a weird light effect act." A review in Will Leonard's "On the Town" in the January 24, 1965, *Chicago Tribune* noted that "Del Close, a way out commentator and comic and actor, is billed as the 'Mad Doctor,' and this time he's just a little further out than we can reach."

By early 1965, Del had used up most of his opportunities in Chicago, and tried to access the likeliest spot for him to begin anew. Though there was still a Second City company in New York, Del had become persona non grata; and he seemed to lack the discipline for stand-up. He was a voracious user of speed, with no sign of slowing his consumption. Finally, the Chicago police suggested that he leave their jurisdiction. Del decided a little more distance might be preferable, so he packed his bags and headed for California.

8

The Merry Pranksters
and *My Mother the Car*

Los Angeles was an obvious destination for Del. He had rejected New York, failed in Chicago, and needed a fresh start. L.A. seemed perfect. Many of his performing friends were already there, lured by money, fame, warmer weather, and a more laid-back lifestyle. He could move west and, with the help of his stand-up and improvisational connections, line up ample TV and film work.

Avery Schreiber had been cast in a new situation comedy, titled *My Mother the Car*. The title and the premise made it an easy target for critics, but it was far from a ratings disaster. It proved particularly popular among children, although it was canceled after the first season of thirty episodes. (Its creators, Allan Burns and Chris Hayward, went on to create, among other series, *The Mary Tyler Moore Show*.)

The show debuted on NBC on September 14, 1965, and starred Jerry Van Dyke as a man whose deceased mother (voiced by Ann Southern) is reincarnated as a 1928 Porter. Schreiber was an evil car collector called Captain Manzini, who would do anything to possess the Porter. Schreiber initially invited him to portray his assistant, but Del was hired as a supporting player and story editor.

Del would appear in three different episodes. The show carried little prestige, but it was a paycheck, and he got to work with Schreiber. He suddenly found himself in some demand in late 1965. He appeared on the spy spoof *The Double Life of Henry Phyfe*, which starred Red Buttons as a humble accountant enlisted as a government spy. He had a particularly memorable scene with Don Adams in *Get Smart* as Minelli in "Aboard the Orient Express," an Agatha Christie spoof. (The episode aired December 11, 1965, just four days after his first *My Mother the Car*.) There was even talk that he might become the series' version of James Bond's Q, supplying gadgets to Smart, but it never materialized.

Del was living with Hugh Romney and his wife, and a few others, who would come and go, in a hotel on Santa Monica Boulevard in West Hollywood that they had dubbed "Misto Acres." (Romney would become nationally known as the emcee at Woodstock in 1969; as Wavy Gravy, he went on to found the expanded counterculture family known as the Hog Farm, and began operating an annual camp for underprivileged children in the 1970s.)

Del's new day job was television, but in his off-hours, he was continuing less conventional pursuits. Romney's version of another oft-told Del story is apparently the earliest and therefore the likeliest. Del found a false ceiling in one of the rooms at Misto Acres, and decided to "set up shop." He created a human-sized web with ropes, then spent hours in it, reading or getting high. Romney recalled: "His black bikini underwear and his black socks with enormous goggles—when you put them on, everything looked like rhubarb on Mars!" He would hang suspended in midair by the intricate web of thick ropes.

Del and the Romneys eventually settled in a large house on Lemon Grove Avenue just west of Western Avenue in Los Angeles. Del was "dabbling in my wife's adopted sister Lona," recalled Romney, and she soon came to live with them. There was soon a regular stream of friends and temporary tenants dropping by the large older house.

Despite a blossoming career as a sitcom actor, Del was not happy about his prospects. "It was an appalling situation," he said. "I would be doing square Hollywood things, trying to shape up and be a Hollywood actor. And Hugh Romney was trying to shape up and be a Hollywood comedian, and he had his hair all blonde."[1]

❖

Working in television would certainly cover his financial concerns, but it would erode his counterculture reputation. Del felt he needed to preserve his integrity. Timothy Leary was coming west to deliver a lecture, so Romney decided to rent the same auditorium and "talk about Silver Meat Cream, SMC: bits of rancid hamburger in gelatin capsules. And for entertainment, we've got rock and roll," recalled Del.[2]

Lysergic A Go-Go, as it was called, was intended as a gentle, respectful put-down of Leary and the then-burgeoning LSD scene, with the over five hundred attendees receiving capsules filled with Safeway hamburger as they entered the incense-filled auditorium. Leary's lecture techniques were parodied, after which the theater darkened and Del trained an ultraviolet projector on the stage, and people danced to a live band while pressurized cans sprayed mist, ropes twirled, and serapes waved under the fluorescent lights.

It was nearly a disaster, underfinanced, but saved by the energy and ingenuity of the performers when nearly everything seemed to go wrong. The original venue canceled the day before before the show, and dozens of hours of work was inadvertently destroyed when someone opened drawers full of exposed but undeveloped film.

Lysergic A Go-Go was nevertheless one of the more influential, if less remembered, events of the 1960s. Del had little interest in rock and roll, but was an enthusiastic supporter of the anarchic spirit the music represented. With that in mind, he decided to incorporate the music with a long-running obsession.

It was with *Lysergic A Go-Go* that Del claimed to have invented the rock and roll light show. At first, Romney called it little more than "giant spot[light]s moving slow." Del had long been fascinated with photography and optics, and collected an assortment of projectors. He dripped various colored dyes onto glass plates and mixed them as they were projected onto walls, bands, and dancers. Del was also experimenting with interferometry, which involved stretching or otherwise altering cellophane and plastics over lights. The word of Del's talents spread, and he would later tell his students how he had done lighting for the Mothers of Invention and the Grateful Dead, as well as *The Phantom Cabaret Strikes Again*, which Del presented with Romney and Tiny Tim.

"I've got nothing against rock and roll," Del recalled. "We'll paint up the dancers, shine some ultraviolet lights on them . . . then I'll do a light show. So we did this 'Lysergic A Go-Go,' the first time light shows and rock ever appeared together."[3]

Lysergic A Go-Go was held on November 26, 1965. The program described it as "an entertainment calculated to astound the senses, based on the manual by Metzner, Alpert and Leary based on . . . the *Tibetan Book of the Dead.*"

The participants were listed under "Who to Blame for What": "Del Close is responsible for the visual effects, using a battery of transparency projectors, UV lamps, a Lissajous wave-pattern generator, and for the 'Retinal circus,' a linear polariscope and a plane interferometer of his own design. He will turn up on stage from time to time as Dwight David Genuine, Azrad the Incombustible, and as himself." The rest of the cast included a guitar player, a conga drummer, a gong player, another color-projection artist, and Hugh Romney (the latter's bio cited his experiences with the original Phantom Cabaret with Tiny Tim and Moondog at New York's Living Theatre).

According to Paul Jay Robbins in the November 26, 1965, *Los Angeles Free Press*, Del was not immune to the snafus that plagued the event.

> Del Close, after explaining the scientific principles involved in his development of interferometry—the adhesive base of the entire show—stepped from the stage to screen his work only to discover that it was gone.
>
> Mere moments before the curtain, some nameless compulsive had tidied up the area and thrown out what appeared to be crumpled cigaret-wrapper cellophane. In actuality, it was supercellophane—specially treated by Close.
>
> The show went on with substitute materials, and the visions which Close conjured onto the screen with a projector have to be seen to be believed. Hallucinatory geometries and nameless colors sing through your eyes and rub a part of you formerly asleep and unsensed. . . . His real work may remain to be seen properly, but what we saw that night was enough to know that Del Close had a good thing going.

Robbins called the evening "an organized trip through the senses— an entertainment predicated on the psychedelic experience where one seeks direct experiences voided of value judgments."

Del later claimed that he brought a much scaled-down version of the show to perform at Lenny Bruce's house; the comedian had fallen out a window of the Swiss America House and wasn't able to attend the original.

◇

Tiny Tim may be best remembered for his appearances in the late 1960s on *Rowan and Martin's Laugh-In*, and his performances of standards from the 1920s or earlier with his falsetto and ukulele; he had a national hit with his recording of "Tiptoe Through the Tulips" and the album *God Bless Tiny Tim*. At the peak of his fame, he married his fiancée, Miss Vicki, on *The Tonight Show* at Johnny Carson's invitation.

Tiny Tim was a friend of Romney's and lived in New York with his parents. "When you called his house and [it sounded like] a man answered, it was his mother," recalled Garry Goodrow. "If his mother answered, everybody thought it was his father." Romney befriended him and made him part of the original Phantom Cabaret.

Before Tiny Tim's national fame, Romney tried to persuade him to come to San Francisco, and arranged for a Rolls-Royce filled with daffodils to meet him at the train station. Instead, he responded with a telegram: "Sorry I can't come. My mother won't let me." Few could match his performance style, and even fewer could match his eccentricities, Del recalled.

> Mr. Tim was something else. He'd cap everybody and blow everybody away. Someone said he's not so much a singer as a haunted house. He'd turn into people like early Bing Crosby or Tex Ritter. 'Cause this falsetto voice is only one of the many personalities haunting the caverns of Mr. Tim's mind. He got his start playing lesbian bathhouses in New York . . . so he basically thought of himself as a lesbian. That's why he wore makeup, to make himself attractive to the ladies. He doesn't say this himself. I told him I was going to tell this truck-driver girlfriend of his. [Tiny Tim falsetto] "Oooh, Mr. Close, if you do that I will melt just like a Hershey bar in the wind."[4]

Romney had convinced Tiny Tim to come to L.A. to appear in *The Phantom Cabaret Strikes Again*. All he brought with him was twenty cans of spinach, and he stayed in the guest quarters at the house on Lemon Grove Avenue, where he would take two- and three-hour showers. *The Phantom Cabaret Strikes Again* was "a rather obscure and very esoteric gig at this little theater [run by] some gay partner of my wife in the answering service business," recalled Romney.

Del contributed the light show and performed as Azrad the Incombustible Persian. (Romney claimed that while they were living together, Del always used to keep gasoline chilled in the refrigerator in case he was suddenly called on to eat fire, noting that he was partial to Amoco. It was likely blended with other flammable substances, because professional fire-eaters—the successful ones, at least—never use pure gasoline in their acts.)

Another highlight of the new *Phantom Cabaret* saw Del shooting electricity through his body with the aid of a 1920s marble-topped contraption. He would clutch a light bulb in one hand, then hold part of the device in the other hand, and the bulb would light up. "He'd get lots of people holding hands and the last person would hold the light bulb, and the electricity would go through everybody," said Romney.

On another occasion, Neal Cassady came to the show and wound up onstage. For reasons that remain unclear, Del and Darden threw a burlap bag around him and carried him off the stage. Other guests would include members of the Grateful Dead and Frank Zappa.

One night, Del began talking with the man who ran the theater's parking lot and found out that he had been a "painproof" for a sideshow—a person who could tolerate extreme discomfort. Del invited the former carnival performer to join the show that night. The man showed up, stripped to the waist, with an old velvet curtain tied around his waist as a sash. "He got this sadistic nurse out of the audience to sew buttons on his breasts, and he was sticking turkey skewers through his stomach," recalled Romney. "You never saw a place empty out so quickly. Tiny Tim was crying, 'Oh, no! Make him stop!' You could hear all the tires peeling out in the parking lot. Everybody wanted to get ten miles away."

The Hollywood Ranch Market was located across the street from the tiny theater presenting *The Phantom Cabaret Strikes Again*. The only place in the area open very late, it was like a beacon to the neighborhood eccentrics, who wandered down the aisles for hours. Tiny Tim soon became a regular, and would buy cans of Popeye Spinach there every night. He so endeared himself to the management at the

Hollywood Ranch Market that on his last night, they let him sing over the public address system. "There wasn't a dry eye in the whole place as he sang *Old Shep*, and *I Didn't Raise My Boy to Be a Soldier*," recalled Romney.

◆

It was the era of the Acid Test, as immortalized in Tom Wolfe's *The Electric Kool-Aid Acid Test*. Romney had introduced Del to the West Coast's nascent psychedelic scene, and they both participated in the group LSD experiments sponsored by Ken Kesey's Merry Pranksters. Del participated in the first L.A. Acid Test held February 6, 1966, at the Valley Unitarian Church. In the following week's *L.A. Free Press*, Paul Jay Robbins called it "a revolutionary concept of the function of the theatre and the relationship of individuals in a society." Nonperformers were encouraged to take part; Robbins noted that Neal Cassady "went out on an hour's worth of fascinating word salad over a mike while interferometric Del Close began casting magical and ineffable colors onto a wall, directed only by his spontaneous explorations of what he was doing. Hugh Romney began a monologue like an incantation while watching a film being shown on another section of the wall."

But LSD was never Del's drug of choice. While living on Lemon Grove during the Acid Test, he was content to rig the light shows for the others, and was the only one allowed *not* to drop acid; he preferred to shoot speed instead. Romney recalled waking up one morning and finding forty people in their kitchen making breakfast: "The Merry Pranksters were staying with us. And Tiny Tim said to me in a puzzled voice, 'Mr. Neal Cassady is looking for some grass—there is a whole lawn of it out front.'"[5]

Although he was a part of the hippie scene, Del was experiencing a clash of cultures, as he later explained to Jeff Lyon in the October 14, 1982, *Chicago Tribune*.

> I walked into one of the Acid Tests wearing my shades, a black suit, thin tie, white shirt, the hipster suit the Blues Brothers wound up later adopting. Neal Cassady is there in a pair of cut-off jeans, and he stopped dead in his tracks. "Hey, what are you trying to do, be 15 years out of date?" So I quickly let my hair grow out and changed my dress style. Protective coloration, see. But honestly, I never took

any of it very seriously. I never gave up on being a beatnik. This whole psychedelic thing was co-opted so quick. As soon as people started wearing beads, they opened up bead shops. It got too commercialized.

Where we used to do mescaline for a day and meditate, these kids got hold of it and just scarfed it down. The beatniks were on a mystical trip. We were the holy barbarians. But the '60s people, they were either politicized or stoned. The beats were apolitical. There was no way to politicize or commercialize them.

Frankly, I thought the whole revolution was a joke because if it had succeeded, look at who would have been running things. It reminded me of the Dada manifesto, "Destroy everything, replace it with nothing."

But Romney had found a lifestyle with the Acid Test, and so the two of them went off in different directions. Del's lack of enthusiasm for Hollywood led him to ingest ever-greater quantities and varieties of drugs, but he knew that if he continued down that path, he would not last long.

I have this image of myself, unable to stand, crawling down the center line of an L.A. freeway, overdosed on speed and LSD, hallucinating like crazy, cars coming by four to six inches from my head. I got out of it somehow. I don't know how. Mostly what I remember is just this moment—you've got to make this like a conceivable part of your normal behavior, so you don't panic.[6]

Del got his pills from a doctor they called Fillmore Testa, whom Romney considered a "sleazo." A favorite was a pill that was Methedrine on one side and barbiturate on the other; Del would carve them in half with a razor blade and swallow whichever half suited his mood at that moment.

On one occasion, Del overdosed after taking pills that he had arranged in brackets not unlike a sports tournament. "I came home and there he was, laid out with his arrangement [of drugs]," recalled Romney. "It was like a Ping-Pong tournament. He had the meds arranged [so that he] he started with eight, then four. He had gotten to the quarterfinals, but he didn't get past the semifinals."

Fearful because of his lack of responsiveness, Romney decided to call John Brent for advice. "John, this is your field of endeavor. What should I do?" he asked. Brent instructed him to throw the *I Ching* on Del's chest. Romney complied, and related the results to Brent. "Well, he's going to be all right then," Brent assured him. "Just stay with it." And Del gradually returned to consciousness. "It was very scary," Romney recalled. "He was cold and waxy."

In his moments of clarity, Del knew that his future lay in another direction. He picked up his weathered spiral-bound notebook and began making notes and observations on the nature of improvisation. His memory was surprisingly good, and he would go through scenes beat by beat, trying to understand the various processes involved. Improvisation had kept him grounded and sane. And now, improvisation would save his life.

9

Paying the Karmic Debt:
With the Committee in San Francisco

Desperation drove Del to approach Alan Myerson and beg for a job. Del knew how he and the others had abused Myerson at the Second City; he even tried to take the responsibility for getting Myerson fired. But in subsequent years, Myerson and wife Jessica moved from New York to San Francisco, where they founded the Committee in April 1963. It quickly became one of the nation's most successful satirical theaters, with a sharp political edge to its comedy and improvisations.

By 1966, Del's options were rapidly disappearing. He had burned bridges in Chicago and L.A., and his speed intake made him too risky to hire. At thirty-two, he was washed up.

> I was in California and in pretty bad shape, really at the end of my rope. And my old lady at the time said "Why don't you call Alan?" I said, "I can't call Alan." Then I thought, "Why can't I call him? Okay, I'll call him. All he can say is no." I just took a mighty gulp, thinking, "If he's willing to give it to me, I'm willing to swallow any bullshit I might have to put up with to pay off the karmic debt."[1]

◆

The Committee theater at 622 Broadway was built on the site of a former Italian restaurant called the Bocce Ball. It was notable for a large enclosed space with a dirt bocce court in the restaurant, where the Italians could play bocce and drink espresso. The Committee leased it, paved it, put in a service balcony and a backstage, and then got a liquor license.

North Beach was a heavily Italian neighborhood. When the Committee took over the Bocce Ball in 1963, many of the old Italian clubs were undergoing a transition, becoming topless bars and nightclubs. The entertainment street of San Francisco was moving north one block from Jackson Street, which was the Old Barbary Coast. Chinatown stopped at Broadway, and the area north of Broadway was where the Italian and Portuguese fishermen worked out of Fisherman's Wharf.

When Del first joined, the Committee was made up of talents including Peter Bonerz (later a part of *The Bob Newhart Show* and a highly respected television director), Chris Ross, Howard Hesseman (of *WKRP in Cincinnati* and *Head of the Class*, as well as such films as *About Schmidt*), Morgan Upton, Stanley Wagner, Leigh French, and Nancy Fish. Other members of the company would include Jessica Myerson, Carl Gottlieb, Roger Bowen, Garry Goodrow, Ed Greenberg, Larry Hankin, Beans Morocco, John Brent, Kathryn Ish, Dick Stahl, Scott Beach, Carol Androsky, Everett Cornell, Julie Payne, Ruth Silveira, Hugh Romney, Avery Schreiber, Dick Schaal, and Jim Cranna. Its reputation was growing, and the group went on to appear on major television shows (*The Smothers Brothers Comedy Hour*) and films (*Billy Jack*), and produce their own film (*A Session with the Committee*) and comedy albums.

From the beginning, the Committee was much more daring and political than the Second City. Del claimed that he had to become a Marxist during the five years he was working with the group. "When I took over The Committee, I had to take over this party line along with it," he explained. "And . . . one of the healthiest things an actor can do is recognize the arbitrariness of his most deeply held convictions."[2] In actual fact, the Committee comprised a wide variety of political ideologies, but it no doubt made for a better story; neither did Del "take over" the Committee, which was always run as a cooperative and ruled by consensus of its members.

Some, like Myerson, Brent, and Bowen, knew Del from the Second City. Writer/performer Gottlieb, who had served as stage manager and interim director of the Committee from 1963 through May of 1965, had heard of him and seen him in a Julius Monk cabaret revue in New York in the late 1950s. "Clearly, he was not yet the legend he was to become, he was just a buttoned-up cool guy," said Gottlieb.

When Del arrived in early 1966, the Committee was planning to open a second theater in San Francisco in which to present scripted plays. The original company focused on the new theater, and a new company took over the shows in the original theater. Del was hired for the new company in the spring of 1966, along with Gottlieb, Hesseman, Wagner, Bowen, Ross, Fish, and French. Myerson was occupied with the new theater, and the director of the new company was Bonerz.

After more than two years, Bonerz had been getting tired of directing the Committee. While Del saw improvisation as a field for experimentation and discovery, Bonerz felt that any discoveries were localized in scene production itself, just as Sills saw scene production as the goal of Viola's games. He was not overly interested in advancing improvisation, but set his sights on a career in TV, film, and theater.

Before moving to L.A., Bonerz joined the new Committee Theatre's cast of *MacBird*, and Del took over, becoming the fourth director of the Committee's original improvisational theater (after Myerson, Gottlieb, and Bonerz). "Del was a leader type, and it was a natural fit for him to be asked to direct," recalled Bonerz. Although he didn't socialize with Del (a rarity among Committee members, Bonerz was married with two children), Del made an impression on Bonerz: "He was unkempt, unruly, snatches of brilliance, very personable, hard to put your finger on, not to be trusted, and always needing some money to go to the dentist—that was their phrase for needing a fix, 'I've got to go to the dentist.' Every couple of days, they had to go to the dentist."

◆

If Del's "old lady" from L.A. accompanied him to San Francisco, she did not stay long. Del was on his own and needed a place to stay. Committee regular Larry Hankin was often on the road doing stand-up comedy while he was with the Committee, living in a large railroad apartment with high ceilings and minimal furniture in North Beach. It only made sense that they should become roommates.

Del and Hankin knew each other from the Second City workshops; during the intervening years, Del's legend had only grown. Hankin had a large hammock stretched across his bedroom, which Del liked to use as well. One day, Hankin came home and saw numerous tiny black dots on the ceiling above the hammock, opposite to the diagonal. He was perplexed. When Del returned, Hankin questioned him. Del explained to Hankin that he liked to shoot up speed in the hammock: "He was cleaning out his needle with his own blood while he was swinging, squirting the syringe up at the ceiling. All the black dots were his dried blood."

Del came home late and slept late, so the roommates saw little of each other. One day, Hankin came home and tried to use the bathroom, but the door was locked. He knocked, but there was no response. Hankin, afraid that his roommate had overdosed, began pounding on the door. Finally, from inside the bathroom, Del quietly said, "Yeah?" Hankin continued pounding until Del emerged, covered with perspiration. He looked at his roommate and said, "Oh, it's you." "Of course it's me!" exploded Hankin. Del said, "I thought you were the police." Upon further questioning, Del explained that he had been hiding underneath their old claw-footed bathtub.

Despite such incidents, they got along well, Hankin swept up with Del's enthusiasms. Del would often talk into a bottle to hear the echo, and his favorite phrase was "Boos Cafe." No one knew what it meant, but Del's delight was infectious. He would grin and say, "I just love the way it sounds, don't you?"

Del was luckier than many to survive his prodigious drug use, including the occasional overdose. Del gave the impression of being reedy and thin, with big black glasses, but was actually broad-chested and muscular during that period. Those who had to hoist him to his feet or walk him around were usually surprised by his barrel-chestedness and upper-body strength befitting a fencing champion. The fact that he survived a drug habit that would have killed most people very early on indicated that his inherited musculature was spectacular. He was an amazing physical specimen.

◆

After a few months, Del moved out. For a while, he shared a two-flat with Garry Goodrow and John Brent; he also roomed for over a year with the piano player for the Committee, who was nicknamed Dr. Gosling Trauma by Brent. Trauma was short and thin, with hair down to his elbows and little owl glasses. Whenever Del wanted company when he was shooting speed and Brent wasn't available, he would seek out Trauma.

The apartment was on Filbert Street, just above Broadway and the Committee's theater. It was wallpapered with blowups of the cartoon strip *Odd Bodkins* by Dan O'Neill, then working for the *Examiner.* Del clipped out obscure news items, then blew them up and pasted them on his walls. He was apparently inspired by Brent (whom Myerson called "the Great Clipper"), who would seize the *New York Times* each day to search for obscure items, clipping them out and posting them in the bar area at the Committee. Other than clippings, all he seemed to care about at home was having a new science fiction story to read, having some pot and a full carton of cigarettes, and the privacy to enjoy it.

Del never lived in the same place for long. His true home was literally the Committee, which let him save money so that he could buy more drugs. There were several places in the theater where he could bunk down, including a balcony at one end of the room that proved impractical as an audience space.

He had girlfriends, but they never lasted long, either. Friends would see Del out with a new girlfriend, looking sparkly and animated. A few weeks later, they would be seen drinking coffee at Enrico's at two in the morning; while the woman would be wan and bedraggled, Del was just as animated as ever. And suddenly, the latest girlfriend would be gone.

◇

Del's contributions to the Committee had become highly valued, if reminiscent of the Second City. He portrayed teachers, professors, and fathers, and did not indulge in much physical comedy. He relied on intellectual, sometimes drug-related humor (often wearing the speed freak's telltale moustache of perspiration while performing).

One of his edgiest, most daring scenes with the Committee was "The Clean-Up" (it is preserved on the Committee album titled *The Wide World of War*). Del and Hankin play junkies who pretend they aren't really addicts, but only use drugs as tools to expand their consciousness. They try to get high and can't leave the room; when one of them offers to sell him his lighter, an outraged Del sputters, "You can't sell fire! It's one of the four elements!"

The junkies have run out of veins, so one of them decides to shoot up into his eyeball (there is a horrific sight gag), and the others are kicking themselves because they hadn't thought of it first. Finally, one of them overdoses, and Del tries to calculate how much he could make selling his friend's corpse to a nearby medical school.

"The Clean-Up" is one of their funniest, darkest scenes, and is Del at his most extreme. He was through swearing at audiences (unless it was in the context of a scene). He didn't have a Sahlins or Patinkin to tell him what to do. He had found a home at the Committee.

When Del started directing the Committee, he stopped performing, though he would still fill in when necessary. His only regular role was in a big act-closing sketch called "Curse of the Mummy." It was structured like a 1930s black-and-white melodrama and set in an English manor, with a sinister butler and a beautiful ingénue. Del portrayed the mummy, who appeared at the conclusion and brought shrieks from the house. He was thoroughly into the part.

One surprise almost backfired, however. Garry Goodrow played an old Egyptian servant in the scene, which featured an elaborate set of doors. Unbeknownst to the others, Del had removed the hinges on the side of the door and put them on the bottom, so that it would *slam* open. On his cue, Del pushed it open, and Goodrow said it missed him by inches: "It would have driven me like a nail into the stage. But, it did scare the bejeezus out of me. I must have jumped three feet in the air!"

Most felt that Del made his biggest contribution to the Committee as a director. In St. Louis, he had lived through the creation of the Westminster Kitchen Rules by Ted Flicker and Elaine May. In San Francisco, he was codifying the rules for improvisation, Del Close style. All of his writings and theories, including those that resulted from his drug-induced reveries, were brought to life with the Committee.

Del was a hands-off director who encouraged his actors to pursue their material. He knew that, under his guidance, they would eventually discover the truth in their work. The company was well balanced, one of the more memorable improvisational companies ever put together. Roger Bowen began with the Playwrights Theatre Club in Chicago, predating even the Compass Players. Howard Hesseman and Carl Gottlieb, who often worked together, had a literary construct and sometimes created as a team. Peter Bonerz had become experienced as a director at the Committee. Del was simpatico with Chris Ross and John Brent as well.

◇

In his workshops for the Committee company members, Del tried to challenge his actors and stave off boredom. Sometimes a workshop would involve physical exercises, and the company would invite the Ann Halperin Dancers (originally brought in by Myerson) to work with the actors.

In addition to the company workshops and rehearsals, Del would also teach a workshop that was open to anyone with cash in hand—wannabes, hopefuls, and hangers-on. The Committee's workshop tradition, similar to that at the Second City, was begun before Del's arrival in San Francisco.

Occasionally, there were opportunities for more promising workshop students to go onstage Monday nights, providing a path for the most talented to join the company. More often, workshops contained students who had done high school plays or tried stand-up comedy. Most of the students had five good minutes that worked for them, a routine or a monologue, and felt they could develop a career simply by refining this one small facet of their talent. "Forget that," Del would tell them. There was no point in relying on their familiar, safe, and comfortable material. He would challenge them, urging them to take chances, leave their comfort zone, and risk failure.

The actors and the students were drawn by his self-assurance, and he rarely gave them a reason to doubt him. "Del had a peculiar sense of macho," observed Alan Myerson. He was ambitious, self-confident, and liked to be the center of attention. Myerson also noted a sense of hubris, an arrogance that went back to the Second City workshops with Viola Spolin, but Del seemed to be pulling it off.

He had planted himself firmly in the center of what was slowly becoming a phenomenon. The Committee was proving that the Second City, the Premise, and the Compass were no flukes. Like many other company members, he shared the vision of improvisation as an end in itself. Unlike the others, he saw that it held the potential to become his life's work. He was not yet the Guru of Improvisation, but the seeds were being planted.

Improvisation did not require him to painstakingly polish material, and usually had a rough edge. As with his unfinished toy train, there were no penalties for leaving scenes uncompleted. In fact, audiences seemed to appreciate the successful scenes more when they could watch their creation.

Del's contributions as a director were not always easy for an audience to discern, but they were often memorable to the actors. Former student-turned-actor Dan Barrows (who later changed his stage name to Beans Morocco) noted that Del started many of his workshops with a trust exercise (originally developed by the Living Theatre), in which he would climb to the upper level of the stage and then fling himself into the waiting arms of his students. He felt it gave them enough confidence to know that their fellow actors would be there for them.

◈

Another legendary Del moment occurred during a trust exercise for a new group in the theater, which had a small balcony eight feet above the stage (accessible by a ladder just behind the doors of the set). When he was excited, Del had a propensity for speaking rapidly, utilizing rather bizarre imagery. He had the students gather below, but when he made his dive, he either hadn't been clear or the students didn't believe he would dive. When he flew off the platform, they didn't break his fall, and he hit the floor and broke his collarbone.

Despite the pain, he didn't want to spook the students, and he saw it as an opportunity to teach them trust and caring for one another on a personal level. He climbed the ladder and dove again. And they missed him again. "Del had all the trust," remarked Howard Hesseman. "He just wasn't quite getting it through to the other people."[3]

As Del would earnestly proclaim afterward, "I would rather suffer the pain of disappointment than carry the burden of distrust." Those who knew only his ego and pomposity had a difficult time reconciling that side of him with his profound, poetic spirit.

After decades of retellings, Del himself would claim that it was, variously, a broken arm, collarbone, or shoulder (Myerson remembered it as a broken collarbone and shoulder). But he remained certain of one thing: "I knew the sixties were coming to an end when they dropped me."

There was another sign that the sixties would not last forever. Gotcha! or Bang! had taken root on the West Coast. The rules were the same as those developed in London in 1962. If you were shot, you had to fall wherever you were, and refusal to fall would break the game. It became even more popular in San Francisco than it had in London. Although it was originally intended as a device to allow spectacular "deaths," it soon became as much about the shooting as the dying. People would send letters ending with "Bang!" and classified ads began appearing as part of the game. But eventually, the game started getting old.

One day, Larry Hankin saw Del getting into a car, wearing a clean suit. Hankin stuck out his finger and shouted "Bang!" But Del said, "No. Sorry." He'd had enough. The rest of the cast was shocked, and word spread quickly. "Did you hear what Del did? He wouldn't die!" Del, who had helped invent and propagate the game, decided to end it. He was the only one who could. "Del had the guts to break the game," Hankin explained. No one else dared to say no.

Another oft-told Del story emerged during this period, when Del was living in an apartment above John Brent on Kearney Street. Brent and some friends were downstairs, listening to music, when they heard strange noises from Del's apartment. "Pace, pace, pace, pace, pace, pace, pace, *thump*!" There was a pause, and then the pacing resumed. After a few more "pace, pace, pace, pace, pace, pace, pace, *thump*!" sounds, they decided to check on Del upstairs. He greeted them, excited (and naked), with "I've just found a way to achieve nirvana!" He explained that by repeating the same sequence of steps in the same place, he could consistently achieve a higher state of consciousness. He offered to demonstrate.

Del led them to an empty room. As they watched, he carefully traced the complicated pattern as he counted out the steps. On the final step, Del's body jolted, his eyes bugged out, and he hit the floor with a *thump!* Brent helped him up as Del regained consciousness. "See?" he said excitedly. Then, Del quickly jumped to his feet and repeated the eight steps once again. As before, on the eighth step, he stiffened, then fell to the floor.

Brent examined Del's trail more closely. As Del again regained consciousness, he said, "See? I've found the sequence of footsteps that allow me to achieve nirvana!" Brent pointed out that on the final step, Del was treading on a worn area of the carpet with an exposed electrical wire.

◆

Most of Del's San Francisco friends were involved with the Committee in some form or another. While that was fine most of the time, it required him to be "Del Close," the larger-than-life figure who always had to entertain and impress his peers. He was careful not to let them see his vulnerable, more human side. How could they respect him if they saw his softer self? It was a lesson he had learned by observing his father, who didn't let down his guard, even in front of his family.

But even while he was ambivalent about playing the role of "Del Close," public figure, Committee member, and counterculture enthusiast, another part of him thrived on it. He lived for the adulation, even as another part of him dreaded the responsibility to uphold his wild reputation. Sometimes he needed to get away from the others. So at night, after a show, he would take some speed, hop on an all-night bus, and ride it until dawn.

On one of these all-night jaunts, he encountered a young man named Hammond Guthrie, and they began talking, discovering that they shared a mutual friend in Hugh Romney. Del wore three pairs of glasses—the frames from one pair of glasses, the lenses of a second pair, which were rubber-banded around the first, but because they weren't strong enough, he had rubber-banded a third set onto the front of those. "He was wearing the pieces from three different sets of eye-glasses held together by colored rubber bands. He sported a long ponytail sprouting from a rapidly balding pate and plainly operated on his own frequency. . . . Together we launched into an all night discourse on the Joyous Cosmologies of Speed."[4]

With Guthrie, Del could leave behind his public persona and be spontaneous, silly, or stupid—something he couldn't do around his theatrical peers; he knew Guthrie would never say "Del isn't as smart as you thought he was!"

Del invited Guthrie to meet his friends at the Committee. When he arrived, he encountered Del in the lobby of the theater as he was affixing a Dan O'Neill cartoon to the wall. He was wearing the inner lining of a football helmet with a propeller on the top of it, which he was constantly spinning.

When he noticed Guthrie, he paused and said, "Wait a minute." He handed the paper to the young man, telling him: "This is all you need to know about morals and life, for the rest of your life. This is the Ten

Commandments of Dolphins." Then he posted it on the wall without another word.

They continued to ride buses together at night, paying 15¢ for a token and a transfer and riding all night, occasionally changing buses on a whim. They called it Rapid Transit Yoga. The two of them also shared an enthusiasm for manhole covers. They would go down by the waterfront at 3 A.M. and make charcoal rubbings of cast-iron manhole covers. Del's collection included rubbings from Los Angeles, Chicago, and New York as well.

Guthrie said that Del once revealed that "all I really want to be is just another guy on the street." "He had tears in his eyes," said Guthrie. "He really meant it." But Del was coming to realize that what he had to give was, ultimately, very important to the future of improvisation. For that, he was willing to be "Del Close."

◈

Del had always been quick to take advantage of the era of Free Love, easily picking up students or waitresses whenever he was in the mood for female companionship. One such encounter, known as the "Coleslaw Story," was presented in *Wasteland* with cowriter John Ostrander, where it was called "Subtext Salad."[5] According to Del, it was based on acting advice by Elaine May, who recommended that an actor have a secret from the audience. Del explained that he had decided to fill his underwear with coleslaw, in hopes of adding an extra layer of depth to his performance that evening. The device worked perfectly at first, and gave his performance an edge. But that edge wore off as the coleslaw reached body temperature. And he eventually forgot all about it.

After the show that night, he picked up a girl in the bar, and she came back to his apartment. As they began to undress, rancid cabbage fell out of his underwear. He tried to explain to the horrified girl that it was an acting exercise, but she quickly ran off. Del is left holding a pair of underwear full of chopped cabbage, wondering what she must think of him, as he realized, "You can't even dignify this with the name 'perversion'!"

According to Alan Myerson, the truth about the "Coleslaw Story" is that it originally happened to John Brent. He filled a baggie with coleslaw and put the cold packet in his shorts, calling it his "Salad in the Pants Theory of Acting." Del may have indeed tried it himself later, but the second part of the story involving the girl feels very much like one of Del's embellishments. Even in anecdotes, Del could find a way to improve on the original.

◈

Del's relationships with the opposite sex were usually casual and brief. He never saw himself marrying again or having another child. He would occasionally pick up a workshop member, but such relationships were purely carnal. It was a post-Pill and prefeminist era. "There weren't many comedy groupies, I know that for a fact!" joked Carl Gottlieb.

> Del was exotic and had good dope, so he could always get one of the girls in the workshop as a partner. But they came and went. A couple of times, I had a girlfriend who had been with Del. They wouldn't talk about him, but I remember them intimating that he was a little bit creepy, that they didn't choose to extend their relationship. Most of them would not want to go climbing in dark spaces, they didn't share Del's enthusiasm for the needle, and for climbing and adventure, so they didn't last long.

Del gained a reputation as a misogynist, and there is certainly evidence for those who would argue this. Very few of his improvisational companies ever had more than one or, at the most, two women, which he jokingly referred to as "nature at work."

> I had no women in San Francisco at some point. I said listen, I gotta have a woman; I'm going to hire the first woman who walks through the door. So I did. . . . I didn't test her out in any way. I figured I was a good enough director so that I could, you know. . . . Anybody can improvise that's halfway sane. The culture spends most of its time telling us we can't. "The entertainer is a specialist; he's different." Well, he's not. We can entertain each other at a very high level of quality. It's much more useful for me as a teacher to treat everyone as a poet and a genius, because they're more likely to behave that way than if they're treated like they're an idiot.[6]

The few women that Del cared for, he virtually worshipped. (Literally, in one case: as a pagan later in life, he worshipped a goddess.) He

Del and George in an undated photo,
looking very much like a young couple
in love. (COURTESY OF CHARNA HALPERN)

was devoted to his mother, and he always claimed that Elaine May and his ImprovOlympic partner Charna Halpern were the only women he ever loved. With few exceptions, that appears to be true.

But Del almost never spoke of another serious relationship with a girlfriend, and many of his close friends in Chicago in the 1980s and '90s never even knew about George. ("My father wanted a boy," she would joke.) She was considerably younger than Del, perhaps as much as ten or fifteen years, but they seemed ideally suited to each other. They genuinely liked each other, and seemed at ease in each other's company.

She appeared at a workshop one day in 1968, wearing her nurse's uniform, and Del and George quickly became a couple. (Alan Myerson was uncertain whether she was actually a nurse, or, like many at the time, simply liked to dress up). His colleagues at the Committee who had seen her predecessors quickly come and go were shocked. Everybody was waiting for the same fate to befall George. Instead, she seemed to take on a wifely role. She moved in, cleaned up his apartment, and then cleaned up Del.

None of his colleagues had ever seen a woman affect Del in the way that George did. Not since Elaine May had a woman wielded such influence over him. Both were physically similar, short, dark women with a personal magnetism. May could be dominant, wielding a caustic, cutting wit feared by her targets, with an intellect second to none. But George was intelligent as well, if in a more intuitive manner. While she may have been more malleable, she was nobody's doormat, and was capable of standing up to Del when pushed too far. Those were important traits for the women in his life. Anyone who did not meet an acceptable intellectual standard or became subservient would eventually be dumped with scorn and derision.

On the other hand, George and Elaine May were as different as they were similar. May was tougher, worldly, driven to success. George was caring and nurturing, as evidenced by her apparent choice of profession, yet she still had the necessary strength to anchor Del, who was prone to becoming untethered from the real world.

Friends of Del who knew George spoke glowingly of her, describing her as easygoing and genial. Del's lifestyle certainly required a caregiver, and a nurse's knowledge of pharmaceuticals may have been a plus for Del. George became his "old lady," a constant presence in his life for the next several years. But years later, none of his friends could even recall her last name.

10

The Birth of Harold, Spidering,
and a Pornographic Western

The Harold was first performed in 1967, under the auspices of the Committee. Created by the company members of the Committee, it marked the first modern step toward long-form improvisation.

Before the Harold was developed, most improvisations were either short two-to-five-minute sketches, quick blackouts, games based on Viola Spolin's work, or the occasional musical piece. Though created on the spot, they were short and unrelated. There had been glimpses over the years of the value of connecting scenes (as in *My Friend Art Is Dead*), but nothing made a lasting impact. The Harold would be a way to combine various devices under one theme, interconnect them, and come up with a lengthy, unified whole.

While the other Committee members helped bring it into the world, it was Del Close who would eventually take it under his wing and nurture it in the outside world, watching it grow into something bigger than most could foresee.

It is debatable whether the Harold would have survived as anything more than an improvisational novelty after the close of the Committee without Del's efforts. What is not debatable is that Del was the one who spent decades seeing the Harold practiced, honed, and redefined as the first significant form of long-form improvisation.

In the years to come, Del would never lay claim to creating and developing the Harold by himself. But when his actors and his other students came to assume that it was all his creation, he was not always quick to set the record straight. In fact, he did have a proprietary interest in its expansion. While the Westminster Place Kitchen Rules were chiefly the creation of Ted Flicker and Elaine May, and so many of the now-familiar games had been codified by Spolin in her *Improvisation for the Theater*, he knew that in spreading the Harold, he could make a truly lasting contribution to the world of improvisation.

Del's involvement in the first Harolds has sometimes wrongly overshadowed that of the entire group. In fact, the first Harolds were very much the creation of the entire ensemble. "Let's not rush to make Del the synthesizer of it all," warned Carl Gottlieb. The companies were collaborative, and Del was one of a company that was finding its way in that direction. Although he was the director, he obviously depended on the interaction of the company.

Under Alan Myerson's direction, the Committee performed two early versions of long-form, predating the Harold, before Del had even joined them. In 1965, the company devised the "Fear, Guilt, and Impotence Collage." It was a compendium of sketches and improvisations, a slide show, primitive audiovisual material, as well as low-technology extras like a slide projector and a tape recorder. The company performed an act-long piece, highly adventurous at the time. The second was a device called the Exorcism. The Committee had also done a series of very long scenes, twenty to twenty-five minutes or even longer, dealing with the issue of reality and the breaking of it, which was part of the zeitgeist that would eventually give birth to the Harold.

The original Committee theater was a proven moneymaker; it was located in the nightclub district with heavy weekend traffic, complete with a liquor license. The members did not want to tamper with their winning formula, yet the notion of long-form improvisation was their Holy Grail. Could a group of people do something together that didn't have a script, outside of what existed in their collective heads?

The entire company knew that a long-form device had to be more than the sum of its parts. Del himself had been pondering the direction of improvisation as he experimented in his workshops. Could there be a way to assemble the parts into one all-encompassing, lengthier form? At the same time, the other Committee members were also interested in long-form. On the day it all came together, it was less a matter of stitching together disparate elements, Frankenstein-like, and more as if, Athena-like, Harold had sprung from their minds fully formed.

According to Myerson, the first Harold was simultaneously developed by a class he was teaching at San Francisco State, a Committee workshop in games taught by Del, and a third class, a musical workshop with selected members of the company headed by pianist Allaudin (Bill) Mathieu. Myerson had his SF State class doing a theatrical collage. (The Committee had experimented with theatrical collages in the past; these consisted of a variety of scenes that were not necessarily connected, not sequential, and all thrown into the suggestion basket.) The scenes all came together that day, combined with games. According to Myerson: "The three of us arrived independently at what came to be called the Harold."

Myerson recalls that he, Del, and Mathieu were chatting casually afterward. "Here's what's going on at San Francisco State," Myerson explained to the other two. While Del was not usually a collaborator, he and Mathieu realized that each of them had, quite independently of the others, hit upon the same concept: an interweaving of scenes that returned, made references to one another, and sometimes directly crossed over. The games served to heighten and crystallize previously introduced ideas, playing in counterpoint to their other characters. It culminated in a whole greater than the sum of its parts.

In addition to Myerson's class at San Francisco State, Ed Greenberg, a student in one of Del's workshops at the time, recalled that it was named in a Committee workshop run by Del, along with Mathieu, and also attended by Julie Payne, Dan Barrows, Joe Spano, and a few others.

Like Myerson's work with the college group, this group took a suggestion one weekday afternoon, and the result was a long-form improvised piece based on a theme. Mathieu's freeform musical brain was perfect for both Myerson's and Del's experiments. It seemed to go on forever, and when they finished, everybody was exhausted from what seemed like an afternoon of improvising. Del was almost literally bouncing off the walls. The actors were relaxing, post-Harold, as Del enthused, "We've invented a new form of theater! This is amazing! This is the future! We've got to have a name for it. What are we going to call it!" And Mathieu, as a satiric comment on Del's state, responded, "Well, Harold's a nice name." Everybody laughed, because it was such a perfect undercutting of Del's enthusiasm. "Harold!" "That's great!" "Perfect! Harold! That's the name!" Del enjoyed the satiric nature of the remark, and embraced the name immediately. It was in the spirit of *A Hard Day's Night*, when George Harrison is asked "What do you call that haircut?" and quips "Arthur."

Harold seemed a perfectly acceptable name at the time, but as it continued to develop, Del feigned annoyance at the frivolous name for his life's work. "It's a stupid name," he admitted, but he never cared enough to try to change it. (Greenberg recalled that a short time later, Del burst into a workshop, telling students that he had just been listening to the Frank Zappa song "Brown Shoes Don't Make It," and reported that it was "a musical Harold," indicating his rapid acceptance of the name.)

Not surprisingly, the memories of others vary, and each of the Committee members at that time has a justifiable claim to the beginnings of the Harold. There was widespread experimentation occurring during that period, and there was not a clear-cut delineation of its birth.

After one particularly fruitful workshop, Del greeted Garry Goodrow at the theater that evening with "We did this thing today that was wild!" The Committee company came in early, and they presented it that evening. It was as successful with the performers as it was with the audience, which had never seen anything quite like it. The company would start by asking the audience to complete a phrase such as "How can I . . . ?" or "I wish I could . . ." The performers would then present a long set of material based on that theme. It didn't succeed every evening, but Myerson didn't want to make the Harold foolproof.

The group normally opened a new show every six months, but at one point, they were having trouble coming up with polished material. After several months, they had one act with three or four good scenes, but no second act, and they had to open. Myerson kept pressing Del: "I don't care if you have a second act or not, you're going to open next Thursday." When next Thursday came, Del and the company were still not finished, so they went out and did a Harold. The audience was buzzing.

◇

Soon, it was all about the Harold. "It was a little bit like a happening," recalled Bonerz. "Certain people liked happenings, and sometimes they were really amazing, and other times, it was just 'Oh, my God, why are they covering themselves with potato soup like that?'"

The regular show, as always, consisted of sketches, but the second act was now a Harold. The long-form piece amazed Avery Schreiber, who had teamed up with Jack Burns by that point. Burns and Schreiber invited the company to open for them at a university show, but Del told him "I don't think so. I'm not ready." Schreiber cajoled and offered to split the thousand dollars they would be getting, and Del finally agreed. "They opened for us," Schreiber would later recall, "and after their performance Burns and I had to wait for four standing ovations before we went out."[1]

The Harold was born around the time when theater games had run their course to the most abstract and incoherent. Spolin was interested in transformation; of course, Spolin was a game player, not a playwright, and she didn't like words.

It fell to Del to use the transformation to advance the story, to create free-flowing improvisation that would incorporate everything the Committee was doing. Del would learn to take Spolin's concepts and give them the hard edge and discipline of down-front performing. At the Second City, Del had been told that improvisation was simply a tool for developing sketches. But he knew that it could be a unique art form, and audiences would buy tickets to watch a completely improvised show.

The North Beach area of San Francisco in the late 1960s was full of distractions. Drugs were prevalent, and women were willing, particularly for men with plenty of drugs. When Del and his friends wanted to see strippers, they did not head over to the nearby Garden of Eden or one of the other topless clubs around the area. Instead, they would announce auditions at the theater, where an array of strippers would come and perform for them, for free, under this subterfuge.

As 1968 came along, Del was doing more directing than acting, so when the performing mood struck, he would perform stand-up on Monday nights, when the Committee was normally dark. At the Garden of Eden, Del would perform in between dancers. Del would wear his brown suit, white shirt, and black shoes, but no matter what he wore, it always seemed to look rumpled. He was rail thin, doubtless as a result of speed. He performed material from his earlier act, including his monologue on beer-can openers that were everywhere until you needed one:

When you open a drawer, they're gone! They've disappeared. On the other hand, take a look in your closet. Where did all those wire coat hangers come from? Apparently, the beer-can opener is the larval stage of the wire coat hanger.

His act included a great deal of conceptual humor. "I remember watching him one night, and he was talking about trying to turn himself inside out," recalls Hankin. "He stopped for a moment, then he said 'Whew, I blew my own mind there for a second!' He smiled, and you could see that the audience got it." Del could truly work the room. He broke the fourth wall and talked to the audience, masterfully controlling them.

Del ruled his workshops with an iron hand. He was delighted to see good scenes, derisive of boring or uninspired work, and abusive of those who dared to make jokes in one of his workshops. He would roar and throw chairs, shouting, "Get the fuck off my stage!" Only the most determined would come back after being targeted by a chair or a particularly pointed epithet. (The chair throwing was apparently confined to those periods during which Myerson was out of town—he would not have tolerated such behavior.)

As angry as he became with actors who were only out for laughs, he always respected those who got his message. Julie Payne was a nineteen-year-old au pair who showed up at a workshop one day and got into a scene. She came down the stairs onto the stage in a robotic walk and said, totally appropriate to the scene, "Klaatu barada nikto." Del was dumbstruck. "What a reference level for a young girl!" He never gave Payne any problems.

Despite egotism and autocratic behavior in workshops, he was also capable of great humility. When students complimented him for his ideas and his brilliance, he would often respond by saying, "Ninety percent of everything I know I learned from Paul [Sills]," or, "I got that from Elaine May and Theodore J. Flicker."

Del liked to experiment in his workshops, both in content and location. One notable session was held on a fishing boat bought by company member Morgan Upton in Sausalito Harbor. The group realized about halfway through the workshop that the boat was sinking. They made it back without incident, and all decided it was a metaphor.

◆

Del quickly befriended Ed Greenberg, which surprised the youth. Del rarely had visitors and never allowed workshop students into his private life, the occasional groupie excepted, but he invited Greenberg to visit. Del's apartment, typical for San Francisco, was a long, narrow place with a bay window; all of the rooms emanated from the long hallway, which culminated in a kitchen at the back. It was cluttered with, among other things, his books, cats, and the paraphernalia he used for conducting light shows. He had collected an assortment of ancient camera equipment, and even converted his bathroom into a darkroom.

Del began to take on the role of mentor to Greenberg, taking care to steer him away from junkie acquaintances. Instead, he focused on books he thought Greenberg should be reading. City Lights bookstore was just a block away, and Del soon introduced him to its treasures. They would wander the store and engage in dialogue. City Lights became Greenberg's university, and Del his professor.

As part of Del became more extreme, another part, the Kansas boy, needed an anchor to stop him from going too far. With Greenberg, he had no need to outdo his most recent drug-fueled adventure. Instead, Del could teach Greenberg to appreciate the finer science fiction novels and his improvisational experimentation. Greenberg was filling the role of the son Del had but preferred not to meet. Del could protect Greenberg, teach him, mold him in the way that Del's own father never did, and Greenberg anchored Del. It was a mutually beneficial relationship.

Greenberg was apparently the first of a series of substitute sons. By carefully handpicking his children, Del would avoid any disappointments that he might experience with his true biological son. If he never met his real son, the child could not possibly disappoint him in the way that he felt he disappointed his own father.

Del kept his friendship with Greenberg separate from the junkies, who were another part of Del's life. Although smoking pot was commonplace in 1960s San Francisco, if he wanted speed and Greenberg was visiting, Del was careful to step into the other room before shooting up. It was more of a token gesture than an attempt to mislead, however. "It was pretty obvious what he was doing," noted Greenberg, who appreciated the admittedly minimal effort.

The two of them even performed some road shows on their own, and their travels were the subject of an unproduced screenplay written years later by Greenberg. The farther they traveled from California, the greater their mystique, and they were viewed as hippies who were touchstones of the whole countercultural movement.

Greenberg's close, quasi-paternal relationship with Del was supplanted to an extent when George arrived on the scene. The young man got along well with George, and the three of them would travel around the Bay Area, often in Greenberg's blue Rambler. During one such trip, Del insisted they stop off and visit Viola Spolin, who was staying at a house in Marin County. The improvisational matriarch mothered Del. When he could not slow down, she snapped, "Lie down, Delbert!" and he immediately dropped to the floor. Spolin ordered him to calm down and relax, and Del happily complied. "She was really very stern with him," Greenberg recalled; once he had settled down, they spent the rest of the evening reminiscing about their days in Chicago.

By summer 1968, Myerson and the original Committee cast had gone to Los Angeles. Many cast members were commuting to Hollywood for ever-increasing TV and film work, and they decided to open a new Committee theater at the Tiffany Theatre on Sunset Boulevard; Myerson and cast members would travel back and forth often between L.A. and San Francisco.

Del was left to direct the San Francisco Committee, and so he turned to his workshops, where he had been cultivating talents like Greenberg, Payne, Ruth Silveira, and Dan (Beans Morocco) Barrows, for replacements. Del transformed the San Francisco Committee to reflect his own interests. By some accounts, the result was disappointing, at least commercially. Whereas the Committee had built at least some of its reputation on political satire, Del did not care for either politics or satire. But Myerson's philosophical ground zero for the Committee was "Let the people find what they needed to find." He respected Del's abilities and was determined to give him enough space for the principle of discovery, which was vital to the company.

Barrows recalled that Harolds didn't work as well in their shows in San Francisco in late 1968 and early 1969 (though they were very well received in L.A.), because audiences were used to scenes. "I remember small houses and doing the Harold without much success," said Barrows. The crowds were also small because it was the middle of winter, a traditionally slow season for the theater. Another group eventually formed from the workshops, solely dedicated to Harolds, called the Experimental Wing, which would travel to colleges to do Harolds.

Along with Harolds, there was some truly exceptional scene work under Del's direction. One of the best and most innovative was a twelve-minute scene with Greenberg and Payne called "Babble," which would end differently each time, depending on how the actors played it or how the audience related to it. Payne played a woman who stayed in her apartment, and worked for an answering service. She has a blind date with Greenberg, and when they get back to her apartment, the girl is not only interacting with the man in the room, but also commenting on about five different levels on their interaction. It was stream of consciousness, and took nearly a year to perfect, but when it was finished, Del told them, "This is as good as minor Chekhov."

◇

In spring 1968, the Committee opened their first show at the Tiffany Theatre in Los Angeles. Gary Austin happened to be driving down the street that day when he saw the marquee reading "Opening Tonight: The Committee." His friend Christopher Ross was in the cast, so he asked Ross for a ticket and sat in the front row that evening (in the same row was Carl Reiner, watching his son Rob, who was in the cast). They watched in amazement. The show consisted largely of set material, though the cast did improvise a transformation, but Austin was so impressed that he went backstage afterward to ask about workshops. John Brent told him to come by on Saturday afternoon. "It'll be run by a Committee member, and it will cost a dollar." Austin showed up the following Saturday; among the fifty or so people at the workshop were Ellen (*Last Picture Show*) Burstyn and David L. (*Laverne and Shirley*) Lander. He began coming regularly; anybody who walked in off the street with a dollar could participate.

During one such workshop, the class was told that someone named Del Close would be arriving that day and would take over the workshops. The class had no idea what to expect, and when Del walked in, they had even less of an idea. He wore black work boots, black pegged pants, a long-sleeved black turtleneck. His very dark hair was pulled back into a ponytail, and his horn-rimmed glasses were held together by Band-Aids and paper clips. He walked up on the stage and addressed the wary group.

Hello, my name is Del Close. I'm going to run the classes. I'm running the workshop today. If anybody thinks he can run it better than me, come on up, I'll be your student. If I don't think you're better than me and I have nothing to learn from you, I will replace you. Now, I make the rules, you will follow them. However, if you break one of my rules and it works, I will applaud you. If you break one of my rules and it doesn't work, I will castigate you. Let's begin.

Del had arrived in L.A., where Myerson was directing the regular show. He was there to hang out, run workshops, and also perform somewhat regularly.

During every workshop, he would light each new cigarette from the end of the previous one. None of his students ever saw Del strike a match, and none ever saw him without a lit cigarette at hand. His insistence on discipline and concentration during his workshops stood in sharp contrast to his casual attitude outside the theater. He had little patience with students who wasted the group's time, and did not shy away from a confrontation when he felt it was necessary.

Austin recalled a typical disruption. One afternoon, Del was sitting onstage before a group of fifty students as one man continued arguing with him. After trying to quiet him several times, Del walked over and stood directly in front of the argumentative student, and then pointed to the two biggest students in the room. "Come here," he called them, and said, "Stand on either side of him." The man was becoming more wary, but remained in his chair as Del called Austin over. Finally, he said, "Reach down and pick him up," and they picked up the unruly student in the sitting position. "Gary, lead the way, take us to the lobby." Austin led them up the aisle of the converted movie theater, and Del asked Austin to open the front door. He told the other two: "OK, take him out through the front door and set him down on the sidewalk." They placed him on the sidewalk on Sunset Boulevard, and he said, "OK, you guys, let's go back in." Del was the last one in, and before he closed the front door, he turned to look at the student sitting on the sidewalk and said, "And don't ever come back."

Del was not always so restrained, however. Another day, a student sitting in the front had so many arguments with Del that every time he opened his mouth, the fifty students would groan. "You're full of shit!"

Del repeatedly told him, and the class's reaction made it clear that they agreed. As they argued, Del demanded that the student "Cop to this!" All of a sudden and without warning, Del picked up the bentwood chair next to him and threw it at the man's head, from the stage down to the front row. The student threw his arms in the air to keep himself from being killed, and caught the chair. Del said, "Now *that's* honest!" The other students all burst into applause spontaneously, as the trouble-maker got up, walked out, and never returned.

◈

A special workshop was held in the tiny green room at the Tiffany. Austin was one of the select dozen invited to participate, so after the main workshop had concluded, the men and women crowded into the room, gathering in a circle around a milk crate in the center of the room, and sitting on counters and chairs. "I'm going to try a few things today, so here we go," Del told them. He asked one of the women to stand on the milk crate, then said, "Take your clothes off." She complied, and stood there completely naked. He then asked her to walk around the circle of the room, naked, and make eye contact with each of the others, insisting that they return her eye contact. After she dressed, he asked a second woman to take off her clothes, and she complied. At this point, the men in the group were terrified that Del would ask them to go next. "We were *so scared*, every one of the guys, terrified that we were going to have to get naked up there and do stuff," admitted Austin. But that was the extent of the nude workshop, except for a final revelation.

Del revealed that he had prearranged everything with both of the women. He had gone to them and said, "Will you do some exercises naked?" and they agreed, so it wasn't a surprise to them. They didn't know what he was going to do, but they knew they were going to be asked to take their clothes off, and they were willing. The actual purpose of the workshop was never made clear. "He would always surprise us in those ways, he would always do weird, bizarre things," said Austin.

Austin began working his way toward the regular company at the Tiffany, even as Del continued teaching him. The young man said the most important device that Del taught him as an actor was what he called the "Fuck it" adjustment: just before going onstage, he would say "Fuck it," and then maintain that attitude the entire time he was onstage. Self-judgment and self-criticism were not allowed until after he was offstage. "I would actually watch him stand before an entrance backstage and say 'Fuck it' before he walked out, and I saw him do the 'Fuck it' adjustment the whole time he was onstage," said Austin. "This was very helpful to me, who, at the time, was very uptight about what people thought about me."

◇

As was the case in San Francisco, Del would occasionally move into the Tiffany Theatre when he was between roommates. Though it lacked a spare room, he made himself at home underneath the stage. The Tiffany stage was about four feet from the floor, and Del dragged a mattress into the crawlspace.

It proved to be a useful place to sleep. When there was a workshop, the students would begin walking around the stage doing their warm-up exercises. It would wake Del below, and he would crawl out from under the stage and start teaching.

The Committee was becoming widely known even outside California with appearances on television, guest appearances in films like *Billy Jack*, and their own record albums and film. So, when ABC began planning a new show for the 1969–70 season, it was not surprising that they would hire the Committee to host the show. It would be called *The Music Scene*, created by the producers of CBS's *Smothers Brothers Comedy Hour*, and would ultimately feature newcomers like Lily Tomlin and David Steinberg. The Committee was signed to perform sketches to introduce the week's hit song, and the band would come on the show and perform it.

To help promote the new show, a photo session was scheduled for the Tiffany Theatre with Cary Grant and the cast of the Committee; Fabergé was a sponsor of the show, and Grant was on the board of directors of Fabergé.

The cast was onstage taking pictures of Grant, the press was there, and scores of cameras were flashing, recalled Austin. Grant was socializing onstage, and very informally taking pictures. He sat in a chair as one actor at a time would come over to say hello, and the press took pictures while they were chatting.

At one point, former Second City actor Lynne Lipton, who had started working with the Committee, was sitting on Grant's lap. Unbeknownst to the group, Del was sleeping under the stage. He heard the

Del as director during his
days at the Committee.
(COURTESY OF CHARNA HALPERN)

footsteps and noise, and crawled out of his lair below them. He stood up onstage and saw Lynne Lipton sitting on Cary Grant's lap. "Cary Grant looked like Cary Grant from the movies," noted Austin, "totally dignified, classy, funny, impeccably dressed and groomed, and he was having a ball!"

Del watched Lipton sitting there for a moment. She then stood up to allow someone else to take her place. Del, although not invited, walked over to the Hollywood legend and sat on Grant's lap. To his credit, Grant never flinched. He did not know who Del Close was. He had simply seen this man, who had just crawled out of nowhere, walk over and sit on his lap. Del was unkempt, uncombed, unwashed, and probably smelled—at least in appearance, he was the anti–Cary Grant. Nevertheless, Grant never showed any sign of distaste, never flinched, never looked down his nose condescendingly. He accepted Del as he accepted everyone else. He sat with Del sprawled on his lap, his arm around Grant's neck, and they talked as the shutters continued snapping.

After the press left, Grant expressed a real interest in hanging out with the Committee. Later biographies, which reported Grant's interest in LSD, may be one explanation for his fascination, but there is no record that Grant ever got together with the group again. (A few days later, the deal between *The Music Scene* and the Committee fell apart when the Committee refused to let the network determine which members would be on the show. Carl Gottlieb and Larry Hankin jumped ship and did the short-lived *Music Scene* anyway; it created a rift between the two of them and Alan Myerson, Howard Hesseman, and others in the company.)

Monday nights soon became as popular in L.A. as they had in San Francisco. The cast of the Committee always had Monday off, but the theater eventually began offering alternative entertainment on Mondays. The evenings became highly popular and featured richly diverse entertainments. Del enjoyed doing light shows for the Monday night festivities (and for their occasional marathon benefit performances, which they called Satirythons, which were held in San Francisco).

Del's passion extended to Disneyland, though he preferred to visit while chemically altered. On his first visit, Greenberg accompanied him, but Disney officials decided that Greenberg's hair was too long, and denied him admittance (they were apparently undeterred by Del's altered state). After a quick trim, the two of them roamed the grounds, Del enthusiastic and excited about everything he saw. The highlight was an attraction sponsored by Monsanto Chemicals, which simulated a trip through the human bloodstream. Del immediately went back for a second trip. Afterward, he ran back to his friends, telling them, "Can you believe that ride where they shoot you out of a hypodermic needle and through the bloodstream!" His companions didn't have the heart to tell him that the giant hypodermic needle was only in his mind.

◇

In the summer of 1968, Chicago was torn apart by the protests during the Democratic National Convention. Many people in later years assumed that Del would have been in the thick of it. (In fact, the closest he came to the 1968 Democratic Convention was in the 1990s, when he was featured as David Dellinger, one of the Chicago Seven, in a play about the conspiracy trial that followed the protests.)

Where did Del actually spend the summer of 1968? "I was a stunt man for a pornographic western," he would explain to friends in casual conversation years later.

In fact, it was not really pornography, nor was it a conventional western. It was what would be considered an "independent" film today, but likely an "underground" film in 1968. Titled *Gold* (also known as *Jacktail*), there is no evidence that it was ever released theatrically. No writer or director is listed, though Bill Desloge and Bob Lewis are credited as "organizers." Garry Goodrow, who costarred in it as Jinks, eventually saw it and called it "an awful, awful movie."

The film is badly shot (with as many sequences out of focus as not), poorly lit, and music tracks and obvious dubbing are dropped in at awkward moments to cover for the often-abysmal sound. The plot ranges from simplistic to incoherent. It starts out as a period piece set in the Old West (though even this isn't clear), but anachronisms soon begin creeping in, with everything from wristwatches to a jeep and soldiers. There is copious full-frontal nudity by both sexes, though most of it is so out of focus that any prurient value is lost.

As the film begins, Del's character (who is apparently called "Hawk"—the soundtrack makes it difficult to discern) bursts out of a wooden coffin with shoulder-length hair, looking skinny and unshaven, with black horn-rimmed glasses. Even there, his energy and charisma are evident. "This is a clean family show, ladies and gentlemen, no geeks, no freaks, no Romneys," he says, addressing the camera. "Now, I would like to play a selection of danse macabre on my head." He begins rapping rhythmically on the top of his head with his knuckles, and as he finishes, falls face forward to the ground.

In another bizarre twist, Del's character becomes a revolutionary, and teaches a follower how to make a Molotov cocktail. As he discusses revolutionary strategy, Del is costumed to look like Che Guevara. The resemblance is more than slight, particularly in a close shot that suggests the famous Alberto Korda photo of the guerrilla leader.

As the film nears its end, Jinks has detained the rest of the townspeople in a wire pen, and it is up to Del's character to free them. He comes across a convenient bulldozer, then knocks down the pen and a shed in which Jinks is hiding.

The real-life events behind the filming may have been more interesting than the result. Goodrow recalls that during the climactic rescue sequence, Del nearly killed him because of his lack of experience driving a bulldozer. Del drove the bulldozer up to the shed and then stopped, as planned. The next shot was to involve Goodrow's character setting off a smoke bomb and breaking out the window in the shed, which was specially rigged to facilitate his escape. At the same time, Del's bulldozer was to crush the shed.

Unfortunately, Del started with the bulldozer in second gear, and proceeded to climb up the side of the building, until it crushed the structure with Goodrow inside: "There was just enough room for me to squat in a little ball by the time they stopped it, and it was right over my head. There was a little opening, which I crawled out of. The cameraman was so frightened by what he saw that he had stopped shooting. . . . It was typical of the way these guys lost good shots, but it was very frightening!"

While *Gold* was not a Committee production, the group was busier than ever with its regular stage shows, TV appearances, and even films; Del did not usually appear on camera, but occasionally directed. In 1969, the Committee decided to send a company on tour to middle America. Del decided to accompany them, with an eye on the performance scheduled for Friday, April 11, at Kansas State University.

◇

After several years, Del would be coming home to Manhattan.

In addition to Del, the company consisted of Gottlieb, Hesseman, Ross, French, and Fish, along with Myerson. Their first show was at the three-thousand-seat field house at the University of Texas at Austin, which Carl Gottlieb called "the best show of my life. Everybody who was there remembers it." The Committee movie *A Session with the Committee* had played for seventeen weeks in the student neighborhood in Austin, so when the company came to town live, they were greeted like rock stars. Instead of an encore scene, the company did a Harold which "went as well as any Harold has ever gone. It was a spectacular evening."

Del did not remind the others that the next evening in Manhattan was going to be a homecoming. He didn't even tell his mother he was coming. They arrived late that afternoon to check into the once-grand Gillette Hotel, which had seen better days. Myerson had bought a bottle of Jim Beam in a ceramic container designed like a hippie in a garbage can, which had amused them all. Del went to the pay phone and pulled out a micro-tape recorder in order to record his call, not uncommon for Del during that period. Just as Del was dialing his mother, Myerson dropped the Jim Beam, which shattered, and the whiskey smell wafted throughout the lobby.

Del claimed it was the first time he had seen his mother in twenty years. This was certainly not true—he was obviously back for his father's funeral in 1954—and he may have invented the "twenty year" story to add to the prodigal son legend.

When he called her, tape recorder in hand, from the hotel lobby, Mildred Close was surprised and very emotional. "Don't blubber, Mom, don't blubber," he repeated into the phone. Finally, he turned to the others, embarrassed. "My mom would like to have us over after the show," he announced, almost as if hoping the group would refuse. But the company enthusiastically accepted.

The seventy-year-old Mildred Close was retired after having worked for the local college and helping part-time as a secretary at the First Presbyterian Church. ("My mother got a job grading papers at a college out there," Del later told the *Chicago Tribune* in a November 4, 1973, profile. "She had to sign a loyalty oath saying she would not attempt to overthrow the government. She wrote me 'Del, honey, I wouldn't know where to start.' I wrote back that she should begin by consolidating her power base and getting control of communications, but I guess she wasn't interested.")

The company members have contradictory recollections of the show at Ahearn Fieldhouse. Gottlieb said that the Committee film had not played much in Manhattan, and the preshow publicity was not as good, so it was underattended and not as much fun as the previous night. Myerson recalled it as a solid success. The local newspaper reported that the company thought it was well done, though the sound system was subpar and many in the back couldn't hear everything.

Afterward, the company was charmed by Mildred Close and her hospitality, though Del was mortified from fear that she might say or do something that would embarrass him. Myerson described it as "very much like a production designer would design a slightly over-the-top '50s suburban home," with plastic flowers and slipcovers. His friends saw a very conventional house with very conventional Grand Rapids– Sears furniture, a piano with a piano shawl, pictures of Del, and a nice little lady puttering around the house.

Myerson recalled her serving cream cheese and cucumber sandwiches. Gottlieb noted that she had also bought everything that she thought Del would like, but because she remembered Del as a high school boy around 1950, there were Oreo cookies, red licorice, Jujubes, and chips, "all kid junk food, stuff that a fourteen-year-old would like." There was no alcohol, but plenty of soft drinks and punch and cookies.

Mildred had invited over a dozen of her lady friends, and when the hippies partied with the old ladies, everyone was on their best behavior. Everyone in the company liked Del's mother, and "the vibe was terrific."

According to Myerson, "I don't know if we bonded with the old ladies, but we maintained a respectful proximity to them."

For Mildred, it was a joyous homecoming. Whatever was said or not said between mother and son, the attendees knew she was devoted to her Delbert. There was a photo of him on the piano that she displayed proudly, a dramatically lit eight-by-ten glossy in which the local photographer was emulating the style of Bruno of Hollywood. To the others in the troupe, he was shockingly handsome, with a strong resemblance to Tyrone Power. "You could have put the picture in a wallet and sold it at Woolworth's, it was that good," noted Gottlieb. "He looked like a Hollywood star." Of course, to Mildred, her son *was* a Hollywood star, and the others couldn't help but notice as his mother doted on him.

Of course, Del was very embarrassed by the whole episode. He didn't want to concede that he had a mother and a home. He had told them of his father's suicide, painting a picture of gothic horror. He was mortified to take them to a perfectly respectable little frame house in a residential neighborhood in Kansas.

Reporter Charlie Eppler, writing in the April 13, 1969, *Manhattan Mercury*, interviewed the prodigal son for a page-one story, complete with exaggerations, with the headline "Local Boy Del Close Returns to Home Town as Director of the Committee."

> Del Close hadn't planned on taking a tour with The Committee, but when he found out the group was headed for Manhattan, Kansas, he just couldn't resist the urge.
>
> The director of The Committee, a group well known on the California coast for its improvising during short skits, is one of those local boys made good products. The son of Mrs. Del Close, 1726 Poyntz, Del returned to Manhattan Friday night for a performance in Ahearn Fieldhouse.
>
> "It was a few years ago when I used to tromp in this stuff as a ROTC cadet," said Close, obviously referring to the dirt floor of the fieldhouse. . . .
>
> "This was our first road tour," Close continued. "We enjoyed it—we wanted to see how it would work out. Every audience is different—an intimate crowd in an intimate fieldhouse is ideal. . . ."
>
> Close has given up being a stand-up comic—he's a full-time director and part-time actor with The Committee. And, who knows, he might not have made it if the big flood of 1951 hadn't come.

"I wanted to go to the University of Denver then," Close recalled, "but when the flood came there went my money. I didn't know it then, but it was probably a big break."

◈

After the Committee tour, the group returned to California. Despite his increasing dependence on alcohol, no one seemed to notice Del's drinking. Many would have a drink or two to relax after a show, and a few used booze to even off the edge of the speed. Del's consciousness appeared to be in a permanently altered state, and he was high most of the time, but it didn't conspicuously impair his ability to function as he needed, at least to his fellow actors. The nonfunctional players were the ones who would drop acid or hallucinogens rather than drugs like smack or speed, which were generally used after the show.

Still, Myerson recalled one startling moment that exemplified Del's immense drug use. While at the Tiffany in L.A., a number of them lived together in a large house in the Hollywood Hills, with a big swimming pool in the back. Del came back to visit on one occasion, and joined them around the pool, according to Alan Myerson: "We were all nude, as was Del, except you could see virtually no white skin on Del, because he was all black and blue. He literally was covered with [needle] marks."

When the Committee first got to L.A., another group of actors decided to find a place to share near the Tiffany, and decided on an old Spanish-style house at 1416 Queens Road, which rented for $500 a month. The occupants included Brent and his girlfriend in one room, Gottlieb in another, Ross in the maid's room, and another bedroom that alternated between Upton and Rob Reiner. Del stayed on the couch during the time he was living there, when he wasn't living at the theater or with a girl. He wasn't particular about where he lived, and usually stayed with whoever would have him.

The communal living arrangements on Queens Road were a delight for them all. The pool table in the dining room was converted into a dinner table, and there would be anywhere from six to fifteen people eating. Because the house was close to the theater, anybody who came to see the show, from Cass Elliot to Blood Sweat & Tears, would go to the house afterward because it was a five-minute walk.

Another of Del's legendary escapades occurred while the group was living on Queens Road, perhaps a logical progression from his spidering in the attic. Nearly everyone with the Committee at that time has their own variation on the story, but the facts are essentially the same.

One night after a show, while Del was living in the theater, the residents on Queens Road noticed a number of sheriff and police cars outside the Tiffany.

Accompanied by Gosling Trauma, Del had climbed into the air-conditioning duct space and discovered it was architecturally connected to an adjacent building. He had climbed into the other space, and when he dropped down into the office, he set off the burglar alarm.

Many years later, Howard Hesseman described the incident in mock-heroic terms:

> Del Close broke down yet another of the walls that separate us all from the unknown. Well, actually, he just put his fist through it—it was only plasterboard, after all—and fumbled with the door's lock button on the other side. Presto! The door swings open to a whole new world. All is revealed. It includes a night security guard, pistol leveled at the two intrepid pioneers. Del attempted, in his extraordinary fashion, to explain their presence to the alert but confused guardian. Alas, the usual entanglement with an unimaginative and authoritarian world-view then proceeded to engulf our hero and his novice.[2]

When Del told the story many years later, he elaborated on some of the details, noting that he was doing a tremendous amount of Methedrine.

> One time, the piano player for The Committee and I . . . were spidering in the attic of the Tiffany Theatre in Los Angeles on the Sunset Strip. We spidered into, unfortunately, the offices of MetroMedia, where we had no interest in being. We just had interest in the attic. And there was this LAPD moonlighting cop there with his big .38 pointing at us suddenly. He said, "All right, I've got you, you burglars!" "We're not burglars, we're great big spiders!" So they took us away to the lockup.
>
> And the thing that I remember most vividly about it is the next morning, after I had managed to come down. It was the Beverly

Hills jail. They serve you steak and eggs in the morning to remind you that you're in Beverly Hills, but they make you eat it with your fingers, to remind you that you're in jail![3]

But the story did not end there, and Del explained that he was arrested:

I was finally charged with abusing a pill with a razor blade. . . . These were pills with one side Methedrine and one a barbiturate. You chopped them in two if you didn't want to take both at once. And I had a prescription. So I was standing in front of a judge, and I was literally sentenced for illegally chopping this pill in two. And in my smart-ass way I looked up and said "You mean, Your Honor, what Abbott Laboratories hath put together no man may take asunder?"[4]

11

Pretty Much a Blur

By the end of 1969, Del's time with the Committee was drawing to a close.

His on-again off-again battle with boredom was on again, and the Committee no longer provided adequate stimulation. He was too weird and erratic, even for Hollywood, and the offers weren't coming in. He continued to ingest massive quantities of drugs, with Methedrine a particular favorite, but to become overstimulated with no way to vent his energy was ultimately frustrating. His recollections in 1978 were typically jumbled.

> I'd ... developed a case of tunnel vision. Partially burned out. I needed a break—a different kind of work. I'd heard Paul [Sills] was on a new trip, something called *Story Theatre*, so I called him up, asked him if he could use another actor. Paul said, "Who'd you have in mind?" I said, "Me." He hired me for his company at the Body Politic.[1]

Although burnout was certainly one reason for Del's departure, he also sought "fresher fields of dopedom," according to Alan Myerson. Del also insisted on laying claim to the authorship of the Harold, and was exasperated when it was constantly refuted by the other company members, Myerson said; he recalled that Del had received an offer in Chicago and decided to move.

From the departure from the Committee to directing at the Second City in Chicago, Del's movements are not always clear, and are not made simpler by Del's own contradictory accounts of this period: "Valium and alcohol—they turn you into an amnesiac. I can read the fine print on some of the memories but it was pretty much a blur."[2]

The one certainty is that Del's tenure with the Committee was ending. He described a disagreement with group members on the nature of guerrilla theater, and claimed that he had decided to put his theories into practice. "My theory was that it's not where you go bother people, but you take your guerrilla and drop him behind enemy lines and see if he can go form a theatre company. So I wound up getting dropped behind enemy lines," he said.[3] In this case, the enemy was the University of Texas at Austin.

> I came with no money and like one or two names and within three weeks I had a functioning company going in a soon-to-be-demolished YMCA . . . and while I was down there, I heard Paul Sills was into a new thing. Now, the last thing I'd heard he was into couldn't have interested me less. It was Game Theatre. John Brent had come back with horror stories: Paul would have you play pussy-in-the-corner, on your knees, and people hit you with a newspaper. . . . I heard he was into another phase—*Story Theatre*. So I took a leave of absence from guerrilla theatre—I was suffering from a broken shoulder, anyway . . . broke it in a trust exercise.[4]

(His "leap of faith" had actually taken place at a Committee workshop in San Francisco months, if not years, earlier.)

A report by columnist Bob Ellison in the February 27, 1970, *Chicago Tribune* provided an update of sorts regarding Del's whereabouts during this period.

> Remember Del Close, the brilliant humorist at Second City a few seasons back? Del's been out in San Francisco for a spell, at The Committee. Well, a few moons ago he got tired of the smog, or something, and split. To go into social work in Texas. Cut his hair and everything. Herb Caen gave him six months, at best. Herb's an opti-

mist. But Del returned to Baghdad by the Bay in days. "I got there," he reported recently, "just as the Y.M.C.A. was being condemned as subversive. The heads were using it for connections. Besides, they weren't giving any Christian services and the director turned out to be Jewish. But don't put Austin down. It's a real boss town, sort of the Berkeley of the southwest."

Del was back in Chicago a month after the *Tribune* column saw print.

Story Theatre began in Chicago in 1968. Paul Sills recruited a group of college students who chose five *Grimm's Fairy Tales*, keeping the original narrative and improvising the dialogue. They worked out of the original Second City building, which was slated for demolition, and charged no admission. They performed during the 1968 Democratic Convention, as police and protesters clashed across the street in Lincoln Park, and the theater often served as an infirmary for the injured. Their work reflected the revolutionary air of the times in the context of the age-old stories.

Sills decided to relaunch it with a new cast in October 1969. He presented *Ovid's Metamorphoses* as the first new Story Theatre production at the Body Politic, a former storefront at 2259 North Lincoln Avenue. It was soon followed by *The Master Thief*. Sills had assembled a company largely from Northwestern University, which included Charles Bartlett, Cordis Heard (then Cordis Fejer), Caroline Jones, James Keach (who was replaced by Gerrit Graham), Molly McKasson, Bernadine Redeaux, and Tom Towles.

Sills's creation struck a chord in Chicago at that time. *The Master Thief* featured *Grimm's Fairy Tales* and *Aesop's Fables*, which included "Henny Penny" done to Country Joe MacDonald's "Feel Like I'm Fixin' to Die Rag." With its revolutionary flavor, it took the town by storm and became a huge hit.

Del, Sills, and Myerson all had different recollections of Del's involvement. Del claimed he had heard about Sills's new project and called the director himself. Myerson simply claimed that Del had received an offer from Sills. But Sills remembered a call from Myerson—Del was at loose ends, and Myerson asked Sills whether he could find room for Del in his company in Chicago. At any rate, Sills invited Del to join the group for its third production, because of his acting skills: "He acted in an old-fashioned, Kansas way, and that's the way I always regarded him. But his wit came through, and he could get a laugh, and if he didn't, then he'd do something about it."

Most of the cast was composed of students at Northwestern University; Del, at thirty-six, was nearly twice their age. All the same, he brought a spontaneity and giddiness to the work, and was not at all threatening or condescending. "He anchored us in an interesting way, because there was now an older person in our company," recalled Cordis Heard. Del and Sills shared a history and were obviously the "grown-ups," but the age difference was never an issue. His quick wit, sense of humor, and quirkiness soon elevated the company to new heights.

The company always labored to find the proper tone when tackling a new story. The group tried to find the joke in the scene, or come up with a song that might help crack the story open for their improvisation. They quickly found that Del was very good at finding the proper flavor. Each scene was completely improvised, which came naturally for Del. Just as important, he could do it quickly.

The third production, *The Parson in the Cupboard*, opened April 15, 1970. The new show featured eight scenes, including "The Little Peasant," "The Two Crows," and "Clever Elsie," along with a Scottish ballad and other selections from *Aesop's Fables* and *Grimm's Fairy Tales*. Sills remembered that Del was particularly memorable in the title story, in which the local minister is sneaking around with the farmer's wife. Del played the parson, who hides in the cupboard when the farmer shows up. At one moment, he jumps out and the farmer cries, "I saw the devil, I saw him with my own eyes! He looked a lot like our parson!" "He could do that sort of thing very well," noted Sills. "That part he was good at, seducing the woman, and fooling around with it. And why not? He was a comic."

The *Chicago Tribune*'s William Leonard interviewed Del about Story Theatre in an April 19, 1970, piece entitled "The Body Politic Exciting, Maybe Revolutionary."

> Sometimes we don't know quite what the story is going to do when we start rehearsing. Sometimes, it seems, it's the audience that tells us what the point of the story is.

He told the reporter that he planned to stay in Chicago for a year, then return to California. For a time, Del and George moved into a storefront on Larrabee Street in one of the few remaining affordable neighborhoods. Del placed an 11½″ by 18″ cardboard sign in the storefront window reading:

The Mad Doctor's Shop and Gallery
2059 N. Larrabee, Chicago
Del Close, Prop.

At the bottom was the motto: "If you can get it anyplace else, you can't get it here."

Del was obsessed by another idée fixe, according to Sills. He was determined to come up with his own version of the Land camera (the first "instant camera," developed by Polaroid founder Edwin Land) and make a lot of money. Sills would occasionally run into Del on Larrabee, carrying around bits of film. "It was very vague, I never made any sense out of it, nor could anybody else," said Sills. Del never tried to sell it anywhere, because he couldn't—Land had patented it. But that didn't stop him from tinkering.

◇

Del and George stayed in Chicago for most of 1970. As Story Theatre continued, Del started conducting workshops across the street. Lincoln Avenue was a bustling scene, with numerous bars and storefronts lining both sides of the street, including the Body Politic, the Kingston Mines, and the Kingston Mines Company Store, a small café attached to the theater just south of Fullerton Avenue. Del spread the word that he would conduct a free improvisational workshop one night a week at the Kingston Mines Company Store, open to anyone, with no limit on the number of participants.

Del's decision to bring the Harold to Chicago attracted a number of students, including Jonathan Abarbanel, Dan Ziskie, Brian Hickey, and Betty Thomas. If he could not take credit as the sole originator of the Harold, he could help it develop and advance.

His motivation was theoretical. He was convinced that the Harold could become a great instrument of theater, rising above its roots in comedy and improvisation. He was determined to progress to a long-form improvisation with some semblance of a beginning, middle, and end. Even though he was immersed in Methedrine, Valium, alcohol, and a vast array of other drugs, he never failed to show up for a workshop.

After training his actors for several months, Del selected a group of students to begin performances at the Kingston Mines Company Store, including Abarbanel, Ziskie, Hickey, Bill Noble, Linda Wesley, Jamie Levin, Keith Schwartz, and William McKinney. He named them the Chicago Extension, because they were an extension of the Harold work of the Committee. The new company moved to a downstairs studio at the nearby Body Politic. Performances were held on the mainstage upstairs, a former bowling alley where pin-spotting arrows were still visible on the floor. They met twice a week for workshops and performed on Sundays.

In the spirit of the 1960s, the Chicago Extension was organized in a socialistic manner, and not even Del made money. Although they did pass the hat, no admission was charged for the Sunday night performances, and there were nights when the company members would stand out on the street to attract audiences.

George was a friendly, if infrequent, presence, but occasionally sat in on a workshop. She understood the work, and was liked and accepted by all. Her larger role was helping Del keep his life organized. George was always his buffer from the real world, protecting him from income taxes and monthly bills, and leaving him to explore and discover.

Eventually, Del began to tire of the Chicago Extension's work on the Harold, and decided to try building long-form improvisation from dreams. Instead of taking audience suggestions, a group member would recount a dream, which would become the basis for a long-form improvisation. It was ideal for private workshops because it didn't require audience suggestions.

◆

Parson in the Cupboard continued through the summer; after the show, Del would cross the street and work with the Chicago Extension. He had even operated a few workshops with the company at the Second City.

But another disappointment was looming. With no warning, Paul Sills left his group of young actors and ran off to Los Angeles. "We were betrayed," said Cordis Heard. "[Sills] deserted us . . . he left us running the show by ourselves." The actors had no idea what was going on and continued performing. Unbeknownst to the group, there had been producers in and out of town who were interested in picking up the show, and Sills's plans for Story Theatre didn't include the original company.

In Los Angeles, Sills made a deal with the Mark Taper Forum, and gathered a cast that consisted largely of Second City and Committee veterans, including Hamilton Camp, Melinda Dillon, Peter Bonerz, Valerie Harper, Richard Schaal, Richard Libertini, and Paul Sand, with Mary Frann and Lewis Arquette serving as alternates. The show previewed for six weeks at the Taper that fall, winning several prestigious local awards. Then it moved on to the Ambassador Theatre on Broadway and was a critical smash, running for nine months with the celebrity cast.

Sills's maneuverings did not go over well with the original cast. They continued the show in Chicago even after Sills had mounted another Story Theatre in L.A. However, Sills had neglected to tell the Chicago company about the Taper (soon to be Broadway) version, and when the original company found out, they understandably felt betrayed. "It felt awful," recalled Heard, seeing the work they had helped to create become a Broadway hit without them. Gerrit Graham said, "We felt swindled, we felt we had been cut out of the money, as indeed we were."

It felt like an afterthought when Sills contacted them in October, after the Broadway show had opened. The Mark Taper Forum wanted a Christmas production of Story Theatre, so Sills came up with a scheme to satisfy the Taper without affecting his Broadway cast. He called the Chicago cast to restage portions of the earlier shows as workshop productions in L.A. "It always felt like, by way of apology, 'You kids can come out here and do this Christmas gig,'" said Heard.

Despite bruised feelings, the cast agreed. After the December 1970 shows in L.A., they hoped to be next in line to replace Broadway cast members, or make up a touring company, though Sills was cagey and indirect with the company.

For Del, the reversal felt even worse. When Sills put together the production for Broadway, he had cast his contemporaries, but left Del to remain with the kids from Chicago.

Dream Theatre continued for a time after Del left town. He prescribed a rotating directorship for the Chicago Extension, telling them "You can do this on your own," and set out for California.

Del and George joined the others in Los Angeles around Thanksgiving to put together the show. There would be little help from Sills, who had not even arranged housing for the group.

The group had to design an upbeat Christmas show for families with children, with no heavy thematic content. Helping to make the transition were two welcome additions to the cast: Avery Schreiber and

Severn Darden, then living in L.A. They put together a new set of stories in no time at all. The Mark Taper show was a "bastardized version" of the Chicago Story Theatre, said Graham. Some of the stories, such as "The Magic Salad," were only ever performed in L.A., and stories like "The Master Thief" were considered much too gory for the holiday crowd.

The Christmas production ran for ten performances, recalled Graham. "We weren't being paid squat. We were marooned in L.A. with no money and no job," though a couple of them were later invited to New York to serve as understudies.

But not Del. As 1971 began, with Story Theatre still going strong on Broadway, Del decided to remain in L.A., where so many of his Second City and Committee cohorts were establishing themselves in TV and films.

It was slow going. Graham occasionally stopped by the Improv on Melrose to get up and improvise with Del and Severn Darden. It was usually dreadful, because they would be drunk or drug-sodden, or the audience wouldn't be hip to what was happening. Del had given up speed for Valium, and his alcohol intake had increased. He was not in the best condition for launching a Hollywood career.

Del and George stayed with friends, but it soon became apparent that they would need a place of their own. They rented a one-story, semidetached place in the flats of Hollywood, bordered by Santa Monica and Beverly Boulevards, between La Brea and Fairfax. It had been freshly painted, with hardwood floors. They had little furniture and no curtains, so they put tinfoil over the windows for privacy.

They were faced with the problem of paying the rent each month, and Del's acting jobs were not pouring in, so Del concocted a scheme with George. Graham received a phone call from Del one evening. "Gerrit? What are you doing this evening? Can you come over? There's something we want to talk to you about, a proposition for you, a chance to make a little money."

Graham, who was constantly broke, agreed to stop by. Del was in the front room and offered him a joint. The smell of fresh paint permeated the place, and George was nowhere to be seen. Soon, Graham's head was spinning from the paint fumes and pot, and he finally asked Del what it was all about.

"How would you feel about being in a movie with George?" Del inquired. Graham said he thought George was great, and he would love to, then asked what kind of a movie. "Well, a porn movie. How would you feel about that?" At that moment, George walked in from the next room, stark naked, to serve as encouragement.

Graham admitted that he was tempted, and said that George did not seem reticent. Del likewise had few hang-ups, and would not have been conventionally jealous. It was clearly a business proposition for the out-of-work actor, presented very matter-of-factly, and there were no indications that Del was interested in watching them perform together.

The young actor responded that he was extremely flattered, but demurred, remembering that the stigma of a porn film was difficult to shake. He suggested that Del do the porn movie with his girlfriend. Del shook his head, lifted his pant leg, and said, simply, "Too many tracks." The subject did not come up again.

There were occasional opportunities to perform with old friends in L.A. When Hugh Romney (by then known as Wavy Gravy) was emceeing at the opening of a new club called the Paradise Ballroom, Del agreed to eat fire as part of the show.

Del quickly captured the crowd's attention with his fire-eating. But the floor was covered with wood shavings, and partway into his act, the stage caught fire. Before it could spread, Romney began rolling through the flames, putting them out, while Del screamed, "Let's hear it for self-immolation!"

◈

Del was based in L.A. throughout much of 1971. He returned to Chicago that summer for a five-week advanced Second City workshop that began on July 19, 1971. An article by Gary Houston called "Second City: Past and Present and . . ." in the August 29, 1971, *Chicago Sun-Times* speculated that the directorship of the Second City was in limbo, and there was some talk that Del Close might get the job, but the report proved premature. Another account claimed that Del appeared with Judy Harris in a low-budget independent movie called *Multiple Choice*, directed by Don Klugman, in the summer of 1971 in Chicago. Another account claimed that in late March 1972, he was stranded in Hollywood. He reported that because he had quit taking speed by this point, his waistline had expanded slightly. "I blew 12 years on dope," he told the *Chicago Tribune* in 1973. "But when somebody says 'Oh, what a waste!' I want to kill him. Pragmatically speaking it *was* a waste. But at the time, it seemed like the thing to do."[5]

By another account, "I was drinking very heavily, and taking Valiums, because I wasn't taking any speed. . . . I've just gone broke rejoining [Actors'] Equity. So I wound up running workshops, and doing this movie, *Son of the Blob*."[6]

Roberta Maguire, who had been studying with Del at the Second City in Chicago, recalled being in Los Angeles at the time, and trying to break into show business, but not having much luck. Del proved difficult to reach, because he didn't have a telephone. Severn Darden gave her a very complicated game plan. "Isn't there an easier way?" Maguire asked him, but apparently there wasn't. Shortly afterward, she stopped in a drugstore to telephone someone. The phone booth door opened, and out stepped Del, who asked, "Want to be in a movie?" She thought, "This is it, this is my dream of L.A." Del recruited her for *Son of Blob*.

◈

Also known variously as *Beware! The Blob*, *Beware of the Blob*, and *Here Comes the Blob*, *Son of Blob* is a low-budget sequel to the classic 1958 B-flick *The Blob*, yet Del always felt proud of it.

The uncredited director was his old castmate from *The Nervous Set*, Larry Hagman, a few years before he would go on to fame in *Dallas*. Del explained: "[Larry] hired all his old friends—those who were willing to work for scale, at least—for *Son of Blob*. It was his first directorial attempt."[7] Del, Hagman, and Burgess Meredith shared a scene in which the Blob ate all three.

Just prior to filming, Del's cat inadvertently scratched his cornea. He was in such agony on the way to the set that the driver finally stopped at a veterinarian's office, where he got a shot and some pills for the pain. He was forced to wear an eyepatch for his role.

Writing about the experience years later for *Wasteland*, Del described what he found to be an unexpected benefit.

> I was no longer in agony—just real pain. . . . Word of my troubles got around the set and everyone started giving me drugs out of sympathy and a weird sense of one-upmanship . . . sort of a "I've got the strongest pain pill" game. I, of course, took them all. . . . They kicked in, and pretty soon, I was feeling no pain. . . .

[Larry said,] "Okay, here's the scene. We're three drunken bums. Burgess, you hate hippies. Del, you accuse him of being aggressive. I keep peeking under the serape, trying to find the bottle of hootch. Del, you hear something. You two send me out to investigate—I get eaten. My screams bring out you two—Del attacks it with a pitchfork, Burgess throws hootch at it. . . . It eats you. We have money for one take."[8]

Hagman was eaten on cue, but when Del attempted to strike the Blob with the pitchfork, he was still disoriented, and stabbed the director in the shoe. Somehow, though, he missed his foot, and proceeded to die on screen and on budget.

His film career was not limited to low-budget features. Some filmographies list him as a cast member of George Lucas's *THX-1138* in 1971. This is difficult to confirm, because he did not mention it to friends, though Ruth Silveira, Scott Beach, and Bruce Mackey of the Committee are credited as "announcers." If Del was involved, it was likely a brief, uncredited voiceover.

Del did play a small part in Lucas's next movie, 1973's blockbuster *American Graffiti*, credited as "Guy at Bar" who watches and comments as Charles Martin Smith's Terry the Toad vomits into the gutter. It's a brief but memorable moment in a memorable film. San Francisco–area filmmakers like Lucas and Francis Ford Coppola often used Committee actors to fill roles in their films. Lucas also cast John Brent (credited as "Car Salesman"), Scott Beach ("Mr. Gordon"), and Ed Greenberg ("Kip Pullman") in the film. *American Graffiti* helped establish the pattern for Del's film career: he would either play big roles in smaller, low-budget movies or small roles in big Hollywood movies. As it turned out, his time in Hollywood had nearly come to an end.

During *Son of Blob*, a few old friends came by to see Del. His workshops in Chicago and the success of a Second City *Hamlet* scene led to a new opportunity. "Second City turns up; they're on tour. I got some of them small parts in *Blob*, and they drove me out to see their show. While I was there, Joyce Sloane asked me if I would come back and take over the directorship."[9]

Before he could begin, though, Del had a few standing obligations. In November 1972, he agreed to direct *The Interstellar Follies* (also known as *The Voyage of the Light-Ship Mariner*), the 212th production of Dudley Riggs's Brave New Workshop in Minneapolis. (By now, he considered himself a "roving director" for the Second City and the Committee.) Based on improvisations, the crew of the *Mariner* hurtles off into space and encounters UFOs, a time warp, a space biker, a flying pyramid, and a "space lump." Along the way, the Brain, the ship's main computer, falls in love with an attractive female crew member who has six PhDs. The entire production was staged with only five actors playing eight roles.

Del told the *St. Paul Pioneer Press*: "This show started out, three weeks ago, as a spoof or parody of [*Star*] *Trek*. I'd always wanted to do a science fiction show. But then we began to improvise . . . and we came up with a show all our own. Forget *Star Trek*. The Mariner pre-dates *Star Trek* by 300 years. And that's technically accurate—based on all the science fiction we dug into."[10]

The program for *The Interstellar Follies* indicated that he would next be directing at the Second City, followed by an appearance on *The Flip Wilson Show* with the Committee. In fact, the Committee had invited Del back one last time. The fabled West Coast company had closed its L.A. branch after two years (and a brief relaunch at the Tiffany in the summer of 1972), and now the original San Francisco Committee theater was slated to close; the Committee would continue to tour several more years, but their home base would be shuttered. One final Satirython was scheduled for January 1973. It was to be a twenty-four-hour around-the-clock show; everybody who had ever worked at the Committee was invited. Del joined them for the performance, then returned to Chicago, where his future awaited.

12

Second City Redux:
Belushi and the Bean Can

"You have a light within you. Burn it out."

By the late 1960s, the Second City had begun a transformation. A new group of actors, younger, more radical, had started to replace the first wave. They were shaped by the Summer of Love, Vietnam, and the zeitgeist of the times. When Bernie Sahlins decided to take his established company to New York in 1969, the longhaired touring company took over the mainstage, consisting of Harold Ramis, Brian Doyle-Murray, David Blum, Jim Fisher, Roberta Maguire, Judy Morgan, and Joe Flaherty. Their first show, which opened on October 15, 1969, was called, appropriately, *The Next Generation*.

It was the first revue directed by Bernie Sahlins, who was energized by the youthful cast. Sheldon Patinkin had left, and other choices had not worked out, so Sahlins gave it a try "by default." He explained: "There was a sense of a clean break needed from the past, artistically, from [the] point of view of personnel, attitudes, the whole thing. It had to be healthier. It was the bourgeoisie reclaiming the lost ground."

It began his direct artistic involvement with the shows, in addition to his responsibilities as producer. Sahlins directed three revues, *The Next Generation*, *Justice Is Done, or Oh Calcoolidge*, and *Cooler Near the Lake*. When he began preparing for the fourth, to be called *Picasso's Moustache*, a new opportunity presented itself.

When Del was doing Story Theatre in Chicago in 1970, a few actors at the Second City lured him back. "I pretty much stayed away from The Second City, remembering the circumstances of my leaving, until a delegation of actors from there came up to me to ask me to run some workshops for them. (Bernie was on one of his extended vacations.) I said 'Sure, for $50 a shot.' I was sure they would turn me down. They didn't. The actors themselves hired me. When Bernie came back and saw what was happening, he gave me his official blessing, validated the actors' move after the fact, and suggested that I continue."[1]

But Del had greater ambitions than running a few workshops, and wanted to direct the next show. Sahlins balked, and Del was ready to walk away. Instead, Sahlins made Del a different offer: "Make me a parody of *Hamlet*."

Once again, the Melancholy Dane stepped in and sent him in a new, productive direction. He *had* to accept the offer. "Ohhh, man. I've only been studying the play since I was nine."[2] This was an ideal opportunity for Del to prove himself yet again.

Del brought his ideas for *Hamlet* to the first rehearsal, and with Fred Kaz and the cast, they began to develop it. Del gave the actors the notion that the actual play was going on back behind the stage. As characters died in *Hamlet*, the actors would enter the scene on the Second City stage, wearing what Del described as "Casper the Ghost" sheets. They were in limbo, and could not go on to Heaven or Hell until someone still alive in the play took revenge for their death. The scene grew increasingly cluttered as people continued to die in the play.

The songs by Kaz proved an invaluable addition to an already great scene. During the rehearsals, Kaz would improvise music for each of the characters. Despite the sheets with eyeholes and faces painted on them, they all sang. Brian Doyle-Murray performed a memorable Bob Dylan parody, playing the guitar and harmonica, complete with harmonica holder, over his sheet. Kaz wrote the company an angry song about revenge, which emerged as the central theme.

Del's return to the Second City excited the cast, impressed by Del's ability to deal head-on with subjects like death and revenge but still get

Hamlet proved to be a constant thread running through Del's life and even beyond, as evidenced by this page from his comic book series. (ARTWORK BY DAVID LLOYD, FROM *WASTELAND* #7 © 1988 DC COMICS. ALL RIGHTS RESERVED. USED WITH PERMISSION)

tremendous laughs. Maguire said that Del was able to provide clarity for the group: "When Del came, I felt like this cool clear water finally was going through my brain. Here was this person who was really teaching us how to give some substance to the work."

Picasso's Moustache began preview performances December 16, 1970, the Second City's eleventh anniversary. According to Larry Townsend's column in the December 18 *Chicago Tribune*, the fortieth revue was rough in spots, but there were two highlights: "A hilarious *Hamlet* song-and-dance skit and the finale, a parody of an afternoon in a teenage drive-in during the 'Edsel and Eisenhower 50s.' Two weeks of

Settling back into Chicago, Del hoped to branch into theater, in addition to directing at Second City.
(COURTESY OF CHARNA HALPERN)

performing before home-for-the-holidays college crowds should tighten the show."

Picasso's Moustache officially opened on January 7, 1971. In the January 8, 1971, *Chicago Tribune* review, William Leonard was particularly fond of Del's brainchild: "The *Hamlet* scene is set in the hereafter, the characters appearing as ghosts, one by one, as they are killed in the familiar course of the play. The complications of who should kill whom below on Earth out of revenge so the spirits can find rest brings a hilarious new viewpoint which overcomes the campiness of the performance."

The opportunity to take over *Hamlet* and rewrite it was empowering. By taking control of *Hamlet*, Del was taking control of his life.

The Second City's *Hamlet* would eventually lead to his return to Chicago, but ironically, Del missed the opening of *Picasso's Moustache* because he was appearing in Story Theatre at the Mark Taper Forum. Del spent most of 1971 in Los Angeles, but he began returning to Chicago more frequently in 1972, and would even direct another Second City show before committing to Chicago for good.

◈

The talent that Del would work with in the coming years was staggering, and included some of the era's most important names in American comedy. But no relationship was more important to teacher or student than the one with John Belushi. Harold Ramis's decision to take a sabbatical saw him replaced by the twenty-two-year-old from Wheaton, Illinois, who would become Del's prized pupil.

John Belushi and two of his friends, Tino Insana and Steve Beshekas, began performing as a comedy group while attending a junior college in the Chicago suburbs. The trio called themselves the West Compass Players, largely because they were from the western suburbs. While attending the College of DuPage, they began performing at hootenannies before going to Circle Campus of the University of Illinois, where they lived in the Taylor Street neighborhood. They rented an old social club and turned it into a coffeehouse, and began performing Friday and Saturday nights. Joyce Sloane came one time to see them perform and issued an invitation: "Hey, you stole the Second City material anyway, you might as well come to the theater."

"John and I would go to Second City. In those days we were under twenty-one, and if you ordered the Irish coffee, you could drink. So, we'd always have Irish coffees and watch the show, and then try and duplicate some of the scenes," recalled Insana (his father was a conductor with the Grant Park Symphony and Lyric Opera, and played piano for their gibberish operas).

When Ramis took his sabbatical, Belushi was hired for the replacement company, Insana was hired to the touring company, and Beshekas was the odd man out. It marked the first time that anyone had been hired and put on the Second City mainstage without going through the ranks. Belushi was quick to capitalize on his opportunity. He was soon able to grab the spotlight from veterans like Flaherty, Doyle-Murray, and the recently returned Ramis, and on June 3, 1971, John Belushi debuted in the Second City's forty-first revue, *No, No, Wilmette*.

Belushi's respect for Del's credentials and anarchic attitude attracted him to the director. Even though Del was in and out of Chicago during 1971 and 1972, he was around long enough to seize Belushi's attention. Del brought a new attitude and approach to the theater. As he told one workshop: "You have a light within you. Burn it out."

Belushi was soon enthralled by the Guru. "He was the first real genius instructor in improvisation that John had ever had," noted Insana.

Belushi loved that Del was a real beatnik, a beat guy from the Beat Generation. He had been in *The Electric Kool-Aid Acid Test* bus with Ken Kesey. Del was the Real Deal. Belushi's attitude was "Teach me." Belushi was fascinated by his lifestyle, his thoughts, his attitude toward drugs as a tool for exploration. In Belushi, Del had found a younger version of himself, funny, talented, and fearless, a doppelganger that he could use to explore his own darker thoughts onstage.

◇

Del directed the Second City's forty-third revue on a trial basis. The cast included John Belushi, Jim Fisher, Judy Morgan, Joe Flaherty, Eugenie Ross-Leming, and Harold Ramis. *The 43rd Parallel or McCabre & Mrs. Miller,* which opened in March 23, 1972, featured some of Del's funniest—and darkest—contributions.

Following the funeral of a friend of Joyce Sloane, the cast began discussing a funeral scene. They were having trouble determining the cause of death, until Del mentioned that he had often speculated about the possibility of death by getting his head caught in a gallon can of Van Camp's Beans. (As he would relate to classes in later years, it was the specificity of the can that made it funny—it had to be "a gallon can of Van Camp's Beans.") The attempts by friends and family to keep a straight face each time they had to explain the circumstances of the death helped make the scene a Second City classic.

With Del and Belushi, death scenes were never far away. Another trademark scene featured Belushi as a taxidermist bringing his girlfriend home to meet his parents. However, she quickly discovers that his parents are stuffed, and that she is apparently next. It was comedy so black that Del's goal was not to get just laughs, but laughs that were also screams. Belushi delivered.

The response to *43rd Parallel* by critic William Leonard could only be called a rave. In the March 24, 1972, *Chicago Tribune,* he wrote that the title alluded to the theater's forty-third revue.

> I have seen all 43, and I don't recall ever seeing a better one.
> This is the sharpest, wittiest, brightest, funniest, cleverest, most brilliant package of satire, corn, pungent comment, and occasional poignancy that anybody has brought to this town in years. It's silly one minute, sad the next, outrageous a moment after that. . . .

There are exactly half a dozen young hams who could go on from here to become stars. They have not only the talent, which is good, but the technique, which is more important, and Del Close, who directed the team, has whipped them into a team that plunks every delicate detail across exactly on target.

This edition is more intelligent than many of its recent predecessors. The Second City has been fun almost always, but it had gotten into a comfortable, fun rut. . . .

This is a thoughtful show, sardonic rather than bitter, its tongue in its cheek but a smile on its face. It moves swiftly, and some of its scenes have more twists and turns and surprises than *Sleuth*. Nobody's going to fall asleep at 10:30 p.m. at *43rd Parallel*! . . .

The Second City never has done its thing better. This is one of the greatest shows in town, and it's great to see the Second City in such glowing health.

With such enthusiastic reviews, it's easy to see why Sahlins was ready to welcome Del back on a regular basis. However, after the opening of *43rd Parallel*, Del headed to the West Coast once more. Kup's Column in the March 16, 1972, *Chicago Sun-Times* reported that "Del Close is parting company with The Second City, where he has been directing, to return to his first love, acting, with The Committee." Whether it was connected to the brief relaunch of the Committee in L.A. that summer is unclear. While Del was on the West Coast, *43rd Parallel* closed after a healthy six-month run; Joe Flaherty and Harold Ramis codirected the forty-forth revue, *Premises, Premises*, which opened September 28, 1972.

In the autumn of 1972 (when Del was in Minneapolis directing for Dudley Riggs), John Belushi left the Second City and Chicago for New York City and *National Lampoon's Lemmings*. From there, he would go on to *Saturday Night Live* and instant fame. It is worth noting that he only performed at the Second City for twenty months, and worked with Del for only a part of that time. It is also worth noting, in light of the events to come, that Del firmly maintained that he did not do drugs with John Belushi during his months at the Second City—that their association was primarily one of director and student. While Del would sometimes socialize with his actors after shows, perhaps even smoking pot, their real friendship did not fully take hold until after Belushi had left the Second City.

The following show, the greatest-hits revue *Tippecanoe and Déjà Vu,* opened on January 17, 1973. The Second City records claim that Sahlins directed it, though the *Chicago Tribune* at that time lists it as a Sahlins-Close codirection, and additional information is sketchy. By the end of the year, Del himself admitted to being codirector of the theater with Sahlins: "That's a semi-permanent job as long as we can tolerate each other," he told the *Chicago Tribune*.[3] Among the nineteen scenes in the show (which featured Jim Fisher, Joe Flaherty, Harold Ramis, David Rasche, Ann Ryerson, Eugenie Ross-Leming, and Jim Staahl) was the *Hamlet* scene, which served as the big production number.

By this time, Del's return to the Second City was a done deal. During his first year, the Second City would be paying him the grand sum of $155.82 per week.

◆

Del and George stayed with Jonathan Abarbanel at his apartment on Deming Place for a week or two while they looked for a place of their own. Because it was a one-bedroom flat, the couple shared the couch in the living room. Abarbanel experienced a few fascinating peeks into the relationship between Del and George. At one point, Del had just entered, and it was obvious to Abarbanel and George that he had just ingested something, even though he was talking and functional. Suddenly, Del stopped cold and fell forward. Because they were not prepared, and because he was not a small man, he nearly fell full-length, facedown on the floor. "We were just barely able to break his fall, and stretch him out, and he came to in a couple of minutes."

Del and George soon left Abarbanel's flat and found an apartment at 3159 North Hudson Street, just south of Belmont Avenue. His relationship with George was warm, if not demonstrative. According to Abarbanel, "Del gave George a lot of credit for keeping his head as together as it could have been at that time, and making sure that his work was organized, and I think she was quite devoted. I don't know how capable Del was of actually loving a woman. I think there was a certain misogyny about him, always."

Whether Del's misogyny was deep-rooted or simply an aspect of his contrarian nature is difficult to determine. For every woman who considered him a misogynist, there seemed to be another who was deeply devoted to him. Roberta Maguire felt that while sexism was rampant at the theater in the early 1970s, Del was one of her biggest supporters. Every job that he couldn't take, he would send Maguire to direct or teach because he respected her talents.

While the question of Del's misogyny is troubling, contradictory, and confusing, he clearly had a voracious sexual appetite. His prodigious drug use had not cooled his zeal by the time he had reached Chicago. Maguire admitted to her own brief affair with Del in the early 1970s. Although Del's sex life was rumored to be dark and disturbing, she said that her own experiences were to the contrary. They slept together a few times out of a genuine affection for each other, and she recalled it as "lovely." Maguire noted that "like a lot of very unique, kinky, brilliant, and pretty disturbed people, I don't think it was very easy for him to get close to anybody." On one occasion, she participated in a threesome with Del and George. She had already slept with him prior to that, so when he asked her, she felt that the three of them shared a certain closeness and agreed: "It was very sweet, actually."

◇

Del's larger-than-life reputation didn't bother the actors or Sahlins, who had tired of directing the shows all by himself: "Close was available, and he seemed to be in good shape. What he did on his own time was his business, as long as he got the job done."[4]

Although Sahlins viewed the direction as collaboration between the two men, whereas Del saw it as his job alone, no one could dispute the results. "It worked out rather well," recalled Sahlins. "Del would dirty things up and I'd clean them up, except that the dirty things were wonderful!"

For the actors, Del was a perfect fit. He would enlist their insubordinate sides in a cabal against the management. "It was very attractive to certain people then, and it remained attractive throughout his career. . . . He had great talent, and one of his great talents was his ability to enlist the bad side of people as something that they should be proud of," said Sahlins. Of course, the Second City audiences were overwhelmingly eighteen to forty-five years old, imbued with the same spirit of insubordination.

Joyce Sloane provided a calming presence, sometimes even a buffer between Del and Sahlins. She was happy to have Del back on a regular basis. The two had gotten along well with Del since 1961, and she was happy to see that he hadn't changed at all. For Del, Sloane filled a somewhat maternal role, although their age difference was not significant. "I always got along very well with him, to the point where he would discuss his mother and his aunt with me," said Sloane. Each year at Christmastime, his mother would send him homemade fudge. It was an annual tradition for her son. He would wait for it, be terribly excited when it arrived, and then bring it over to the theater to share it.

Del firmly established his reputation during his ten-year stint at the Second City. It was also the period during which Del's downward spiral accelerated. His alcohol abuse was taking a toll and threatening his health, his ability to function, and his relationship with George. His drug use was still more of a tool to foster creativity than an impediment at this time, but his suicide attempts would also begin again.

The stories that would become legends were beginning to swirl around him, nurtured by Del; they would follow him to the end of his life and beyond. With every piece of extreme behavior, real or exaggerated, his mystique grew.

13

Valium, Vitriol, and
Ancient Egyptian Opium

The Second City renaissance was under way. While it had always had stars, not since the early days had there been such a consistently high level of talent about to reenergize the entertainment industry, led by names like Belushi, Aykroyd, Murray, Candy, and Radner, all Second City alumni, all former students of Del Close.

Bernie Sahlins took the resident company to New York in early 1973, and the touring company was moved up to the mainstage, under Del's direction. Del had run workshops for most of the group, which consisted of Bill Murray, Betty Thomas, Tino Insana, David Rasche, Ann Ryerson, Jim Staahl, and John Candy. The new mainstage company took over the "best of" show while developing material for their first show.

Bill Murray had joined the touring company in 1972; his older brother, Brian Doyle-Murray, had been a part of the *Next Generation* cast and appeared in five revues, leaving in mid-1971. New to the group was nineteen-year-old John Candy, discovered by Del, Sahlins, and Sloane during auditions for the new Toronto Second City. Del immediately requested that Candy move to Chicago and join the mainstage, where he performed for the next year and a half before joining the Toronto company. (Dan

Aykroyd was also hired at the same audition and remained in Canada to perform in Toronto, along with Valri Bromfield, Gilda Radner, Flaherty, Doyle-Murray, Jayne Eastwood, and Gerry Salsberg.)

At first, Del's behavior was not markedly different; if he was mad, he was mad in a positive, creative way. "That's why he was there. He was a genius, and what are you going to do with a genius? They crack every once in a while, and they come back," noted Insana.

Del's reputation had grown, in part for his work with the Harold. It became a point of contention with Sahlins. The producer was not a fan of improvisation, while Del always tried to insert more improvisation into his shows, before relenting under pressure from Sahlins. At one point, he even inserted a Harold into the regular revue. "That was the first time we actually had long-form improvisation in a Second City show," recalled Insana. "We did that for a while, and eventually we slid it out after a few months' run, and put some scenes in there. But to open a show with a Harold—that was pretty daring!"

Del ran workshops to develop the material generated during the nightly improvisational sets that followed each show. He would usually begin each session with a monologue, and the cast loved hearing about the old days with the Second City and the Committee—the girls, drugs, and improvisation. Despite their fifteen-year age difference, the cast considered Del to be one of them.

Second City piano player Fred Kaz had joined the theater in the mid-1960s. Kaz would run the musical numbers while Del directed scenes; they rarely worked together on the same piece. If Kaz came in with a big musical number, he would rehearse with the company, and Del observed a "hands-off" policy. Kaz would sometimes hold rehearsals on his own, and Del would not interfere unless it pertained to matters like blocking. Del and Kaz were kindred spirits, both from the Beat Generation, and the relationship soon developed into trust and long-term friendship.

With the launch of *Phase 46 or Watergate Tomorrow, Comedy Tonight* on August 15, 1973, Del would continue to vindicate Sahlins's decision to hire him. The following day, *Chicago Sun-Times* reviewer Glynna Syse wrote that while the absence of Watergate sketches disappointed her, "I had gone prepared to enjoy myself and the mission was accomplished. Close has gathered together what I think is the best group of actors the theatre has had in a couple of years." Syse particularly enjoyed a group therapy session consisting of two people. William Leonard, writing in

Fred Kaz, Bernie Sahlins, and Del Close pose outside of Second City in the early 1970s. (COURTESY OF CHARNA HALPERN)

the August 16, 1973, *Chicago Tribune*, was not as enthusiastic, calling it "typical" and "less than exciting," but "still a joy."

> They are a splendid, energetic, imaginative, and beguiling company, under the directorial guidance of Del Close, who is a real veteran of Second City. The material is not always as good as their efforts (in fact it bogs down badly on half a dozen occasions), but these players never let their own momentum vanish. . . . Having witnessed all 46 of the Second City revues, we'd rate this about midway in the playhouse's register of entertainment value. The writing, if not the direction and playing, looks a little tired at this point in time.

The decision to avoid Watergate scenes was deliberate. As Del told columnist Aaron Gold in the August 3, 1973, *Chicago Tribune*, "We're not doing any Watergate shtick because we're tired of it—and our company is no longer a bunch of angry actors."

Del had showed Sahlins that the success of *43rd Parallel* was no fluke. He told *Chicago Daily News–Panorama* reporter Jack Hafferkamp in a December 15–16, 1973, piece on the theater's fourteenth anniversary: "It's beginning to dawn on me that I don't know what I do. I just get in there and mess around. Maybe that's one reason why I'm growing steadily crazier." (In the same piece, Del commented on the name of the theater: "The idea was to take the banner of your enemies and wave it as your own. That's how Second City was named.")

The director and cast of *Phase 46*, including *(front, left to right)* Del Close, Betty Thomas, Ann Ryerson, Jim Staahl, *(back row)* Bill Murray, David Rasche, Tino Insana.

(COURTESY OF CHARNA HALPERN)

❖

With *Phase 46* a success, Del had time on his hands, and decided to fill it by directing his first scripted play at the Body Politic. Written by Dick Cusack and starring Byrne Piven, *The Night They Shot Harry Lindsey with a 155 MM Howitzer and Blamed It on the Zebras* opened on October 18, 1973. The cast also included Richard Kurtzman, Mike Nussbaum, and Del's former Second City castmate Mina Kolb, who played a sweet little old lady who is entangled in the world of international arms dealers.

Del told the *Chicago Tribune* that he was taking a naturalistic approach in his direction: "I spend most of the time telling the actors to do less. The secret of farce is to say preposterous lines with complete sincerity, and *let* the audience laugh, rather than trying to make them. If actors attempt to decorate lines, farce becomes overly baroque. Rule One is never joke the jokes."[1]

Years later, Kolb admitted that she didn't understand the play, but did recall a young member of the supporting cast, one of a pair of turbaned Hindus who didn't even have lines. He was a former Second City dishwasher, soon to make his mark as a writer, named David Mamet.

William Leonard's review in the October 17, 1973, *Chicago Tribune* called the cast and the play fun, if not deep: "Del Close, who has directed countless revues, staged this, his first play script, with an emphasis on all the right spots, so these caricatures approximate characters. . . . Dick Cusack, the author, has a lot of funny ideas and some mighty flighty dialogue, but he has overloaded his play. It tries to do too many things, all for the sake of fun, and some of them get lost. It's a fine couple hours of fun, it looks good on Lincoln Avenue, and that's as far as it goes."

Del admitted in a profile in the November 4, 1973, *Chicago Tribune* that his earlier ambition to change American theater was a little unrealistic: "It was a typical megalomaniac speed freak kind of thing. I have enough on my plate right now. And I'm thinking a little smaller. Rather than having great ambitions for things I probably won't accomplish, I'll do what I can. Perhaps something fresh will grow out of that." What was not apparent from the newspaper accounts, however, is that Del wasn't capable of finishing the play, let alone changing American theater. During rehearsals, Del was drinking heavily, and Byrne Piven had to take over as director. Del had stopped showing up, and was fired halfway through the rehearsal schedule, noted Kolb: "I don't even know if he cared, because he was drinking so much."

◇

The exact reasons his drinking increased are unclear. He may have been replicating his father's drinking patterns. His mental demons were starting to recur. Whatever the reasons and the timing, the most destructive force in his life was alcohol. It was eroding his ability to function at the Second City and in his life.

It became too much for George. She had so often served as his buffer from the realities of the everyday world. For years, she did her best to catch him whenever he threw himself off the precipice, but she had finally had enough. The next time he fell, she would not be there. The exact reasons for their split are unrecorded, yet painfully obvious: she had become fed up and couldn't take it anymore. Despite her nurturing qualities, Del had finally worn her down. Her happy-go-lucky spirit had always enabled her to take everything with huge grains of salt. Finally, she tired of it. Friends who knew the couple were amazed that she had lasted as long as she did.

Del and George,
in happier days.
(COURTESY OF CHARNA HALPERN)

Their breakup left Del even more embittered. He may have blamed George for abandoning him—she was the only person who had been able to hold him together for the past several years. Del rarely mentioned their relationship afterward. But as resentful as he may have been after their split, there was more to the story than he wanted to reveal. After his death, hidden deep within one of his scrapbooks, was a spiral-bound page with photographs of Del and George. They reveal a beautiful young woman with long dark hair, miniskirt and boots, cigarette, and, in every photo, a wide, infectious smile. She is walking down the street, drinking coffee at the outdoor café at Enrico's, and outside the Body Politic in Chicago. In two other photos, she is hanging on the arm of a grinning, clean-shaven, fashionable Del Close (wearing a suit and tie), and they look very much like a young couple in love. Whatever the circumstances, whatever his public posturing, he kept the photographs and the memories to the end.

◇

In late 1974, Del moved out of the place on North Hudson Street and into a coach house at 1617 North Wells Street, across the street from the Second City, in the heart of Old Town. The hippies and head shops had given way to gentrification, but it was still well suited to Del, who had given up driving. Just a few steps away was a Walgreens, on the northeast corner of North and Wells, handy for cigarettes and snacks. On the opposite corner was a Lums restaurant, and a few doors west was the Old Town Ale House, where a hand-painted mural saluted famous Chicagoans (a portrait of Del would soon be added to the display). In the other direction was the Stagecoach, a coffee shop derisively referred to by Del as "the Roachcoach," though that didn't stop him from becoming a regular. The Earl of Old Town, also located across Wells Street from the Second City, was a mecca for folksinging, and often featured local favorites like Steve Goodman and John Prine.

Del rarely had to venture more than a few hundred feet beyond his new apartment. After the Second City workshops, he could stop in at the Earl for a drink, then walk past the neighboring Kamehachi restaurant to the black iron gate that led to his building. His ground-floor apartment faced the same tiny courtyard as the kitchen of the sushi restaurant (though after one too many raids by Del's cats, the kitchen help learned to stop leaving the door open). To leave no doubt as to the new tenant, he placed his "Mad Doctor" in the window.

Not long after he moved in, Del became friends with an aspiring young folksinger named Jamie Swise, who often sang at the Earl of Old Town. When Del was in rehearsals at the Second City, he would run across the street to the Earl during breaks to have a triple JB and Coke and visit with Swise, who often rehearsed there. He became convinced that Swise was his son, so when Swise's schoolmarmish mother came to the Earl to hear her son play on Christmas Eve, Del approached her. "Where were you in 1952?" he wondered, asking if he might have gotten her pregnant. Mrs. Swise was quick to assure him that his theory was incorrect.

◈

While Del had held himself together during *Phase 46*, he was not quite as circumspect when work began on the next show, *Et Tu Kohoutek*. "The first show was exciting, and we all learned, and everything really came together," said Insana, who called it "the most wonderful time of my life." But when Del started running 10 A.M. workshops for *Kohoutek*, he was increasingly drunk or sleeping on the floor by 11 o'clock.

The cast was only aware of his problems with alcohol, though he continued to dabble in drugs like Valium. When he occasionally obtained a handful of speed, he would work with the cast until the middle of the night. He would often run backstage and fire the whole cast. "You're all fired! You're done, you're fired!" he would shout, then pause and add, "All right, rehearsal after the show."

The Second City companies bonded like families, rehearsing together during the day, performing together at night, and after the evening's show, doing workshops and going out together to socialize. But not all was peace and harmony within the groups, recalled Joyce Sloane. "I remember once he said to me, 'Am I allowed to fire an actor the night before opening?' And I said 'Not if it's David Rasche.' And it was." Rasche's father was a minister, and his training was theology, so he had the nerve to ask Del Close "Why?" Del didn't feel the question was necessary.

Still, turmoil did not wipe out the many happy memories. The entire cast was over six feet tall and none were Jewish, so they became known as "the Tall Goyim." (In response, Sahlins allegedly quipped, "There goes the neighborhood.") Del felt that it would be a good idea to feature a sketch in which the entire cast tap-danced. Without a clearer idea than that, the cast began tap lessons from well-known local dancer Lou Conte of the Hubbard Street Dance Company. He was serious about dance, but the cast was looking for laughs and trying to do shtick. Years later, Conte still remembered them, telling Insana, "All you guys drove me crazy!"

At one of Second City's annual Thanksgiving parties, Del decided to resurrect his fire-eating act. Everyone had brought a dish to Betty Thomas's place on St. Paul; Del decided to do his "famous flambéed pudding," and ignited the drapes. The fire department had to be called.

Del's fascination with fire had not subsided. One Saturday, he decided to show off for the students. Sloane arrived at the theater just as Del was being led down the stairs; his entire arm had been on fire. "Well, it almost worked," he told her.

Despite the behind-the-scenes commotion, *Et Tu Kohoutek or Take 47*, which opened on January 31, 1974, proved just as successful as its predecessor. In the *Chicago Tribune* review the next day, William Leonard was enthusiastic.

> Del Close, the director, told us before last night's opening that he thought this one was much better than the last one. We'd pay the production a bigger compliment than that. We'd say it is just as good as the last one and several of the preceding capers under Del's direc-

tion. For consistency is the jewel that has made the Second City great—not intermittent flashiness. . . . Another wonderful aspect about the sophisticated crazy house on Wells Street is the uncanny span of its interests. . . . A male cop gives a rape victim a hard time, telling her she asked for it; then a male rape victim comes to the station, a policewoman tells him the same thing, and the male cop doesn't think that is fair. . . . William Murray shows us how fantastically banal a nightclub singer can be. . . . There is the old "Reunion" that falls flat—that must have been in at least 46 of the 47 Second City shows. . . . Members of the cast . . . are as good as any other predecessor troupes.

In the February 4, 1974, *Chicago Today*, reviewer Marilyn Preston wrote:

With a deep bow to director Del Close's wizardly tutelage, I've come to expect, and respect, the mixed bag of blessings Second City consistently offers. . . . Straining to put a point across . . . in their two obligatory serious vignettes [referring to a high school reunion scene and another on the "changing neighborhood mentality"]. . . . But generally, they manage to pull off a very entertaining evening.

Terry Curtis Fox, writing in the February 8, 1974, *Reader*, noted that "if *Et Tu Kohoutek* is not quite the riproarer of a show that a much-needed new direction should be, it is certainly the most ambitious Second City offering that I have seen."

The Chicago critics could not agree on the stronger and weaker scenes; Preston and Leonard loved Bill Murray's Vegas lounge singer and didn't care for the class reunion, while Fox loved "Reunion," which opened the show, and hated Murray's now-famous lounge singer.

The new show drew solid audiences the first part of the year, but the follow-up to *Kohoutek* seemed to be taking forever. Del was having trouble developing the next revue. According to Insana's particularly harsh assessment, just before Del left the Second City in 1974, "he was a pathetic drunk, slobbering, unconscious, drinking during workshops till he passed out before noon." At that point, he was drinking cognac in the mornings. He would break into the Second City bar, pull out a bottle of Courvoisier, empty it before noon, and then pass out cold. As much as they loved working with Del, it had become a challenging experience.

"He made it a point to touch each one of us. We had our own private moments with Del. We all loved him, and he broke our hearts."

The Second City in Chicago was becoming desperate for a new show. To boost the attendance, an exchange program was worked out that sent Bill Murray, Betty Thomas, Ann Ryerson, Paul Zegler, and Mert Rich to the Toronto Second City. The Canadians, including Dan Aykroyd, Gilda Radner, Eugene Levy, John Candy, and Rosemary Radcliffe, traveled to Chicago for four weeks; on August 6, 1974, they opened in the forty-eigth revue, titled *The Canadian Show or Upper U.S.A.*

Two months after their return from Canada, the Chicago company finally mounted a new show with a largely new cast. *The First 100 Years or So Far, So Good* opened on October 10, 1974. Del was again credited as director, and the cast included newcomers Don DePollo, Michael Gellman, Deborah Harmon, Doug Steckler, and the returning Betty Thomas and Mert Rich. The following February, the same cast was featured soon after that in the fiftieth revue, *For a Good Time Call DELaware 7-3992*, the title both referring to the phone number for reservations and serving as a nod to the director. Critic Jon Anderson wrote in the February 7, 1975, *Chicago Sun-Times* that it was "crisp and colorful, fast and funny," citing sketches featuring Richard Nixon as a used-car salesman, and another with DePollo and Steckler planning to escape with the *U-505* German submarine on exhibit at the Museum of Science and Industry.

But Del was still restless. When Barbara Harris returned to Chicago for a visit, she was amazed and impressed at the shows Del had mounted, and sought him out after the show. She found him in the bar after the show, pacing. Wanting to help him relax, she told him about her interest in Krishnamurti, and suggested that if Del read his meditative works, he might calm down. He told her, "I've read everything Krishnamurti's ever written about relaxation and meditation, and all I do is pace when I read him!'"

❖

There were indications that Del missed stand-up comedy and performing in general. Gellman, who had replaced Bill Murray in *Kohoutek* and was now a mainstage regular, was the youngest member of the cast, and enjoyed spending off-hours with Del.

One afternoon, Del asked Gellman whether he had ever seen him doing stand-up comedy in New York. Gellman pointed out that he was only twenty years old. Del jumped to his feet, and he and Gellman ran outside. Del shouted "Cab!" They rode down to a small working-class tavern where twenty postal workers were sitting at the bar. Del climbed into the window area of the former storefront and called out, "Excuse me, can I have your attention?" Gellman feared a hostile reception, but Del launched into his stand-up comedy routine. Twenty minutes later, he finished to plentiful laughter and applause. Del said, "Thank you very much. We must leave. Come!" He whisked Gellman out of the little bar and shouted "Cab!" and they returned to the apartment. When they arrived, Del turned to him and said, "And *that's* how you do stand-up comedy!"

◇

On August 3, 1975, the *Chicago Sun-Times* ran a humorous piece that Del had written on the upcoming Bicentennial in hopes of gaining more publicity for the next revue, the fifty-first, *Once More with Fooling*, which was about to open. "Second City's Satiric View of Bicentennial" was a rarity for Del; he wrote very few such essays, and this is one of the only ones known to be published.

> Well, here we go again, folks. The Second City's 51st show in 16 years on Wells Street, *Once More With Fooling*, opens Thursday.
>
> In keeping with our tradition of delivering barbs left, right, and center, radicals, liberals, middle of the roaders, and reactionaries all take their lumps—starting with our most recent national absurdity, the Bicentennial.
>
> It's hard to satirize such a self-satirizing phenomenon. How can you get goofier than boldly reproducing "Washington Crossing the Delaware" on your toilet seat cover? I'd rather celebrate the 1500th anniversary of the fall of Rome to the Visigoths in 476 A.D.
>
> It's a grim business, this being funny. Every time you come up with a strong satiric idea, the world tops it. None of our reactionary military characters in the past decade could top the real-life line that came out of Vietnam: "We had to destroy the village in order to save it." And who could stay ahead of Watergate, or even stay abreast?

Once More with Fooling saw another rotation of the cast, with new-comers George Wendt, Ann Ryerson, and Miriam Flynn joining DePollo, Gellman, and Rich. The August 8, 1975, *Chicago Tribune* review by Roger Dettmer declared: "These Fifty-Firsters, as Del Close has directed them, are notably proficient at producing explosions of startled laughter." The subject matter of the revue was turning toward local politics once again; among the highlights noted were Michael Gellman's newscaster (report-ing the upset of the then-six-term Mayor Daley), Ryerson's new police cadet and Wendt's police captain, DePollo's traffic court judge, and a series of Bicentennial TV commercials.

George Wendt had been hired for the mainstage from the touring company in August 1975 for *Once More with Fooling*. Wendt, who would go on to fame on *Cheers*, first encountered Del in 1973, when the Com-mittee was playing the Quiet Knight on Belmont Avenue with a com-pany consisting of Larry Hankin, Jim Cranna, Dan (Beans Morocco) Barrows, Julie Payne, and Ruth Silveira. Wendt had never seen the Com-mittee and was in awe of the five-member company; he was startled when someone in the back started heckling the performers. "It turns out that was Del," noted Wendt.

The fifty-second revue, *East of Edens*, was credited with direction by Sahlins; Del was spending much of his time helping the Toronto company with a new show that would be sent to Chicago. Critic Linda Winer, writing in the February 27, 1976, *Chicago Tribune*, called *East of Edens* "mostly forgettable": "Most of the first act is clever and funny. . . . The second half starts strong—with a manicurist who has a job-related taste for the organic—before the material turns quickly into waste."

After a few weeks, the new show from Toronto, *Foreign Exchange*, came into Chicago; it would run from April 15 through May 2, when *East of Edens* would return. In the cast were future *SCTV* stars Andrea Martin, Catherine O'Hara, and Dave Thomas.

The next three Second City revues were all well received by critics. *North by North Wells*, which opened July 29, 1976, featured a travelogue through suburbia, two sportscasters in a three-hour telecast of a boxing match that ends in the first round, a parody of Woodward and Bern-stein's *The Final Days*, and Don DePollo as aging folksinger Leadlips. Will Leonard wrote in the July 30, 1976, *Chicago Tribune* that "while the gambits may be familiar, the faces are new, and Del Close, that wildly imaginative director, has staged this one with an especially exhilarating joie de vivre. . . . This revue stands up to match the enviable quality of all the Second City shows since 1959." And the August 2, 1976, *Chicago Daily News* said that "this is a show that gives some special twists to many contemporary themes."

The same cast opened the next revue, *Wellsapoppin'*, including Shelley Long, Miriam Flynn, Steven Kampmann, Don DePollo, Eric Boardman, and Will Aldis. It was dedicated to the memory of critic William Leonard, who had attended all fifty-three previous revues. Larry Townsend reviewed the fifty-fourth for the February 25, 1977, *Chicago Tribune*, praising the ensemble cast and the scenes, including "Socrates Is Dead," which dealt with the recent death of longtime mayor Richard J. Daley. And in the February 18, 1977, *Chicago Daily News*, Sydney J. Harris raved: "The talented and energetic youngsters keep coming, the skits and blackouts seem to have an inexhaustible source, and altogether it reminds one more of a family reunion than a successful commercial enterprise. . . . Del Close's direction is unflaggingly tight and pointed."

Although Del was officially the director, Bernie Sahlins was stepping in more often. When things got too difficult, Del would be temporarily suspended, but he continued to run workshops at the Second City to earn extra income, keep busy, and work out improvisational theories. His reputation continued to grow, and he won a prestigious Joseph Jefferson Award for directing the 1977 revue, and shared a Chalmers Award for the part he played in directing the Toronto Second City in 1977.

◇

Larry Coven, a recent college graduate, was hired into the touring company in late 1975, and promoted to the mainstage in mid-1977, where his castmates included Shelley Long, Miriam Flynn, Steven Kampmann, and Will Aldis. Coven and Del soon became aware that they both had a keen interest in science fiction and horror. Del had always been a fan of intelligent science fiction that pushed the concepts of the mind and broadened the possibilities of man. His love of horror came from a deeper, darker place, and he was particularly drawn to the works of H. P. Lovecraft and Clark Ashton Smith. He loved the language and concepts they brought forward.

Through workshops and rehearsals, Coven and Del were becoming close, though Del was more cautious. When Coven made a remark that clearly assumed they were friends, Del snapped, "What makes you think I'm your friend? Do you think you're Severn or something?" A day or two later, though, he took it all back, saying, "Yeah, I apologize. We are friends."

After his breakup with George, Del had allowed Jamie Swise to become close, and now Coven had broken through as well. Del may have viewed the two initially as surrogate sons, in the same way that Ed Greenberg had become close to him, but Coven would remain close to Del to the end of his days.

Reports on Del's capabilities during this period vary greatly. Nate Herman, who appeared in *Sexual Perversity Among the Buffalo* (and would later direct at the Second City), said that the Del he knew in 1977 was not dysfunctional, but working to the best of his abilities. "I never saw him in the foggy periods. I have nothing but fond and fine memories of the guy."

In fact, the night Herman quit the show after a fight with another member of the cast, Del rallied to support him. Del stopped by his nearby place on Wells Street and begged him to return. They called other friends over and stayed up until four o'clock in the morning playing Del's word-association game. "It's one of my cherished memories, and it's a game that, if you don't understand what's going on, you don't understand what's going on! He doesn't teach it, he just says, 'We're going to play it,' and he starts."

Coven likewise never saw a workshop when Del was unable to function, although there were occasions when Sahlins took over the workshops without explanation. There were times, however, when Del would push the glasses back on his head and say, "Well, I've got to go feed the cat." The students knew it meant he was going to get a drink.

Del made a halfhearted attempt to curtail the use of drugs around the theater by insisting that the actors could not be stoned for rehearsals. "His note to the cast was always 'Back time your drugs,'" noted Gellman. If the marijuana they were smoking at the time lasted an hour and a half, they could not smoke it less than two hours before they were due at rehearsal. He considered this to be "working straight," with little regard for the fact that it remained in their bloodstream for a long time afterward.

His use of drink and drugs proved divisive for the Second City casts. Some, such as Gellman and DePollo, were devoted and would defend him against all attacks, while others only tolerated him because they were being paid.

◆

It was soon an open secret at the Second City that, after *Phase 46*, Del was having trouble finishing a show. He was brilliant when helping the cast develop ideas, but when a revue needed more polishing, Del was either not interested or not able. He would claim that a show was ready to open when Sahlins, Sloane, and many others felt that preparations, like his kindergarten toy train, were far from complete.

Inevitably, Sahlins would step in for the final polish. Unfortunately, this would have an ever more detrimental effect on Del, who viewed it as interference. But instead of confronting Sahlins, he would walk away and continue drinking. It became a downward spiral. The more he drank, the less capable he was of finishing a show; the more Sahlins would take charge, the more Del would drink and become even less capable.

"Del was just uninterested in the kind of donkey work involved in passing from pure inspiration to perspiration," noted Sahlins. He felt he was improving the shows, and was genuinely surprised to hear many years later that Del had been upset. "I always thought I added to his work. He saw magic where it didn't exist."

It didn't help that Del and Sahlins had virtually nothing in common outside theater. "I don't know how Bernie and he ever had a conversation," said Swise. "They were absolute opposites." Of course, the answer was that they came together over the work. It was their lone point of agreement, but for years it was enough.

How much Del's shows needed "fixing" is a matter of dispute. When Del felt a show was ready to open, he simply declared it finished and stopped coming. But other people, including good friends, supported Sahlins; he had a formula for shows, and Del did not agree with formulas. Danny Breen recalled that Del would usually say, "Well, I'll just go crazy now and they'll send me home." George Wendt felt that Del's biggest creative shortcoming was that he didn't have the discipline to open a show or decide on a running order that fit the mold: "That's no doubt in great part because Del was not a mold kind of guy. Del was always outside the box." Selecting the opening and closing sketches and the running order was an executive, left-brain process more suited to Sahlins. Del was a creature of the right brain.

But many of the best Second City shows were collaborations between Del and Sahlins. "Bernie was very necessary," said Fred Kaz. "If we had let it flow as much as we at times wished to, I'm not sure we'd have survived."

Even Larry Coven didn't see Sahlins as interfering. Del would come up with brilliant scenes; Sahlins would come in at the end. Sometimes Del would be upset, but other times it was valuable advice: "They worked pretty well as a team. . . . There was basically a mutual respect there."

George Wendt felt that Del was invaluable for building scenes, but finishing shows was not his strong point: "Bernie and Del were a great team in that regard. While Del would take us all on flights of fancy that turned into wonderful theatrical moments that came completely out of left field, Bernie had a real clear idea and had the executive ability."

Even when he disagreed, Del didn't argue with the producer. Instead, he would opt for more passive-aggressive tactics; he would suddenly stop attending rehearsals, increase his drinking—or even attempt suicide.

◈

When he returned to the Second City in the 1970s, his suicide attempts had abated, but they were back again. They were one way to lash out at perceived injustices, and were clearly attention-getting measures. After swallowing a handful of pills, he would immediately get on the phone to inform friends. According to Breen, Del was not visibly morose or depressed; he was having a good time, and had no reason to kill himself. "It was like a kid acting out, he didn't get his way. It was little incidents that set it off, stuff that shouldn't have, but did."

Among those Del resorted to calling upon was Joyce Sloane. On one occasion, he told her he needed money to pick up "his medicine" and left the theater after Sloane gave him the money. A few minutes later, the phone rang. "Well, I've tried it again, so I'm calling to say good-bye," Del told her. She immediately called an ambulance, and everyone from the theater ran across the street. As they were putting him in the ambulance, he turned around to Sloane and said, "My respiration should stop at any moment now."

Larry Coven blamed alcohol for an attempt not long after he joined the Second City in 1975–76, as a result of which Del was hospitalized. Del explained that he thought of suicide as rebirth in a certain sense. Michael Gellman believed that Del was flirting with death in an attempt to understand why his father had killed himself.

He was always trying to go right up to the edge of death and look over the edge. I thought that's what the Harold was all about, exploring how the brain worked. He was constantly trying to figure out how the human mind functioned chemically and psychologically, and figure out how someone could kill himself. Everything he did in improvisation was about exploring the human brain and the workings of the mind. I thought his entire artistic existence was all about the brain.

One of his most exotic explorations began when Gellman was visiting Del at his apartment on Wells Street and there was an unexpected knock on the door. A voice called, "Del, it's John! Open up!" Paranoid, Del asked, "Who?" "John! It's Brent! Open up!" "Who?" "Brent! Open up!" "Uh . . . Brent's in New York." John Brent had, in fact, told Del he was going to be in New York, which made Del more suspicious than usual.

After a lengthy exchange, Del finally began undoing the chains and locks on his door as he talked with his friend. "Brent? What are you doing here? You're in New York!"

"No, man, I'm not, I'm here! I was at the Metropolitan Museum of Art!" responded Brent, excited and giddy.

"You were at the Metropolitan Museum of Art and you had to come to Chicago?"

"Yeah, man!"

"Uh . . . John, you're not making any fucking sense. What are you talking about?"

"Dig, man, the mummy case was open! They were cleaning the mummy case!"

"And you had to come to Chicago? You're fucking nuts, Brent!"

"No, Del, look!"

Brent reached into his pocket and pulled out a small object that he displayed before Del.

"Uh, John, that appears to be an ancient Egyptian opium pipe."

"Yeah, man!"

"You stole an opium pipe from a mummy at the Met? And you came to me with it!"

"Yeah, man!"

"You're a true friend. John, there appears to be some shit left in the pipe."

"Yes, Del!"

Del turned to his younger friend and said, "Gellman, you don't use needles, do you? You better split."

The next day, Del was two hours late for rehearsal. Gellman and DePollo were commiserating: "Oh, this is going to be really bad." When Del arrived, he was considerably worse for wear. "Sorry I'm late," he told them. "I don't feel very good. It was either the two-thousand-year-old opium I shot, or the ham-and-cheese sandwich I had at the Roachcoach."

Growing up with his father, Del had learned to take extreme measures when he was in need of attention. Although he apparently never used the tactic when his father was still alive, the boy who could not get enough attention had grown into a man who knew how to get plenty of it.

14

The *Clockwork Orange* Treatment

S*aturday Night Live* would have as much impact on the Second City's reputation and renown as its premiere on Broadway fifteen years earlier. The cast, including John Belushi, Dan Aykroyd, and Gilda Radner (Bill Murray joined the following season), brought a new flurry of national attention to the Second City. And the bright young stars would be quick to acknowledge Del in their rise to fame, even while Del was little able to handle the spotlight.

Del had little interest in mainstream fame. He shunned the second-lead-in-a-sitcom type of fame, but was drawn to anything that would reinforce his counterculture credentials or establish his reputation as the paterfamilias of comedy's new generation. "Laughter is a response to gestalt formation where two previously incompatible or dissimilar ideas suddenly form into a new piece of understanding—the energy released during that reaction comes out in laughter," Del philosophized in an interview in the "Comedy Roots" column for the December 26, 1977, issue of *New Times.* "Our favorite kind of laugh was what we used to call the mystery laugh. That's when you say some perfectly straight line on stage, and the audience just cracks up. Then you realize 'Ah, that was funny.' We find the best laughs by accident in most cases."

The dark side or the evil nature to which Patinkin and a few others had referred rose closer to the surface. He was not the wise guru of improvisation, dispensing nuggets of wisdom for students to carry along to network television stardom. He wanted people to be respectful, if wary. He wore a T-shirt that read "Junkies Give the Best Shots."

Just as his students were becoming the hottest comedy performers in America after the October 1975 premiere of *Saturday Night Live* (at first called just *Saturday Night*), Del couldn't get an acting job. He simply couldn't pull himself together. He often relied on Swise for support.

One evening, Del called Swise, saying, "I'm bleeding." Swise found the door half-open and entered, calling his name. Del was inside, naked, bending over a pile of apparently useless items. While trying to find pieces to make a kaleidoscope, he had fallen and cut his head. It was bad timing, he told Swise: "I'm going to be trying out for the part of Einstein at 9 A.M." He would need to be downtown, cleaned up that next morning. "How much Placidyl did you do?" asked Swise. When he figured out that Del had taken a twenty-four-hour dose, he realized there was little chance of him passing for Albert Einstein, so he put him to bed and left.

The next morning, he dutifully arrived at seven-thirty, banged on the door, and finally dragged Del out of bed for the audition. "I'm going up against [actor Richard] Henzel, and Henzel might look like Einstein, but I think like Einstein," Del said as he got ready. "Not today you don't," answered Swise. He took Del to the Stagecoach, where he ordered three fruit plates. (He claimed that some time ago he had written Adelle Davis for a junkie maintenance diet, and she said that fruit would be good for him.) He thought that if he ate three helpings of canned fruit, he would be straight. Swise loaded him into a cab and sent him downtown, but it was the last he heard from Del about Einstein.

Although Swise did not indulge in drink or drugs, he soon learned about the properties and effects of all Del's favorites. Another call came during the winter. Swise arrived to find Del in his courtyard, naked, standing in a snowdrift and screaming as he complained of chest pains. Swise suggested that his problem might be that he was standing out in the cold without any clothes on, screaming. He led Del inside and explained that if he truly believed he was having a heart attack, then they should call the EMTs. "But they'll see my old track marks," Del protested. Swise assured him that no one would really care. An ambulance arrived, and a medic who looked like a fresh-faced twenty-year-old ex-cheerleader carefully checked Del, who was draped across the couch, and told him that he had not suffered a heart attack. "Aren't you going to say anything about my track marks?" The young paramedic told him no, and then picked up her bag and walked out. She was not going to admonish him about his drug use, and he was not going to have the opportunity to defend it. Del was terribly disappointed.

Although Del's paranoia was increasing, at one point he decided to revive his stand-up career. He made an appointment with his old friend and former Second City actor Dennis Cunningham, who was now a successful Chicago attorney. He walked in and handed him a hundred-dollar bill. "Do you accept me as your client?" he asked, and a puzzled Cunningham said, "Of course! Why would I not? You don't have to pay me!" Del insisted he take the money, explaining that he was going to appear in a new club that had opened in a former grocery store on Lincoln Avenue, but he was worried he might get arrested. Cunningham went to the show the first evening. At one point, Del called out, "Is my lawyer in the house?" Cunningham answered in the affirmative, and he continued his act. Nothing happened. He continued with his routine, which involved a scientific description of the laughter reflex, explaining what happened neurologically when people laugh at something funny.

Del was only trying new material. After seeing close-up the legal trouble Lenny Bruce had gotten into—and the notoriety it netted him—he decided he would take no chances. But Del had nothing to worry about, noted Cunningham, who was more concerned about his apparent paranoia. Del's foray into stand-up was short-lived and soon forgotten.

Although his continued drug use was beginning to have an effect on his ability to perform, Del was still able to attract young women. He would occasionally dally with students who were brave enough to follow him across the street. One minor scandal involved a beautiful girl, married to an attorney, who emerged from his apartment after two days, during which her husband had been searching for her. For some women, Del apparently exerted a charisma that could overcome his roach-infested apartment and head-to-toe scars.

The condition of the Wells Street apartment deteriorated rapidly. Trash piled up, there was no attempt at dusting or cleaning, and even the bravest souls would avoid his bathroom. The Orkin Man refused him. "It would *rain* roaches in that house," noted Swise.

During this period, Mildred Close paid a visit to Chicago for an unspecified reason (possibly something as auspicious as a Second City opening). She was nearly eighty years old. Friends who observed the two of them together said that he was a different person when he was with his mother, on his best behavior.

Yet Del was always capable of thoughtful gestures. One year, near the end of September, he phoned Swise and suggested that they go to Wrigley Field during the Cubs' final home game of the season. They hopped in a cab and simply strolled in during the fifth inning (the Cubs were so far out of contention that no one cared). They watched a few innings, then he walked up to the booth to say hello to announcer Jack Brickhouse, and then he jumped in a cab and headed home.

Del once called Swise and suggested they go to see *Close Encounters of the Third Kind* on the big screen at the Esquire Theater. During the first show, there was a mother in the audience with a crying baby. Del stood up, his voice booming: "Boil that child in oil!"

◈

In the wake of the success of *Saturday Night Live*, Sahlins and Toronto Second City producer Andrew Alexander agreed that it was a perfect opportunity for a Second City TV show. Despite occasional local specials, the Second City had not conquered television. But Alexander worked out a deal with a Canadian TV station, and so in 1976, Del, Sahlins, and several others flew to Toronto for a creative meeting to discuss ideas for the possible series. Del would later maintain that he came up with the premise for the show, an assertion that was apparently exaggerated. Sheldon Patinkin maintained that he was the one who said, "Why don't we do something about a day's programming at a TV station?" while Del then added, "It should be a bad UHF channel." "We created the idea together, although I don't get much credit for it," noted Patinkin.

SCTV's original writer-performers were alumni of the Chicago or Toronto companies, and included John Candy, Joe Flaherty, Harold Ramis, Rick Moranis, Dave Thomas, Eugene Levy, Catherine O'Hara, and Andrea Martin. When some of them eventually left, their replacements included such talents as Martin Short, Robin Duke, and Brian Doyle-Murray. Since he was unwilling to move to Canada, Del's participation was restricted to a few minimal writing contributions, which he would send in from Chicago.

Eventually, Sahlins and Sloane sent Del to Toronto to direct their new production for Alexander. In 1976, author Jeffrey Sweet was at work writing *Something Wonderful Right Away*, his definitive oral history of the Compass and the early days of the Second City. When he asked Del to participate and record interviews with him, Del was quick to agree, and invited him to watch a rehearsal with the Canadian cast, which then included Thomas, O'Hara, Candy, Martin, and John Monteith.

When Del arrived, Sweet got the impression that Del didn't want to be there, but decided to run the session anyway. Del said, "I'm going to teach you how to make someone mad at you onstage." The company members asked, "Why would we want to know that?" But Del assured them it was well worth learning. "While you're in the scene, you say, 'Why are you mad at me?' And the more they insist that they aren't mad at you, and the more you insist that they are mad at you, the madder they'll become." The group acknowledged that projecting an emotion onto the other person could be a valuable lesson.

Del then announced that he was going to teach them a new game called Autobiography, using the company to re-create an episode in someone's life. When no one volunteered, Del led them through a version of his father's suicide. Thomas said, "Well, Del, you're right, you do know how to make somebody mad at you onstage." And they all walked out on him. Del went off to dinner with Sweet, commenting, "Well, I think that went rather well, don't you?" Sweet recalled: "He was very hyper, and talking about scientific theory and literary theory and seemed to be very chipper. When I got back the next day, I'd heard that he'd made another suicide attempt."

It was obvious that Del was very needy, and in bad shape. One night, he arrived in the middle of winter with no shoes, in a cab, threatening to kill Alexander. Candy and Patinkin had to take him back to his hotel room, pack everything up, and get him on the next plane to Chicago. That included emptying the dresser drawer of his hotel room, which he had converted into a cat box and filled with kitty litter. (The Second City was banned from the hotel as a result.)

When he gave his lengthy interview for *Something Wonderful Right Away*, Del professed boredom and frustration.

> My job here now is covering home plate. If Chicago falls, the whole thing falls. To some degree, it's a Red Queen's race—you run so hard to stay in the same place. We have a constant turnover of actors. It's amazing to me the level of quality we've been able to maintain.[1]

He claimed that the Second City had become more about maintenance than innovation. "At the beginning, in Compass and the first days
of The Second City, we had a definite sense of being part of the process
of history in the making—hanging ten out there in the front of something, forging away into the unknown. Now, to some degree, the thrill
of discovery is gone."[2]

Even then, in 1976–77, Del was certainly capable of brilliance. During one Chicago workshop, he told a group of young students, "If you're
a good enough improviser, you can take any line that somebody hits
you with, and by your response, you can give it direction and make a
scene." He lined up the students on the stage, and one after another,
they would give him a line, and he would immediately respond with
something that would indeed make a scene. One person decided to be
a smart-ass, and gave him a bland "Hi, Del." He said, "Sure, you say that
to me this morning!"

◈

It took time for George Wendt to adjust to Del's style in workshops
and rehearsals. There were no rules, to the extent that Del would either
ignore scenes or give copious notes on scenes that were eminently ignor-
able. It was ultimately enlightening and discouraging for the company,
said Wendt: "You'd do a brilliant scene, and you'd know it was great, and
the audience would know it's great, and you'd be very excited, and you'd
come backstage, and Del would say, 'Nice work in the psychiatrist scene.
Unfortunately, Mike and Elaine did it in 1958.'"

Del and Sahlins had complementary strengths and weaknesses,
noted Wendt. Sahlins insisted on academic sketches and references, a
bow to the University of Chicago intellectuals who supported the Second City in its early days. Sahlins preferred the opening scene to be
a cast scene that set the tone politically and upped the stakes for his
University of Chicago contingent. Wendt lamented that "up in Canada,
Marty Short's got the hair eight feet tall doing Ed Grimley, and we're trying to do Socrates, because Bernie insisted upon it for his U of C crowd!
Consequently, the Canadians were hilarious; everyone fell in love with
the Canadians. We were always trying to do something meaningful."

Both Del and Sahlins agreed that the level of the material had to
be kept high. "Don't tell me it works for the audience, that's never good

enough," they would tell the cast. "It got a laugh? Don't tell *me* it got a laugh!" It had to be cool and hip for Del, the right *kind* of laugh.

Del and Sahlins clashed over the sketches that would go into each show. Del insisted that the performers work at the top of their intelligence. Even so, Sahlins vetoed some of Del's favorites, still concerned about the University of Chicago crowd that made up much of each opening night audience.

Del knew that the U of C crowd wasn't enough. If there was a really cheap blackout that would get a huge laugh, Del would be the first one to say, "You've got to put that in. It's very funny and it gets a huge laugh." Sahlins, more often than not, would prefer an obscure joke about a philosopher. Del and the company found it immensely frustrating. They, too, wanted a smart show, but they also wanted as many laughs as possible.

One such blackout always got big laughs in the late-night sets, but Sahlins never let it in the show. It was called "Looking." The men in the company lined up along the upstage wall, backs to the audience, as if they were standing at a urinal. One of the men becomes irate and screams, "You looked at my dick! You fag!" The others would calm him, and another man would say, "No, it's a scientific fact, it's just a curiosity thing." As the lights went out, all of the men were looking at one another. "It would get a huge laugh. Del defended that from the get-go, saying, 'No, that's funny! It works!' and Bernie never let it in a show. Shows often needed those huge laugh blackouts," said Breen.

The cast inadvertently got their revenge one night. A critic from a London paper was in the audience, unbeknownst to the cast. The cast did a cheap, scatological improvisational set, and the critic wrote of his huge disappointment at going to see the Second City. He was particularly horrified by a cheap bit from Tim Kazurinsky and Breen, the latter of whom reflected: "It was Bernie's worst nightmare! He was livid for a really long time, he was really disappointed. . . . Del found that amusing. 'Oh, fuck him!'"

Directing at the Second City usually involved about six weeks of rehearsals, and during the 1970s, a new show would run for about six months. After a new show opened, Del had time for a variety of odd jobs, but spent much of his time conducting workshops nearly year-round. Occasionally, a number of students would form their own group and begin performing independently of the Second City.

The first successful group to spin off the Second City workshops was the Reification Company in late 1974; for several years it became a true alternative to the Second City. After Del's Saturday workshops, the class would go across the street to the Earl of Old Town or the Sneak Joint (a bar just a few steps away from Del's front door). "This guy, Sylvester, asked Del if he had any funny people, because he was thinking of opening a club," recalled Bernadette Birkett. After briefly quitting the Second City following a disagreement with Sahlins, Del helped them form the group. They began working at Sylvester's on North Lincoln Avenue, opening the last week of 1974.

The Reification Company became true rivals to the Second City, with a younger following, and less mainstream audiences. Del brought the bulk of his Saturday workshop there, and eventually pared them down to the core group, which included Rob Riley, Mark Nutter, Tom Tully, Danny Breen, Nonie Newton, Mary Gross, Rick Thomas, Norman Mark, Bill Nigut, and Birkett.

Still, Del did not serve as the group's official director. Del would either lend his approval or say, "This doesn't work; I don't know what you're thinking." They were a burr in Sahlins's side, even as they became media darlings, garnering great reviews, performing sketches, improvisations, and quite a bit of musical material. Carol Kleiman wrote in the November 26, 1976, *Chicago Tribune* that "the group is beginning to mesh, and their good feelings about themselves and each other [are] contagious." Del and Don DePollo inevitably left the Reification Company to go back to the Second City; they needed the health benefits that the more established theater could provide.

Tim Kazurinsky, who would go on to *Saturday Night Live* and screenwriting success (*About Last Night . . .*), joined the mainstage in 1978 during *Sexual Perversity Among the Buffalo*. He often shared the stage with Wendt, including a memorable scene in which he sat on Wendt's lap as a ventriloquist's dummy. Their workshops with Del were inconsistent, but when he was on, Kazurinsky said, he could "say things and whip an entire class into such a frenzy that you were so focused, and the doors—Aldous Huxley's *Doors of Perception*—would slam open in your mind, shafts of light, 'Oh, *that's* what it's about! *That's* how to do it!' . . . and it would become so clear as to why you were there, and what it was all about. He's one of the few geniuses I've ever met."

For both Kazurinsky and Wendt, doing Del's Harold was the ultimate experience in improvisation, one that they didn't perform often enough. The best scenes they created came out of improvisation, according to Wendt.

> The richest laughs of any Second City revue, I can almost guarantee you somebody didn't write that on a typewriter. Ninety percent of those came out of the collective unconscious on the evening that it happened, and boy, you never forget those! You don't have to write those down. Those get seared into your consciousness! Harold was like jumping out of an airplane! You've got to do or die. It's like being thrown into the water, you've got to swim or not! The intensity of the pressure to create is liberating.

◇

Around the middle of 1977, Del returned to Kansas for a twenty-five-year class reunion at Manhattan High School. Del went early to visit his mother, who had moved out of the house on Poyntz to a rest home in nearby Abilene. During his visit to Manhattan, most of his time seemed to be spent "trying to find drugs," recalled one classmate. He did relate some of his post–high school experiences to his junior high dancing partner, Donna Fearing, telling her that he had been exempt from the draft for psychological reasons. He also related his encounter with the psychiatric nurse who had borne him a son while trying to "cure" him. Fearing wondered whether he was referring to homosexuality but didn't ask. She thought Del was deliberately trying to impress her with his wild life after leaving their hometown.

◇

After the reunion, Del returned to Chicago, attempting to resume workshops while Sahlins directed the new show. Danny Breen recalled that Del was "kind of a mess" by the end of 1977. The same year, Breen, Wendt, and stage manager Joel Bloom were living in an apartment in Old Town ironically called "the Energy Center," where they had parties every night. When they were selected to host the annual Second City Thanksgiving party, it was the first time they cleaned it in a year. Throughout the party, Del continued to look at people and say "Oogabooga!" while accompanying it with a hand gesture implying a whammy. The residents had a pot plant growing in a planter by the front window.

In the middle of the party, Del suddenly dropped his pants and urinated on the pot plant. "This is what they do in Mexico to make it grow better!" he announced. The next day the plant was dead.

During the same period, Jim Belushi was learning the ropes, just as Del's problems were coming to a head. Belushi had met Del years earlier, and when he began to aspire to the Second City, Del took him under his wing. Del would proudly tell classes that the first time Belushi ran offstage, he excitedly said, "This is better than fucking!"

The younger Belushi was devoted to Del, and his mentor felt the same way. "Del was very nice to me. He was very complimentary of my work," said Belushi. "He really guided it, and he never had a harsh word for me. He never hurt my feelings, he totally believed in my work. He gave us great outs in scenes and directions. He was very respectful of me and my talent."

By the time they first started working together in late 1977, Del was hitting bottom, and Belushi was still fiercely supportive of his mentor. "He was going through a real drinking phase. I think this was part of his isolation," said Belushi. "He managed to piss everybody off in the theater and push everybody away from him, from Miriam Flynn to Will Aldis, and definitely Bernie and Joyce. To the actors, he was caustic. But I loved him, I accepted him for however he was."

Belushi happened to be at the theater one day when Del had been fired for his drinking. He was walking in just as Del was being kicked out. "As I turned the corner, he was walking out. I said, 'Del, I know what's going on here, everybody's talking about you, it's a tense time. I want you to know that I trust you.' And he goes, 'You trust me, huh?' 'Yes, Del, I do.' And he kicked me right in the nuts, and he walked away. 'You trust me, huh?'" Afterward, in an alcoholic haze, Del claimed he didn't remember anything about the incident.

Finally, whether the result of alcoholism, schizophrenia, or simply misogyny, even Swise had enough. The final straw involved a friend of Swise's who was sitting quietly at a table at the Earl of Old Town one afternoon. Del came in for a shot of JB, and Swise introduced the two of them.

Del said something that was kind of hostile. She came right back on him, and just cut him up, but harmlessly. He jumped up and he pushed her, ass over head, off that chair, and stormed out. And I

Del before the "Schick Clinic."
(COURTESY OF CHARNA HALPERN)

was in shock. She was crying, not because it hurt her, but because it scared the hell out of her. And I was apologizing, because I introduced her to the guy. He had gone back into his little thing, and he was gone for two days. When he came out, I said "Del, how could you have done that?" He pretended he didn't know what the hell I was even talking about.

For Coven, the most unsettling times with Del likewise involved alcohol, when he would go into what Coven called his "devil mode." Though it happened very seldom, early in their friendship it terrified his friend. "He would start recalling things he had done long before I knew him, and he would be so evil, it would just scare the fuck out of me! He would tell me things that he did, stories about things he did with Elaine May, and things he did to twelve-year-old girls—I have no idea if it's true, but what was scary about it was that he wasn't just telling me a story, it was this personality of his that came out. I was really frightened to be there."

◇

By 1977, Del had given up most drugs except for pot and codeine, but alcohol was destroying him. He didn't complain about the alcohol impeding his abilities, but did mention the possibility of quitting. It had become a problem, because he kept getting suspended from the

Second City, and that was his only income by then. No one else would hire him.

He had been making halfhearted efforts to cut back or control his drinking. While directing the Second City company in Toronto, he had hired a large, menacing bodyguard called Tiny, and ordered Tiny to prevent him from drinking any alcohol. It appeared to be working, but by Saturday night, Andrew Alexander saw Del sitting by himself at the bar with a drink in his hand. When he asked about Tiny's absence, Del replied, "I gave him the night off."

Del knew that he would be spending the rest of his life working in cabaret theaters that sold liquor, and decided to do something practical to stop drinking. He was haunted by another reason as well, which he confessed to Charna Halpern years later. He did not want to be lying in the gutter some day and have someone come up and kick him, saying, "Hey, are you Del Close? I'm your son." The specter of his own father and their relationship still loomed large, and, at least with regards to alcohol, he would no longer allow it to perpetuate.

Del tried to find something on which to fix the blame for his drinking. He tried to hold the Second City responsible, even though he had started long before he returned to Chicago. "I would always be criticized for drinking, but whenever I came out of the room, there would be someone with a drink for me," he told friends. The paranoid, suspicious side of him felt that the Second City must want him well enough to be able to direct their shows, but to remain an alcoholic so that he couldn't go off on his own with his brilliant talent—so that they could keep him for pennies.

Whether it was pressure—or an ultimatum—from the Second City, or a personal epiphany, Del made the decision to stop drinking. Despite his suspicions about the Second City, it was clear that everyone at the theater supported his decision to embrace sobriety.

An initial attempt to quit with the help of Alcoholics Anonymous had little effect, and he was left with a less than flattering opinion of the group.

I'd gone to A.A., a useless bunch of whining assholes, peddling this ersatz pseudo-Christian cryptomonotheism. You have to hit rock bottom, then they've got this pattern you follow. And every one of them falls off the wagon. And they insist you spend all your time listening to these boring assholes tell each other what a bad time they had drinking. I had a great time drinking. Some of my best conversations . . . you'd laugh about your despair. Because everybody I hung out with was hooked—"Well, my liver's going; might as well have another drink."[3]

After AA, sterner measures were obviously called for. Del called an old friend who had successfully quit, and he suggested the Schick Shadel Hospital (Del usually referred to it as the "Schick Clinic" or the "Schick Institute") in Fort Worth.

I called Severn and said "How'd you get off booze?" He directed me to this clinic in Texas. They dry you out for three days, give you a little bit of booze so you don't go into hideous withdrawal. And then, they shoot you up with these chemicals. It makes you violently, violently ill—intergalactic nausea. Nobody on earth has ever been that sick.

Then you drink highly dilute, warm, and slightly salted versions of whatever drink you like, and ooh, you throw up for about an hour and a half. Then they put you in bed and give you sodium pentothal. Which gets you whacked; this is the reward part of the therapy. It could also be used as a hypnotic, they can sneak past the censor by giving you posthypnotic suggestions. So they come at you every which way.[4]

Del called it the "*Clockwork Orange* treatment," in which understanding why people drink is less important than stopping them from drinking. He was forced to consume enormous quantities of everything he had been drinking, which was virtually everything in a bar; the doctors even had to go out for a bottle of green Chartreuse. After drinking and vomiting it all, he was sent to bed, where he experienced convulsions because of his high susceptibility. The same treatment was repeated for five days, and supplemented with medical lectures on alcohol. Del was particularly interested to learn how, unlike heroin and cocaine, alcohol affects not just one or two organs, but the entire body on a cellular level, making withdrawal particularly painful.

The two weeks of aversion therapy in January 1978 proved a success. He was overwhelmed by the sense of optimism he felt as he walked through the hospital. No one's belief systems were threatened, and the

Del at the "Schick Clinic."
(COURTESY OF CHARNA HALPERN)

entire course of treatment was paid for by his Actors' Equity major medical insurance. For the rest of his life, if he inadvertently drank or even got too close to alcohol, even someone who'd had a drink, he would immediately become ill.

During his rehabilitation in Texas, he faced another, less critical problem. He had been working with an improvisational group at the end of 1977 called the Impeccable Warriors. Unfortunately, just before their first big show, Del had to leave for Texas to undergo his aversion therapy. The group was worried; not only was Del their director, he was also scheduled to appear onstage, hosting and doing introductions, explanations, and stand-up.

He still felt tremendous loyalty to the performers, but he would be in the Schick Clinic the night of their performance. So he devised a solution—he would phone in his performance. Literally.

As the audience filed in, they saw two stools onstage, with a speaker on one of them. There was a telephone line attached to the speaker.

Del waited at the pay phone in Texas as the show began. Recalling his folk club days, in which music and comedy were used to complement each other in performance, Jamie Swise opened the show with a song, and then Del's voice came out of the speaker. "This is our show, and I'm supposed to be there, but I'm in aversion therapy in Texas," he told the group via long distance. As he delivered his long-distance monologue, patients walked by him in the hospital corridor, and Del would stop and talk to them as they went past.

His sobriety was his first step toward a new life. It had never occurred to him that so many of his problems derived from the fact that he was a drunk. When Del returned to Chicago, he was content for his demons to spring from nonalcoholic causes: "I progressively got more capable. You still go crazy, and you do weird, self-destructive stuff. But you do it on a more interesting level."[5]

15

"Junkies Give the Best Shots"

"A lot of people still regard me as an asshole, but I'm a sober asshole."

Del Close had returned to Chicago sober, determined to regain control of his life. Self-destruction was deeply ingrained, but his father's shadow was fading, and he could see the new possibilities available to him.

Even though he had stopped drinking, he indulged in whatever drugs came his way. He explained that they were tools to free his mind and boost his creativity, but he never discussed their usefulness in quieting his inner pain.

He still had the need to rebel against the real world. In his apartment, cleanliness was next to impossible; he tended to wear his clothes for days or even weeks in a row until they became unwearable, then he would throw them out and buy new ones.

Jim Belushi noted that the sober Del Close "wasn't so nuts." Giving up drinking was the first step, though the road to respectability would take years. "Alcohol wasn't his drug," explained Belushi. "[After alcohol,] he wasn't so crazy and unpredictable."

Del gave Belushi some valuable career advice. Belushi had the opportunity to do a network TV show called *Who's Watching the Kids?* but didn't want to leave the Second City or Chicago. He explained his predicament to Del in the back kitchen at the Second City. Del listened carefully, then asked: "What makes you think that Second City is the only place you can learn to be an actor? There are thousands and thousands of actors out there that are very good that didn't go through Second City. They had to learn somewhere, Jim." For Belushi, it was all the permission he needed to go out and do the series.

Del's guidance as a director is something that Belushi and many other students have used throughout their careers. Del rarely talked about acting or performance. Instead, he would discuss the context and meaning of a scene. "To this day, doing this TV series [*According to Jim*], I'm doing the same stuff: What is the scene about? What are we trying to say?"

Sobriety meant that Del was much more together, projected his ideas much more clearly, and had a much clearer aim in life. Larry Coven felt that "none of the drugs he took ever hurt him, except for alcohol and cigarettes."

◇

On his return to the Second City, Del discovered that he was still on a "leave of absence." He had directed the fifty-fifth revue, *Upstage, Downstage*, in July 1977, but Sahlins took over the direction of the next show before Del left for the Schick Clinic. *Sexual Perversity Among the Buffalo* opened in February 1978 with newcomers Jim Belushi, Nate Herman (who was replaced by Tim Kazurinsky), Audrey Neenan, and Maria Ricossa, along with Coven, Will Aldis, and Don DePollo. Although Del helped shape the material, much of the work fell to Sahlins. The show is still noted for the "White Horse Tavern" scene, made famous by Belushi and Aldis, about two brothers who meet for drinks, discussing life, death, and Dylan Thomas.

By summer 1978, Del's "leave of absence" was over, and he was in charge of the next revue. Del now had enough energy to rehearse with the Second City cast during the afternoon, conduct evening workshops with a troupe called Del Close and the Control Group (which sprang from one of his workshops), and still attend the Second City's late-night improvisation sets after the shows. Some thought that his sobriety made him less artistically volatile and "dehorned" him; others found that his workshops became more focused.

The resultant Second City show, *Another Fine Pickle*, opened October 5, 1978, receiving an enthusiastic review on October 7 by the *Chicago Tribune's* Larry Kart.

> Always topical and usually very funny, Second City sometimes tries a little harder and comes up with a show that does much more than a comedy troupe reasonably can be expected to do. *A Fine Pickle . . .* is one of those shows. . . . *A Fine Pickle* zeroes in on the curdled idealism of our antipolitical times and accurately diagnoses the pervasive malaise of the forlorn late 1970s.

Kart praised Will Aldis and Larry Coven's "Grant Park," featuring a nostalgic look at the 1968 Democratic Convention by a present-day insurance salesman and an accountant. A particular favorite was "Pheasant Run," with Audrie Neenan and Tim Kazurinsky as a married couple at each other's throats rehearsing a seduction scene. Wendt portrayed the world's first test-tube baby. Del inserted his own program note, warning that it was the first show he was directing sober, and "he hopes it doesn't show."

Freud Slipped Here opened the following April with newcomers Bruce Jarchow, Nancy McCabe-Kelly, and Breen joining Kazurinsky, Coven, Neenan, and Wendt. Kart, writing in the April 18, 1979, *Chicago Tribune*, called it "consistently amusing," but not as strong as the previous two revues.

> I especially miss the wrought-up thematic drive that director Del Close brought to *A Fine Pickle*. Close is the man behind *Freud*, but this show is almost benign, with too many joke-oriented bits, no real focus, and only two of the extended comedy-drama scenes that Second City does so well.

From day to day, there was no telling how constructive Del would be as a director, even though he was capable of "amazing moments of brilliance." "Del would give you a note that nobody on the planet would be able to give you except Del, and all of a sudden, everything would crystallize with whatever it was you were stuck on, or he would send us in another direction with a scene that we would never have intended, and made it much better," said Breen.

But not all of his suggestions were helpful. While preparing the follow-up to *Freud*, the cast lacked a closing scene. One night, Jarchow talked the others into improvising a piece in which they all portrayed walruses. The following night, near the end of the first act, Del burst into the green room with an inspiration. "I know what we're going to do. I want everybody to play the entire second act as walruses!" When Tim Kazurinsky came in, Breen panicked: "He wants us to be walruses!" Kazurinsky responded, "Call Bernie." Breen slipped away to the nearest pay phone at intermission and called Sahlins: "Bernie? Uhhh . . . Del wants us to do the second act as walruses." "I'll be right over!" Del was irate and disappointed that Sahlins did not allow it to happen, shouting "What do you mean they won't be able to do it as walruses!"

Despite the lack of walruses, the twentieth-anniversary show, *I Remember Dada or Won't You Come Home, Saul Bellow?* was well reviewed in the December 12, 1979, *Chicago Tribune* by Kart, who believed that it could measure up against any of the previous shows. The stars of *Dada* included George Wendt, Tim Kazurinsky, Mary Gross, Nancy McCabe-Kelly, Bruce Jarchow, and Danny Breen. Singled out were "Would You Be Mime?" in which Kazurinsky and McCabe-Kelly discover that college-aged daughter Gross wants to become a mime; "Amtrak," in which Breen and McCabe-Kelly relive railroad fantasies; and "Regression," as Breen tries to move back in with parents McCabe-Kelly and Kazurinsky. The highest praise was reserved for George Wendt as Cardinal Cody, confronted by McCabe-Kelly's pregnant woman who is hoping for a church wedding. According to Kart, Wendt "performs here with the glee of a floating soap bubble, crooning dotty asides to his crosier as though it were a two-way radio that directly connected him with the Lord. Here is a benchmark performance, indeed, a scene in which a satirical premise is etherealized into pure abstract hilarity."

The Second City casts were never really intimidated by Del's sometimes-brusque demeanor. They became frustrated because the rehearsal process seemed to take forever. Sometimes Del wouldn't show up at all, and Sahlins would take the company next door to That Steak Joynt, and then they would go home. By the late 1970s, the rehearsal schedule could be prolonged by four to six weeks when Del was in charge.

Despite his shortcomings, though, Del was still able to teach them some of the most important principles of comedy, from such concepts as working at the top of your intelligence and respecting the audience's intelligence, to the importance of the straight man. No one at the Second City ever wanted to be the straight man, but Del impressed upon them that if a scene is going to work, someone has to be setting things up. Del often served as straight man himself, whether it was in *How to Speak Hip* or Committee sketches, and Breen referred to him as "the best straight man he ever saw."

◇

One unanticipated result of Del's sobriety was a renewed interest in his acting career: "When the booze stopped, that's when I got back on stage. I could act again. I didn't have pictures, didn't have a resume, I had a T-shirt printed: Del Close, AEA, SAG, AFTRA," said Del.[1]

In 1978, Gregory Mosher became artistic director of Chicago's Goodman Theatre, and Del got an audition for an upcoming show. "I did this complicated, weird audition. And they asked me to come back and read for the Ghost of Christmas Present," said Del. "So I started acting at the Goodman."[2] Interviewed for the November 5, 1978, *Chicago Tribune Magazine*, he told Jon Ziomek: "I thought it would be a contrast to move from bare stage cabaret theatre to a full-blown theatre production. And whether anybody likes it or not, I am a fixture in Chicago theatre."

The *Tribune* article followed Del during one of the last workshops of the Control Group (his *Christmas Carol* rehearsals would force him to give up the group). "Other men have lived lives of quiet desperation," he told the reporter, "I have lived a life of wild desperation." The upbeat piece, titled "The Dinosaur of Improvisation," offers a quote from John Belushi: "I like the man's style. He can create with you, unlike so many other directors. He can motivate people. He's been my biggest influence in comedy."

The short feature is a seldom-seen look at the post-rehab Del in late 1978. The writer even follows Del to his small Wells Street apartment after the two-hour workshop, describing how he would pace from living room to kitchen to bedroom, charitably omitting the squalor of his living quarters.

Del gets into character—
and makeup—for
A Christmas Carol.
(COURTESY OF CHARNA
HALPERN)

The Goodman's annual holiday production of *A Christmas Carol* in December 1978 was Del's first significant nonimprovised Chicago theater production as an actor. It was the initial step in what would be a respected acting career.

A Christmas Carol marked Mosher's first opportunity to work with Del. Four years earlier, when Mosher arrived in Chicago at the age of twenty-four, people told him, "Hey, you have to meet Del Close!" The young man visited the Second City, where Del left quite an impression on him; he returned frequently to watch the improvisation sets.

After they met, people began telling him, "You've got to give Del Close a job!" Yet Mosher didn't even consider auditioning Del for a role at the Goodman until 1978, because he thought of Del as a teacher and a Second City director, not an actor. When Mosher decided to stage *A Christmas Carol*, he introduced Del to director Tony Mockus. "Del came in and did one of those amazingly creative Del moments during his audition, and Tony just said, 'Yeah, great, you've got it! Let's go to work!'"

When Del was drinking, he was incapable of remembering lines and blocking, and now his acting comeback literally hinged on the show. Mosher was unaware that Del had just been through such a difficult personal period, nor was he aware of his drug use, but everyone seemed to sense the importance of the play. Occasionally, someone would say

"This really means a lot to Del," but nothing more was spoken. Mosher simply felt that Del was the best man for the part. "My feeling was, we were just lucky to have him, nobody's doing anyone a favor here. There was zero charity effect—it was just 'grab the guy!'" said Mosher.

The Ghost of Christmas Present was a good, strong supporting role, and Del made the most of it. He was buried within the huge robe and beard, but it also freed him to do what he thought appropriate. He had been doing invocations as part of his workshops, in which the actors would conjure up the spirit of a person or theme to solve a problem, and he took a similar approach after he was cast.

> The first step is to find out what the character really is: Is he some sort of symbol? Locate the archetype and you're right next door to the god. . . . It was very clear the Ghost of Christmas Present, I mean, those three spirits have no place in the Christian pantheon. Also, what's being undertaken in the story is a process known as the hart hunt. A process we refer to as magical memory, going back over your life in great detail with the help of someone and finding out where the trauma is in your life, which is precisely what they do with Scrooge. . . .
>
> Of the old gods, who was I playing? I came in laughing, covered with ivy, sitting on barrels of food, wine, beer . . . Bacchus, certainly. I don't know any invocations to Bacchus, but he is the same figure as Dionysus.[3]

The production of *A Christmas Carol* was a gamble, and the cast was unsure whether the show would work—right up to opening night. When it began to snow just after six o'clock, the company decided it was a good omen. But all was not well backstage prior to curtain time. Del was missing.

The Goodman board threw a dinner for their backers at the University Club before the premiere; there was much riding on this production. At 7:30, Mosher was called away from the table and told, "Del's not here." He went back to the table, where he was sitting next to *Chicago Sun-Times* theater critic Glenna Syse, who said, "Hmm . . . something looks wrong." Mosher whispered, "Del's not at the theater." A look of sadness and concern, pained empathy, crossed her face as she said, "Oh, poor, poor Del." Syse could only imagine the demons that were plaguing him. Mosher recalled: "To have the critic for the *Sun-Times* saying it—

she didn't say, 'What are you going to do?' or 'How's your understudy?' She didn't care about the play. She cared about Del." In the end, Del made it in time, and the cause of his lateness was forgotten. The reviews came out and they were glowing. Del's reviews were tremendous.

If he was nervous, it didn't show. He seemed completely comfortable in the role, save for his nearsightedness. Del would wear his glasses up to the last moment before he stepped onstage, then give them to a stagehand. Only then would he start his character's laughter offstage, careful that it didn't set off his smoker's cough.

Del and William J. Norris, who played Scrooge, entered together on a movable platform with a man inside it, pushing it around the stage. Del always worried while sitting on top of the moving platform eight feet high without his glasses, but he never fell.

During *A Christmas Carol*, Del met a young playwright named John Ostrander, and their shared love of science fiction and comic books helped to cement their friendship. Ostrander, who had scored a success at the Organic Theater with his play *Bloody Bess*, shared a dressing room with Del.

Del channeled Bacchus each performance; he was not interested in the Christian aspects of the show, and wore an inverted pentagram under his T-shirt in the costume. It delighted him to think that whatever Christian activities the others might be engaged in, he was doing a vaguely pagan ritual. Del would return for the Goodman's annual *A Christmas Carol* each season though Christmas 1984.

◈

Del did his best to abstain from drugs during the run of the show, but was not as discriminating around the Second City. There was every indication that the now-sober Del was apparently trying to fill the gap left by lack of alcohol with an even greater reliance on drugs.

> Wouldn't you know, right after I got off booze this old friend set up a Methedrine factory in his kitchen and decided he was going to make me a customer. I got a little peeved at the guy because he so clearly pressured me into it and I'm fairly amenable. Getting off dope is a lot easier than getting away from your friends who are dope fiends. 'Cause they resent the fact that you're straight now. Oh, they hate it.[4]

But drinking no longer posed a problem for Del. After the show each night, the Second City cast would always visit the back bar to fill their glasses before receiving the director's notes. According to George Wendt, the motto for the cast was "$300 a week and all you could drink," and as Del would be giving notes, he would smell the alcohol on their breath and turn away or ask them to move back. "Unfortunately, there was still every other drug under the sun for which he did *not* have aversion therapy," said Wendt. While rehearsing, Del would disappear for a few minutes, then stagger to the center of the stage and "make some lame excuse about feeding the cats."

The Second City was forced to go to great lengths to circumvent his more creative measures to get high, to the point of chain-padlocking the refrigerator where they kept the whipped cream. The waitresses would come in that evening and try to make an Irish coffee. With Del having inhaled the propellant in order to get high, the cream would just drizzle out. "He would go through cases of it," said Wendt.

Del never lost the capacity to surprise his Second City peers. On one occasion, Del and Wendt were sitting on the theater's bench behind Fred Kaz, watching the improvisation set. A table on the upper level, near the light booth, was getting raucous, so Del walked over to them. Wendt continued watching the show, when he suddenly noticed a brawl had broken out. He ran over to the commotion, and to his surprise, found that Del was winning. "[Del] had the other guy's shoe off, and he was beating the guy over the head with his shoe. We had to drag him off!"

No one who was there could forget the day that Del "died." He was late for rehearsal one afternoon, so Coven and Breen crossed the street to Del's apartment to retrieve him. Although it was the middle of winter, his door was wide open and his cats were wandering in and out. The two stepped inside, hesitant to go any farther, but they could hear the shower running, so they approached the bathroom door. Coven began knocking, calling, "Del? Hey Del?" Breen kept his distance as Coven slowly pushed the door open, then let out a blood-curdling scream: *"Del's dead!"* Breen and Coven scrambled out of the apartment, running back to the Second City screaming, *"Del's dead! Del's dead!"* Stage manager Larry Perkins shoved them away, barking, "Get out of my way!" He walked over to the apartment, calling, "Del? Del?" Del was lying on the floor of the shower. The stage manager shut off the water, and Del opened his eyes. He said, "Oh, I was cold last night, so I got in the shower to warm up."

◆

Del was now reaching the point where he couldn't deliver. After he returned from Texas, he had been relatively clear and productive, but his increased drug intake made him "crazier than ever." His usage only intensified after some new neighbors moved into the building next to him. John Belushi and Dan Aykroyd were virtually given carte blanche by Mayor Jane Byrne for their upcoming film, *The Blues Brothers*, to be shot all over the Chicago area. Their base camp for the cast, crew, and their friends would be the Blues Bar, the former Sneak Joint, only footsteps across the courtyard from Del's apartment. When they weren't filming, they were usually hanging out at the bar, where there was music, plenty to drink, and, inevitably, drugs.

Though he didn't spend much time in the bar, Del enjoyed having his friends near, and having Del next door undoubtedly made his former students feel at home. In Bob Woodward's *Wired*, he recounts an incident in which John Belushi and his wife, Judy, stopped by Del's apartment. Belushi was going to be rehearsing a dance sequence and wanted a shot of speed; he knew Del was an expert at handling needles and would give him the injection quickly and painlessly. "Junkies give the best shots," Del told his guests.[5]

Despite his portrayal in the bestselling book, Del was quick to point out that his drug relationship with John Belushi was only during that one period in the summer of 1979, during the filming of *Blues Brothers*, and he insisted that he had not introduced Belushi to habits that he did not already have. In fact, Del's house became a refuge for Belushi whenever he simply wanted to get away.

> My house was next door to the Blues Bar. So you had the Blues Bar to get away from the public, and you had my house to get away from your friends.... The one thing I didn't get ... there's this little image of me shooting up America's hero in his flabby ass. Well, why am I doing that? They didn't mention that that was because he was trying to work on coke. You got to work on something that will keep you going all day. Well, shit, I know how to do that. Take this. Ahhh.

Because there's no way to balance coke intake. But you take a hit of speed, you're going for eight hours.[6]

Although the *Blues Brothers* filming may have been a distraction, Del still plunged back into the Second City, conducting workshops and taking the reins of the mainstage productions.

◈

In September 1980, a classically trained nineteen-year-old actress named Meagan Fay was hired for the mainstage company. Her brother Jim, a company member who drove her to the theater to meet with Sahlins, had recommended her. As she met with the producer, she noticed a man with dirty clothes and hair, glasses held together with tape. "This is Del!" Sahlins kept insisting. She finally signed a contract to appear on the mainstage, but when she began walking down the stairs to leave, Del stopped her. As she stood on the first landing, Del pushed the tape-covered glasses back up on his nose. He took off the jacket of his tracksuit and removed the filthy T-shirt beneath it. Then he dropped his trousers down to his ankles, and turned very slowly with his arms outstretched, so that she could clearly see all the sores that covered his body. When he finished, he pulled up his pants and put on his T-shirt. He said, "I just wanted you to see my 'tracksuit.'" She ran outside crying, where her brother Jim staunchly defended Del, whom he called a genius.

It was undoubtedly the reaction that Del was hoping for from the naive teenager, who had never before improvised, yet was now one of his cast. Fay took over for McCabe-Kelly in a show that featured a retrospective of sketches, and the cast, which also included Breen, Lance Kinsey, Bruce Jarchow, Rob Riley, and Mary Gross, developed new material for the upcoming revue *Well, I'm Off to the 30 Years War*, which would be directed by Del and open at the end of the year.

Fay had no trouble with the scripted material, but was too afraid to try improvising for the next three months. Del never said anything, as if this was to be expected, until one night he looked at her and said, "Well, I suppose you're going to start talking one of these days," and left. Finally, she did an improvisation with Riley and Kinsey that got a very good response from the audience. Del met them backstage and Fay expected a comment from Del. "It had been a good scene and been my idea, so I was quite proud of myself. He completely ignored me and looked at Lance and Rob, who had not done a lot in the scene in my estimation, but they were good and it was a good scene, and said wonderful things to them about how great it was. Then he turned to me and said, 'And you, uh, try it again sometime and paint your nipples green.' That was my directorial debut from Del."

The incident led to another altercation with Sahlins, however, who was furious because that was the only note that Del had for the girls. After their confrontation, Sahlins took over the direction of the show.

The incident eventually helped Fay earn Del's respect, however. Later, they tried improvising the scene again. It worked well, and the actress was obviously making great strides. As she stepped offstage, Del was standing there. She said, "Hey, I took your note. It really worked!" She knew she had worn him down when he fell over laughing.

While many at the Second City considered him a misogynist, Del respected those women who he felt had earned it, including Fay. The "paint your nipples green" comment would never be repeated, because he liked her work, and they could sit and talk about scenes. Del saw that she could do it, and congratulated her on the fact that she didn't play "women's roles," she created different dynamics, and did it as a woman, but without being "the mom" or "the girlfriend." Once she had earned his respect, Fay said she never had a problem with him. "People were saying he was a misogynist. I kept thinking, 'Well, he isn't with me.'"

By the end of the 1970s, drugs seemed to be more prevalent than ever at the theater. But unlike the 1960s, it was taking on a much more reckless, self-indulgent nature. Audience members were applauding scenes by hurling bags of coke and pot onto the stage. It was decadent at best, disturbing at worst. No one at the Second City imagined that the deadly bubble was about to burst.

16

Saturday Night Live,
Tennessee Williams, and the Cleanup

By the late 1970s, Del knew his days at the Second City were numbered. He was all but asking to be fired. Frustrated at having to follow Sahlins's rules, he began to cast about creatively in other directions.

Del tried writing, but since he lacked the discipline and self-control, he needed a writing partner. With Larry Coven, he began submitting material to Dave Thomas at *SCTV*, for which they were paid $1,000 a week. At the time, they were the only two contributing writers who weren't permanently based in Canada. But shortly after they were hired, Don Novello came in as the new *SCTV* producer. He didn't know who they were, and the opportunity soon vanished.

Del collaborated on an HBO pilot with Jamie Swise, but the latter soon discovered his partner's limitations. Swise did all of the writing; Del never put pen to paper. Instead, he would talk and throw out ideas, like "Attack of the 50-Foot Grandma," and leave it to Swise to flesh out the idea. The project went nowhere.

Del was a brilliant teacher and director, but he was not a creator. Inspiration came slowly. He could take good ideas and improve them, or watch a scene or improvisation and immediately analyze it and make it better, but he seldom originated or initiated scenes. Even his best-known stand-up comedy routine, his bit about beer-can openers being the larval stage of coat hangers, was cribbed from an award-winning 1950s science fiction novel, according to Swise: "I never called him on it, but a friend of mine who was also a fellow science fiction person said, 'I've heard that someplace else before.' And he got the book and showed it to me. I didn't ever say 'Del, you stole that.' But he stole it."

◇

Del's reputation had been growing in some influential circles. *Saturday Night Live* had begun its sixth season, its first without Lorne Michaels, and also its first without Second City performers. Belushi, Aykroyd, Radner, and Bill Murray had all departed, and the show was suffering. In an interview with Ed Bruske in the November 25, 1979, *Washington Post*, Del underscored the effect of the changeover:

> That's when *Saturday Night* started to go, when they started using writers to come up with the material. Those people were all trained in improvisation and when they stopped doing that, the show lost something. . . .
>
> There are two watershed marks in contemporary comedy. The first was Shelley Berman considering a glass of buttermilk. The second was Danny Aykroyd putting the fish into the blender. . . . A lot of the stuff *SNL* was doing came out of *National Lampoon*, comedy based on outrage and bad taste. Murray, Belushi, and Aykroyd, those guys are the brotherhood of rage. They all did some pretty weird things.

Critics were savagely denouncing Lorne Michaels's replacement, Jean Doumanian, and there were even rumors of cancellation. Among NBC's solutions: hire Del Close. "When *Saturday Night Live* was in serious trouble, they called me up in the middle of a season when Jean Doumanian was still producing," recalled Del. "My mission was to come save *Saturday Night Live*. I don't know that I actually did it, but the show is still on the air. That was the job. The job was not to make it good, the job was to keep it on the air!"[1]

When Del got the call in December 1980, he agreed to come to New York and join the show. "The reason that I went to *Saturday Night Live* to begin with, is that Jean Doumanian . . . had made a lot of questionable decisions, to put it mildly. I liked the woman a lot, and my job was to try to make her decisions work, rather than sit there and carp about her being a bad producer," said Del. "But she did hire a bunch of people that didn't know how to work together, and my job was to come in and try to give a semblance of a feeling of a company."[2]

Doumanian's comedy credentials were shaky, but when he met her, Del was complimentary.

> A neat lady; I liked her a lot. I mean, just because she had no sense of humor didn't mean she could not run the show. That's what you hire experts for. All she was doing all day was keeping the network off our backs. If she'd had the support Captain Queeg had, she would've come through the hurricane.[3]

After the fifth season ended, the cast had been replaced with unknowns like Charles Rocket, Denny Dillon, and Gail Mathius, along with then-supporting players Eddie Murphy and Joe Piscopo. No one knew how to best utilize Del's talents at *SNL*. He wouldn't be a writer or a performer, but a comedy coach. He became the "house metaphysician," and he began teaching the cast to improvise with the intention of developing material:

> They made some of the silliest mistakes . . . before the show started, they would expect the writers to create material; it would stack up and give them a sense of futility. "We don't even know who the fucking cast is, yet we're writing 'cause we're on salary?" So I had the actors improvise in front of the writers, and ba-boom, the material started pouring out. The next thing I suggested was we should rehearse once before the camera blocking. Radical things like that.[4]

◈

Doumanian's reign would soon be ending. On March 9, Del conducted a workshop with that week's host, Robert Guillaume, and the cast and writers. At the same time, Brian Doyle-Murray, accompanied by his girlfriend, Sarah, and his younger brothers, Joel and John, stopped by the *SNL* offices. Doyle-Murray, who was writing for the show, went off to get his paycheck, while the other three waited behind.

Although Joel Murray had been to New York City before to watch his brother Bill on *SNL*, this was his first visit as an adult, and everything was electrifying. But everyone else seemed anxious. Joel found himself being introduced to a man named Del, who had a beard, a dirty dark shirt, and dark green pants that had been pinned shut with several safety pins. "I don't think that was a punk accoutrement, they looked purely for function. I remember being introduced as if I knew him already, like 'And you guys know Del, of course.'"

Del was roaming the floor, looking for cigarette papers or a pipe with which to smoke some pot. "Hey, Murray boys! Have you got any skins? You got anything for me?" When they told him they had nothing, Del was off again. They continued waiting in what turned out to be Doumanian's office, when Del returned a few minutes later, brandishing a pipe. "Success!" he called as he sat down at the desk and filled the bowl. Just as he was lighting it, Doumanian walked in, near tears, and said, "Del, it's not a good time!" Del exhaled a large cloud of smoke: "For *you . . .*"

The younger Murrays left the room, and it soon began to fill up again. Doumanian announced that Brandon Tartikoff had fired her. At the end of the meeting, Letty Aronson announced that it was Del Close's birthday (his forty-seventh), and a cake was brought in. The group sang "Happy Birthday" to Del and toasted him with champagne, and he in turn toasted Doumanian.[5]

"She was fired on my birthday, which was an interesting subtext," said Del. "Everybody was called into her office, they're all crying and carrying on. Jean announces that she's gotten fired, and all of her staff's in tears, and she says 'But don't be sad—it's Del's birthday!' They bring in a birthday cake, and everybody's crying and cutting the cake—it was one of the strangest birthdays I've ever had in my life!"[6]

Following a brief hiatus, Chevy Chase hosted the next show, and then a strike by the Writers Guild shut down production for five months. When Del returned to New York that fall, *SNL* had been reinvented once again. There had been another massive housecleaning. Dick Ebersol had replaced Doumanian, and only Murphy and Piscopo remained from the previous season's cast. The strike had allowed the show to reboot. Del found some familiar faces that season in Second City veterans Tim Kazurinsky, Mary Gross, Tony Rosato, and Robin Duke, who were new members of the cast. Nate Herman had joined the show as a staff writer alongside Doyle-Murray.

"When Dick Ebersol took over as producer, he decided that I should come along with the package, because at least I was smart enough to recognize that Eddie Murphy and Joe Piscopo were extremely talented, particularly Murphy," said Del.[7]

> Ebersol realized that he needed people who knew how to work together, so he hired Mary Gross and Tim Kazurinsky, on our suggestions, Bernie and mine, and then picked up two people from SCTV and The Second City in Toronto. So, instead of the people he had before, he added four Second City types, [including] Robin Duke and Tony Rosato from Canada. Originally, he had wanted Catherine O'Hara and she had said yes, but Michael O'Donoghue just scared her to death! Michael and I got along famously, we're both sorry that we didn't have a chance to work together.[8]

But Del was not keen on relocating and the following season decided to stay in Chicago. He assumed his *SNL* days were finished, particularly when he heard about the financial arrangements.

> I decided that I didn't really want to do it. I certainly didn't want to move to New York, and when they offered me the salary that the acting coach would get, I realized that I'd have to borrow $200 a week from Bernie to live in New York at that salary! So I stayed here with Second City and did a fourth year of *A Christmas Carol* at the Goodman.
>
> Then, just as happened the year before, I got a phone call in early January saying, "We're in trouble, Close, come to New York and work as acting coach." So I did, this time doing some writing as well with Brian Doyle Murray, because I had kind of carte blanche, I could do anything. My main job was acting coach, but the contract said "duties include, but are not limited to, those of acting coach," which meant that I could screw around with any department of the show that would let me do it. And since I got along fairly well with folks, they did indeed listen to me a little bit and let me screw around. But I wouldn't move to New York, so I had to commute two or three days a week, which was kind of interesting, particularly in that terrible weather.[9]

Unfortunately, he now had little or no authority, and Murphy and Piscopo often ignored his workshops. He made what he considered one of his major contributions when he stopped Eddie Murphy in the hallway and, pulling off pieces of his prosthetic makeup, told him, "People don't want to see Stevie Wonder. They want to see *you doing* Stevie Wonder!" Nate Herman recalled: "The mindset there was heavy prosthetics, and I always thought it was a little over the top, just remembering Chevy Chase doing Gerald Ford with nothing, no makeup. When Piscopo did Sinatra, you couldn't see Piscopo under the prosthetics. I mean, they just went prosthetic-crazy."

◆

Even worse for Del, the drug culture at the show had worsened, and he soon developed a cocaine habit fueled by his television salary.

> I would come in at 11 in the morning and there'd be some writers; they . . . had been there since ten the previous morning. . . . They'd say "Come in here, Close, we've got to talk about this concept," 'cause I was, like, being the ombudsman between the actors and writers. And they'd say "Do these lines or we won't be in the same space, man." So I wasn't too hard to convince, you know, but on the other hand I was waiting until like five or six in the evening . . . cause we were very high, but we were cutting the gig. But, ah, it was too much.[10]

"I swear, I've never seen a situation in which it was obligatory to take as much cocaine as some of those writers would," said Del. "And it's movie star coke there, it's like 85 percent [pure], so you wind up blitzed all the time. I did maybe three grams a week when I was there, and [one of the producers] would go through that much in a day! He was just completely wired! Ebersol was about the only one who wasn't out of his gourd most of the time, and the actors didn't really—but Good Lord, you'd turn around a corner, and I think there were pages at NBC that were putting themselves through college selling cocaine to everybody on the 17th Floor or Studio 8H."[11]

Del was making more money than he had ever known in Chicago. He began buying volumes of rare, collector's editions of science fiction and horror classics, knowing that what he didn't spend on books, he would spend on cocaine. In the past, he had always avoided a cocaine habit, but now he had the environment, the means, and the requisite lack of willpower. He was soon buying a gram a day, and was becoming dependent. Worse, the cocaine was affecting his work, and the show had been infected by what he called "coke writing": "Ideas tend to slip sideways and ridiculous puns get taken literally. The gesture is never completed. The thought's never fulfilled."[12]

The circumstances of his departure aren't clear. Cast members recalled that one day he simply wasn't there. After returning to Chicago, he stated: "I didn't think they needed me this year [1982–83], and I don't know whether they did or not. We just didn't bother to communicate."[13]

His unique communication situation didn't help. During one trip to Toronto to direct a Second City show, Del claimed he had allowed friends to stay in his Chicago apartment, and they ran up a $600 phone bill. He didn't feel like paying it, and so decided that he didn't need a phone anymore. "For six months, I think I was the only person working in network television that didn't have a phone. I would occasionally get messages from Ebersol or Grant Tinker. They'd leave them up at the Earl of Old Town. The bartender picked them up for me. 'You got a call from NBC, Close!'"[14]

◇

Del left New York with an expensive coke habit. "I enjoyed working on *Saturday Night Live*, but it's not the sort of thing you want to do very much. It's much more fun to say you've done it than it is to do it."[15]

His future at the Second City was more uncertain. He continued as director while working on *SNL*, though Sahlins was still stepping in often. If his elevated cocaine use wasn't causing enough trouble, his workshops were now becoming problematic. There were rumors of devil worship in his workshops, altars to various lower deities. In fact, Del's intent had likely been misinterpreted. It was true that he had become a witch—although he would sometimes point out that the correct term was actually "Wiccan." Far from devil worshipping, Del described it as a religion whose adherents worshiped Mother Earth, praying to a goddess who represented its spirit.

Del had decided that the Wiccan "map of the spiritual territory seems to work reasonably well."[16] Some of the appeal was no doubt in the shock value in telling others that he was, indeed, a witch. If pressed, he would explain that the Wicca religion was all about Earth worship with a female deity, which usually shocked those who had heard of his misogynistic traits. He once said that their ceremonies usually consisted of many middle-aged women dancing around in basements, hitting their heads on the exposed pipes.

He had even incorporated some Wiccan ideas into workshops, with improvisational exercises like the Invocation. One day, Joyce Sloane was sitting in her office when actor Michael McCarthy came in, obviously disturbed. "Joyce, do you realize what Del's doing in that class? He's invoking the devil!" Sloane looked up at him. "Michael, Del is like a film festival. Ninety-five percent of it is bullshit, and five percent of it is brilliance—you just have to wait for that five percent."

Del had continued directing the mainstage revues between *SNL* commitments, although Sahlins was still stepping in toward the end of the rehearsal process. Whether due to outside distractions or fatigue, the sixtieth revue, *Well, I'm Off to the 30 Years War or Swing Your Partner to the Right*, which opened October 8, 1980, received a lackluster review from *Chicago Tribune* critic Larry Kart, who noted that the show "seems almost as off its feed as we are. Not that there aren't a number of fine sketches here. But like most of the productions that Del Close directs, [it] tries for cumulative effects, and in this case the effects don't quite accumulate." Kart noted that the disparate cast consisted of three newcomers (Meagan Fay, Lance Kinsey, and Rob Riley), three holdovers (Danny Breen, Mary Gross, and Bruce Jarchow), and returnee Jim Belushi, citing the mixture as a possible problem. He enjoyed "Happy Birthday James Joyce" but cited its weirdness. "Fine as all this creepy stuff is, I suspect that it sprang more from Close's mind than from those of the performers, which gives the show an oddly distracted air, as though the cast hasn't yet grasped the mood of the material. Perhaps *Well, I'm Off* just needs more time to percolate—either that, or a much stronger dose of supporting weirdness from the environment."

The next revue, *Miro, Miro on the Wall*, opened June 25, 1981, between Del's two stints at *SNL*. It was the final revue that Del would be officially credited with directing—and also one of the best-reviewed. Susan Dugg, John Kapelos, and Rick Thomas joined the cast, while Mary Gross, Rob Riley, and Bruce Jarchow departed. Kart hailed it on June 27 as the best revue since *A Fine Pickle* two years earlier, because it similarly reflected the mood of the nation.

But *Miro* goes even farther, the idea being—when one links the skits together—that right now the national self-interest amounts to the self-interest of each individual in the nation. These are, in other words, very mean times. And the big scenes in *Miro* portray America's return to the "I got mine and I want yours too" ethic in all its glory.

Kart praises "Mom's House," about an unpleasant family attempting to take the rest of their father's remaining possessions, a political "Ballet," and "Walnut Room," in which one patron tries to help liberate the forlorn son of a suburban matron during lunchtime at Marshall Field's. Referring to the punch line of the last scene ("Your mother's a bitch. Here's 50 bucks. Run away from home."), the critic said:

> That line, that sketch, and the entire show amounted to a liberating insistence that naked power must be kicked in its naked behind. Obviously stimulated by their material, the cast, directed by Del Close, was in top form. Rarely at Second City have I seen such detailed work around the edges of each scene, such shared confidence in each performer's acting abilities. From the top on down, the company ought to be proud of *Miro*. And those who think that Second City no longer has guts had better think again.

So impressed was Kart with "Walnut Room" that he wrote a feature for the July 26, 1981, *Chicago Tribune*, interviewing Del, Sahlins, and the cast, analyzing the thought process involved in its formation. The scene involves a matron (Mary Gross) whose verbal abuse of her son (Lance Kinsey) is finally noticed by a man at another table (Jim Belushi). She is receptive to what she perceives as his advances, and gives her son just enough money to go off to a movie at one of the city's seamier theaters. Belushi's character delivers his slam-dunk line to the son, tells off the mother, and sticks her with the check. Based on a real incident witnessed by Gross, it had a cathartic effect on the audience.

The cast told Kart that Sahlins was initially excited about the scene but started having doubts, while Del was always confident about it. "I think Del has a better perspective, having been an actor. He realizes the pain you go through trying to recapture the initial feeling you had. Whereas Bernie is more likely to give up," said Gross. Fay appropriately uses a fencing metaphor: "If Del doesn't like a scene, he has a rapier-thrust approach. He attacks from within. Bernie just used the old sledgehammer."

As Del explained that his role was to support the actors and help them develop a structure, the schism between Sahlins and him became clearer.

> The actors have the worst seats in the house—they're onstage. They need that extra eye out front. I'll tell you the truth, one reason I'm very fond of the scene is that I don't like women very much. I get a sadistic glee out of seeing the **** kicked out of that ****. It's very antifemale.
>
> Bernie hates the scene, though. It makes some kind of statement that he doesn't like. He kept saying "It's another scene about a damn kid." So I had an unfortunate double job. I had to simultaneously shape the scene and fight to keep it in the show. . . .
>
> Do I think this show has a nasty edge to it? Well, Bernie felt that we weren't doing a show that represented Second City, and he threw out about two-thirds of the material we had been working on, which looked at the time like very vulgar material. But when you add intelligence to vulgarity, which is basically what we did, you get viciousness.
>
> I sometimes feel that we're helplessly in the grip of the national or local mood, that it will speak through us no matter what. And Bernie was trying to fight it, while I was trying to go with it, which made for a hellish experience.
>
> But truly I'd rather fight with Bernie than agree with other people. You hear me complaining about him, but it's like one uncle complaining about another uncle. We're not going to do anything about it.

Sahlins responded defensively to the charge that he did not like the scene, even as he admitted that he wasn't initially enthused.

> I think the scene is theatrical, skillful, and certainly worth its stage time. But to say that I'm not fond of it would be a mistake—I just didn't share everyone's total enthusiasm. I feel it's a little too much like a sitcom. . . . I'm always leery of scenes in which our actors play kids. Not only is it an easy game, when you're playing way beneath

your age, it's got to be external. The characteristics you're exhibiting do not come out of you but are externally observed.

So getting back to "Walnut Room," because the audience obviously likes it, that means there's a lot for me to learn from that process, from agreeing that perhaps there's a deficiency in me someplace. But don't spread the fiction that I dislike the scene; it's just not one of my favorites . . . now I like it a lot better.

The creative friction between Del and Sahlins may have been frustrating for both men at times, but it resulted in some of the Second City's finest work.

If *Miro, Miro on the Wall* marked Del's last Second City revue (save for a onetime return in 1989), he was going out on a high point artistically. He would continue to help Sahlins direct the mainstage shows over the next two years, but his ten-year reign as director was ending.

◇

Del had been in Chicago in the fall of 1981, in time to encounter another prominent theatrical personality. The Goodman Theatre was holding a soiree in honor of Tennessee Williams, and Del, apparently leaving a *Christmas Carol* rehearsal, made another memorable first impression. Williams was in Chicago for the rehearsals and opening of his final play, *A House Not Meant to Stand.* Goodman artistic director Gregory Mosher was an eyewitness.

Del was in a rehearsal room, and the cast was in the inner sanctum working. To exit, Del had to pass through the Goodman Café, or cocktail area, where an event for wealthy donors was being held that evening. One of the guests was talking to Williams when Del walked by, and the playwright was a few feet away. She graciously said, "Mr. Close, my name is so-and-so, and I just want to tell you how thrilled we are at the Goodman, that you are here with us." She extended her arm, on which there were several jangly bracelets. Del extended his arm, out of which came a cockroach.

The woman quickly pulled her hand back and her drink went flying. Mosher recalled: "She was very startled, and then she was very embarrassed. She walked away out of embarrassment, not out of rudeness. And Del stood there, slightly startled. I'm not sure he even knew about the offending animal. And Tennessee walked over and said, 'I like the way you did that, boy! That had *style!*'"

The Tennessee Williams story has become part of the canon of the Del legend. What has been forgotten, and was rarely even mentioned by Del himself, is that Williams soon became a fan.

Williams began coming to the Second City, and was apparently fascinated by Del. He was in Chicago often during the mounting of his new show, and often visited the Second City to watch improvisation sets and pal around with Del. "I remember him being around quite often. . . . He just thought Del was the craziest, funniest, oddest person he'd ever met. I remember looking out several times and there, on the bench next to Del, would be Tennessee Williams," recalled Meagan Fay. Their budding friendship was short-lived, however; Williams left Chicago after the play opened, and died in February 1983.

◈

Del's services were still in demand for workshops, but his hitch as the Second City director had run its course. It looked as though he might give in to Methedrine and cocaine, when an unexpected tragedy struck.

On March 6, 1982, the body of John Belushi was discovered in a bungalow at the Chateau Marmont in Los Angeles. Everyone at the Second City was stunned by the news, and the press was soon swarming. Larry Coven and a few others walked across the street to Del's place and locked themselves in to avoid the press. There, they sat and exchanged grim jokes as a coping mechanism to stave off their grief. In later years, Del would frequently mention that "after he died, the first thing I heard was 'Well, the bean can got 'im.' I didn't give him the drugs, but I gave him the bean can."

The sad circumstances of Belushi's passing have been detailed elsewhere; the coroner ruled that he had died of an accidental overdose of cocaine and heroin. John Belushi was buried on Martha's Vineyard, three days later, on March 9. It was Del's forty-eighth birthday.

Though Del had occasionally observed Belushi's drug use, his death nevertheless came as a complete shock. He had already started to feel that he, too, was "going over the edge," but called Belushi's death "the big signal."

The afternoon of [Belushi's] memorial service, I had my shaving kit with a hypodermic needle in it, and I took it out and threw it in the street. Well, that's enough of that, thank you.[17]

He also stated that he had learned everything that he could as "that [drug] person." He had run out of drugs. Del did give Belushi the bean can, in that he had encouraged the permissive atmosphere around the Second City. Until John Belushi died, Del enjoyed his part in the creation of this flourishing universe. Afterward, everything began to change. Until Belushi, virtually no one from the Second City had died; even the founders were still alive and well. But Belushi's death was the wakeup call, for the Second City and for Del in particular.

◇

In another interview taped years later, Del would say he "gave up drugs for John Belushi. It was the least I could do." Of course, for Del, "giving up drugs" had a looser interpretation than it would for many people. He continued smoking pot until his lungs could no longer manage it, and he was amenable to other substances that became available. He was fond of psychedelic mushrooms and hash, but from that time on, he apparently stopped injecting drugs. He joked that he simply didn't have any veins left. "There comes a time when you just can't do it anymore," he would explain; "There aren't many fifty- or sixty-year-old junkies."[18]

By that time, of course, Del had virtually stopped injecting drugs anyway. Larry Coven, who was as close to him as anyone during that time, noted that he never saw Del with any needles. Jonathan Abarbanel ran into Del near the Belmont "L" shortly after Belushi's death: "He said, 'I'm cleaning up my act. I've decided I want to live.'"

But he still had an expensive cocaine habit and a lack of willpower. He refused to consider a typical support group to break his addiction. Instead, while conducting a workshop in Canada, he chose a less common method of quitting cocaine.

"I was just doing far, far too much, so I had this brainstorm," said Del. "I managed to get off alcohol by doing the aversion therapy trip down at the Schick Clinic. How am I going to get off coke? Well, I joined this coven of witches in Toronto, wearing a pentacle. There's a little altar in the other room. Well, it's witchcraft: 'Blessed be, and do what thou wilt shall be the whole of the law.'"[19]

The Wicca in Canada agreed to conduct a banishing ceremony for Del (he sometimes claimed that, in exchange, he had to agree to become the warlock for their coven).

> Whatever you want to banish from your life, you symbolize; it's this rock in one hand and a candle in the other; and you use the energy of the group to imprint on these objects, and then hurl the objects into the fire, and dance to exhaustion and leap through the fire and carry on, all this great outdoors witch stuff. And I came back to Chicago, and the first thing I knew, I'd bought another gram, and I'd done it up my nose, and I thought "Well, shit, obviously it didn't work." . . .
>
> And another couple of days went by, and I'd done maybe, you know, two and a half grams. And then three weeks went by and suddenly I realized I hadn't had any for two and a half weeks. I'd gotten some that was bad, made me ill, and one of the connections got busted; every time I wanted any, it wasn't available; when it was available, I didn't want it or just experimentally was saying no to see if I could. And before I knew it, I just wasn't doing it anymore. I called the high priestess in Canada and said "Is this the way it's supposed to work?" And she says "Well, yeah, it takes about three weeks for it to work its way through your unconscious. It took me that long to get off heroin." So this former junkie kicked the same way I just kicked, hmmmm. So it was not a matter of witchcraft works, ooga booga. I had accepted the images of the universe of the pagans, to the point I was allowing [them] to work in me.[20]

Del wondered whether the spell he had put on himself had actually affected all the coke dealers in Chicago, and he joked that he had inadvertently ruined the coke for everyone in town. "It also gave me a little respect for the powers of the unconscious, that it's not like A A , where you have to struggle every day not to drink. You just put this image in your unconscious somehow or other, and it works in its own way, and pretty soon you're not fucked up anymore!"[21]

Del was invited to conduct an invocation at a downtown art gallery for Halloween 1982. The candlelit ceremony pleased the crowd, except for one short, dark-haired woman. The group stood in a circle around Del, who was holding a magic wand. He began to invoke gods from the East, North, and South, then asked a few improvisers on hand to invoke a mythical god.

Charna Halpern recalled that it felt "eerie" in the room. At the time, she was into meditation and had been taught to "white-light" herself as a form of protection against evil spirits. Angry that Del would leave a room full of people unprotected, she backed up to the end of the room, so as not to be affected by his conjuring.

Halpern approached him afterward, obviously agitated, and scolded him. Del was condescending and dismissive as he asked her name. When she identified herself, he immediately recognized the name. Halpern had recently begun working with David Shepherd on something called the ImprovOlympic; Del was unimpressed.

But Halpern challenged him. "You've got a lot of nerve doing something like that without protecting the people in this room!"

"*I* protected the *building*," sneered Del.

"You can't do that!" snapped Halpern.

"Yes I can!" insisted Del, and Halpern indignantly walked out. She was no expert, but most of her anger was at the fact that she knew Del didn't like her.

◇

Del's ten-year tenure at the Second City would not officially end until December 1982, though he had been on shaky ground throughout the previous year. He was supposed to direct the follow-up show to *Miro, Miro* (which would ultimately be called *Glenna Loved It or If You Knew Sushi*), which opened in February 1982. But during rehearsals, Del experienced what Breen called "another meltdown," and Sahlins replaced him as director.

In autumn 1982, Del was again put in charge of the next revue (to be called *Exit Pursued by a Bear*) and went through yet another "meltdown." He was fired—and this time it would stick. Sahlins finished directing *Exit Pursued by a Bear*, then brought in Ed Greenberg as the new Second City mainstage director. Afterward, Greenberg noted that "Del claimed he was the only person who was ever fired from a job, and allowed to handpick his successor."

Del's departure was fueled by his behavior. His creative philosophy had never changed. Del had not tried to inject improvisation into the shows, simply because he knew it would not be allowed by his boss. But Del would forever maintain that improvisation is an art form in itself;

for Sahlins, it was only a tool to create scenes. It is a debate that continues in improvisation circles and shows no sign of letting up, despite Del's decades of work.

Sahlins maintains that if an audience is enjoying an artistic experience, they don't really care how it was created, that how it relates to their lives is more important than the fact that it is being made up on the spot.

> It's the difference between a presentational form and an artistic one. It's the difference between a sword swallower and an actor. It's "Look, I'm improvising" versus "I'm inviting you to an idea of the world." And most improvisations fail most of the time. On some level they work, on the game level, but not the theatrical one ... someone onstage with whom you identify as a character, what happens to that character happens to you, it must be done with great verisimilitude and integrity and with concision, which you can't accuse an improvisation of doing.

As justification, Sahlins cites a speech from *Hamlet*, act 3, scene 2, in which the title character admonishes the performers of his play within the play that if they are substituting "the methodology for the thing, and the methodology becomes the thing, then you're doing a disservice to the work, because it's not the best you can do." In Shakespeare's words:

> Let those that play your clowns speak no more than is set down for them: for there be of them that will themselves laugh, to set on some quantity of barren spectators to laugh too; though, in the meantime, some necessary question of the play be then to be considered; that's villainous, and shows a most pitiful ambition in the fool that uses it.

But others disagree with Sahlins's interpretation of the lines in *Hamlet*. Roberta Maguire parses it to mean that Hamlet advises not to let clowns/actors improvise within a scripted play—to speak no more than is set down for them: "He is talking about the propensity of some performers to steal focus for themselves at the expense of the play. He is saying nothing about improvisation as a separate art form."

◆

Despite this major disagreement, Del's departure from the Second City was not about improvisation. If they were opposed in their philosophies of improvisation, they had long since discovered a way to work together. Sahlins says he always respected Del's intelligence, humor, and quickness, but he was simply out of control, and it was hurting the theater. Others felt that Del was somehow being blamed for John Belushi's death.

The final split may have come from an unexpected source. Danny Breen was not slavishly devoted to Del, but their relationship was usually affable, although Breen's complete indifference to science fiction would sometimes annoy Del. When Breen joined the mainstage company and they began working together regularly, however, the friction increased. One afternoon during a rehearsal, Del walked into the office where Breen's two-year-old son Spencer was playing on the floor. "Take that thing out of here!" he bellowed, driving Breen's wife, Nonie Newton, to tears. It was the last straw, and Breen decided to quit. "Bernie said, 'What would it take for you to stay here?' I'd been there a pretty long time at that point, and I said 'Well, Del would have to go,' thinking 'That'll never happen!' And Bernie went 'OK,' and I said 'What?'"

As in the case of his sudden departure from *Saturday Night Live*, his colleagues were unaware of an inciting incident. One day he was there; the next he was gone. There was no traditional Second City farewell ceremony with a pie in the face.

Although Del was ready to leave the Second City, he couldn't bring himself to quit, and forced Sahlins to fire him. When Del finally got his wish, his relationship with Sahlins immediately improved. "I met him at the [Old Town] Ale House and I said 'Del, this can't go on.' And actually, he was nicer to me after that." There was no big blowup, said Joyce Sloane. "It was just time. The work was suffering—that's really the judge of everything, what happens on the stage."

To the surprise of everyone, particularly himself, Breen became "the guy that got Del fired." Del continued to hold workshops at the Second City, and a week or two after he was fired, students from the workshops were reporting that he had some of them performing magic spells to hurt Breen, his wife, and Meagan Fay, who he felt had gotten him fired. (Company members Rick Thomas and John Kapelos took Del's side.)

At first no one could believe Del was really gone, because he had been fired regularly in the past. But Sahlins had been preparing his dismissal for some time, and Breen provided him with the provocation.

"Bernie was definitely ready [to fire Del], he even said it to me," said Breen. "[Bernie] probably thought that he could always bring Del back if he wanted to."

From Del's perspective, it was art versus business, and the long-standing disagreement with Sahlins over the value of improvisation. In an interview just after leaving the Second City in February 1983, Del said that his role in *A Christmas Carol* was a turning point.

> Lo and behold, I got the part of the Ghost of Christmas Present. I had not managed to ruin the voice in all those years of abuse! So that was kind of my road back. And the soberer I got, and the more successful Second City got, the more we all realized that we were just repeating ourselves over there. For the public, it's a trivial little disagreement, for [Bernie and me], it's a great crisis of artistic vision. And it was mutually decided that, since I was so heavily into experimentation and the use of improvisation to find out more and more about what constitutes a human being, and Second City is more into success and auditioning for television, that I am no longer the director that they need over there, because I am still up for improvisation and experimentation.
>
> Right around Christmas, Bernie and I had a meeting, and what we did was, we just recognized what everybody else knew, which was that our views of how to do Second City these days were just too divergent. Rather than sit around and bitch at each other—golly, like trying to direct shows with Bernie!—he would try to compensate for what he thought were my mistakes, and I would try to compensate for what I thought were his mistakes. In the meantime, we would drive a company of actors absolutely nuts, because he would say "Now really, what Del wants you to do here—" So it was just nuts, it was like a schizophrenic situation. What you need in a situation like that is one strong director who sets the goals and makes a lot of the choices for the actors, and then lights the fuse and gets away.[22]

Del would be free to delve into the mystical aspects of improvisation. He felt that "improvisation so clearly calls upon higher powers of the mind," a school of thought never encouraged at the Second City.

> My mystical orientation was tolerated and chuckled at by the producer. Bernie was just a businessman. When I first came back to

Second City after leaving The Committee, I thought that I was just going to be handed the theatre on a platter here and do another renaissance, like we did with The Committee, and let the chips fall where they may. No. I was just hired as a technician to put on a show, so whatever experimentation that I did—and I did a lot of it—was in the workshops.[23]

Of leaving the Second City, Del would often explain, "I got tired of cutting the comedy salami." At the end, he simply shook hands with Sahlins and they wished each other well. "Thanks for giving me a place to recover from the '60s," he told Sahlins. He would head into 1983 with no alcohol, no cocaine, and no Second City. What he would emerge with would surprise everyone who had ever known him.

17

The ImprovOlympic

Del's options were few. The Second City, *Saturday Night Live*, and *SCTV* were no longer possibilities. Aside from *A Christmas Carol*, his acting career had stalled. He would have to pay the rent with more workshops, which might be more difficult to maintain without a current Second City affiliation.

In February 1983, just after leaving his ten-year stint at the Second City, Del had a chance encounter with college student named Bob Odenkirk. The younger man had just interviewed Joyce Sloane at Second City for a college radio station; although she was warm and cordial, afterward Odenkirk felt uncertain about his own prospects for performing.

He walked to Barbara's Bookstore, where he picked up a copy of Keith Johnstone's *Impro*. As he paged through the book, he heard the girl at the counter speaking with a customer whom she called "Del." Recognizing the name, Odenkirk asked, "Are you Del Close?" When Del said "Yeah," Odenkirk said, "I just interviewed Joyce Sloane. Is it OK if I interview you, too?" "Sure! Perfect timing." Del explained that after quitting *Saturday Night Live*, Second City, and cocaine, he was about to embark on a new journey, and felt reinvigorated.

They walked to his Wells Street apartment. The round window in the front door was broken out, letting in the freezing February air. Del saw the student staring at the window, and explained that a jealous husband had broken it the previous year on New Year's Day. "I've left it open as kind of a memorial. It was the coldest day of the year, twenty-six below zero, and I suddenly didn't have a front window." He explained that he kept it that way because his cats liked to get in and out easily.

The suburban boy from Naperville felt intimidated. He declined Del's offer of pot and they sat down for a lengthy interview. Del talked about quitting cocaine, witchcraft, Second City, and the Committee. Leaving the Second City, Del explained, all seemed to be part of a pattern in his life. "I noticed that I'd been drunk [at the Second City] for five years, and in the process, I managed to mount some very good shows, thank you. But I figured I owed them the same amount of time sober that I was there drunk, and that period of time has just now come [to an end]," said Del. "The Committee ran for ten years and closed. After it closed, I came to Chicago for ten years—it's like in terms of ten-year cycles. Five years drunk, five years sober at Second City, it all comes to a big ten years. Five years at the Goodman Theatre, that's the close of that cycle."[1]

Del revealed that he had been eyeing Crosscurrents cabaret, just off Belmont Avenue, as a possible venue for classes and an upcoming show. He had already performed two nights at Crosscurrents with Paul Krassner. The club's owner, Tom Goodman, had asked Del to put together a group that could write and perform a new show every week. Rather than the typical "And now ladies and gentlemen, we take you to . . ." Del preferred to look at the performers as musicians, a band that approached conceptual comedy like jazz.

Del preferred struggling organizations, admitting, "I'm just not comfortable with successful operations." While his attitude toward the Second City could be viewed by some as sour grapes, he felt that the theater had been creatively stagnant for years, and only stayed open for commercial reasons. "In reality, if it were not such a sound business proposition, Second City probably should have closed . . . because we've done nothing but repeat ourselves for the last six or seven years," said Del. "So long as the shows are not so much worse than television, [audiences] won't be disappointed."

Odenkirk's encounter with Del changed his life. Coming minutes after the interview with Sloane, which left him feeling very uncertain about his chances of making it in the world of comedy, Del's energy and enthusiasm convinced Odenkirk to pursue his own career.

The Post-Rational Players, 1983:
(left to right) Warren Leming,
Larry Coven, and Del Close.
(COURTESY OF CHARNA HALPERN)

Goodman's offer led Del to form the Post-Rational Players with Larry Coven and Warren Leming, performing written sketches with an improvisational feel. Coven did most of the writing; Del contributed ideas and scripted a couple; Leming wrote songs and one or two other pieces. The Post-Rational Players began as part of a Friday-night variety show, then started their own revue titled *Three Brains, No Waiting*.

❖

Crosscurrents was located on North Wilton, a stone's throw away from the bustling intersection of Belmont and Sheffield in Chicago's Lakeview neighborhood. Not yet gentrified, Lakeview was a mixture of liquor stores and pawnshops, along with a few more upscale institutions like Leona's Italian restaurant and Ann Sather's (which feature Scandinavian favorites). It was a melting pot of ages, nationalities, even sexualities.

Originally a Swedish Women's Temperance Hall, Crosscurrents offered an eclectic mix of entertainment, including blues bands, performance artists, stand-up comedy, and more traditional theater. A bar and a cabaret theater were located on the main floor, and two upstairs rooms served as rehearsal space or classrooms.

The Post-Rational Players became known for their edgy humor and their music. One of their most popular pieces, written by Coven with Del as straight man, was called "The People Upstairs," but soon became known as "Baby Seals." Outrage against clubbing baby seals was at its peak at that time, and Del, as straight man, heard Coven's outrage at his upstairs neighbors, who were keeping him up at night because they were busy slaughtering baby seals. It became their signature piece.

But another comedy theater had also settled in Crosscurrents.

Several months earlier, Charna Halpern had finished Josephine Forsberg's Players' Workshop and was directing a Second City children's show. Having just read Jeffrey Sweet's *Something Wonderful Right Away*, which included interviews with Del Close and David Shepherd, she learned that Shepherd was in Chicago, auditioning actors for a play called *The Jonah Complex*. She recalled that Shepherd had attempted something called ImprovOlympic in Canada, and began to think: "I have an improv troupe, and Dan Castellanetta has an improv troupe and Frank Farrell has an improv troupe. *We* could do that ImprovOlympic, I could be performing anytime I want. *That's* what I want to do. I'm going to run ImprovOlympic!"

Halpern drove to the auditions at Victory Gardens Theater, where Shepherd agreed to work with her on a revived ImprovOlympic, and she began assembling teams to play Spolin's games. The shows attracted audiences, but Halpern soon decided to cut ties with Shepherd; she suggested that he continue his revival efforts in New York, leaving her to run the Chicago ImprovOlympic on her own.

By early 1983, she had chosen Crosscurrents as a base and decided she was through with partners. She was aware of Del Close, and had vivid memories of their encounter at the Halloween ceremony in 1982, but because she had allied herself with Shepherd, Del wanted nothing to do with her. He felt that anybody working with Shepherd had to be an idiot. Unbeknownst to Del, Halpern had sat in on one of his Second City workshops and watched a Harold, but was unimpressed. It had gone on and on. She went next door for lunch and returned forty-five minutes later—the same Harold was continuing.

So Del was convinced that Halpern was a twit; Halpern was convinced that Del's passion, the Harold, was tedious and unworkable.

Halpern had been running the ImprovOlympic in Chicago for nearly a year without Shepherd, and was getting tired of the games. It simply wasn't enough of a theater for her. She had a team of rabbis who couldn't perform on Friday nights, a team of psychologists, a team of local TV reporters. Del was performing once a week with the Post-Rational Players. When she suddenly ran into him at Crosscurrents, her first thought was not of a potential partnership, but "Maybe I can steal something from him!"

She was certain that Del wouldn't remember her from the previous Halloween; desperation and boredom compelled her to approach him with an offer: "How'd you like to make $200 and some pot?"

"Doing what?" he responded cautiously.

"Teaching one three-hour class," said Halpern.

"Can I do anything I want?"

"Yes."

"Can I invoke demons?"

Yes, said Halpern. Obviously, his memory was unimpaired.

Del decided on a different approach for his ImprovOlympic workshop. He decided to embarrass Halpern by teaching the invocation, because, as he explained to the class, he had "met Charna Halpern, and she didn't know what I was doing, so maybe I better show you what I am doing." Halpern and the class were amazed and impressed. Afterward, she told him that she had gone as far as she could with her training, and there just had to be something more from improvisation. Del was impressed: "Well, you're not a twit after all."

Del was determined to raise the level of Halpern's games and turn them into an improvised theatrical experience. He later recalled:

> They were developing scenes based on games. My perception of this whole tendency was, this is theatre reduced to a party game. The idea is to take these games and combine them in a way that they are sufficiently elevated to call them theatre.[2]

Halpern was less than excited when Del suggested the Harold, but Del agreed that "it never works, it's unteachable and unplayable, but if we made a structure, maybe we could come up with something." Del recommended that she close down her "little game theater" while they figured out a structure. It was less than a formal partnership, and more of an agreement to work together. Del didn't care to talk about money, so Halpern decided they should split everything.

◆

Even as the new ImprovOlympic was getting on its feet, another opportunity presented itself at the Goodman Studio. Del was invited to costar in a new one-act play with Peter Falk. The author was Elaine May.

The offer from the Goodman must have been welcome, but the chance to work with Elaine May was irresistible.

> Suddenly I'm being directed by Elaine, whom I have always loved and will never stop loving, and at one point she says, "Gee, you're a very good actor." And it had never occurred to me that I really might be.[3]

Elaine May's *Hotline* was one of three one-acts performed at the Goodman Theatre from June 3 through July 7, 1983, along with David Mamet's *Disappearance of the Jews* and Shel Silverstein's *Gorilla*. While Art Wolff was the director of record for *Hotline*, May soon took charge of her own production.

Hotline takes on impersonal urban institutions in the story of a suicidal prostitute who forces her problems on a bumbling, novice suicide counselor. Del didn't even have to audition for the show, but was regarded as part of the acting family of the Goodman.

"We knew Del was going to be solid and fine, and Del was the least of the things anybody had to deal with, including getting the script right and Peter learning the lines that Elaine was changing every day," recalled Mosher.

The evening of three one-acts ran during the summer, at the same time that the Post-Rational Players were performing late-night shows. Del invited the cast and crew to the show one night, and Coven even went barhopping with Del and May on several occasions. There was little talk of the past, though there was some discussion of *Hotline* and the Post-Rational show. They would tell each other silly jokes and schmooze. At one bar, a rat ran under their table. Coven freaked out, while Del and May thought his reaction was simply hysterical. Coven recalled: "They were clearly still close. Elaine and Del seemed like good old buddies."

◇

Although the Post-Rational Players would continue until the end of the year, Del's attentions were increasingly drawn to Halpern and the

Peter Falk and Del Close
in a scene from Elaine
May's *Hotline* at the
Goodman Theatre.
(COURTESY OF CHARNA HALPERN)

Del with the cast of *Hotline*.
(COURTESY OF CHARNA HALPERN)

ImprovOlympic. Sahlins had always insisted that audiences would never sit through an entire show made up of games and unscripted material. The Second City company would only improvise after two acts of polished sketch comedy, but their Dirty Little Secret was that the improvisation set each night wasn't always improvised. Because it was being used to develop possible scenes for the next show, audience suggestions were often shoehorned to fit sketches currently under construction. Only the games were truly improvised.

It was difficult to argue with the success of Sahlins's approach. Audiences were bigger than ever, and a spin-off theater, the Second City e.t.c., was launched in September 1982 next to the original.

But Del felt the Second City shows had become prepackaged. He missed that spark, the unpredictability, the freshness, and the originality of true improvisation. Bernie would argue that improvisation was not always safe. For Del, that was precisely the point. If an audience sees the actors creating something before their eyes, they are immediately more invested in it. Unlike a scripted scene, there are no guarantees that the actors will lead them to a safe conclusion, so when they succeed, the payoff is bigger. Even when they fail, audiences are more understanding, because they have been a part of the process.

Del would tell his classes, "We all know how to get laughs from an audience. It isn't hard. But I want us to get cheers!" He was determined to prove that audiences *would* enjoy a completely improvised show. The ImprovOlympic offered him one more chance to prove it.

After a great many years, his personal life was under control. Although he was still tripping occasionally, smoking pot, and taking Valium and mushrooms, none of them seemed to have a debilitating effect. He was ready for a new start, and felt no need to engage in the risky behavior that had nearly killed him in the past. He had survived.

It was challenging to attract students to the ImprovOlympic. Following Del's departure, the Second City began offering workshops of its own, three eight-week sessions taught by Don DePollo. Business was good. But Halpern took advantage of every opportunity to publicize the new-and-improved ImprovOlympic, and her knack for promotion began to pay off. The ImprovOlympic was presenting shows Tuesday nights at Crosscurrents, and newspapers and radio began paying attention, even though most of the groups competing, such as Friends of the Zoo, did not develop from ImprovOlympic classes.

By the end of the first year, however, audiences thinned and performances ended. The Post-Rational Players finished their run at Crosscurrents, and the group had effectively ended. Nevertheless, the Improv-Olympic managed to attract just enough new students to keep it afloat.

I was among the new students in January 1984 for Del's Monday night class. Bob Odenkirk was a fellow student; just as my own encounter with Del at a party led to my taking classes, Odenkirk's meeting drew him to Crosscurrents for the eight-week sessions. Del rarely acted in a scene during the class, but didn't hesitate if it would illustrate a point or provide an example. We experienced such an instance during our first session. It was a memorable moment for Odenkirk: "The difference between him doing the scene and all of us was so huge, the world that he brought onto stage as an actor was so complete and real to him that it made me go, 'Oh, I see, *that's* how you do it.'"

Odenkirk was eventually hired as a writer for *Saturday Night Live*, went on to cocreate *Mr. Show*, and even, with the support of Joyce

Although the Post-Rational Players would disband, Del's friendship with Larry Coven would continue to the end of his life.

(COURTESY OF CHARNA HALPERN)

Sloane, performed on the Second City's mainstage. During one summer hiatus, a group of *SNL* writers, including Odenkirk, Rob Smigel, and a then-unknown Conan O'Brien, wrote and performed *The Happy Happy Good Show* in Chicago. One of the sketches featured a troupe of improvisational puppets called the Impettes; one of the characters was based, of course, on Del.

◇

By the end of 1983, Del decided to concentrate on the more advanced students, and asked Halpern to start teaching the introductory classes. He knew that the Harold was the key to establishing improvisation as its own art form, if only he could discover a loose-but-reliable format that could be repeated with infinite variations, with a reasonable degree of success.

To achieve this, he studied one of Halpern's ImprovOlympic games called the Time Dash. At first glance, it merely seemed like another in a series of Spolin's improvisational games. The Time Dash involved a series of scenes, normally beginning with two players. As soon as the actors established a scene, it would advance in time and resume. Then the players would jump ahead once again, and the audience would see the culmination of the scene. The principle is simple—the actors advance one relationship or situation through time. (The variations are many; the scenes need not progress forward in chronological order.)

Del saw the possibilities inherent in the format. As he saw actors perform scenes 1-A, 1-B, and 1-C, he decided the hipper choice would be to mix it up. Three pairs of actors would continue to perform three

Time Dashes, but they would reorder and intersperse the scenes. Audience suggestions were still obligatory, but his actors would treat them in a different, hipper, manner. Sometimes they would begin by hitting the suggestions head-on, but more often, they would begin scenes as far away from the literal suggestion as possible, then begin moving slowly, inexorably, toward the players' personalizations of the suggestions.

The structure appeared airtight, provided scenes were done correctly. The players could not make jokes, which was too cheap and easy a tactic. Connections were the most acceptable way to elicit laughs from an audience, provided the scene work could stay on a high enough level.

Del preferred heightened, even poetic language. He insisted on emphasizing the intelligence of the players. With few exceptions, it was the Compass Players and the Second City, along with trailblazers like Lenny Bruce and Mort Sahl, that pioneered the idea that the comedians were the smartest ones in the room. "Always play at the top of your intelligence" was a mantra his students would hear often. At the same time, he also claimed to be "sick of wit," which he felt was too often wit for its own sake, a ploy that hampered growth and discovery.

He was fascinated by left-brain right-brain theories, and focused on Betty Edwards's 1979 book *Drawing on the Right Side of the Brain* as a method of nurturing creativity. He was determined to learn how to dull the left side of the brain to make the right side kick in and do something brilliant.

He also experimented with rituals and invocations in problem-solving. For Del, an invocation was an attempt to explore or answer questions inherent in the theme. If the theme of a Harold was "apple," then Del would encourage the improvisers to address it by personalizing it, heightening language, speaking to the incarnate Apple in an attempt to make the mundane profound. (A general rule of thumb was to make a profound suggestion into something mundane, and vice versa.)

At the heart of each scene were the basic principles developed by Elaine May and Theodore J. Flicker, the Committee, and the Second City: Less is more. Take the active choice. Follow the fear. And agreement. *Always* agreement. So important was the latter that Halpern decided to name their company Yes & Productions.

By mid-1984, Del had settled on a structure for the upcoming Harold performances. He would use a group of six to eight students for each Harold, now based on the Time Dash game. He would utilize three groups of students, each performing a three-part Time Dash that would be woven into the others, reflecting themes, characters, and other connections. Group 1 would still perform scenes 1-A, 1-B, 1-C, but they would be intertwined into one larger whole with the three scenes of groups 2 and 3. There would be an opening game, however, a word association similar to the classic Game that Del had played in the early 1960s at the Second City, to inspire and suggest ideas.

The Harold would consist of the opening word-association game, followed by the first three scenes (1-A, 2-A, 3-A), followed by continuations of those scenes (1-B, 2-B, 3-B), culminating in the final set of scenes (normally 1-C, 2-C, 3-C). By the final set, players in one scene would often discover they were connected to players in another scene.

This more formalized construction for the Harold was not the only difference. While the structure was based on the Time Dash, the content was an act of defiance against the comedy norms of the time. Del and the group had arrived at a new approach to dealing with the age-old issue of timing. He called it Slow Comedy. As he described it to the *Chicago Tribune*, he could no longer watch a situation comedy, and had lost his feeling for most improvisation, because he had become "deaf" to the timing.

> Even when the jokes are different the timing is the same. . . . It is always one . . . two . . . joke . . . repeat. The laughter is a knee-jerk reaction and the comedians, who since the '50s have been perceived as these sort of whimsical wimp types, go through the motions. The comedy needs some depth and more wit. We got to think about slowing our comedy down by maybe a factor of eight. What we found was we were getting a different type of laugh.[4]

The idea was for each actor to slow down the response time when given a line of dialogue. Instead of going with the first, knee-jerk response, which was often a cliche, or even the second response, which audience members might anticipate, Slow Comedy encouraged the actors to wait for their third, even fourth or fifth response. Responding to a simple statement like "The doctor will see you now" would elicit different replies when slowed down. The immediate response of "Thank you nurse" or "Shall I bring my sample?" might take a different turn in Slow Comedy, perhaps "How much longer have I got?" or "Glad to hear his retina damage has healed," or "I'd like to raise him $20."

Del was excited by the prospect of unveiling his new experiment before an audience:

> We are mining an area of comedy that has never been mined before. What we are doing is we are taking improv comedy one step further; we are doing something that has never been tried before, and it is really very, very exciting. . . . We are going to try to draw the audience in . . . using a game of complex word associations. When they see a good intellectual-emotional move, we want them to cheer. There will be a good 30 seconds between responses and the audience is surprised by the answers, and they are not clichés.[5]

The ImprovOlympic Presents Harold premiered at Crosscurrents on October 1, 1984. Slow Comedy eschewed cliches; its disadvantage was the long pauses in anticipation of what was, with any luck, the next bit of brilliance. The slowness that gave it a distinct feel also limited its theatrical potential. Although it was a unique and worthy experiment, it was simply too . . . slow. By December the show had closed.

Far from being discouraged, Del was invigorated by the experience. He had established himself with Halpern and the ImprovOlympic, and had a venue for his theories and experiments.

18

Roaches in the Dental Floss

Del wanted a renewed acting career. His workshops and the Improv-Olympic occupied the inquisitive, curious part of his mind, but he needed more. Acting would allow him to perform, to play, while developing characters and relationships with fellow creative talents. He knew his talent and potential, but the biggest theatrical challenge would be to convince the Chicago acting community that he was now functional.

A Christmas Carol was fine, but that was once a year, playing the same role, and it had ceased to challenge him. Other opportunities would occasionally surface, but most proved insubstantial. In early 1980, he wrote:

> Saturday night at a party at my house, [Tim Leary] asked me to go on the road with him for a few days as his opening act—he's working saloons as a Stand-up Philosopher. That's where Lenny [Bruce] and His Royal Highness [Lord Buckley] wound up, having started as bur-lesque comics. Maybe Tim has that to look forward to. The first date in a three-date series was called off—Duffy's in Minneapolis already had an opening act—a male stripper—and didn't want another one. Yesterday we were supposed to be in Milwaukee, and tonight Madi-son [Wisconsin], but no word has come. He accused me publicly . . .

of changing his life by luring him into the counterculture with *How To Speak Hip*. I, in turn, speculated on what might have happened if, on his first acid trip, instead of picking up the Bardo Thodol he'd read *Winnie the Pooh*. We got along famously, but maybe he's one of those people who re-evaluates his decisions when the drugs wear off. Takes all kinds.[1]

In early 1980, director Gregory Mosher cast him in *Bal* (formerly *Baal in the 21st Century*, an adaptation of Brecht's *Baal*), which opened in March 1980 at the Goodman Theatre. Jim Belushi, who starred in the production, considers it Del's acting comeback. When Belushi and Mosher were discussing casting possibilities, Del's name came up, and they decided to give him a shot.

Del wrote in an unpublished essay: "I play a near-psychotic named Duzack, who dominates the first scene, is passed out cold in the second, and disappears forever, skipping the curtain call so as to make it back to the Second City in time to watch the improvisations and give notes."

According to Mosher, Richard Nelson's adaptation of the Brecht play *Baal* was not a success, although Del acquitted himself well. After the second preview, when it was obvious that the audience truly hated the show, the actors were all gathered onstage and Mosher asked, "Del, why do you think the audience doesn't laugh?" Del dryly replied, "Well, it's not funny."

Nothing could help the chaotic production. Del was amused by the turmoil around him, and while the others didn't know the production had collapsed until the first performance, Del saw it all coming. He remained slightly off to the side, albeit "in a perfectly civilized and nice way, never truly distancing himself or looking down on it, just laughing!" Despite Mosher's recollection of the show as a mishmash of acting and writing styles, the show was not universally reviled by critics. *Chicago Tribune* critic Linda Winer called *Bal* a "very good, very uneven new play," with positive words for both Del and Belushi, who plays the title character: "When we first find Bal, he is wearing a sweatshirt and gorging fine sausage at a party peopled by cardboard socialites out of early Albee. Del Close, who is perfect in comic stupor, delivers tautologies about rational man and plays radical chic host to his newest discovery."[2]

Still, Mosher claimed that "for a long time, it was the gold standard for the worst show in Chicago theater history." The cast and crew were not amused, but it didn't bother Del. In the middle of one scene, in a way that made sense to him (although it was certainly not indicated in the script), Del's character started to sing "Deutschland über alles." While it wasn't necessarily appropriate, it was the least of their problems, and so it stayed in the show.

Del shared a dressing room with Belushi, who observed the actor renewing his craft. Del loved the regularity of his new acting job, getting ready for each show and discussing his performances with his former student. His acting career was slow to develop, despite his participation in *Christmas Carol*, *Bal*, and *Hotline*, but he began to get more interesting auditions.

> I let it be known I was shopping for a major supporting role. And my dresser for *Christmas Carol* was with the Remains [Theatre], and he said "Would you like to read for Kit Carson?" Then *Time of Your Life* opened on my 50th birthday, about the biggest omen I've ever run into.[3]

Although favorably received in his previous productions, William Saroyan's Pulitzer Prize–winning *The Time of Your Life*, directed by Donald Moffet, would be Del's breakthrough to the mainstream Chicago theater community. The Remains Theatre Ensemble was hired en mass to stage the production at the Goodman, headlined by William L. Petersen as alcoholic philosopher Joe, Amy Morton as fallen woman Kitty, and Dennis Farina as bartender Nick. Kit Carson, the displaced mountain man, was exactly the sort of fat, juicy supporting role for which Del had been looking.

He built his character using a familiar device, walking into a rehearsal and telling Moffet that he had invoked the spirit of Kit Carson the previous night, and found an archetype for his new role, admitting that it was "a character that was going nowhere with my ordinary acting skills."

> First, I had to figure out who Kit Carson was. What was his function? To get G.I. Joe ready for World War Two, to demonstrate some people needed to be killed, basically Hitler. But was he out there doing it obviously? No, he was not. I figured out Kit Carson was Mars, God of War. But I didn't want his warlike personality; I wanted his devious propaganda personality.[4]

Del played up the more mystical aspects of his role preparation.

> Certain flattering descriptions of the god; you remember, of course, that you're speaking to yourself. . . . You get into the character of the god. And you get, like, some good advice, or ill, you know; sometimes they're not crazy about it, these guys, they're not always jovial. Well, at any rate, Kit Carson literally walked in the door, sat down beside me, told me all the mistakes I was making, and left. So was he there or not? It's easy to take magic and reduce it to psychology. When you practice it you realize it's psychology elevated to something else.[5]

The Time of Your Life, which opened March 12, 1984, (just three days after Del's fiftieth birthday) was a solid success. The next day, the *Chicago Tribune*'s Richard Christiansen called it "simplistic and sentimental baloney. But it is also a wonderful, joyous work of theatre, and I have the feeling today that the world is a little better place in which to live now that the Goodman Theatre has revived it for us in such a loving and life-giving production. . . . Del Close, in the role of his lifetime, spins those incredible tall tales of the old timer Kit Carson with devilish glee. . . . All hail to them all . . . who have fashioned a beautifully crafted production out of the dreams and dust of this once-in-a-lifetime play."

His success in *Time of Your Life* drew increased attention from agents, but Del instead appointed Halpern his manager, and one of her responsibilities would be to deal with the agents and business matters. Del simply wanted to act.

◈

The film and television work had been slim after he had moved back to Chicago. He appeared in a peculiar, X-rated documentary called *A Labor of Love*, codirected by Robert Flaxman and Daniel Goldman, which chronicles the making of an explicit film dealing with surrogate parents. The soft porn movie deals with a man who can't get his wife pregnant. At one point they visit a group of male prostitutes, and one of the "young" studs is a leather-clad Del Close. (The producers eventually scrapped the explicit footage and released it as an R-rated drama called *Whose Child Am I?*). Del also made a brief appearance in 1981's more respectable *Thief*, starring James Caan as a safecracker who agrees to do a job for the mob. Jim Belushi costarred, though he was not involved with Del's hiring as Mechanic #1.)

It was not until his success in 1984 with *Time of Your Life*, when Chicago's TV and film industry picked up, and Halpern took charge of his acting career, that his film career began to build. He was cast in *First Steps*, a 1985 TV-movie starring Judd Hirsch and Kim Darby. Set in a laboratory with cages of small animals, the gray-bearded Del, wearing a white lab coat with a large black snake draped around his shoulders, walks Hirsch through the lab as the latter asks for a suggestion regarding animal subjects.

"Well, we got cats! And I'd recommend Ketamine as an anesthetic. Now, it's hallucinogenic—heh, heh!" chuckles the zoologist, as he puts the snake back in its cage. "You've never seen a cat grin? Well, give it a shot and you will!" Hirsch's character thanks him and the zoologist flashes another devilish grin. "Now, it's potent stuff—I'd be careful if it was a cat o' mine!" he cackles, as he latches the cage.

Though it was a brief scene in a TV movie, Del seized as much focus as was appropriate. Afterward, he told his classes that the snake was nauseous during the shooting, paraphrasing the show business joke: "What, and give up the snake vomit?"

Halpern and Del began developing a television project for WMAQ-TV, the local NBC affiliate. Looking for what was then considered important public affairs programming, the station approved a one-hour special on teenage alcoholism called *No Laughing Matter*, which would air March 16, 1985. It included comedy sketches and more serious interview segments to make its point about peer pressure to drink and alcohol addiction. It was familiar ground for Del. Halpern rounded up a highly talented cast that included Larry Coven, Rob Bundy, Lili Taylor, Anne Morgan, and Tim Kazurinsky, back from *Saturday Night Live*, along with Del.

◆

In February 1983, Del had been interviewed for Bob Woodward's *Wired*, the controversial biography of John Belushi that did not shy away from Belushi's drug experiences. The debate that followed the book's release in spring 1984 was particularly intense in the Chicago area, where Belushi grew up and came of age.

The cast of *No Laughing Matter* consisted of *(back, left to right)* Rob Bundy, Anne Morgan, Del Close, Charna Halpern, Larry Coven, *(front)* Tim Kazurinsky, and Lili Taylor.
(COURTESY OF CHARNA HALPERN)

The *Chicago Tribune* ran a front-page series after the release of *Wired* that included some critical remarks from Del. When the *Washington Post* reporter came to Chicago to promote the book, the radio station WIND-AM invited Del along to "debate" Woodward.

A funny thing happened on the way to the debate. Del had second thoughts about disputing the accuracy of the book, and instead of arguing with the reporter, he decided to follow his own improvisational teachings about agreement. In short, he would "Yes and" Bob Woodward.

The Steve King show was live at 11:00 A.M. on June 6, 1984; King initially welcomed Woodward alone, then brought Del into the studio. King stated that Del had disagreed with *Wired* in that week's *Chicago Tribune* but now seemed to be nodding in agreement. "In the words of Pontius Pilate, I find no fault with this book," replied Del. King asked if that marked a turnaround in his attitude about the book. "Well, I'm a magician. I can change my mind," joked Del.

At that point, King's anticipated debate was defused, and Woodward addressed Del: "There was a magnetism that you saw in [Belushi], and you told me, and I say in the book, 'He was in italics, and everyone else was in regular print.'" "That sounds like I'm a little bit condescending to Harold Ramis and Joe Flaherty and so on, but I think they all know what I mean," responded Del. "Yes, he was in italics and the other people were regular people, but they were still a rather higher order than regular people."

Woodward then got to the point: was what he wrote in the book true as Del knew it? "Yeah. Many of the things that I said in the newspaper were nitpicking basically, and I could continue to pick the nits, but I won't, because it's not really worth it," said Del. "What you end up doing is standing there with a crash helmet waiting for the bulldozer. I mean, this is the guy that brought down Nixon, after all. I'm going to pick nits with Woodward? Goodness gracious!"

King noted that in the earlier segment Woodward said that he felt the book was a fair total portrait of John Belushi. Did Del agree? "If we want Belushi's humor, we're going to have to write our own book," answered Del. "However, Bob managed to catch—Mr. Woodward— managed to catch the humor in *Saturday Night Live* sketches, and I must say, that yes, I probably do think he gave a total fair portrait, and I'll even go further and say that the real picture was probably far uglier . . . than presented in the book, yeah. Not only that, if I was in John's position, I would have made his behavior look conservative by my own."

A moment of shocked silence followed. Del had managed to "Yes and" both Woodward and King. The pair finally responded by asking about drugs and show business, with Woodward asking Del, "What did you see? What do you know?" "Well, this might seem a trifle bit unresponsive, but I'd like to try to follow some of my own directions," said Del. "First, conflict is rather tedious, nobody likes an argument, so let's see if we can come to an agreement. Second, agreement leads to action. Possibly some action we might take is to clean up the industry a little bit, design it so we don't kill each other quite so often and quite so painfully."

Woodward raised the point that John Belushi had become a symbol of youthful rebellion, even subversion. "I had just come hot from the revolution when I arrived in Chicago in 1973, I had been directing the Committee for five years, which was this highly political version of what Second City was doing, and you know, I was a friend of Lenny's, a friend of Lord Buckley's, and a stand-up comic myself. I bumped into John when he was twenty, and certainly he imprinted on me like a baby duck. 'Oh, I want to be that!' You know, if somebody with larger appetites and greater faith than I, that's what I did—they croak! There's a whole quantum jump, a whole order of drug use—I used to think I did a lot of drugs. Dear heavens!" gasped Del, with an astonished laugh. "I've never seen such a situation in my life! I feel like what I really am, the little guy that lives in the back of the alley and smokes a joint occasionally."

King next asked Del about his own problems with drugs and alcohol, which Del readily admitted. "Yeah, I have. . . . The only one that surprised me was booze, because they don't warn you about it being an addictive drug," said Del.

The host then opened the phone lines for a few questions from listeners, and Del responded to the heated comments the book had aroused: "As painful as it is, reading the book is like not only having John die, it's like watching him slowly tortured to death before your eyes. It's a painful experience. No wonder we respond emotionally."

The show concluded when Woodward had to rush to another interview, and Steve King thanked Del for his candidness. "Yes and" had resulted in something more interesting than argument. Even though his own drug use had dwindled in the last couple of years, he refused to repudiate any of it. He did, however, tell his class, "The advice I gave Belushi made him a star, it didn't kill him."

◇

Del was now determined to take control of his life and his life's work. Halpern was stepping up, taking on some of his responsibilities, and cushioning him from others. She was providing him with what he had always needed and was now, finally, ready for: someone who would allow him to indulge his creativity, experiment, take improvisation to the next level, and at the same time make sure his electric bill was paid.

Del was cultured and incredibly charming when he chose to be, but his lifestyle choices and his contrarian nature left her work cut out for her. There was no better example than his apartment. The first-floor flat on Wells Street, behind the Japanese restaurant and across from the Sneak Joint/Blues Bar, was legendary for its slovenliness. After ten years in the same location, it scarcely appeared habitable. One single black extension cord trailed into the bedroom from the apartment upstairs; he would give the occupants a few dollars each month to pay his portion of the utility bill. Del referred to this as "borrowing a cup of electricity" from his neighbors.

Due to the limited nature of his power supply, he was not able to turn on the light and watch television at the same time, so it was normally dark throughout the flat. His TV set had seen better days. The makeshift antenna seemed to pick up more snow than picture, and was sensitive to the slightest movement in the room. The channel selector dial was only a distant memory; whenever Del wanted to change the program, he had to use the pliers that had been set aside for that purpose.

Of course, the lack of light was a boon for visitors after dark, who were prevented from getting a clear view. The omnipresent cockroaches had become so accustomed to the squalor that, instead of scattering when the light was turned on, they seemed indifferent.

His bed was a mattress on the floor, a concession to his hippie days. (At one point, he had written in marking pen on the ceiling just over his head, "Your name is Del Close. You live here." Most of his friends felt it was probably for show, but could never be certain.) Virtually all the spare room in the apartment was taken up by books and bookshelves, predominantly science fiction and horror, but with everything from science texts, EC Comics reprints, and biographies jammed into the available areas. He had accumulated many valuable autographed volumes and limited editions and was careful to segregate them as much as possible.

What little wall space was not covered by bookshelves was filled by theatrical and vintage rock concert posters, and original artwork by artists as varied as Peter Falk and serial killer John Wayne Gacy Jr. Pagan altars were scattered about the living room, and memorabilia was everywhere.

Fortunately, the kitchen was seldom used for food preparation. Del ate most of his meals out, normally at the Stagecoach. He often brewed coffee, though frequent visitors learned to check their cups before he poured. In the back was another makeshift altar, ostensibly to worship his pagan gods. It served to freak out the easily offended, though whether that was the chief intent is unclear.

The most objectionable room was unquestionably the bathroom. Those who used it took care to touch as little of it as possible, and would avoid it in the future at all costs. Few used it more than once.

Anything that remained in the apartment for long was covered in a thick layer of cat hair. Overall, the stench of cat urine and (often) the litter box permeated the poorly ventilated apartment. Del would welcome visitors at the kitchen table, sweeping aside handfuls of old clothing from a chair so guests could sit. At night, the lack of light forced him to greet his company in the bedroom, huddling around the TV as if it were a campfire. Del never seemed to feel self-conscious about his surroundings. Anyone visiting was expected to take his hospitality as they found it—and Del always did his best to make his guests feel welcome with coffee and pot.

When Halpern first walked into the Wells Street apartment, her first reaction was understandable: "We've got to get you out of here!" Del resisted, but Halpern implored him. "Del, there are roaches in your dental floss!"

Of course, Del's cats had adjusted well to life in the middle of Old Town. Del loved to tell of the exploits of his cats, who kept the area free of birds. Del proudly told his classes that his cats would kill birds and bring them to him because he thought they must see him as their god. Therefore, whenever a cat brought a dead bird to him, he would do a dance to thank the cat for its gift.

The animals even contributed to his growing legend. Once Del's cat brought in a still-living bird and dropped it at his feet. Del picked it up, telling Halpern, "Let's go take it out [in front of the Wells Street place] so that the cat doesn't get it." The two of them walked out to the street just as two students were walking by. They said "Hi Del," and he said "Hello." As they watched, he gestured with his hand, and the bird flew away. They walked away stunned, eager to pass along the story.

Just as strange was the day he heard one of the cats returning home. It sounded as if it was dragging something, so Del walked out of the bedroom to the front door to investigate. There the cat proudly dropped at his feet a dead octopus. The cat had crept into the kitchen of the Kamehachi Restaurant, the back door of which faced Del's courtyard. One of the chefs had apparently left the octopus sitting out, and Del's cat made the lucky discovery.

Despite Halpern's persistent entreaties, Del refused to move. Finally, they compromised. Halpern would allow him to stay, provided she could hire workers to clean regularly. Unfortunately, the work involved in cleaning the place was more than anyone cared to undertake. Most took one look at the place and refused the job. Finally, she found some cleaners who were willing to try. They were devout Christians, however, and so wound up running away screaming after they discovered the altar and learned that they were in the home of a "devil worshipper."

Halpern was more successful in other areas. Del refused to do laundry, and wore the same clothing until it became too worn, too odiferous, or otherwise objectionable, then threw it out and bought more. Halpern attempted to teach Del a better way. Once, after she got him new clothes, the two of them went to lunch together. While they were eating, Del spilled mustard on his pants. "See?" he showed Halpern. "What's the point?"

Del also refused to open a bank account, and kept his money in his "stash box," a small wooden box that he also used for pot. His reasoning was that if he were walking along the lakefront with his bankbook in his pocket and fell in the water, he might lose the bankbook and never be able to get his money again. Eventually, she convinced him otherwise.

He also eschewed telephones, which meant that anytime Halpern or anyone else had to contact him, it would require an inconvenient drive to Old Town from the Lakeview neighborhood. Del refused to consider a telephone. As he explained it, if the president was speaking on television, and Del didn't like what he was saying, he would be morally obligated to phone in a threat to the White House, and he would undoubtedly be arrested. He felt that he would not be able to control this urge, so he was better off without a telephone.

But Halpern was persistent, and they struck a deal. Del would eventually get a phone, but he had to promise to first call Halpern before he phoned in any threats to the president. In turn, Halpern promised to either talk him down or take responsibility for his incarceration. And so Del got a telephone.

◇

As the ImprovOlympic continued, so did the whispers about a romantic relationship between Del and Halpern. Del did little or nothing to discourage such speculation, preferring to let others make their assumptions. Finally, however, he confessed that he was in love with her, even though he feared rejection was inevitable. Indeed, as much as she liked and admired him, Halpern could not reciprocate.

They sought a way to deal with their feelings. Del felt that they should keep their personal relationship separate from their work, because it was important for them to stay together. If they had an affair, he said either he would kill her or she would be grossed out, so it would be better to avoid the possibility.

Eventually, they reached another agreement. In public, at least when Del was around, Halpern would not be with any other man. Del wanted others to believe that they were a romantic couple; although he would not directly say they were together, he allowed others to make the assumption.

It was a complicated compromise. If she started dating someone, her boyfriend would not be allowed to go anywhere with Del and Halpern. If she could not be his in actuality, Del was determined to give that impression to others. At least in public, he was strong, virile, able to attract a woman more than fifteen years his junior. The arrangement was fine with Halpern, but Del soon found himself in the unfamiliar position of allowing himself to be weak and vulnerable. For someone reputed to be hardened and cynical, Del opened himself up to Halpern early in their relationship. "There was a point in the very beginning where he kissed me a few times and told me he was celibate—this was one of the very first times that he told me that he didn't think anything should happen with us," said Halpern. He was frustrated because, despite his wild sexual reputation, drugs had betrayed his body and he couldn't offer her a real relationship.

Their agreement would soon be put to the test. Halpern began dating one of the students. Del did not react immediately; he had always gotten along with the student in the past and even praised his work. In addition, he proved to be a talented piano player, and would accompany the performers.

Finally, when he moved in with Halpern, it became too much. Del's demeanor around him became insulting, even openly hostile. When the couple broke up, the other students and performers breathed a sigh of relief. "I had a couple of guys say to me that as long as Del is alive, you will never have a boyfriend," said Halpern. From that point on, her relationships with others were kept out of sight.

◇

After *The Time of Your Life*, the world of Chicago theater had opened up for Del. He set his sights on *Hamlet*, which was being staged in 1985 at the Wisdom Bridge Theatre, with direction by Robert Falls and Aidan Quinn in the lead role. Del decided that if he couldn't play the noble son, he might be able to play the wicked father figure.

> I thought "Well, maybe I can play Claudius." So I'd been running into Bob Falls. . . . So I asked to read Claudius. Which I did, rather badly. So I thought "Well, fuck it . . ." Terribly disappointed, but . . . it wasn't the role of Hamlet, just an attempt to get in a damn play. So Charna got a call, would I read for Polonius? I was always annoyed when I'd see a production that they would play this guy like an old fool. Kind of a sight gag who dodders on every now and then, does something dumb, dodders off. I'd play him like an intelligent human being. It turned out that was precisely what Falls wanted. Falls says "What's your conception of the 'words, words, words' scene?" And I said it's like one of those Victorian psychologists; they bring a mad person in and poke him with a needle . . . for Polonius's lecture on man. And Falls got interested at that point. He did a lot of checking around—is Close, you know, can he, like, function? So, ah, it ran a reasonably triumphant run. So I thought, all right, I was getting serious attention from theatre heavyweights; obviously I don't have anything to worry about.[6]

With a $150,000 budget, it was at that time Wisdom Bridge's most expensive production, and director Falls spent six weeks in rehearsals with the cast. Nominally a "modern dress" production, it featured television monitors (King Claudius's initial entrance is staged as a modern media event), slide projectors, and even TV newscasts, with a blaring rock soundtrack. Hamlet begins his famous soliloquy by spray-painting "To be or not to be" on a wall.

In the February 1, 1985, *Chicago Tribune*, reviewer Richard Christiansen wrote:

> Pocked with flaws, streaked with invention and emblazoned with daring . . . *Hamlet* is blessed and cursed by its passionate desire to throw fresh, startling light on Shakespeare's tragedy. . . . When Quinn is focused, when Falls' bold imagination punches the right note and when [Michael] Merritt's design suddenly illuminates the text, this *Hamlet* sparks with excitement. It does not hold together

as a consistent piece of work, but some of its fireworks are memorable, and it passes the crucial test of reminding us once again of what a great play this is.

He noted that the casting of Del was a masterstroke.

Falls has hit home with one exemplary character concept, and, in Del Close, he has a shrewd, seasoned actor who can make it work. Polonius, as Close plays him, has wonderful little bits to emphasize his petty, devious nature. He fiddles absentmindedly with a calculator, records his daughter's conversations, without her knowledge, on a tape recorder, and he officiously shushes Hamlet when the young prince begins to get unruly in a court scene. Close really does freshen and reinforce his lines with remarkable variation of cadence and change of pitch.

When one of the props malfunctioned, Del's Polonius was even able to deliver an often-quoted ad-lib: "Flick thy Bic once again!" (After the show, a woman was reportedly heard asking, "Was that line really in the play?")

With some comparing his Polonius to Henry Kissinger, Del discussed other possible political comparisons in the February 19, 1985, "INC." column in the *Chicago Tribune*: "Claudius is Nixonian, Gertrude is a mixture of Nancy Reagan and Pat Nixon, and Hamlet is like one of those Kennedy kids." Del also discussed delivering some of the most familiar lines in the English language, such as "to thine own self be true," in a way that makes them sound fresh: "The way Aidan and I deal with overly familiar lines is to try and sneak them by you, just say them with emotional honesty and clarity. By the time the line is over, you think 'Hey, I just heard a famous line.' In the theatre it's called 'the illusion of the first time,' making a line sound like it just occurred to the speaker. When I say 'Though this be madness, yet there is method in't,' I originally intended to deliver the first part of the line and then turn to the audience and see if I could get them to say the rest in unison."

Years later, Del explained his approach to the character to Jeffrey Sweet. "Well, I think people make a mistake with Polonius. They think that Polonius is this dumb guy, but he's Claudius's chief advisor, and Claudius is no fool, so he can't be a dumb guy. So I decided I was not going to play him dumb. He's a smart guy who says dumb things. Why does he say dumb things? He's one of these people who babbles in front of royalty, and he *knows* that he's babbling when he's saying this shit in front of royalty, but he cannot be silent in front of royalty. He feels that he has to fill that void."

So impressed was Christiansen by the images of this four-and-a-quarter hour production, he returned six weeks later to see whether the show had grown through the course of its run. The March 17, 1985, *Chicago Tribune* printed his conclusion, confirming "this production's limitations coupled with a quickening of appreciation for its considerable leaps of imagination. . . . [Falls and Merritt] have made some brilliant choices in their concept of the play. . . . Happily, Del Close appears to have resisted the temptation to broaden his already sly, shrewdly hammy portrayal of Polonius, and his line readings are the best in making the Elizabethan language startlingly contemporary. . . . Long after many smoother and better productions have faded in memory, I'll continue to recall vivid bits from this *Hamlet*. . . . This is a *Hamlet* that's going to last, flaws and all."

Critics and audiences alike applauded the production and his Polonius, and he was honored with a Joseph Jefferson Award, the Chicago equivalent of the Tony Award, for his performance.

◈

With his stage career reignited with 1985's *Hamlet* in Chicago, he took on another role later that year for the Steppenwolf Theatre and director Frank Galati, playing stuffy millionaire Mr. Kirby in their production of Kaufman and Hart's *You Can't Take It with You*. The show, which opened on December 1, also featured Jeff Perry, John Mahoney, Amy Morton, Randall Arney, and Laurie Metcalf. The entire nineteen-person production was praised by critic Richard Christiansen in the December 2, 1985, *Chicago Tribune* for its mixture of the screwball and the sentimental.

> The Steppenwolf Theatre version . . . captures both the timelessness of the play's immense good will and the innocence of its era, when we could still make jokes about Communism and capitalism and being on relief. . . . The play and the production keeps us in their grip from start to finish. One minute we're weeping with laughter as [Bradley] Mott throws the stuffed-shirt Mr. Kirby Sr. [Del Close] to

the floor in an impromptu demonstration of Roman wrestling, and the next we're brushing aside a tear as Grandpa gathers the family around the dinner table and gently asks God to give them His blessing. Lovely, just lovely.

Del followed *You Can't Take It with You* with a role in *The Tempest* at the Goodman the following spring, again directed by Robert Falls. His theatrical revival was obviously moving into high gear. By the mid-1980s, Del had been liberated. Although he could never forget his past, his father's memory would never again oppress him so deeply. He was no longer a slave to his addictions. He had found a new direction and a means to pursue his life's work in improvisation. He had found a new partner, and if it was not a perfect relationship, he could live with it. And now, he had found a revitalized acting career, winning awards for his role in the greatest play of them all, *Hamlet*.

Del had transformed his character, often thought a doddering fool, into a wise, if flawed, counselor. Del empathized with young Hamlet, and aspired to Claudius, but would find his salvation in Polonius.

19

The Return of the Harold,
the Baron's Barracudas, and Charna

Even though his acting career was rapidly catching fire, Del still had not forsaken improvisation. It seemed that his success in one area only served to stoke his creativity in other areas.

By early 1985, Del had begun working on a new approach to the Harold. Many of the earlier students, including Bob Odenkirk, had drifted off, while newer ones were climbing on board. New in class were Mark Beltzman from Detroit, Chris Barnes, newly arrived from New York, an actor calling himself J.J. (John Marshall Jones) who had worked with Del in *Hamlet*, and two locals who had recently roomed together at a Loyola University program in Italy, David Pasquesi and Joel Murray.

During their first workshop at Crosscurrents, Pasquesi and Murray received a suggestion for a scene about two men suffering from hangovers after a party. Later, unaware that they had previously performed on a cable program, Del told the class, "Look at these guys! They're slow, they're not going for jokes!" When the class finished, Del took Murray aside. "Well, I have a long history with your brothers, and they've done very well by me, and I would offer you a scholarship if you would like to come here and take the classes. I really like that Pasquesi guy. I'll tell you what, I'll give you both classes for half price." Although Murray had just gone from an offer of free classes to half price, Pasquesi was delighted, and both of them committed to studying with Del.

Del's determination to devise a foolproof method of presenting Harolds saw him develop numerous variations on the Time Dash. The structure was becoming more like a pyramid, with many scenes at the base, tapering off to one or two at its closing. Del wanted to use the vast array of games in his arsenal. Even the term "game" was limiting for the Harold, because it could envelop everything from Spolin's examples to one-time devices developed in front of audiences. The best games would illuminate a theme, make connections between scenes, challenge actors to think on a higher level.

Del still demanded that students work at the top of their intelligence, and he did not suffer fools. He usually offered a short break in the middle of his three-hour workshops. But one night, shortly after the second half began, there was a stranger sitting with the group. Del stopped his lecture in mid-sentence.

"I'm sorry, but are you in this class?" he asked warily.

The stranger admitted that he wasn't, but explained that he was a friend of one of the other students. The other student spoke up, saying that he had thought it would be OK if his friend sat in. Based on Del's reaction, it obviously wasn't. Del explained that it was a closed class, but the intruder did not move. "We're trying to build trust within the class, so that we can make some advances. Push the work forward," Del continued, still calm.

Inexplicably, the stranger remained.

"Lose the fucking friend!" snapped Del, his voice beginning to build in anger.

Silence. Finally, Del had had enough. "Of course, if some people are not able to understand that, then I'm just going to have to throw out the fucking rude asshole!"

The rest of the students were frozen as they watched, yet unable to look away from the confrontation. Del was apoplectic as he finally erupted.

"Fuck off, turkey!"

At last, the stranger slunk away silently, Del glaring, and every other eye in the classroom upon him. As he left the theater, Del began to calm down. "Rude fucker!" he muttered, and resumed his lecture to the relieved but still tense class.

Many of the students in that workshop session cited it as the most memorable, if frightening, moment in class, watching the color rise up from his neck and screaming the fierce *"Fuck off, turkey!"*

Such incidents were highly rare. Crosscurrents was his turf, and he always asked the class's permission before visitors were admitted. There were ample rewards for the students who stuck with it, who would retire to the bar for hours after class, most nights trying to comprehend what had just happened. More than once he would leave them gasping, "I don't believe this! He just handed us the whole key to comedy!" Favored students would stop by his apartment, often bringing a joint, like an offering, in exchange for more knowledge.

Del usually needed a ride to Crosscurrents from Old Town, and several students witnessed a strange phenomenon in the busy neighborhood. When picking him up or driving him home, it seemed like his students *always* got a parking place outside his entranceway. "Every time you drove him somewhere, you would pull up and it was like a bad Hollywood movie. All of a sudden there was a parking space big enough for a Winnebago," joked Murray.

The wisdom that Del imparted during his classes had an important effect on Murray, who would go on to be a regular on *Dharma and Greg* and *Still Standing*, always playing a character not far removed from his real-life persona. "Wear your character like a thin veil," Del advised Murray. "Find out what's inside you and what's true, as compared to working so hard on the fake. Nobody's going to pay you to be a sixty-year-old man." Murray took his advice to heart, and has worked steadily ever since.

Del's influence on Pasquesi would become even more important as the two of them spent more time together before and after shows at Crosscurrents. One evening, before a show, Del approached him as he was drinking a large glass of liquor. "You're pretty good. You ever try it without that?" asked Del. Rather than suggesting that he quit, Del challenged him to stop using alcohol as a crutch. "See if you can do it without that, and then you'll know it's you, and not the liquor." From then on, Pasquesi would never go onstage at Crosscurrents while drinking.

About four years later, Pasquesi noticed that his drinking was causing problems and, based on Del's experiences at the Schick Clinic in Texas, began to consider aversion therapy. He spoke to Del, who allayed his fears in what was as close to proselytizing as he ever allowed himself: "Just because you're not drinking doesn't mean you're not going to be an asshole." Pasquesi was comforted by his advice and stopped drinking on May 1, 1988. In ten years, Del had gone from a stumbling drunk to what was, for him, a champion of sobriety.

During a break in another class, Bill Russell, a new student at the time, experienced the more mystical side of Del. He had recently found the Committee's *The Wide World of War* record album, and was particularly taken with the scene about the junkie buying pot and a lighter, to be told, "You can't sell fire! It's one of the four elements!" Although there were no credits listed, Russell thought he recognized the voice, and so approached Del during a break outside Crosscurrents.

"Say, Del, when you were in San Francisco—"

"I was with the Committee, yes."

"Well, there's this—"

"Oh, *The Wide World of War.*"

"Uh-huh . . . I really liked—"

"Oh, the bit about selling fire! That was one of my favorites too."

At that point, Russell walked away, taken aback. He decided that either one of Del's many skills was the ability to read minds or he had simply had many similar conversations with other people.

Although Del's principal work was with the Harold, it was a broad enough umbrella for a variety of experiments and theories. If he was reading a psychological text with a principle that might apply to a scene, or if a science fiction novel was rooted in gestalt intelligence that might be applied to a game, Del would walk into class that evening ready to try it. Every workshop was different.

Finally, he decided that the work was good enough to perform for audiences. With Halpern, they put together the first house team of the ImprovOlympic, consisting of Mark Beltzman, Chris Barnes, Tara Gallagher, J.J., Joel Murray, David Pasquesi, Jade Wells (briefly), and myself. The new team would be the tent pole for the new franchise, performing alongside teams being developed in classes.

The members sat in the bar to decide on an appropriate name for the fledgling team. Del had previously recounted a story about a phone call he had received years earlier in New York. He was asked, "Can you do a song in the voice of a fish that sounds like Bela Lugosi?" Of course, Del said yes, and soon found himself in a recording studio, performing a song titled "I'm the Toughest Creature in the Sea" as Baron Barracuda, villain on the *Diver Dan* children's TV series, when the original voice performer was unavailable for the record. Gallagher suggested they

An early grouping of the Baron's Barracudas, circa May 1985, featuring *(back, left to right)* author Kim "Howard" Johnson, Becky Claus, J.J. (John Marshall Jones), David Pasquesi, *(front, left to right)* Chris Barnes, Mark Beltzman, and Honor Finnegan. Missing: Joel Murray, Tara Gallagher. (COURTESY OF MARK BELTZMAN)

call themselves "the Baron's Barracudas." Although Gallagher did not remain long with the group, the name stuck.

Del would introduce each performance of the Harold by talking about the work and performing stand-up. Then two or three teams, including the Baron's Barracudas, would each perform a Harold. The audience would then vote for their favorite, and all the players would perform a group game like freeze tag.

The competitive aspect of the show bothered Del at first, but he soon reconciled his feelings. "The reason we remember the ancient Greek plays is because they were winners at competitions," he would explain.

The work drew the attention of some of the Second City's young turks, giving Del's upstarts even greater confidence. They were attempting something new nearly every show—and succeeding. Del was giving his students ridiculous assignments every week in class, dealing with areas such as archetypes or invocations. "It was blowing us away that we were pulling it off!" recalled Murray. One night, Del told the group "All right, we have twenty-one minutes left. I want you to do a twenty-one-minute Harold." As the performers finished the Harold, he pointed to his watch and said, "Twenty-one minutes. Who's got a joint?"

◆

Most of the Chicago improvisational community seemed to drop by for the Tuesday night contests. The audience scored each team from one to five points. The crowd soon began looking for more than simple laughs,

The Baron's Barracudas, phase two: *(back, left to right)* David Pasquesi, Steve Burrows, Brian Crane, Bill Russell, *(middle, left to right)* Judy Nielsen, John Judd, Honor Finnegan, *(front)* author Kim "Howard" Johnson. (COURTESY OF CHARNA HALPERN)

applauding for connections and intelligent gameplay, and hissing for negation. "It was like playing Operation onstage. It was fun, the whole community supporting each other that way," said Murray.

One initial difficulty was that there were simply not enough players trained at a high enough level to mount more teams. In the beginning, the Baron's Barracudas usually faced either Apocalypso, a team assembled from a more recent group of students, or Pigwings, a team of performers from the nascent Improv Institute, who were talented improvisers, though not trained by Del.

Even the Baron's Barracudas experienced some growing pains. Beltzman, Barnes, and J.J. left when they had the opportunity to join a Second City touring company. Joel Murray left temporarily to shoot a film, and Halpern merged what was left of the Baron's Barracudas with Apocalypso. Surprisingly, the new Baron's Barracudas, consisting of Stephen Burrows, Brian E. Crane, Honor Finnegan, John Judd, Joel Murray, Judy Nielsen, David Pasquesi, Bill Russell, and myself, became just as strong, or even stronger, than the originals.

Murray returned and was immediately hired for the Second City touring company. Pasquesi continued working with Del, but was eventually hired by the Second City. Torn between their loyalty to Del and their desire for a paying gig, they found themselves returning to Crosscurrents as time allowed. Nielsen eventually bowed out, but the core of the team remained firm, and Pasquesi continued to perform whenever the touring company's schedule allowed.

Del's dispute with Sahlins continued from a distance, but he was confident in his own skills. When Sahlins argued that improvisation didn't work more than half the time, Del would counter with "Well, we just put up three more Harolds that all worked, so I think his average is quite off!" Del never objected when one of his actors was hired by the Second City, however, knowing the value of a paying gig.

◆

As a venue, Crosscurrents was less than upscale. The windowless theater was painted black and poorly lit, which no doubt covered a multitude of health and building code violations. The performers overcame such physical limitations as a pole stuck near center stage, a primitive sound and light system, and a particularly memorable evening in which a rat dashed across the stage, with a cat in hot pursuit.

Each Tuesday and Saturday, the Baron's Barracudas would compete against other teams, often sharing the space with dubious blues bands and an eclectic mixture of stage shows (including the long-running *A Couple of Blaguards*, with the then-unknown Frank and Malachi McCourt). At one point, during failed negotiations with Crosscurrents, classes were held in various bars along Clark Street. One memorable evening, the class was left standing outside a bar just north of the Metro, while Halpern negotiated with the bartender to allow us to hold classes there. But somehow, the classes would always return to Crosscurrents.

The Baron's Barracudas began to develop the group mind for which Del had long been working. I often found myself serving as a narrator for our various spot operas or musicals, and was astonished at how the group was able to comply with the most perplexing challenges. If an actor needed a rollaway couch, three of us would instantly appear to somersault into place, opening the bed.

One of the more misused rules of improvisation is "There are no rules," but students study long and hard to master the other rules before they dare to implement this one. Ironically, "no rules" is actually a rule based on agreement: if the actors find themselves agreeing to disregard a rule, they may proceed as they like. The Baron's Barracudas found themselves disregarding rules with abandon, and they made it work. In one scene, Brian Crane was trying to sell a car to Steve Burrows, but Burrows said, "That's not a car." Crane mimes a book and responds, "According to my improv book here, that's a denial." Burrows responds, "That's not a book, that's a hamster." They had built a scene on negation, but it worked because they had obviously agreed to play the denial game.

Spontaneity was often the key to a successful Harold, which helped support Del's eternal argument with Sahlins. Some things worked extremely well when improvised, but could not be successfully duplicated in subsequent Harolds. One evening, when a scene had obviously come to an end, I stepped behind a flat, placed both of my shoes on top of the flat, and began a scene called "The Nike Family." Other shoes soon joined the scene, and even got cheers from the audience. A couple of weeks later, needing to end a scene but stuck for an idea, the Nike Family returned. The reaction was still positive, but the sense of invention was missing. Finally, weeks later, the Nike Family reluctantly returned for the third time. The audience was amused, but the repetition had drained it of the creative energy. Still, Del appreciated the thought process that created such games.

> What we want people to understand is the way Viola thought when she invented her games, the way I thought when I invented my games. We want our students to understand that it's a matter of instantly adapting something to the circumstances, so that no game is ever done without the knowledge that this game is being played to illuminate a particular point. And that point is usually the theme that the audience suggested.
>
> There's a game that came up maybe three times in one of the Harolds which became progressively less interesting because it was repeated. It's a game where people offstage use shoes on one of the upper levels of the stage. So you just see a shoe up there talking, and another shoe—we'd call them the Nike family. You know, Mr. Nike, Mrs. Nike and the children. And another peculiar shoe will come in, and they'll have a reaction to it, you know, basically just using the shoes as props. That's not a game you'd ever teach to someone—it just happens.[1]

While the original group felt like a collection of very talented individuals, the new Baron's Barracudas were a team. Halpern continued to hustle for opportunities. One evening, she walked up to us and proudly announced, "We're going to London!" Apparently, a wealthy woman from Evanston had enjoyed the show so much that she vowed to take us to England to perform. The trip failed to materialize (though not until after Burrows had borrowed money for the trip from his grandmother).

But the Harold was growing. One summer, a group of students from Yale joined us, calling itself the Purple Crayon; their Ivy League competition was written up in the *New York Times*.

Del began inviting guests to the classes to share their expertise in different areas. Jamie Swise, who had by then developed his own line of games, came to discuss their relevance to the type of improvisation we were doing. Actor Richard Henzel conducted a session on masks (an aspect of Keith Johnstone's book *Impro* in which Del did not feel skilled). Michael Flores, whose knowledge of psychotronic films and Japanese anime appealed to Del, came in for a session, but none of the guests would stay long; Del seemed to best use them to spark his own ideas. (Del went on to participate in Flores's Psychotronic Film Society and the Church of the Sub-Genius for several years, even writing a regular column for the newsletter.)

The Baron's Barracudas began teaching and directing other, younger groups, with talents like Tim Meadows, Mick Napier, and Andy Dick. On Tuesday nights, Bonnie Hunt and Mike Myers were among the then–Second City actors who would bring along teams. Certainly the most celebrity-heavy was the week that Bill Murray brought in actors to learn improvisation.

One day, Del reported to Halpern that he was going to have to throw himself in front of a bus. He had gotten a notice from the IRS informing him that since he had failed to file his income taxes for several years, he now owed $20,000 in back taxes. Del had never bothered to pay his taxes because he never thought he would live long enough for the IRS to catch up with him. Halpern accompanied him to a meeting with the IRS, and afterward, they had dinner with Bill Murray. Halpern brought up the IRS matter, and Murray was happy to loan "Uncle Del" the $20,000. Del felt an obligation to pay him back, and eventually they worked out an agreement. Murray was interested in the idea of improvising a film, and knew that there was no one better to teach it than Del. Murray would bring in a group for a week of training with Del, and in return, they would call it even.

Murray's group included his brother Brian Doyle-Murray, C. Thomas Howell, Jamie Gertz, Bud Cort, Olan Shepherd, and Dana Delaney, along with Sydney Pollack, who would presumably direct the resulting film. They worked throughout the week, developing a film story about a convict released from prison who returns home. At the end of the week, the Baron's Barracudas joined the Hollywood actors in a lengthy workshop, eventually mixing the groups and splitting them in half to perform two Harolds. Though they all enjoyed the experience, plans for the improvised film were ultimately shelved. "They were better actors than you guys, but not better improvisers," Del told the Baron's Barracudas after the Hollywood group had left. "The acting in their scenes was better, but the improvising wasn't any better."

◆

Del usually delivered an original monologue before each performance. The subjects ranged from everyday frustrations to profound thoughts. But on January 28, 1986, the mood was different. The space shuttle *Challenger* had exploded earlier that day, killing all seven astronauts, including schoolteacher Christa McAuliffe. Though an audience had shown up, it did not appear to be a night for comedy. Even the Second City had closed the day John F. Kennedy was assassinated, and the mood was much the same.

When some of the performers assumed we would cancel the evening's performance, Del's immediate reaction was "Why would we cancel?" One of them said that because all of these people had just died on the space shuttle, nobody was in a laughing mood. "Precisely the night for comedy!" responded Del. He knew that he could go up onstage on an average night and get laughs with little effort. But tonight? People were challenging him to go out and get a laugh, so he knew he must. In addition, he felt responsibility for his performers. He couldn't send them up there on their own without some assistance. The elephant in the room that evening had to be addressed, or the cathartic effects of the comedy would be stifled. And so, at the appointed time, Del walked onstage.

"When you were children, how many of you had little CO_2 rockets?" he asked them. The audience was taken aback. A few of them knew where this was going, and laughed nervously.

"How many of you got bored after a while with CO_2 rockets?" The laughter began to grow, and a few people raised their hands.

"And how many of you people, when you got bored, taped a grasshopper, or another living thing, to the CO_2 rocket?"

Mildred Close, still active, sharp-witted, and funny in her eighties. (COURTESY OF CHARNA HALPERN)

And the laughter began to flow. It was a healing laughter, which let the audience members release their feelings since learning of the *Challenger* explosion, and led them to an understanding of human nature. It was ultimately inspirational. He went on to tell of his experiences as a test subject for NASA, being injected with LSD-25 and laughing hysterically at the words "chicken salad sandwich." He had won the audience over, and the improvisers went on to a successful night of Harolds.

It was a few weeks later, on March 8, that a more personal tragedy struck. Mildred Close died in a retirement home in Abilene, Kansas. Halpern received the call the next morning, and since Del still did not then have a telephone, she asked Pasquesi, who lived near his apartment on Wells Street, to convey the sad news. He ran down the street and knocked on Del's door. He said, "Del, I have some bad news for you." Del responded, "No you don't. My mother's dead." Somehow he knew, even though he didn't have a phone. As he explained, "I was run over by a psychic freight train last night." Pasquesi was shocked, but also relieved that he didn't have to deliver the information.

There was a show scheduled at Crosscurrents that Saturday evening, but no one expected Del to attend. Nevertheless, he took the stage to deliver a memorable stand-up eulogy. "My mother died this morning," Del told the audience. "She was eighty-five. And this is the day before my birthday. I figure it was either extreme consideration on her part or extreme viciousness. I'm sure she didn't want to screw up my birthday, but nevertheless, she wanted to make it easy to remember."

He went on to recall his mother, the funny one of the family—how, just two years before she died, she had written a poem about losing your memory and mailed it to him. It was, he noted proudly, eight stanzas long and perfectly rhymed. And one last time, whether as an invocation or a tribute, he recited, "Dainty determined Demona, daily defying death, as she takes her own life in her hands and loops the loop in a hollow ball."

It was funny, but as Del would later put it, "not a bunch of grotesque death jokes. It was sort of a comic tribute to the kind of imagery I had inherited from my mother. . . . I like to do stand-up comedy dealing with crises."[2] Various people—including Carol Burnett and one of Del's heroes, Lenny Bruce—have been credited with saying that comedy is tragedy plus time. With the *Challenger* disaster and his mother's death, Del had been able to remove the element of time from the equation.

◇

Not long afterward, Del finally consented to moving from the Wells Street apartment. Most of his work was now being done at Crosscurrents, and Halpern lived near the cabaret theater. Del had run out of reasons for staying in Old Town, but still resisted. "It'll be too difficult. I have too many books; it'd be like moving the Chicago Public Library."

Halpern finally put her foot down. She hated bugs, and was scared to death to go inside. She finally begged *"Please* let me move you!" and found him a large first-floor apartment directly across the street from her place. Del never saw it until the day he moved in.

Halpern recruited several students with cars (myself included) to help with the move. There were countless boxes of books, scattered photos, and other memorabilia, though little in the way of clothing or kitchen supplies. When most of the larger items had already been moved, the floor was littered with fascinating scraps of paper, photos, and unusual knickknacks. Chris Barnes, Richard Laible, and I were picking up items one evening, ready to move another load, and were astonished by what was scattered about.

There was a primitive, makeshift projector that he explained he had used for light shows for the Grateful Dead. Laible found a color photo of Del with an attractive dark-haired woman. ("Who's this, Del?" "That's my ex-wife." "She was really good-looking." "I know, that's why I married the bitch.") And stuck partially beneath a radiator was a faded color Polaroid. On closer examination, it was Del with John Belushi. "I think I'll keep this one," he declared.

After most of his things had been removed, Burrows, Laible, and Russell (with Del's permission) went through the old apartment. Russell recalled one lasting souvenir: Burrows took a Polaroid picture of Del's refrigerator freezer, which had never been defrosted. Del had propped a can of Diet Coke between the top and bottom layers of frost to keep it from freezing completely solid.

The new apartment was located directly across from Halpern's place on Racine Avenue, just north of Belmont. Crosscurrents was four and a half blocks east. Racine was quiet and residential, while Belmont was bustling. At the southwest corner of the intersection with Racine was the decrepit Bel-Ray Hotel. The southeast corner was the site of a 7-Eleven, which Del would come to rely on for cigarettes, snacks, and occasionally meals.

The stretch of Belmont along Racine and Sheffield was a neighborhood in transition. Belmont was feeling the effects of Wrigleyville's gentrification, though it would be slower to change. Del usually favored the small Mexican restaurants over the other ethnic restaurants and pizza places, though he would sometimes pick up a deli sandwich or coffee elsewhere. Of all the businesses along Belmont, however, there was one clear favorite: The Stars Our Destination bookstore. Now he could avail himself of science fiction just a couple of blocks from his home.

The new apartment, a first-floor walk-up, was bigger, more spacious and open, with higher ceilings than the previous one. There were so many walls that even he didn't have enough books to cover them all. The front door opened into a large living room area, which for a long time was filled with boxes from the move; it was literally years before they were all unpacked. The far end of the living room joined a dining area with what was presumably intended to be a wet bar. Del converted this to an altar, where he would keep incense, statues, and other Wiccan objects. Del burrowed into the bedroom off the kitchen area in the back.

Much as she tried, Halpern could not convince Del to use a bed, and his mattress would always remain on the floor ("He wouldn't ever go for it," said Halpern resignedly). He would lie on the mattress reading, able to watch TV at the same time. He was happy. Everything he needed was no more than a short walk away, including Halpern. He settled in nicely. Halpern was right.

Although their relationship continued to cause complications, they both reaped the benefits. She was opening his eyes to the traditional, middle-class world, and Del was discovering that—maybe—it wasn't that bad. She tried to show him that he could live in a cleaner apartment and do laundry. She bought him a big TV, a remote control, and a reading pillow. He was amazed by it all.

In turn, Del gave her theater instant credibility, and would take improvisation to the next level under the auspices of the ImprovOlympic. Now that Halpern lived across the street, she could keep an eye on Del, and be there when he needed her. Of course, any romantic entanglements might be scrutinized by Del. He knew that she was free to date whomever she pleased, but he didn't want to have it going on around him.

There were no more suicide attempts. Del explained to her that he was a different person under different drugs. When he was drunk, he was violent and angry. He was another person when he was on speed. But when he was smoking pot, he liked himself, and he felt that he was a better human being than when he was straight.

◇

A couple of years after the incident with the piano player, the possibility of a serious relationship arose for Halpern. An artist named Steve volunteered to paint some backdrops for a show, and Del suggested that he stay at Halpern's place during the week that it would take to finish the work. The two of them became infatuated with each other, and he invited her to Wisconsin for the weekend. The night she left, Del was given a few hits of speed. He took them all at once and called Halpern, threatening to leave if she didn't come back. "I had nightmares, I was crying. I was really upset," said Halpern.

She cut short the weekend and returned to a very emotional Del. She learned that Del had not shown up for his class, and an assistant who went to Del's house had found him crying. She ran to Del's place and walked into an empty apartment. Del had thrown everything out of his apartment in an attempt to clean it. There was nothing in the living room but a chair, in which Del was sitting when she came in. Crying, he asked how Wisconsin was. He was crashing on speed, so Halpern tried to cheer him up. Del continued to tell her how he loved her. When she heard him saying, "I'm not sure I want you to be with somebody else, and maybe we should be together," she was taken aback. "There was a point where he wasn't sure. And I was scared, because it could have been

Del Close and Charna Halpern.
After a sometimes-tumultuous
period of adjustment, they
found a way to make it all work.
(COURTESY OF CHARNA HALPERN)

really bad. I didn't feel that we should be together," said Halpern. She called a student to help put his belongings back in his apartment. When she was ready to leave Del, he was still very depressed, so she invited him back to her apartment for the night. He came but was depressed and still crying. This was not the man she knew. He kept repeating that he loved her.

The next afternoon, she received a phone call from Del and a psychiatrist friend of his named Jeff, asking her to meet with them at Del's place. She returned to Del's apartment and sat next to Del on the side of his bed, while Jeff sat on a chair facing the pair. They were about to have a counseling session.

Del was still extremely depressed, telling her he loved her and didn't want to lose her to anyone. Halpern said she loved him too, but that he had made a lifestyle choice whereby he planned to be alone. She explained that she wanted to get married someday—and was not celibate. However, she promised him that their feelings for each other were very special and they would always be together, no matter what.

The next day, Halpern got another call from Del. It was the same man she had known before. He was fine and chipper. When she dropped over, he lifted his shirt and showed her lines all over his chest made by a sharp knife. She was upset and asked what that was about. He said that when a shaman is stuck somewhere, as he was, there is an inner journey from which he must escape. He escaped and this ritual was part of it. He was now fine, and nothing of the previous few days was ever mentioned again. Del liked Steve, but when she became involved with him, he disowned Steve as a friend. Steve agreed that as long as Del was alive, she would never have a boyfriend.

◇

Though she had some trepidation, Halpern decided that it was time for Del to meet her traditional Jewish parents. Although she wanted them to like each other, she also knew the chances of that were slim. Del was a former junkie who loved to get a rise out of people. Halpern was late, and when she arrived at That Steak Joynt, Del was already sitting with her parents. Del had rolled up his sleeves and was showing them his very prominent track marks. Halpern hastened to add that Del was no longer shooting up. "I know," her mother said. "He told me."

Her parents wondered about his favorite comedians, asking, "Do you like Jerry Lewis at all?" "No." "Why not?" "Because he's Jewish." Halpern bit her tongue. She knew Del was only making such statements to provoke a reaction. Fortunately, so did her parents, and they took it in the spirit that Del had intended.

While sitting at the table, Del noticed a ring that her father was wearing. Del said, "Oh, I see you're a Mason." Her father acknowledged that he was, and Del asked what degree he was. Upon learning that he'd attained the thirty-third degree, Del said, "Oh, my. I never even got that high. Well, Charna, you'll be amazed to know your father is even more of a magician than I am. If you think I'm powerful, you should see the things your dad does." She didn't know what he was talking about, and Del told her that being a Mason was very mystical and secretive. Her father sat there silently when she questioned him. Del became more excited. "Your father can't answer your questions because he is sworn to secrecy. But if you think I am scary, you should know the truth about your father. In fact, *I am your father!*" She was frightened and confused. She looked at her father for some assurance that Del was crazy. Her father looked back and shrugged: "Well, you wanted me to like him."

Against all odds, they became friends, and managed to get along through the years. Her parents figured their daughter would be afraid to tell them how she felt about Del, so another night at dinner, her mother opened the subject by saying, "Del, Jack and I want you to know that if you'd like to marry our daughter, it's OK with us." Without missing a beat, while eating his soup, Del replied, "*No*, thank you."

Despite any romantic feelings, they were becoming family. At holidays, they were always together. Halpern realized that Del was increasingly relying on her in his day-to-day life, but she didn't mind being his buffer against the outside world. She knew that Del needed to be sheltered, needed to exist on a different plane. She kept one foot on the ground, because if she let go, she felt like he would fly away. She would take him to a movie or dinner, make sure his house was clean, make sure he got his medicine and other important things. When his microwave or air-conditioner was broken, she would take care of it for him. In addition, she got an accountant to do his taxes so that he wouldn't get in trouble with the IRS again.

She also helped him grow more self-reliant. He learned that he could get to auditions by himself, on time, and remember to bring his headshots. He began taking his own messages. When she began serving as his manager, she would set up his appointments, but eventually, he began to take charge of his own life. "He'd say 'I have an audition today,' and I could go 'Really? Cool!' And he always made it. So I did teach him to live a little bit normal in this world."

Halpern said that Del was proud of a psychic link that existed between the two of them. One incident occurred after they had been working together for a few years. Halpern had hired Shelley Berman to teach a 9 A.M. workshop at Crosscurrents. There was no plan for Del to be there, as he always kept late hours.

At that time, Halpern was practicing meditation. The night before the workshop, she'd lain down on the bed and closed her eyes to begin to meditate. As soon as she closed her eyes, she was certain she saw Del's face clearly in her mind. It spooked her and she opened her eyes, but when she closed them again, there he was. She decided to let this continue. "In my mind, I said 'Is this you?' He said 'Yes.' I couldn't understand how I could even see this face, as I hadn't even begun to get into the meditation." Finally, she said, "If this is really you, come to Crosscurrents in the morning and then I'll believe it."

The next morning, Del was standing in front of Crosscurrents when she arrived. She asked him to come into the lobby to talk. He didn't seem surprised and just shook his head yes. She had to know why he was there, so she said in a vague manner, "Did you by any chance visit me last night?" He said, "No, but you visited me." He shook his head and continued, "Let me tell you something that a wise teacher once said to me. If you don't know what you're doing, don't fuck with it." With that, he got up and left the building.

20

The Brain of the Galaxy

Del had been a comic book fan while growing up in Kansas. He was lukewarm about superhero comic books, though he loved *Tales from the Crypt* and other EC comics of the early 1950s. Except for underground comics of the late 1960s and early 1970s, his enthusiasm for the form lay dormant. But in the early 1980s, as the Harold and Del were revitalizing each other, Mike Gold, John Ostrander, and I reawakened it.

Mike Gold was a fixture of the Chicago counterculture from an early age, most prominently as Abbie Hoffman's assistant during the Chicago Seven conspiracy trial that followed the 1968 Democratic National Convention in Chicago. Del first met Gold at a conspiracy trial fundraiser held at the Second City in 1970; John Belushi had contributed a pirate shirt to the fashion auction, and when no one bid on it, Del gave it to Gold.

In 1983, Gold cofounded an independent comic book company called First Comics. One of the writers was John Ostrander, a playwright and actor who had befriended Del during *A Christmas Carol*. Ostrander was confident he could interest Del in writing with him. Del was intrigued by the potential of comic books, feeling very strongly that although they were looked down upon by the mainstream, they were a genuine American art form.

Ostrander created a hero called *Grimjack* for First Comics, but Gold rebuffed Ostrander's ideas for an anthology backup feature. In desperation, Ostrander blurted out, "I can approach Del Close and see if he's interested in cowriting." Gold suddenly became very interested. Ostrander was experienced enough to make certain that they would have a publishable script for *Munden's Bar*, the name of their new series. "The whole basis for Munden's was a bizarre bar owned by Grimjack in the ever-shifting multidimensional city of Cynosure, a place Del had been living for years," cracked Gold.

Munden's Bar was inspired by the Bucket of Suds, a late-night, weekends-only establishment that did not appear to have been cleaned in decades. The owner distilled much of the liquor, and drinks were ordered by taste rather than by traditional names. Rows of ancient, unmarked bottles and Mason jars lined the shelves in front of the long, browning mirror. The customers included several prominent rock stars who made it a point to visit the Bucket whenever they were in town. Although Del was sober, he was more than familiar with quirky little bars, and had enough raw material from his drinking years for endless stories.

While never a disciplined writer, the ideas flowed out of him, and the two made a good team. They often met at the Old Town Ale House, because the idea of writing a bar story while they were in a bar appealed to them. Other times, they would work at Del's Wells Street apartment, but Ostrander was always careful to use the bathroom elsewhere. "I used the toilet there once, and never again," he noted. "Of course, Del was cackling at me, 'Now don't let the rats bite you!'"

Munden's Bar continued for several years, but Del's interest in it eventually faded. Deadlines and Del didn't always get along well together, and sometimes Ostrander would have to write solo. The comic book series was just one more example of his struggle to finish things. Gold's transition from First Comics in Chicago to DC Comics in New York gave Del enough reason to step back from the series, but he was growing bored with comics in general.

◈

I had been a student of his for more than two years by this point, and our mutual enjoyment of edgier entertainment helped Del and me forge our friendship. When he moved to his new apartment on Racine Avenue, across from Halpern, he was only two blocks from my apartment. I began to take advantage of Del's always-warm hospitality, and my proximity seemed to help him adjust to the new neighborhood.

Because he had no telephone at first, I had no way to call, but he seemed to enjoy my dropping by, often with books or videos. I can never remember a time when he didn't seem genuinely glad to see me at the door. Kicking aside the piles of unwanted mail that had accumulated under the mail slot in the front door, he would invite me in, usher me past the still-unpacked boxes in the living and dining rooms to the kitchen and bedroom in the back of the apartment—the only rooms where he had furniture.

He would always offer his guests coffee, which he would brew himself, and often a hit of pot. He seemed to keep the new place clean enough for guests to accept his offerings, although he once announced of his coffee, "I have figured out how to brew it to have the maximum diuretic effect."

One day, I brought him a few copies of a DC title called *Swamp Thing*, transformed by British writer Alan Moore into a superior work of horror. I returned later to find Del effusive in his praise of *Swamp Thing*. One storyline dealt with a convention of serial killers, a subject that increasingly interested him. Another story, dealing with aliens, was a thinly disguised Pogo Possum story, and Del quickly admitted that he was in tears by the time he had finished it (it was one of the few times I ever saw his emotions flowing so freely). More, he begged. Bring me more.

Comic books were undergoing a renaissance of sorts at that time. In addition to *Swamp Thing*, DC Comics was publishing *Watchmen*, Moore's innovative adult take on the superhero genre, and Frank Miller's four-part graphic novel *Batman: The Dark Knight Returns*, which was also setting the world of superhero comics on its ear with its grim and gritty tale of a middle-aged Batman forced to come out of retirement. Del particularly relished a scene of the Joker killing Cub Scouts with poisoned cotton candy. Comics were becoming hipper than ever, he was discovering, and he would once again become a part of it.

Although they were no longer cowriting *Munden's Bar* stories, Del and Ostrander were still keen to work together on the right project. While Ostrander was visiting Gold in Connecticut, they came up with the idea for a new series during a rainy walk around a duck pond. They wanted to do a horror anthology, with psychological rather than traditional horror, raising the bar with each successive issue. They spent

Del finally met Don
Simpson, one of the
artists on *Wasteland*,
in 1994.
(AUTHOR'S COLLECTION)

several hours working out the format. Instead of an artist-of-the-month, there would be a set team of artists, starting with David Lloyd (of *V for Vendetta*), George Freeman, William Messner-Loebs, Don Simpson, and color artist Lovern Kindzierski.

"As we got together with Del, it eventually became what we decided was black hole comedy, in that sometimes the humor was so dark that no laughter actually escaped the event horizon," noted Ostrander.

The new series would be titled *Wasteland*, although Del hated the name. His choice of titles was "Misogynist Funnies," but Gold and Ostrander pointed out that they would rather alienate people *after* they had bought the book.

The idea was for Del to cowrite one or two of the three stories each issue. The horror stories would differ from more typical mainstream horror, however. "We're calling attention to that which is horrific in our own society," explained Del. "[It's] horror as a way of looking at the world . . . the horror of bureaucracy, of late-night 7-11s."[1] For DC, *Wasteland* felt like an anarchic, underground, independent comic.

In addition to the horror of the everyday, however, he was focused on the supernatural: "I have more intimate familiarity with [the supernatural aspect] than John does, being a witch, so a lot of the stuff I expect I will be doing is not precisely what you'd call pagan propaganda, but propaganda for the kind of wide-angle thinking that includes multiple realities. . . . I suspect there will be many stories in *Wasteland* where the stories will be presented as horror stories, but if you reverse them, you'll discover that they're something else again. They are propaganda for another way of thinking."[2]

"Life's Illusion" was *Wasteland*'s tribute to science fiction author Philip K. Dick's most paranoid fantasies.

The first issue of *Wasteland*, cover-dated December 1987, led off with stories of a deadly psychedelic mushroom and a futuristic society where retroactive abortion is legal up to the age of nine. But the final story in that issue would truly set *Wasteland* apart. "Sewer Rat" featured Del strapping on roller skates, tying an acetylene torch on his head, and skating through the sewers, shooting at rats as he was confronted with largely psychedelic imagery. As Del explained, it was autobiographical.

> Now you can read this as a pro-drug story or an anti-drug story: there's no real position taken. The experience was strenuous to go through—it was not necessarily horrifying to me—although it's totally horrifying to anyone I've ever told it to. "What, you've lived through those things?"
>
> It was great fun to me, but to keep it fun I just had to make it part of my normal everyday reality, which is the point of the story. . . . If you're sufficiently flexible to convince yourself that this is normal, then you have a good chance of getting out of it.[3]

From that point on, nearly every issue would feature an autobiographical story of Del's past, sometimes exaggerated, sometimes all too true.

DC's publisher, Jenette Kahn, reportedly hated the series from the very first issue, recalled Gold—so they knew they were on the right track. The retroactive abortion story, which was carefully calculated to set the tone of *Wasteland* by offending just about everybody, upset her so much that she never read another issue. "That, of course, gave us enormous freedom—and we took full advantage of it."

The *Wasteland* writing process for the two of them would vary wildly. Sometimes they would actually sit and either do the full script or plot together. There were many times when they worked things up entirely together.

By this point, Del had moved to Racine Avenue, and they would often work at a coffee shop on Clark Street that was convenient to both of their apartments. One day, Del made a confession to his partner: "Look, I've gotta talk to you. I gotta warn you about me." He proceeded to tell Ostrander that he wasn't always a very good partner, that there had been problems in the past with some of his partnerships, and that they had always ended badly. "I thought I had to warn you." His part-

Wasteland artist David Lloyd illustrated an interview with Del for a feature in the *New Theater Review* in 1988 that included this quote from serial killer John Wayne Gacy. Del also incorporated the same Gacy quote into a story in *Wasteland #7*, causing much controversy.
(COURTESY OF DAVID LLOYD)

ner said, "OK, so I've been warned. Can we get on with it now?" They resumed their writing. Del did not elaborate, but Ostrander suspected he was referring to his partnership with John Brent; Del had made comments about betraying Brent in the past and had been paying for it, but the exact cause of their falling out is unknown.

Shortly after Ostrander married Kim Yale, they stopped meeting in barrooms and coffee shops. Del would usually come over to their place to write. The first time that he came in, Kim was overattentive: "Oh, Del, can I take your coat? Want a cup of coffee? Can I get you some water? Can I get you this? Can I get you that?" He just looked at her and raised one eyebrow and said, "Kim, don't get all wifey on me now!"

One of Del's favorite *Wasteland* stories appeared in issue #11. He giddily described it to me immediately after scripting it: "A boy sees his high school biology teacher pinned down on the middle of the basketball court, after he's cut open and dissected by the boy's father. And that's only the first page!" Del explained that he and Ostrander had begun with that opening image for the story, titled "Dissecting Mr. Fleming,"

Del in *Ferris Bueller's Day Off*, as Mia Sara's high school English teacher. Note the plug for the Harold, which was then running at Crosscurrents, on the chalkboard.
(COURTESY OF CHARNA HALPERN)

and had to work out where to go from there. It ends up as a gruesome, yet heartwarming tale of a father and son's bonding experience.

After eighteen issues, *Wasteland* was canceled, though not because of low sales. Gold himself canceled the title because it was taking Ostrander longer to write a single nine-page story for *Wasteland* than an entire issue of any of his other assignments. Gold explained: "John was starving to death doing the best work of his life." Del was becoming so busy with his acting and workshops that he struggled to find time for *Wasteland*. As proud as he was, he was ready to end it as well.

◇

The success of his stage roles (particularly 1985's *Hamlet*) had launched Del into a television and film career at a dizzying speed. Del was a fresh fifty-two-year-old face, and the summer of 1986 kept him busy with roles in three movies.

Ferris Bueller's Day Off, written and directed by John Hughes, starred Matthew Broderick, Jeffrey Jones, and Mia Sara in the tale of a teenaged slacker's adventures while cutting class. Del is featured in a small but notable role as "the world's most boring high school English teacher." As he reported to our class after filming, he "sneaked a Harold commercial into that one." In fact, a close examination of the chalkboard behind him includes, inexplicably and in large block letters, the word "Harold." In *Date Night*, written by Al Franken and Tom Davis, Del plays a cranky

Del on the *Untouchables* set and in character as 43rd Ward Alderman John O'Shay, holding his envelope full of cash. (COURTESY OF CHARNA HALPERN)

man. And Paul Schrader's *Light of Day* features Michael J. Fox and Joan Jett as siblings in a rock band whose family problems begin to intrude; Del's portrayal of Dr. Natterson was the most serious part he had done to that point.

But bigger things were yet to come. Brian De Palma's *The Untouchables* took over Chicago for weeks; Del's only scene was a memorable one that garnered him much attention. Playing an alderman, he bursts into Elliot Ness's office, where he attempts to bribe the lawman. Later, Del was delighted at playing a scene with Kevin Costner, and joked that Andy Garcia, Charles Martin Smith, and Sean Connery were "all background players in my scene!"

Starlog editor David McDonnell obtained a still from the film, and I had it framed as a gift for Del. After his death, the image was bequeathed to me, and I discovered the following message written on the back:

> With Elliot Ness (& gang) on the set of *The Untouchables*—film version—here's where I utter the title of the movie—"What're you guys—untouchable?" The character's name and title was Alderman John O'Shay, but I added the line "John O'Shay, alderman, *43rd ward*"—making the character, in effect, Paddy Bauler, the alderman famous for the line "Chicago ain't ready for reform." The costumers were unaware that part of the alderman's costume was a pinkie ring—to their credit, when I asked for one, 4 trays of rings appeared in 30 seconds. [Name Withheld] asked me to score him some pot—

all I could get was ¼ ounce of hashish, which I delivered the following day. Charlie Martin Smith and I were in a scene together in *American Graffiti*.

While *The Untouchables* was one of the biggest films of the year (winning an Oscar for Connery), Del had an even bigger role in another Chicago period piece. *The Big Town*, directed by Ben Bolt, was the story of 1950s Chicago crapshooters. With a stellar cast that included Matt Dillon, Diane Lane, Tommy Lee Jones, Bruce Dern, Tom Skerritt, Lee Grant, and Suzy Amis, Del's role as Bible-thumping gambler Deacon Daniels gave him several opportunities to flex his acting muscles. The film itself was well reviewed as well. Gene Siskel and Roger Ebert each gave it three and a half out of four stars; Siskel called it "a surprisingly effective drama,"[4] while Ebert said it was "a great-looking movie that never steps wrong. . . . The story is predictable, but the style had me on the edge of my seat."[5]

Del was also landing occasional on-camera TV roles. The First Comics title *Sable*, created by Mike Grell, became a short-lived one-hour adventure series for ABC, premiering November 7, 1987. Jon Sable, played by Lewis Van Bergen, was children's book author Nicholas Fleming by day and a mercenary by night. *Sable*, which ran for seven episodes and costarred Rene Russo, featured several Chicago actors in smaller roles, including Lara Flynn Boyle and Neil (*Scrubs*) Flynn. Del appeared in episode 4 on November 28, in which a serial killer hires Sable to protect his next victim. Had the series continued, Del would almost certainly have become a recurring character, portraying Fleming's publisher, Middlebury.

❖

With increasingly steady film and television work, Del continued to take control of his life, which even extended to his housekeeping, recalled Richard Laible. Del was about to leave town to film *The Big Town*, and Laible was a struggling would-be actor with no money. "I've got all this laundry here, I'll give you $100 if you'll go do my laundry," Del offered. A hundred dollars seemed a fortune to him at the time, so Laible promised to wash everything before Del returned. He filled up six huge garbage bags full of clothing, including twenty-year-old T-shirts that would be considered vintage collectibles. He wasn't familiar with Del's old habits,

Del Close found his TV and film career revitalized thanks to Halpern and the emergence of the ImprovOlympic.
(COURTESY OF CHARNA HALPERN)

and didn't realize that when his clothes got dirty, he would simply go buy more. Del would buy a three-pack of underwear, and wear them much, much longer than intended without washing them. "Mick [Napier] used to call him 'Smell Clothes' instead of 'Del Close,'" joked Laible.

With the dirty laundry bagged, he took a cab to a nearby Laundromat. The years of unwashed clothing filled fifteen front loaders. Some of it needed to be dry-cleaned. Laible ended up spending $90 to get Del's clothes laundered, and with the cab fare, he broke even. But he was meticulous. All of the shirts and pants were folded, even the underwear.

When Del returned, he looked at the piles of clean, folded clothing, astonished. He kept repeating, "I can't believe you did it like this!" Laible admitted that he had spent the entire $100 doing it, and Del gave him another $200.

❖

By the end of 1986, Del's latest rehabilitation had proved successful, but he was not content to rest on his laurels. He was demonstrating that audiences would come to see an entirely improvised show. With Halpern's support, he had halted his self-destruction, and was ready for new challenges.

Del had not directed a scripted show since leaving the Second City, but decided the Baron's Barracudas were up to the challenge. He thought about *The Interstellar Follies*, the show he had directed for Dudley Riggs in Minneapolis in late 1972, and borrowed from the story of a crew on a spaceship that had several strange encounters during their deep-space voyage.

He was fascinated by the idea of re-creating a star field in a very low-tech manner, an image suggested to him in a cloud of marijuana smoke. In examining his own interests at the time, there would almost certainly have to be something about then-President Ronald Reagan, and he also determined that the public was beginning to develop a fascination with serial killers. In creating his heroine, he incorporated his newfound love for Japanese anime, which had been kindled by his involvement with the Psychotronic Film Society.

Finally, Del called a meeting of his cast. The show would include the Baron's Barracudas, then made up of Steve Burrows, Brian E. Crane, Honor Finnegan, John Judd, Bill Russell, and myself, to be joined by Richard Laible and Mick Napier, with Charles Silliman on piano.

Del presented his ideas to his cast: the new show would be a show-case for its only female member, and would be called *Honor Finnegan vs. the Brain of the Galaxy*. It would celebrate his love for science fiction and dark, edgy humor with the story of an alien intelligence that threatens to destroy the world, and the "spunky little chick" launched into space to convince it to spare Earth. A dream sequence during the interstellar journey provided an opportunity for a trio of sketches.

Del outlined his ideas and encouraged the cast to script them, and soon the pieces began to come together. A narrator (played by myself) appears throughout the show with monologues that explain the history of post–World War II relations between Japan and America, as seen through the Godzilla films. Judd, as Reagan, selects Finnegan as the likeliest candidate to save the planet, as she is subjected to indignities from the press corps, the president, and even her own family. She sings a love song to Godzilla just before she is launched into space through a starfield created with penlights held by the cast during a brief blackout, a low-tech yet startlingly effective technique.

During the voyage through deep space, Finnegan visits rock and roll heaven, where she is serenaded by Elvis (Burrows), who tries to sell her souvenirs ranging from Elvis hair spray to Elvis refrigerators. Next is a support group, where the members cheerfully back up each other as

The poster for *Honor Finnegan vs. the Brain of the Galaxy*, illustrated by noted Chicago artist Mitch O'Connell.
(AUTHOR'S COLLECTION)

they describe their rationales for serial killing, until Ed Gein (played by myself) describes his crimes in a song-and-dance format, proving too much for even the worst of the other real-life killers. Finally, Finnegan visits the set of a game show (hosted by Russell and Laible) called *Celebrity Dogfuck*, in which the dogs of celebrities engage in sex.

Finnegan eventually confronts the undulating Brain of the Galaxy (played by the rest of the cast), convincing it to spare the Earth, not because of the innate goodness of humanity, but because of its evil. No matter how badly you try to exterminate us, she warns the creature, some of us will survive, and "We will hunt you down and burn your children in their beds!"

The show opened in February 1987 at Crosscurrents. The reviews were positive to mixed. Lawrence Bommer in *The Reader* wrote:

> When a comedy names itself *Honor Finnegan Vs. the Brain of the Galaxy*, subtlety ain't its strong suit. Instead, its edge turns out to be a wacky, infectious inventiveness, with all the spontaneity of

improv humor and the well-orchestrated laughs of a finished script.
. . . Despite or because of a go-for-broke nutty shamelessness, along
its crazy course, *Honor Finnegan* hits several hard (and very few)
easy targets. . . . This goofy, silly-smart, and semi-lethal satire falls
on its face far less often than it doesn't.[6]

One of the more memorable evenings occurred that April. My
friend Graham Chapman of Monty Python was in town that weekend,
as was Bill Murray, and they both attended Saturday's performance of
Finnegan. Afterward, a small group drifted over to my apartment on
North Racine for drinks and snacks. Everyone sat in a circle in the living room as Del held court, telling stories and having a grand time. Del
and Chapman, who didn't drink, talked about being recovered alcoholics, while Murray largely listened. Del seemed to be in awe of Chapman;
he would still pontificate, but if Chapman had something to say, Del
stopped and listened.

Honor Finnegan vs. the Brain of the Galaxy closed July 4 after
five months; though Del considered a follow-up show to be called
Yuppie Ninjas, he soon became too busy. But the closing of *Finnegan*
marked the beginning of the end for the Baron's Barracudas. They
had reached what was then the glass ceiling at the ImprovOlympic,
and gradually went their separate ways. At that point, there was no
new ground to conquer at the ImprovOlympic. By the end of 1987,
the group had gradually dissolved. No superstars emerged from its
ranks, but many achieved professional success. Joel Murray built a
solid sitcom career on such shows as *Dharma and Greg* and *Still
Standing*, where J.J. was an occasional guest star. Mark Beltzman
was a semiregular on *According to Jim*, and Chris Barnes was a
regular on *Life with Bonnie*. John Judd became a highly respected
stage actor, as did David Pasquesi (who is also one of the top voice-
over artists in the nation). Steve Burrows became an accomplished
commercial and feature director (*Chump Change*). With the departure of the Baron's Barracudas, Grime and Punishment, including
Laible, Mick Napier, Dave Razowsky, and Tim Meadows, became
the new house team of the ImprovOlympic, with new teams being
formed regularly, such as Floyd's Toothbrush, with Noah Grego-
ropolous, Madeline Long, Alan Leib, Matt Need, Andy Dick, Scott
Markwell, and Meadows.

Madeline Long, Andy Dick, Noah Gregoropoulos, Scott Markwell, Matt Need, and Tim Meadows were part of the second wave of the Improv-Olympic as Floyd's Toothbrush.
(COURTESY OF CHARNA HALPERN)

In a response to a class reunion announcement, Del wrote a letter to former Manhattan classmate David Dary, postmarked July 14, 1987, summarizing his ongoing resurgence.

> Aug. 15 I go into rehearsal for the Goodman Theatre prod. of Peter Bernes [sic] epic plague comedy, *Red Noses*, And immediately after the show closes (on Samhain—the Witches' high Holy Day—also known as Halloween) Then I'm off to New York to direct at Lincoln Center. . . . It's a "Mock Opera" called *Ron Giovanni*. . . .
>
> Gee, I'm having *fun* in my old age! (Teaching, too, of course, always teaching.)
>
> I owe you a long letter about Life, Art, & how much I admired your ham Radio rig when we were slightly younger—something other than a résumé of my current activities. . . .
>
> Please David, give my best to all at the reunion—I'd love to come, particularly since I don't imagine I'll be around for the 50th. I'm perfectly healthy, but I'm a heavy smoker & my life-styles have doubtless taken a physical toll that I'm as yet unaware of. (never use a sentence to begin a preposition with!)

His career was taking off in ways that he had not dared to hope a short time before. He would more frequently be called away from the ImprovOlympic for stage and theater, but with the talent assembled there and Halpern's organizational skills, he knew it would stay on course.

21

Chris Farley, *The Blob*, and Farewell to Second City

On the opening night of *The Tempest*, in the spring of 1987, Del received a call at the Goodman Theatre. Was he interested in directing political satire at Lincoln Center in New York? After assurances from Halpern that the ImprovOlympic could manage without him for a few weeks, Del signed on.

The story of Ronald Reagan selling his soul to the devil was called *Ron Giovanni*; it was written by Tony Hendra, well known for his work with *National Lampoon* and *This Is Spinal Tap*. It would rehearse in New York in November and December, and open in January at the Mitzi Newhouse Theater.

Gregory Mosher, Del's former director from the Goodman, had become artistic director at Lincoln Center. When Hendra first brought the project to Mosher and asked about a possible director, he replied, "I think there's only one guy." Del was excited about the show, but Mosher recalled that "there was no sense of him being flapped," unlike Hendra, who was "really wound up." Their contrasting attitudes struck Mosher as highly appropriate for the project: "I knew that the best thing for it would be barely controlled chaos."

Del began by casting several established Chicago actors, including Bruce Jarchow and Rob Riley, along with national musical talents like Meat Loaf and Karla DeVito, then threw himself into the rehearsal process. But as it progressed, one problem was becoming apparent. As edgy and extreme as they tried to make the material, the real-life Reagan was outdoing them. Whenever they felt they were parodying Reagan to the nth degree, he would do something even more extreme, such as laying a wreath at a cemetery for Nazi storm troopers in Bitburg. They would throw up their hands and say, "Well, that's better than what we have, and he did that with a straight face!"

I was visiting New York in mid-December, and Del invited me to their first complete read-through of the show. I watched as the highly talented cast ran through the show from start to finish. The show was very funny, with some biting satire interspersed throughout. The only criticism I could offer was that the send-up was not as pointed as it could be. As a tag line for the show, Del had always liked "Tired of political satire? Try a little treason . . ." But at this point, the show fell short of the treasonous.

Del and I attended the DC Comics holiday party that weekend. When I arrived, Del was in high spirits, telling stories to amazed guests. He was introduced to a woman claiming to be a countess who was involved with DC's foreign publishing department, and I was later startled to see them jitterbugging on the dance floor.

Then Del saw Gold talking with publisher Jenette Kahn. She didn't like *Wasteland*, but was still aware of Del's reputation and wanted to meet him. Del's attitude toward authority figures was that they were usually funny and irrelevant, and certainly not worthy of automatic respect. Nevertheless, Del made a beeline to them and started performing acrobatic tricks with his ever-present cigarette—bouncing it off his tongue, and rolling it around his mouth while flipping it so the lit side was in his mouth. Gold recalled that "Del kept on flashing impish looks that showed enormous power right behind the surface, as intimidating as they were cute. Before the one-sided conversation ground to a halt, Del made a perfectly timed exit."

Afterward, Del and I went back to his suite, where he allowed me to sleep on the couch for a couple of nights. Del sheepishly told me that he was expecting a phone call from Tony Hendra; if the phone rang, he asked me to intercept it and say that he was unavailable. I gladly agreed and soon fell asleep, interrupted only by the sound of Del talking in his sleep in the next room.

The next day Del explained. Just three weeks away from the first public performance, Mosher suggested they approach it like a Second City revue or *That Was the Week That Was*, leaving half the show intact, but putting in a new half hour or forty minutes of material every week. Hendra claimed it simply wasn't possible. Mosher insisted, "All I can tell you is, what Reagan's doing is funnier than what's on the page." Del simply sat quietly, listening.

After Hendra left, Del sat in Mosher's office and they wondered what to do about *Ron Giovanni*. Finally, Del told Mosher that he agreed: "I think you're right, but look, it's all the same to me. I don't care. It might be great, it might not be great, but you're not going to hurt my feelings if we don't do it, so don't keep doing it for my sake. I have plenty to do back in Chicago. It's not going to change my life one whit." Del didn't try to defend the show, which Mosher interpreted to mean that Del thought it was the proper decision to close the show. Mosher noted that it was "the only show I've closed in rehearsals—but I think that people should close shows in rehearsals more often!"

After the meeting, he and Mosher had decided to pull the plug on the show, unbeknownst to the writer. Hendra wanted Del to intervene in hopes of reviving the project, and Del was ducking his calls.

In an interview that I conducted with Del the following spring for *Starlog* magazine, he elaborated further on the demise of *Ron Giovanni*.

> Tony [Hendra], to this day, does not know that I was the one that said "Let's trash this fucker!" It doesn't really matter, because some-one had to say it, but I was still presenting myself as one of the fellow victims there, as you may recall, for all the Marx Brothers numbers we were doing around DC that time, you answering my phone in my hotel room![1]

◆

I didn't find out a possible explanation for the late-night talking until years later. Halpern had been traveling with Del earlier that year, but was apparently a light sleeper. Del had been hired by Andrew Alexander to teach a workshop in Canada, where he and Halpern shared a hotel room. Del slept in the twin bed on the right. He was asleep, and Halpern turned onto her right side and saw Del on his back, his hands moving around in the air. It was dark, so she couldn't see whether his eyes were closed and never even thought to look. She assumed he was doing something spiritual, and turned over and went back to sleep.

Months later in New York, he was given an efficiency apartment. Halpern came to visit, and when she got up in the morning, Del was sleeping on the couch with his back to her, but his hand was moving around over his shoulder. It seemed to recognize that she was in the room, and it stopped and waved at her. She said, "Good morning," and Del turned and said, "Oh, hi, honey," as if she had just woken him up. She didn't understand how she could have awakened him since he had waved, but she simply shrugged it off.

That night, they were in their beds when Halpern turned over and observed his hands moving in the air again. Suddenly, the hands both stopped in midair and slowly turned toward her, as though looking directly at her. Like puppets, they said, "You're dead! You're dead!" Frightened, Halpern immediately woke Del up and told him his hands were threatening her. He said, "Don't worry about it, I have everything under control." Nevertheless, she asked him to stay awake while she slept, so he turned on the lamp and read while she went back to sleep. The next day, she asked what that had been about. He didn't want to tell her, and when she persisted, he said in a booming voice, *"They don't want to talk about it!"*

◆

The collapse of *Ron Giovanni* led to one of Del's most prominent film roles.

> I called up my agents and said "Well, I just pulled the plug on a show. This project's dead—what am I going to do now?" feeling kind of forlorn and stranded in the Big City. "We have an audition for *The Blob.*" [Director] Chuck [Russell] was coming to New York to see somebody, Paul McCrane or Jeffrey DeMunn, people he eventually wound up hiring from New York. He was auditioning all over the country, LA, New York, not Chicago as it happens.
>
> I thought this was some sort of omen, because . . . three weeks prior to that, I had written a Blob story for *Wasteland*—I think it was

in the last issue, "The Eye, Like Some Strange Balloon," where my cat had scratched my cornea and forced me to appear in *Blob 2* with an injured eye in an eyepatch. I thought there was some sort of omen hanging over this thing, so obviously, I'm going to get the part in *The Blob*. So I walked in and laid some comic books on Chuck, and sure enough got the role![2]

The remake of *The Blob* was a major Hollywood SFX release starring Kevin Dillon, Shawnee Smith, and several highly respected character actors, directed by Chuck Russell (*Nightmare on Elm Street III*). Del was immensely proud of the film. His was a solid supporting character, and it remains his largest role in a studio film.

On May 7, 1988, after the filming but before its release, I sat down with Del to conduct a lengthy interview about his experiences on the film for *Starlog* magazine, in which he recounted the making of the film from his perspective.

As it turned out, Chuck had seen me in *The Untouchables* on his flight in to New York to audition me, so I was fresh in his mind. It was nice to have a big-budget audition tape directed by Brian De Palma!

Del's character, the Reverend Meeker, is a constant background presence, transforming from a small-town minister to an apocalyptic, fire-and-brimstone preacher.

Reverend Meeker isn't a big part—I'm never on screen for more than 30 seconds at any given moment. They keep cutting to this preacher who keeps doing kind of interesting things: Why do they keep cutting to this guy? What is the significance of this dude? And eventually we find out, right at the end of the flick. When I met Chuck, I was waving the script around in one hand, and I said "So Meeker inherits the Earth!" Later, he told me that was when he knew I was the right guy for the part.

On January 11, 1988, the 150 cast and crew members reported to the Travelodge on location in Abbeville, Louisiana. Del would spend fourteen weeks on *The Blob*, by far the longest time he had spent on a film location and far surpassing the three-week stint in Toronto for *The*

Big Town. Most of the filming took place at night, so the group usually slept during the day. To Del, it felt much like summer camp in Kansas. Everyone left the doors to their motel rooms open, and cast and crew would walk from one room to another. On nights off, they would stay up all night and watch videotapes, often eating crayfish, the local delicacy. "The second thing they ask you down there is 'You et mudbugs yet?' The first thing varies, but the second thing is always 'Have you eaten mudbugs?'"

The night before his first scene, Del was nervous, and he wanted to make sure he didn't make a mistake on the set. He met with Russell late at night in his motel room to discuss the significance of some of his speeches, which included biblical quotations and discourses from the Book of Revelation. Del tried out various line readings and approaches for the character for forty-five minutes. Finally, Russell stood and said, "Well, we've got to knock this off, because I have to be up at four." Del suddenly realized that Russell, who had to be up in just three and a half hours, had done him a much bigger favor than he had realized. "He was really gracious, and he gave me that time just before we started shooting, even though he would have rather been in bed sleeping at that time."

In the later part of the film, Del's character is burned, so he had to undergo a lengthy makeup process, in addition to working with on-set special effects. He sat in the makeup chair for five and a half hours for the burn makeup, and seven and a half hours for the healed-burn makeup, and the near-constant poking and prodding by the makeup technicians started to get to him.

> I go home at night, and I'm falling asleep, and it's like riding a motor-cycle for eight or nine hours, and you get to the motel, and you get off the motorcycle and you're in bed, and you're still seeing the road coming at you and you're still feeling the vibrations. I went to bed that night, and I could still feel these guys going poke! Poke! Poke! Poke! The phantom poking around the head!

Del's past experience as a fire-eater and human torch would come in useful on *The Blob*, because Rev. Meeker is supposed to catch fire after a man with a flamethrower on the other side of the screen explodes. Unfortunately, there were complications after Del's stunt double didn't catch fire immediately.

They couldn't blow the guy up again with the flamethrower, so they blew my stunt double up and they really set him on fire! But what was missing was the moment where you see the flames and the Reverend. In the big-frame shot which they can only do once, he didn't catch on fire big enough or in time—in fact, Chuck said he looked like he could be waiting for a bus before he caught fire!

I must have said at some point to Chuck that I would prefer not to get set on fire, I would prefer to be doubled in that stunt. And he said, "Yes, of course you are going to be stunt doubled for that shot."

So I guess my aversion to flame got somehow magnified down the line. Chuck says, "He doesn't want to get set on fire." Another guy says, "Oh, he *really* doesn't want to get set on fire!" And the third guy says, "He's terrified of being set on fire! Fire really freaks him out!" So the assistant director says, "Oh, we're only going to set you on fire a little bit at this point, for this insert." And I had heard none of this other, and I said, "Oh, can't you give me a little more of that gel? Because this is like an insert." And he was trying to freak me out, but I wasn't playing the game. They were not aware that I had done human torch work in the past!

Really, at my advanced age, I am not crazy about doing human torch stuff again. On the other hand, when I did my human torch, I never had the kind of protection that these guys did, either! I think I would be just as averse to being set on fire as just about anyone else at this point, except yeah, I kind of wish they would put a little fire on my shoulder, just to give the impression that I'm doing my own stunts, even though anybody in their right mind knows that you don't do that.

The number of actors who actually performed as human torches is undoubtedly few, and most, like Del, gave it up before middle age. In the wake of *The Blob*, Del was trying to give up smoking, explaining that he was only allowing himself one cigarette per hour, down from three and a half packs a day. He also lost twenty-five pounds during the course of the filming, at the request of Russell, dropping from 198 to 173 by the end of the shoot.

I've given up a lot of things. I've given up drugs—not because I dislike drugs, and not because I've reformed, certainly, it's just because you can't do it after a while! You don't keep being a dope fiend into your grave, or into your old age, at any rate. If you happen to survive drugs, as I did, and you're in your fifties now, you can't have any veins left! So the same way I avoid drugs, it's sort of like common sense, I avoid fire as well. I suppose if I were to do a movie about junkies, I'd say "Yeah, yeah, I can shoot up!" Well, I probably couldn't—I couldn't find a vein. I'd have to get a vein double in for me, somebody who could tie up and actually manage to get the needle in there! They get body doubles for chicks with tits, I suppose they could get vein doubles.

The closing scene of the film belongs to Rev. Meeker, and Del makes the most of it. The seeds are planted for a sequel in which Meeker will unleash the Blob on the world once again: "If there's a sequel to the new *Blob*, I don't see how they can avoid using me. It's safe to say that I survive the Blob—sort of."

Unfortunately, while it received mostly good reviews, the box office was simply not strong enough for a sequel. But for Del, *The Blob* may have been the personal highlight of his movie career, and the film he enjoyed the most. During the filming of *The Blob*, he asked for some tentacles. Later, when he took Halpern to see *The Blob*, he secretly held on to the tentacles until the moment where a girl is coming out of the sewer, and the Blob is reaching down to touch her head. Del used that carefully chosen moment to utilize his own Blob tentacles. Halpern screamed in the theater as she discovered that the Blob was crawling down her face. He had worked out the scheme for months, and when she screamed in the theater, it made all of his planning worth it.

❖

Life returned to normal after Del finished *The Blob* and came back to Chicago in early 1988. During the filming, he didn't know what he was going to do when he returned to Chicago, although he hoped to do a play. "Like most Chicago actors, the real reason I'm doing movies is to be able to afford to do plays, except I don't have a play to do," he explained. "The last show of the Goodman season is *Pal Joey*, and they heard me sing in *The Tempest*, and they're probably not going to want me!"

Despite his prediction, however, Del was soon being directed by Robert Falls in the Goodman's production of *Pal Joey*, with choreography by Ann Reinking. *Pal Joey* opened at the Goodman on June 3 and ran for two months; the Steppenwolf's Kevin Anderson played the title role in the 1940 Rodgers and Hart musical. By an odd coincidence, Del discovered that Falls, who had cast him as con man Ludlow Lowell in *Pal Joey*, was a college classmate of Chuck Russell when they both went to the University of Illinois.

Halpern was able to cover for him when other opportunities arose, and he did the same for her. In his fifties, he had decided that he wanted to be an actor again, and he was succeeding. He didn't have to choose between teaching improvisation and theater or film. He discovered he could have it all.

◆

As the ImprovOlympic became more established, new talents came looking for Del. Actor Pat Finn had just finished at Marquette University, along with his friend Chris Farley, and they were both determined to do comedy. They signed up for classes at the Second City, attended one of the shows, and afterward ran into Joel Murray. Farley begged Finn, who knew Murray, to speak to him for advice. Murray told him it was really pretty simple. He needed to work with Del Close at the ImprovOlympic. From that point on, working with Del became a top priority for Farley.

Farley idolized John Belushi. Though Belushi was gone, his "biggest influence in comedy" was still around, however, and doing some of his most innovative work. Years later, after *Saturday Night Live*, Farley was effusive, respectful, almost worshipful of his director, teacher, and friend in a June 26, 1992, conversation. Farley had little performing experience before moving to Chicago, aside from working for the Ark Theatre for a year in Madison, Wisconsin.

One night, Farley went with friends from his Second City class to watch Harolds, and began classes with Halpern afterward. "I just wanted to meet [Del] so badly," said Farley. "He was teaching classes at the Second City then. I remember just seeing him walking out, and following him down the street, never being able to talk to him because I hadn't met him yet, and wanting to talk to him so badly. Oh, man, I was just in awe of him, this guru of improvisation."

I was one of the students standing in the back of Crosscurrents when Farley attended his very first class with Del. The newcomer clearly made an impression on everyone there that night. He tried to impress Del with "as much sweat and blood as I knew how—and ignorance, because that's all I had. . . . I remembered he told Belushi to attack the stage, which I read in *Wired*, so I tried to attack the stage like Belushi."

Indeed, Del turned to us and said, "Wow, I haven't seen that kind of energy onstage since Belushi." But it was unfocused energy, and Farley needed to learn how to balance the energy with control. Del's first advice to him was, "Settle down, son; you're sweating too hard. You're like the guys we strap onto the front of a battleship when we go into battle. Fearless, but you have to have some control, too."

Farley was nothing but generous in his praise. "Del is the greatest teacher I've ever known," he said. "I owe everything to Del. He brought me to Second City, and he taught me everything I need to know."

Del and Halpern took Farley under their wings. Del eventually got him hired by the Second City, and they remained close. After Farley was hired by *Saturday Night Live*, they took him out for a farewell dinner at a fine restaurant to wish him luck—and to help teach him manners. Farley drank his beer so quickly that it spilled out the sides of his mouth. "Jesus Christ! No one is going to take it away from you! Slow down," Del urged him.

Halpern explained that they wanted to discuss his bad-boy behavior so that he could curb it in New York. Farley pulled out Halpern's chair at the restaurant to seat her in a gentlemanly way. Once she was seated, noticing that the floor was slippery, he whipped the chair across the floor with Halpern in it while Del continued eating his bread without missing a beat. "He's hopeless," Del said.

Chris Farley's *Saturday Night Live* debut was on a show hosted by actor Patrick Swayze, who was also an accomplished dancer. The writers created a memorable scene in which Farley and Swayze would audition for a slot with the Chippendales, but Farley was very upset that he had to dance bare-chested alongside Patrick Swayze. He called Del and Halpern to complain that they were "making fun of the fat boy." Del told him to dance the best he could and pretend he was lighter than air, to be the best he could be and not let them turn him into a cliche. Farley took his advice, and became a star.

But Del was not afraid to criticize his former student. After *Beverly Hills Ninja* opened, Farley called to see whether Del had seen it. Del said, "You owe me two hours of my life back."

◈

Even though he was only in his mid-fifties, Del had a powerful sense of his own mortality. On the evening of August 16, 1985, Halpern had been sitting with Del in the bedroom of his Wells Street apartment when John Brent's picture fell off the wall above his bed. Del was surprised, because the picture had been up for years. He called Halpern the next day to ask whether she remembered the picture falling the previous night. She said yes. He said he had just found out that Brent had died the previous day.

Brent had been one of his closest friends, but the two had experienced a falling-out of sorts. The circumstances are unclear, but Del felt a strong sense of regret. In an undated letter written to Brent's son, but never mailed, Del recounted some of his friend's final days.

> A couple of years ago I met this actor-producer who . . . claimed to know John better than I did. Perhaps he did, but it was a different John. This was after John had had major heart surgery, in fact a few weeks before he died. The guy said that John's attitude toward death had changed—He'd been writing down ideas—John had—for a sit-com set in a hospice for the dying (well, they put one in a Nazi prison camp!) but had given up the concept because he now found "there was nothing funny about dying." Well, as I said, we knew two different Johns—and there were a *lot* of Johns!
>
> One can enter a life from any point—cigarettes, for instance. I'm told that while in the recovery room after heart surgery, John was valiantly puffing away on a cigarette, horrifying the nurses.[3]

In August 1988, Mary Jo Henderson died in an automobile accident. Though he rarely mentioned her name, Del was deeply saddened by her premature passing. He had seldom, if ever, been in contact with her since their days together in the St. Louis Compass, but what she represented was still very important to him.

Around that time, Del wrote a story for the fifteenth issue of *Wasteland* that involved a retelling of his beloved *Hamlet*, beginning as Hamlet jumps into Ophelia's open grave to debate with Laertes as to who loved her more. In "Crocophagia, or Hamlet in Aegypt," Prince Hamlet promises to eat a crocodile to prove his love for Ophelia, and sets sail with his friends for Egypt to make good on his pledge. At the conclusion of "Crocophagia," we see a dedication: "This story was inspired by the death of a woman for whom, in mourning, I ate a crocodile. Del Close."[4]

Del often confided to friends that he expected to be dead by the time he was fifty-four years old. His father had killed himself when he was fifty-four, and Del did not expect to outlive him. But by March 9, 1989, Del was surprised to find that he had made it to fifty-five, and thus outlived his father. It called for a celebration; as he told his friends, "I never expected to do any of this 'getting old' shit. I thought I'd be dead by now!"

Del was accomplishing his life's goals. He was a survivor. But fate still had one more twist in store for him, and it came in the form of an unexpected phone call late in 1988 from Second City.

◈

The Second City, that once-stodgy bastion of comedy, was loosening up. In 1985, producer Andrew Alexander and financier-partner Len Stuart bought out Bernie Sahlins's interest in the Chicago Second City. Though Sahlins was a fixture, even an icon, he would no longer be calling the shots.

Change came slowly at first. By June 1988, the seventieth revue had opened; Mike Myers and Bonnie Hunt led the cast in *Kuwait Until Dark or Bright Lights, Night Baseball*. When Sahlins declined to direct the next Second City revue, Joel Murray and David Pasquesi went to Joyce Sloane and suggested that Del might be available. Sloane had been considering a shakeup, a new wave, at the theater, in part because of the effect the upstart ImprovOlympic was having on the Chicago improvisation scene. Alexander had been hiring Del to conduct workshops for him in Toronto in recent years. Now the timing was right for Alexander and Sloane to stir things up in a big way. Would Del be interested in coming back to direct one final Second City show?

The offer surprised both Del and Halpern. The Second City had been hiring away ImprovOlympic performers, but this was an opportunity to more directly challenge the status quo. Del was uncertain at first. After all, they were the competition. But Sahlins was now out of the picture. Del could stage the show that he wanted, without interference. Halpern encouraged him to consider the offer seriously, perhaps giving them a set of conditions, first and foremost of which would be hiring his own cast.

"Hmm, then we could put up our own people, like Farley, Pasquesi, Joel Murray, Tim Meadows," he mused. It was an opportunity for Del to push his former students to the mainstage. "We could hit them up for a lot of money, too. I'll bet I could ask for more bread than most directors do!" he added. So with his conditions met, Del tacked his cast list on Joyce Sloane's door.

By that time, Murray was understudy to Kevin Crowley, who was leaving the mainstage, and Pasquesi was taking the place of Myers, who had just been hired for *Saturday Night Live.* Farley had just been hired for the touring company, and Meadows was replacing Aaron Freeman.

Del was keeping a promise to Tim Meadows. When he was directing *Honor Finnegan vs. the Brain of the Galaxy*, Meadows came to the first rehearsal, and Del said, "You're not in this." It was an uncomfortable moment for everyone, particularly Meadows, who said, "Oh, I didn't know that." But then Del told him, "I promise the next show I direct, I'll put you in it." And so, Halpern called Meadows and "Guess what? You're going on mainstage and you start rehearsals next week!" It was the first he had heard of it. Refusing to believe her, he said, "That's crazy! That's ridiculous! That's not true!" Then he ran into Sloane, who hadn't heard anything about it yet. He called Halpern again and said, "Joyce doesn't know anything about it." But Halpern insisted that he show up at the Second City the following Monday for rehearsals.

There was a new regime in place at the Second City. Del was directing a company comprising Farley, Meadows, Murray, Pasquesi, Joe Liss, Holly Wortell, and Judy Scott. Del's return to the Second City gave it a sense of occasion. Sahlins and Patinkin were seldom seen around the theater, so the production would be the sole product of Del and the company.

While some things were dramatically different, others changed very little. The company struggled to find a two-woman scene. Every night, Del's note was: "We need you two girls to come up with something. You girls put something up every night, and you'll find something that you like." In the end, there was not a two-woman scene in the show (Murray said they simply didn't develop anything strong enough for the show), and Wortell and Scott were not happy with Del.

Del was not terribly helpful to the women, according to Pasquesi, but it wasn't as clear-cut as boy-girl, because four of the five men had worked with Del in the past for lengthy periods. A shorthand had developed between Del and Murray, Pasquesi, Meadows, and Farley, as well as the sole cast member of the previous mainstage show, Joe Liss, which made it easier for the men to work together. Del wrote on a piece of paper the different functions within the cast—earth, air, fire, water, and also spirit—giving each of them an element. The two women were excluded.

The men of the company were prolific in generating material. Del told the cast that he viewed the job of Second City director as someone who tells the actors what they are doing, *not* telling them what to do. "Timmy and Joe Liss and I were doing a scene in a pickup truck, and the next day Del was talking about it as 'that gun control scene,'" explained Pasquesi. "We said 'What are you talking about?' 'That one's about gun control.' 'Oh, OK. Sure.' He was great about giving direction in the same way: 'More speed.' 'More amphetamine.' That's what he'd say, he'd use terms like that, which I understood."

To Del, everyone had a different function, and the whole was always greater than the sum of its parts. "Together, we'll do things together that are impossible with a bunch of individuals. If you're a bunch of individuals, you can only be as good as the sum of individuals, but if we are truly a group, then far greater things can be accomplished," he told them. Del also urged them to keep their minds open with regard to the more mystical elements: "While we're working on this show, I think you'll notice a lot of coincidences that are difficult to explain. When your mind is looking for the connections, you'll see the connections. When you're doing things like putting up a show, your mind is thinking different ways, and because you're thinking different ways, you're able to see different things."

The Gods Must Be Lazy opened on March 8, 1989. Del likened the show to a train wreck, because instead of starting the show with three blackouts and ending with a cast scene, it began with a two-person improvisation and a cast scene game-song, and ended with a blackout. Del explained that it was "like a train running into a wall. Splat! It's over. Send 'em out to the road." Pasquesi's favorite scene was the opener. Traditional Second City rules dictated "you don't do strong characters until they've gotten to know you, and you don't improvise until you've done a couple of strong scenes." Pasquesi started by portraying a homeless character, and Murray and he started the show by improvising.

Another acclaimed scene, often used later in touring company shows, teamed Murray with Farley. Murray played an Irish father picking up his son at the drunk tank. It was a first-time improvisation, and when the pair had finished, Del said, "Script that, that's fantastic."

The father is obviously a drunk himself, while the son is a fledgling drunk; the man has lost his wife, and is desperately trying to prove that he's not an idiot. All of the father's lines, like "Drinking is our life, and gosh, you've got to know how to do it right," and "Moderation, you've got to learn when to say no, or just beer . . ." betray no thought about quitting or getting help. It concludes with the father saying, "Let's get out of here," and the son says, "I'll drive." The father nods in agreement, and the audience bursts into applause and laughter because the son, already arrested for driving drunk, now has to drive them home.

Farley was featured in an Elvis scene; making Farley a hero was a high priority for Del. He also wanted to show audiences that Murray and Pasquesi were so brilliant that they could open the show simply by sitting there with a newspaper and talking, improvising their lines.

Del was happy with the show, and critics tended to agree. The next day, the *Chicago Tribune*'s Richard Christiansen wrote: "Under Del Close's direction, the whole Second City mix has the standard quota of low spots, and a few exceptionally funny and inventive high points, including a startling mondo bizarre appearance by Elvis Presley in a small-town café and hilarious nightclub routines by Ulysses, Atlas, Polyphemus, Cyclops and the rest of the Greek-myth gang in a smoky little boite called Pandora's Box. The new cast also reinvents the familiar with the unique blend of its physiques, personalities and tastes (which are fairly randy)."

And in the March 14, 1989, *Daily Herald*, Tom Valeo wrote, "This is the freshest, most original show Second City has created in years. . . . The main credit goes to Del Close who, with this show, demonstrates the power of pure improvisation."

As good as the show was, the unfinished toy train from kindergarten had not disappeared. "I didn't think *The Gods Must Be Lazy* was polished," said Murray. "I thought it could have been better. We just threw some stuff up." Del would often tell the cast, "Oh, yeah, that's great, just script that, that's it." Other times, he wouldn't say anything or he would disappear, and the cast failed to get the legendary direction they had been hoping for.

None of the cast but Liss were familiar with the traditional Second City process, so they didn't realize how much material could be refined during the improvisation set after each show. Murray felt the subsequent show, *It Was Thirty Years Ago Today*, which wasn't directed by Del, improved on *The Gods Must Be Lazy*, while Pasquesi noted that he wasn't disappointed in *Gods*, even though Del stopped coming to rehearsals during the last two weeks before it opened.

The Gods Must Be Lazy, the Second City's seventy-first revue, was Del's last show for the theater, though he made himself available for workshops and other Second City events, including occasional celebrations at the theater. Later in 1989, Del attended the thirtieth-anniversary celebration, where he expressed his relationship with the theater: "Second City is like the Masons or the Mafia. Once you're a member of it, you're never *not* a member."

22

Workshops, Reunions, and the Family

By the end of the 1980s, Halpern was determined to find the Improv-Olympic a permanent home, but it would not be easy. Crosscurrents closed, forcing the group to occupy a dizzying array of spaces over the next few years. They briefly moved to the cavernous Ivanhoe Theatre on Wellington, where the owner welcomed them until they could find a more suitable space. After four weeks, they landed at Orphan's, a bar on Lincoln Avenue, where a back room with a stage set up for bands was converted into a theater.

The group then moved to a trendy club at Jefferson and Lake streets called At the Tracks, where they performed on weekends. (For a brief period they also worked Tuesdays at the cabaret formerly known as Crosscurrents, which had reopened as a blues bar called Cotton Chicago.) Next, the theater landed in an unused upstairs banquet room at Ciao, an Italian restaurant on Wells Street. In early 1990, they moved to the basement of Papa Milano's at Armitage, Sedgewick, and Lincoln avenues, where they stayed until the end of the year.

Workshops were likewise being held wherever Halpern could find the space, though the ImprovOlympic teaching program at that time was limited to workshops taught by Halpern, performer-director Noah Gregoropoulous, and the advanced class taught by Del.

◇

It was a time of upheaval, and Del was restless as well. Although he had shunned television decades earlier, he even went to California for the TV pilot season. He flew out to audition for the character of a bartender named Del in an unsuccessful pilot. The part had been based on him. He didn't get the role.

It was typical of his Hollywood experiences. While younger actors go to L.A. to seek their fortunes, Del was fifty. Even worse, he didn't have a car and didn't drive, and had to rely on friends to be driven from audition to audition. Being a small fish in the big Hollywood pond did not sit terribly well with him. He enjoyed being a guru, so it was a humbling experience. As he later told Ed Greenberg, "I used up ten years worth of favors in three weeks."

According to Fred Kaz, who had retired from the Second City by that time, they met one day at Severn Darden's. Del couldn't decide whether to stay in Los Angeles or return to Chicago. "I threw the I Ching for him at a blessedly auspicious moment," said Kaz. "It was unmistakeable. Go."

In 1989, while the group was at Ciao, Del decided it was time to leave the ImprovOlympic. At the beginning of his regular Monday night class, he explained to the students "My time is finished here." He had thrown the runes, and decided they read, "You've done your work, the Harold is over." Halpern was taken aback; she had no idea Del was going to make such an announcement. That night after class, she had a long talk with Del. "That's ridiculous! Do you think that's all you have in you, that you can't teach us something else or create more? I think it's a personal thing. We're doing something important here, we're creating more than just Harold." She did her best to convince him that there was still much more they could accomplish together with the ImprovOlympic. Del relented, and agreed to remain.

Ironically, Del then was hired for the Neil Bartlett adaptation of Molière's *The Misanthrope*, directed by Robert Falls. This version, featuring Kim Cattrall, was set in the world of show business. It was to be workshopped at the La Jolla Playhouse, which meant Del had to travel to California to rehearse and open the show there before it was presented at the Goodman Theatre in Chicago. It would require him to be away for two months, but Halpern gave him her blessing. Many of the students at the ImprovOlympic did not realize that, despite his announcement in class, Del had not left the theater permanently, and students who had gone through the first two levels of classes and were preparing to work with Del were irate. But two months later, he did indeed return.

Del was back in time for the stint at Papa Milano's. He wore a rubber band around his wrist, and whenever the urge for smoking came upon him, he would snap the band sharply. The momentary pain was intended to take his mind off the desire for a cigarette. Unfortunately, he had an unusually robust tolerance for pain, and eventually gave up trying to quit.

◇

After years of upheaval for the ImprovOlympic and for Del, Halpern found a space upstairs at the Wrigleyside Bar on North Clark Street, beginning a multiyear run. Eventually, a space opened up on Belmont Avenue, very near to Del's and her own apartments, across from the Theatre Building. It was small, no more than fifty seats, but the iO Annex was enough for a few shows and classes while they continued performing at the Wrigleyside.

The work kept advancing as well. While the Baron's Barracudas were the first masters of the form, Halpern explained, the form was evolving and growing. Other teams arose to become dominant for a time. Grime and Punishment was followed by Fish Shtick, which spotlighted Chris Farley, Ian Gomez, Brian McCann, and James Grace; and Tequila Mockingbird, which included Dave Koechner, Jim Carrane, and Noah Gregoropoulos.

The next team to establish itself would be Blue Velveeta, with a lineup that included Kevin Dorff, Jay Leggett, Mitch Rouse, Brendan Sullivan, Susan Messing, Brian McCann, and Tom Booker. Ironically, Blue Velveeta took over the space at Papa Milano's at the end of 1990 from the ImprovOlympic. The group was so far ahead of the other teams that the feeling at the time was "Why do we need Charna Halpern?" But Blue Velveeta eventually imploded. It left Del displeased with the way Halpern was abandoned by her former charges: "Isn't it wonderful that we gave them something they loved so much that they were willing to stab us in the back for it?"

Fish Schtick consisted of *(back, left to right)* Brian McCann, Pat Finn, Randy Hassan, Leo Ford, Ian Gomez, *(front, left to right)* Cici Lubin, James Grace, and Chris Farley. (COURTESY OF CHARNA HALPERN)

Blue Velveeta included, among others, *(back, left to right)* Brian Blondell, Jay Leggett, Susan Messing, Mitch Rouse, Tom Booker, Brendan Sullivan, and *(front)* Kevin Dorff. (COURTESY OF CHARNA HALPERN)

After Blue Velveeta, groups like Mr. Blonde and Frank Booth followed in the early 1990s, but the most dominant group of that era was arguably the Family. It started as the Victim's Family, but following the tragic death of member Rick Roman, the name was changed to the Family. After several personnel changes, it ended up with members Matt Besser, Ian Roberts, Neil Flynn, Ali Faranakian, Miles Stroth, and Adam McKay.

Stroth, who would later serve as manager of the ImprovOlympic, vividly recalled his first class with Del at Papa Milano's. The group waited in the basement, and when Del showed up, the room went quiet. Before he could start speaking, an attractive young waitress walked through the back of the class and up the stairs. Del kept his eyes on her the entire time. When she was out of sight, he turned to the class and said, "Well, she was pretty enough to kill."

Roberts saw his first show at Papa Milano's and began classes with the ImprovOlympic, but soon discovered he wasn't prepared for Del. In the middle of a scene in which he was trying to impress his teacher, Del stopped it to berate him: "Oh, all right, all right, stop. Well, you've ruined a perfectly good game with your inane pop references!"

The students who ultimately succeeded were those who learned from his criticisms. Those who didn't would seldom last long. He was brutal to those who resisted his advice. Del's usual reaction to those who consistently made jokes or refused to listen was to issue them an immediate refund, usually in front of the entire class. On one memorable occasion, Halpern entered the class and noticed that one of the new students had disappeared. Del explained that he had written a refund check. "But Del," protested Halpern, "he hadn't paid me for the class yet!" Del shrugged. "Well, it was worth it just to be rid of 'im!"

The early classes at Papa Milano's were eye-opening for Matt Besser. One night, a *Sun-Times* reporter was interviewing Del and some students, but she obviously knew little about improvisation. Though they needed all the publicity they could get at the time, after two questions Del said, "You obviously don't have any idea what you're talking about. Why don't you go research a little and come back later when you have some knowledge?" Besser observed, "He's one of the few teachers that would tell you 'No, that's terrible. That was awful.' And I think at a certain point, you need that if you're really going to take this thing seriously."

Del tended to lecture for thirty minutes or more before beginning exercises with the students. The brightest realized that there was usually a correlation between the lecture and the stage time that followed in each workshop, though it was not always immediately clear to the class. "[It] was usually him telling us about some book he read on the bus, or some interaction that he saw," recalled Peter Gwinn. "There was some element of that philosophy or interaction that he wanted to reproduce onstage, so it was more mindset preparation."

After his return from L.A., disagreements between Halpern and Del were rare, and they always managed to work them out, as with an offer from Southern Comfort to sponsor a comedy tour. At first, Del was opposed, arguing, "Oh, yeah. Let's sell alcohol to kids, that's a great idea, you know, I used to be an alcoholic." Halpern said, "Yeah, but maybe it's a way of letting them atone—they're spreading the word of improv around college campuses, and they're giving us a lot of money. It'd be really good for the theater." Eventually, Del gave in.

In June 1990, they announced the Southern Comfort Team Comedy Challenge, intended to be a national search for the best improvisational comedy team in the country, culminating in national championships early the next year in Los Angeles. They enlisted Mike Myers as the official spokesman for the contest: "People are addicted to the excitement of team sports, so why shouldn't they love yet another team challenge that involves victory, defeat and performance?"[1]

Most of their disagreements involved business. Once, during a big business meeting in L.A., Halpern was hoping to reach a deal. She watched in horror as Del told them, "Oh, absolutely not, I would never do that!" She was kicking him under the table until he finally said, "Thank you very much, gentlemen, I'm not interested," and got up and walked out. She knew when she could and couldn't push him, and each of them somehow knew when to give in to the other.

While Del could occasionally be intimidating, he would always listen to reason. There were times when he would say, "No, I absolutely won't budge on this," and Halpern had to listen to reason as well. She knew that he could simply fling a "Well, thank you, goodbye" and walk out. She knew when he was never going to budge on a matter. With Southern Comfort, she thought, "Well, let's look at it *this* way," and Del responded with one of his harrumphings, which meant that he was giving in.

◇

When Andrew Alexander began developing TV projects, he kept Del in mind. In 1990–91, Alexander executive-produced a syndicated series called *My Talk Show*. The five-day-a-week series starred Cynthia Stevenson as a Wisconsin housewife who found herself with her own talk show, shot in her living room, with her friends and neighbors as her guests.

Much of the series involved Alexander "trying to shoehorn Second City scenes into this talk show," recalled Danny Breen. Alexander brought in numerous Second City alumni to fill in various roles, including Del, who was eventually chosen to serve as a crazy, rabble-rousing neighbor who jammed the broadcasts to deliver rants and comic monologues.

The format was perfect for Del, who didn't want to leave Chicago for any lengthy period. He could write and perform his own material, shoot it in a Chicago studio, and have it sent to the production office. Del invented a character called Chauncy Julius Oldphart, eventually changed to Ozzie Mandias, and began writing politically incorrect social commentary, with subjects ranging from Ronald Reagan and Clarence Thomas, to Scientology and psychedelic toads.

My Talk Show marked the end of Del's career as a recurring character on a TV series, but he continued to appear in scene-stealing smaller roles in films and series shot in Chicago throughout the early 1990s, often portraying pompous authority figures. He had a small role as Dr. Stone in the 1989 *Dream Breakers*, a TV movie starring Robert Loggia, Hal Linden, and Kyle MacLachlan. He appeared as Frank in 1989's *Next of Kin*, which he referred to as "that hillbillies versus the mob" movie, and he also had a role in 1990's *Opportunity Knocks* as Williamson, Dana Carvey's obnoxious boss. He was also featured prominently as H. R. Rineman in 1992's *The Public Eye*, starring Joe Pesci as a 1940s tabloid photographer.

In 1993, Del appeared as Col. Robert McCormick, legendary publisher of the *Chicago Tribune*, in an episode of the syndicated TV series *The Untouchables*, inspired by the success of the De Palma film. The series ran for two seasons, from January 1993 to May 1994.

Of course, many of his parts were also cut. He was sent on location to Mexico for 1989's *Fat Man and Little Boy*, starring John Cusack, where he portrayed Dr. Kenneth Whiteside in the story of the development of the atomic bomb. Despite weeks on the set, he almost disappeared from the final theatrical release, visible only as he answers a door in long shot. His lines were also trimmed from Penny Marshall's *A League of Their Own* in 1992, though he is seen in a meeting with Walter Harvey (played by Garry Marshall). But film work was slowing down in Chicago, and Del would content himself with local theater jobs.

Although he would miss the Hollywood paychecks, they were little more than a way to subsidize his art. The jobs he cared least about, the television and films, paid the best, while those that he was most passionate for, the theater and workshops, paid the least. Richard Laible once noted that with all of his movies raising his profile, he could charge more for his classes. "Just the opposite," Del responded. "I only do these movies to make money. What I love to do is teach classes. Now that I'm making enough money, I can actually charge less."

David Pasquesi *(left)* with Del in the Remains Theatre production of *The Chicago Conspiracy Trial.* (COURTESY OF CHARNA HALPERN)

If improvisation was his life's work, the theater was his first love. In the summer of 1991, he was cast as David Dellinger, the senior defendant in the Remains Theatre production of Ron Sossi and Frank Condon's *The Chicago Conspiracy Trial.* Based on the actual transcripts of the Chicago Eight (later seven) trial following the 1968 Democratic National Convention, the production, which opened September 22, featured a cast of thirty-six actors, including former students Bruce Jarchow as lawyer William Kunstler and David Pasquesi as Abbie Hoffman.

It was also when the teacher-student relationship between Pasquesi and Del turned to friendship. They spent more time together, and Del would even visit his residential neighborhood for barbecues. He seemed to enjoy it greatly, even taking pleasure in playing with Pasquesi's two young sons. "When Giancarlo was just learning how to speak, I came around the corner, and Del was trying to make him repeat 'Daddy is a junkie.' His defense later was, 'Well, at the time, I didn't know it was true!'" Pasquesi laughed.

The pair even put together a two-man show, *Del and Dave in Rehearsal for the Apocalypse,* during the run of *The Chicago Conspiracy Trial.* The late-night short-run (ten performances in five weeks) show was presented the following year in the Remains space, and consisted of individual prepared monologues rather than improvisations. The two of them would sit in Del's kitchen at night after the performances of the *Conspiracy Trial,* since neither of them would go out to the bar; the show developed from their talks.

Del still appeared semiregularly with the Steppenwolf company during the early 1990s. He was in their production of *Harvey* from November 1, 1990, through February 28, 1991, which was directed by Austin Pendleton and featured Randall Arney, Sally Murphy, and Rondi Reed. Two years later, he was in 1993's *Ghost in the Machine* during its April 15 through May 5 run, directed by Jim True-Frost and featuring Arney and Martha Lavey. Later that year, Del was featured in the world premiere of Steve Martin's *Picasso at the Lapin Agile*, directed by Arney for the Steppenwolf's Studio Theatre. Opening on October 23, 1993, the cast included Tracy Letts, Shannon Cochran, Jim Ortlieb, Philip E. Johnson, and Del as Sagot.

Del returned to the Goodman the following year for *Merchant of Venice*. Acclaimed director Peter Sellars helmed the production, which opened on September 30, 1994. Del was cast as the Duke of Venice, and also portrayed the (typically) blind Old Gobbo, whose son, Launcelot Gobbo, was portrayed by Philip Seymour Hoffman. Del found Sellars exasperating at times, and delineated his thoughts about the first week of rehearsals in a 1994 Labor Day letter to Larry Coven.

> Peter Sellars has this vision of how it's gonna go, and by golly, it's gonna *go* that way! It's as if he's playing every character. There will be no set—much to the annoyance of George Feypin, the putative designer, just a bunch of tables set C. R & L [centerstage right and left] roughly parallel to each other, and with a bunch of caskets lying around in the middle. (The caskets of gold, silver, and lead are full-size *caskets*!) In the first part of the show, when not in Belaine (Belmont), we're in Shylock's bank. Old Gobbo doesn't encounter Launcelot in the street, but comes to bug his son as he works at a computer in a bank. Instead of the son fooling with the blind father, we have the non-blind (Sellars—"Of course you're not blind—you see very clearly.") father, a "homeless" bum *by choice*, harassing his yuppie son about his lifestyle. The change of subtext works for about ¾ of the scene, but where it doesn't, you could get an emotional hernia tryin' to bend the words to Peter's meaning. I got *really stoned* t'other night and *almost* figured out how to do it—but so far, some of Shakespeare into Sellars simply won't go. (Probably this will change.) Peter is happy to paraphrase the lines, showing how clear his ideas are—but one is tempted to say "Okay, Peter, now try it with the real words!"
>
> The actors in this production are stunningly good—I'm *way* outclassed.

There are mikes everywhere, and video monitors, and actors with videocams following each other about. Peter to Del (as Old Gobbo): "You don't have a mike—you're a poor man." A poor man with a loud voice. I discover that the word *poor* projected from the diaphragm will dislodge my upper plate. Hazards everywhere.

The trial scene is designed to look like the O.J. Simpson/L.A. Riots courtroom. I suggested that when Shylock reveals his knife it should be taken from a large manila envelope. Didn't even rate a chuckle from the director.

Peter's a little wiry guy with that weird brush cut, careful to project a hail-fellow-well-met jolly and caring attitude, taking 30 folks out for dinner and saying "Just tell me if you're bored—I don't want anybody to be bored," but underneath he's *fierce*, armed with his vision, not only of the play, but some sort of primitive Christian-like communitarian spiritual vision and he'll *crush* you if you get in his way, because he's *right* and has a lot of moralistic ammunition to *prove* he's right. Well, no arguments from me—he *is* a better man than I am, as I said, but despite all the Bibles, Korans, Talmuds and Bhagavad Gitas lying on the library/research table, I haven't bought into his worldview, and I'm not precisely sure what it is, to be frank. . . .

Peter's the kinda guy that no matter how light or trivial the conversation, he always, always, *always* has the last word.

After the Chicago run, *Merchant of Venice* went on a successful European tour (originally scheduled for three weeks, it was extended to five before it even opened).

In September of the following year, Del returned to the Goodman for his last Shakespearean production, *All's Well That Ends Well*. Director Mary Zimmerman set the play in the late seventeenth century, and the production received, at best, a mixed review from the *Chicago Tribune*'s Richard Christiansen. In the October 3, 1995, review, the critic, who admitted it was one of Shakespeare's "problem plays," cited poor casting and noted that many of its orations were not clearly delivered. He did single out Del as an exception, however.

The actors, using a contemporary conversational rhythm for the Shakespearean verse, sometimes discover quick bursts of humor and meaning in their lines (Del Close as an old lord of the court is particularly tricky in his line readings). And Zimmerman, when she has the chance to present an attractive picture, as she does in the final lines of the play, comes through with a gracious ensemble tableau.

◇

In July 1993, Paul Sills organized a pair of benefit performances in Door County, Wisconsin, where he was conducting workshops. The Second City alumni would include Severn Darden, Dick Schaal, Mina Kolb, Paul Sand, Valerie Harper, Hamilton Camp, and Avery Schreiber, as well as former Sills actors Lewis Arquette, Garry Goodrow, Rachel Keene, and pianist Fred Kaz.

Author Jeffrey Sweet was invited to attend by Barbara Harris; she had previously told him that they could ride with Halpern, who would be driving up with Del. But there was an unexpected problem: Del had not been invited to perform, so he refused to go. The next morning, Halpern pulled her car in front of Harris's apartment, and Del was in the backseat, grumbling, "Nobody's going to keep me from seeing my friends! Fuck Sills anyway!"

During the drive to Wisconsin, the topic turned to the Second City performances in London during the Cuban Missile Crisis, and Del told them about the game in which they would point fingers and "shoot" each other. "Is it true that you once fell down seven flights of stairs?" Harris asked him. With a chuckle, Del replied, "I don't know where these stories get started. It was only five."

The subject only served to remind Del of Sills again. "Sills never got the idea of this game. He said you shouldn't be killing each other, you should be kissing each other, this should be an exchange of love. He doesn't understand. You only kill the ones you love."

When they arrived for the Early Second City Players Reunion, they learned that the July 23 and 24 performances would consist mostly of theater games under Sills's supervision. Although the first performance was wonderful, Del was frustrated, and still felt an urge to perform with them on the second night, so he approached Sills with an idea. "You know, Avery and I used to do that thing about the computer answering questions, where Avery mimed being the computer. Avery's here, why don't I join you and do that for the second show?" Sills said, "That's awfully generous of you, Del, but I think we've got the show that we want. We're all set here." Del walked away muttering, "Fucking asshole, fucking asshole . . ."

Nevertheless, the following night's show was also delightful. But even when the group retired to a nearby pizza place, Del was still irritated, grumbling into his beard. Then he looked across the table at Dick Schaal, who smiled back at him. And so Del pulled out his finger and said "Bang!" Schaal flew up from his chair and died a spectacular death. And Del finally smiled. "After thirty years, they were still playing by the rules of the game," noted Sweet.

◈

Late in 1993, I began hosting an hour-long pop culture radio show, sponsored by Moondog's Comics, on WCBR-FM. Each show included an interview with a pop culture star in the first half hour, and a noted comic book creator in the second half hour. When I learned that the in-studio guest for the show on December 11 would be Tiny Tim, I immediately invited Del along to let them catch up after twenty-eight years.

After picking up Del, we drove out to a suburban hotel, and I met Tiny Tim in the lobby. He was wearing a sport coat and incredibly potent cologne, and carried a ukulele in a brown paper shopping bag. As we walked outside, I informed him that I had brought along an old friend whom he hadn't seen in a while. Del turned to face him, and Tiny Tim looked puzzled. Del had a long gray beard, and his hair was shorter than it had been. "It's been a number of years," said Del, smiling and extending his hand. "Mr. Close! Mr. Del Close! Praise the Lord, it's Mr. Del Close!" Tiny Tim grinned and pumped his hand. Tiny Tim always called everyone "Mister" or "Miss," so it didn't surprise me when Del immediately referred to him as "Mr. Tim."

The two of them began to reminisce as we drove. They compared notes about the time the Grateful Dead came down for a midnight show, the period in which Tiny Tim lived in the guesthouse behind the house where Del was staying, mutual friends like Lenny Bruce and Ken Kesey, and the visits by the Merry Pranksters. All too soon, we arrived at the radio station, where we met my wife, Laurie Bradach, cohost Gary Colabuono, and comic book guests Joe Quesada, Jimmy Palmiotti, and *Wasteland* artist Don Simpson.

As the show began, Del spoke:

I see a ukulele there that looks very much like the ukulele that I glued back together with Elmer's Glue when someone sat on it out on the West Coast in 1965, when Mr. Tim and I were doing *The Phantom Cabaret Strikes Again* out there! Mr. Tim is probably the most exciting entertainer I have ever worked with in my entire life. He's the only entertainer I know who can open a three-hour show, three heavy acts come on, and then Mr. Tim can come on and close it, too! . . . Nobody's ever brought me to tears with "Goodbye Old Paint" except Mr. Tim!

Del revealed that Lenny Bruce had told him how the last thing he would listen to before going to sleep at night was a tape of Tiny Tim. "There was an article in *Ramparts* magazine [referring] to Mr. Tim as 'a haunted house,'" noted Del. "These 78-rpm voices come singing through Tim almost as if it's a séance. . . . You can almost hear the scratches in the records through the voice."

After Tiny Tim mentioned Spider-Man, I asked whether he was around when Del used to do his own spidering. "I don't think Mr. Tim knew about spidering," said Del. "I once got arrested for overspidering. Spidering consisted of taking an enormous amount of methamphetamine hydrochloride and climbing from attic to attic. The attics in San Francisco tend to be connected, so if you get into one attic, you can spider from one attic to another, and sometimes you can spider for a whole block."

Del also informed everyone that "you could list your name in the telephone directory under any name at all so long as you absolve them of any legal problems you would have. I wanted to list my name as Spider Spider Spider, but, they couldn't get all three spiders on one line, so I was listed as Spider S. Spider."

After another version of the "spidering" story, more comic book discussion followed, as Joe Quesada mentioned *The Dark Knight Returns* and *Watchmen*, the two comic book stories that got Del interested in the field once again. "I just have this weird feeling about comics, that it's kind of like Elizabethan theater just before Shakespeare. We're waiting for the first really great graphic novel to come out and grab everybody's attention and convince everyone all at the same time that this is indeed an art form," said Del.

Tiny Tim *(center)* entertains Del *(right)* and the others in the radio studio with "When Will the Sun Shine for Me?" On the same show, Del revealed that Lenny Bruce liked to fall asleep at night listening to Tiny Tim. (AUTHOR'S COLLECTION)

"I've been quoted as saying that *Dark Knight* and *Watchmen* are the *Sgt. Pepper* and the *White Album* of our industry. I think there's a next step that has to be taken," said Quesada.

"Yeah, that's the one I'm waiting for!"

After another song by Tiny Tim, the show wrapped up and Del promised to return in the future. I drove Del and Tiny Tim back as their stories continued nonstop. They even briefly discussed ex-wives, as I reflected that the two of them might have been as ill-suited for marriage as anyone I've ever known. Tiny Tim, who married "Miss Vicki" live on *The Tonight Show*, revealed that "the marriage was over the minute the [TV] lights were out." Whenever I climbed into my car for weeks afterward, I was still overpowered by the scent of Tiny Tim's cologne.

The following month, Del did another appearance with guests Beverly Garland, star of numerous low-budget horror films, as well as *My Three Sons*, and comic book creator Jim Starlin. Del was scheduled to appear again on the March 5, 1994, program. Unbeknownst to him, I had planned a surprise party on the air to celebrate his sixtieth birthday. The on-air guests who would be calling in included Chris Farley, Howard Hesseman, and *Wasteland* collaborator Ostrander.

Then, the day before, one of Del's best-loved students, John Candy, died of heart failure. Although Candy was certainly overweight, his sudden death came as a shock. I called Del after I heard the news; he apologized, not feeling he could go on the air, even after I revealed the surprise I had planned. Farley likewise canceled. I told Del to listen in nevertheless. Howard Hesseman paid loving tribute to Del and related stories of their days at the Committee.

The second half of the show featured John Ostrander discussing *Wasteland*, and how the literal truth of stories like "Sewer Rat" was ultimately less important than what appeared on the page—that some details were changed for the sake of the medium. "After a certain point, [detail] almost doesn't matter. There are certain mythologies that start to come up. A good myth always starts under the basis of what is true, then gets to what is psychologically true, and that's what the whole thing wound up being." In the end, beyond any factual discrepancies, what are left are wonderful stories.

23

"Close, You've Gone Sane!"

The ImprovOlympic had settled in at the Wrigleyside. Long-form had found a familiar niche, with shows based on the Harold, but there was little new to shake up the status quo. iO student-performer Mick Napier had founded the Annoyance Theatre, presenting original shows like *Splatter Theatre* and *Co-Ed Prison Sluts* with an improvisational feel, and the Family was drawing a devoted following at the ImprovOlympic.

Del's classes were still well attended, but the fire that had driven him in the past was burning low. Complacency appeared to be setting in, and many believed Del was content to ride on his own coattails as the Guru.

The early 1990s saw a long-form explosion in Chicago, in part because of a new group calling itself Ed, which came out of Evanston's Piven Workshop. It startled ImprovOlympic regulars. Ian Roberts of the Family attended the final performance of Ed, and came into class raving about the show, but found Del unimpressed. "I think it really ticked [Del] off, because none of them were iO people," recalled Roberts.

Several members of Ed then joined with ImprovOlympic veterans to start a group called Jazz Freddy in 1992, selling out weeks in advance, and receiving national press.

The success of Ed and Jazz Freddy lit a fire under ImprovOlympic. Surprised to see how rigid and resistant to change so many other students and performers had become, Del decided to use the Family to loosen up the form. After nearly four decades of improvising, he was still in the forefront of innovation. Del considered past long-form experiments in which an audience member would discuss his or her day and the company would extrapolate from the experiences; there was the idea of improvising a movie; and even acting out dreams, which went back to the days of the Chicago Extension.

Until that point, the most successful teams at the ImprovOlympic had nowhere else to go within the organization—a problem that dated back to the Baron's Barracudas. But Del realized that Improv-Olympic didn't have to be a student show that stopped after a stint as the house team. The emphasis on traditional Harolds would have to change; the ImprovOlympic was not the only game in town anymore. It even affected the Second City, which brought in former ImprovOlympic students like Noah Gregoropoulos and Mick Napier to direct long-form improv shows there. The newspapers proclaimed, "Second City wakes up and smells the coffee."

◆

The new shows with the Family would be another turning point for the ImprovOlympic, as Del resumed the direction of improvisational shows for the first time since Blue Velveeta. The first two shows would feature the Family, which consisted of Miles Stroth, Ali Faranakian, Neil Flynn, Adam McKay, Matt Besser, and Ian Roberts, doing the newly developed long-forms and a traditional Harold in *Three Mad Rituals* and *Dynamite Fun Nest*.

Del's first attempt became known as the Spineless Harold, a faster type of long-form. He declared, "We don't have to do this three-beat structure." The group started playing with tag-outs, in which one actor would "tag out" another performer in an existing scene to further the action and heighten the meaning. The Family became known for being fast, just as Jazz Freddy was known for being slow.

The first successful long-form performance piece to follow the Harold was the Movie, as presented by the Family. Del was frustrated by the limitations of improvisation, that his actors couldn't do special effects or scenes on a grand scale. The Movie included elaborate description, as the performers narrated improvised stage directions like "The camera booms in; we see a fire in the distance; we can't really tell the size of

The Upright Citizens Brigade, *(left to right)* Matt Walsh, Matt Besser, Ian Roberts, and Amy Poehler, was an offshoot of the Family. (PHOTO BY BRIAN HUS- KEY; COURTESY OF THE UPRIGHT CITIZENS BRIGADE)

it. As we move closer, we find that it is not a campfire, but it is a house burning." The first public performance of the Movie was at a memorial service for Rick Roman, and the Family succeeded on the highly emotional occasion.

The Movie was the second successful long-form format that truly worked, and people were talking about it. The success of the Movie led the Family, under Del's direction, to put together a program that would highlight the Harold and two new kinds of long-form improvisation. *Three Mad Rituals* consisted of the Movie, the Harold, and the Check-In Deconstruction, scenes based on a one-sided re-creation of someone's day. It eventually required a group member to commit to going out and having an exceptional day, to prevent the resulting improvisation from being too boring.

Three Mad Rituals was followed by *Dynamite Fun Nest*, a name derived from a "word ball" that Del had given to Halpern. The Family continued to perform the Movie as part of the new show, and added the Check-in Expansion and the Horror to the new show. The Horror was performed just before the intermission, noted Stroth, and "every show we lost two or four at intermission."

The controversial Horror, also known as the Expressionistic Horror, was a favorite of Del's; the inevitable walkouts after each performance delighted him. Each week, a series of scenes was based on a newspaper article about a tragic, horrific event. Del told them, "I want to do an improv form which is not comedic. In fact, I want to take the most horrible article in the paper and try to embody everything that's horrible, exponentially, about that article." Del enthusiastically supported it. "The first two pieces, everyone laughed and clapped, then [when we did the Horror] there was silence, creeped-out silence, and all you heard in the back of the theater was *Ha! Ha! Ha!* Del just loved it," recalled Roberts. "You could do stuff about pedophiles, about child murderers, about fires where everyone had died." Most of the audience was disturbed and puzzled by what happened, and even some members of the Family hated it. "Charna hated that thing, and it was really a crowd-alienator. . . . It was very dark, incredibly dark," recalled Gregoropoulos.

After *Three Mad Rituals* and *Dynamite Fun Nest*, Del began working with groups other than the Family, gravitating toward those who were slightly askew, odd, or uninhibited. One of his eight-week sessions reflected his fascination with chanting. He told his class that there was really nothing very amazing about it: "If you pay attention to the chanting in the movie *White Zombie*, it's really just half of the people going *Ooo baba lala* and the other half going *Chaca chaca chaca*. That's all the chanting's going to be." He divided the class into groups and assigned each a segment to repeat in order to give a ritualistic feel to the improvisation. The students soon lost their sense of time while chanting. "At the beginning, when we were chanting, he'd say, 'How long do you think that went?' And we'd say, 'Maybe five minutes? Ten minutes?' And he'd say, *'Forty-five minutes!'*" said Roberts. It eventually transformed from pure chanting to spinning off improvisational scenes. Del found it all fascinating.

The Family eventually drifted apart because of various outside factors. Toward the end of *Dynamite Fun Nest*, Kelly Leonard took over as producer at the Second City, and several members of the Family were hired. The mainstage show at the Second City was revamped, and the result was more like long-form improvisation. Immediately after Adam McKay directed there, he was hired for *Saturday Night Live*.

Del never bore a grudge against the Second City, and remained friendly with Alexander and Leonard. One day, Leonard informed Del that he had done his thesis on the Beat Generation, and they talked about Kerouac, Ginsberg, and a number of the lesser-known Beats, including John Clellon Holmes, the man who coined the phrase "Beat Generation." "The next day, I came into my office and a brown paper bag was on my desk," recalled Leonard. "Inside was a first-edition copy of Holmes's novel *The Horn*. No note, no nothing. I left him a message to thank him, but he never called me back or took credit for the gift."

◈

During the run of the Family, Besser, McKay, and Roberts founded the Upright Citizens Brigade, which focused on sketch comedy. After the Family broke up, Besser and Roberts pitched the idea for an Upright Citizens Brigade TV show to Comedy Central in 1996, with a cast consisting of Besser, Roberts, Matt Walsh, and Amy Poehler. They wanted to turn the Harold into a sketch show for television, but TV shows were twenty-two minutes long, and the Harold was usually at least thirty or forty minutes. They sat down with Del at the Salt and Pepper diner next to the theater and asked how they could fit a Harold into twenty-two minutes. Del responded "Condense time!" by using video editing and cuts that can't be done onstage. The group insisted that Del be hired to do the introduction and voiceovers for the *Upright Citizens Brigade* TV show; the Upright Citizens Brigade eventually founded theaters in New York and L.A.

Miles Stroth remained at the ImprovOlympic, assisting Halpern in nearly all aspects of the business, including the bar, the training center, the box office, and the nightly shows. There were new shows, new classes, and an energized Del to keep pushing the form forward.

Perhaps the most successful during this post-Family transitional time was the Armando Diaz Theatrical Experience and Hootenanny, a long-form that began with a monologue delivered by one of the players; the other players would then begin improvising around incidents and themes suggested by the monologue.

Other iO classes focused on the Dream Harold. Del battled the perception that the Dream was nothing more than a glorified freeze-tag, and made it more long-form while weaving more ideas through it. Other workshop exercises were variations of the Harold. There were experiments with Improv Tragedy, inspired by the Horror. There were Backward Harolds with the opening at the end. "We had to think of themes backwards," recalled Peter Gwinn. "Instead of generating information to pull from later, we had to think about what the themes were in the work we just did, and weave that through the opening."

◈

Halpern made a business decision of her own in 1995, looking once more for another space for the ImprovOlympic. She found it, surprisingly, just a stone's throw away from the Wrigleyside, at 3541 North Clark Street, in the shadow of Wrigley Field. After pitching the idea to her cousin, he bought the building and then leased it to Halpern.

In March 1995, the ImprovOlympic Theatre opened at last. In fact, the building contained two theaters, each with a full-service bar, along with offices and rehearsal rooms for classes. The first floor theater could seat eighty, and proved handy for classes as well as shows. The upstairs theater held one hundred seats salvaged from the old Chicago Stadium. It was named, appropriately, the Del Close Theater.

Del was proud to have a theater named after him, particularly because, as he was quick to tell friends, "I didn't have to put any money into it! I didn't have to donate anything to get my own theater!" He would often mention that his theater had seats that had watched Michael Jordan play basketball.

◇

Del's interest in directing grew. Through the mid-1990s, he continued to be involved with theater and films, and he also stayed active socially. During that time, when my fiancée and I operated a comic book and science fiction art gallery in Chicago, Del was a jovial presence at all openings and related events; after we married, he presented us with a very thoughtful wedding gift: a bust of Ed Gein. But even though his sociable side was dominant, he stayed true to his public persona, one that had no affection for children—at least in front of other people.

He had grown apart from Jamie Swise, who had gotten married and had a baby, which was anathema to Del. One day, Swise was pushing his year-old daughter's stroller down Belmont Avenue. Del was sitting inside a Mexican restaurant with Mike Flores from the Psychotronic Film Society, when Swise waved and called out "Hi, Del." Del pointed his finger at the baby as if it were a gun and said "Pow!" Swise simply continued walking. It was the type of thing Del would do to show off in front of friends like Flores, without considering its effect on his long-time friend. Swise felt a twinge of disappointment and sadness at seeing Del still going for the quick laugh at the expense of their one-time friendship, so he moved on. He wasn't interested in allowing Del to make his daughter the butt of his jokes.

Del was content for people to believe that he hated children, just as he didn't care whether he was labeled a misogynist; it was a part of his public persona. It continued to stem from his own feelings of guilt about being a burden to his parents.

When he was alone with friends and their children, he was normally respectful. Only when he had an audience did his behavior toward children turn hostile. The whole truth was a bit more complicated. Although Del had always been very well behaved when visiting the Pasquesi family, one evening, when my wife and I and some other friends were visiting during the Christmas season, things changed.

When David Pasquesi was out of the room, Del made some unkind remarks to their four-year-old son, Giancarlo. His wife, Joan Marie, said something to Del, who ceased, but then, when both parents were out of the room, Del could not resist performing. "Who comes down the chimney on Christmas Eve? Satan!" he told the boy, who stood up to him, insisting, "No, no he doesn't." The other guests were uncomfortable watching Del cross the line, and David quickly returned. When he asked Del about it, Del was very dismissive. "All I can figure out is that he had to keep up that persona in front of people. He was always fine when it was just us, but he wasn't fine when there were other people there," said Pasquesi.

After that evening, Pasquesi saw little of Del, and they drifted apart. Only when they were both doing shows at the Goodman was the rift mended. Del was offstage for most of *Merchant of Venice*, while Pasquesi was across the hall doing a show in which he only appeared in the first and last scenes. They rekindled their friendship in the green room of the Goodman and started spending time together once more.

◇

Del's misogynistic reputation seemed to lessen in his later years, though the opportunities to clash with female actors were fewer, because he could generally pick and choose his students. No matter the gender, he respected toughness and intelligence, and would savage anyone who fell into trite or cliched roles.

In the early days at the Second City, Del often disliked the choices that women made onstage. Accustomed to working with Elaine May, he didn't like students who immediately fell into the roles of wives or girlfriends, considering these choices boring and unimaginative. Only years later, when women made stronger choices and gender roles were evolving, did he become interested in the women. That was why he wanted to build a show around Honor Finnegan, a "spunky little chick," and why he was delighted by ImprovOlympic performers such as Susan Messing, Melanie Blue, and Tina Fey. "It wasn't a matter of hating women, because he would respect anyone if they deserved respect," explained Halpern. "If there was a man who didn't deserve respect, he wouldn't like him, either. 'Stop being stereotypical and do something interesting, and then I'll realize that there is some interest in you.' That, I think, was the problem."

◈

During his last two decades, Halpern saw sides of him that he was not comfortable revealing to anyone else—some vulnerable, others, like the "talking hands" episode, frightening. He could be sentimental and emotional with her to the point of tears, apparently schizoid at other times. He loved to surprise her, sometimes buying her unexpectedly thoughtful gifts. "He bought me a velvet watch with diamonds around the face once for Christmas, and he did a beautiful presentation. He really took the time to do it, and no one would think he would be that romantic."

Del would occasionally exaggerate incidents, or allow others to exaggerate them without correction, which, to Halpern, was all part of the legend. To her, his varying versions of his father's suicide were "building the mystery of Del." "He told us he was there when he saw his dad die, and we kind of figured out that he wasn't, so who knows? Why did he want us to be horrified? Why did he want us to think that he sat there watching it?" There were other incidents as well, including a far-fetched story seemingly calculated to provoke her reaction. The two of them had just seen a film about a killer who felt he became stronger with each life that he took. Del claimed that this was indeed what happened when one took a life, while Halpern insisted he didn't know what he was talking about. So he tried to convince her that he had taken part in the murder of another child a long time ago. "Yeah, I had a little to do with that," he told her. Halpern felt it would have been impossible for Del to have done what he claimed, and that he wanted to seem evil for some unknown reason.

While some extreme statements appeared intended to provoke a reaction, others likely reflected his desire to play devil's advocate. "It wasn't a question of shocking as much as Del felt he had to take the other point of view of any conversation, because *somebody* had to," said

Halpern. If someone was condemning Hitler, or any unpopular figure, Del would find a reason to defend him for the sake of argument, because, in his opinion, "*somebody's* got to take the opposing view."

That kind of off-center thinking served him well in his creative life. When his students were faced with a problem, he would urge them to discard their first thought, because it was likely too obvious. Instead, Del would urge them to make the *opposite* choice. He never thought in the conventional way.

◆

The exercise called the Invocation involved performers invoking an object or person. In a three-stage process, the students would first describe it, then talk directly to it with gradually heightened language, and finally worship it. There was even an occasional fourth stage in which the players would become that object or person.

During one workshop in the 1970s, Del agreed to perform it for his students, and decided to invoke himself while being taped. He delivers a frank assessment of his own talents and abilities, admitting that while others would find success and fame through him, it would never be his.

> He was a young comedian.
> He didn't know what he was doing and got into show business for all the wrong reasons: ego satisfaction, the fact that it was too easy, very easy, very easy to impress, very easy to generate a little easy charisma.
> But then he began to learn.
> You! You! You asshole, you began to learn.
> You stayed in your work too long, until it was too late, and then you began to realize what you'd gotten yourself into. You surprised him! You took a step he didn't expect, and you committed him to something that frightened him to death.
> Thou art my higher nature, and I have become thee,
> Much to my surprise.
> I know who thou art.
> Thou comest and takest my body and my mind and use it for thy purpose with my wholehearted permission.
> I am the messenger.

I am not what he expected to become.
There is no enlightenment or reward in this life for me.
I am the messenger. I am the channel. I am his final doom.
I am the door through which you will pass, but he may not.
But he understands. I am the messenger.
Nothing less. But nothing more.

◈

By the mid-1990s, mortality was beginning to weigh on Del. The decades of smoking were finally taking their toll. His efforts to quit were unsuccessful, and he continued to borrow cigarettes from students when Halpern was not around.

Worse, he continued to lose his friends and even his students. Severn Darden, who had introduced him to improvisation, died in late May 1995 at his New Mexico home. A star-studded memorial service, coproduced by Janet Coleman and Garry Goodrow, was held for Darden in New York. As Del spoke about his friend during the service, he broke down crying on the stage of the Walter Kerr Theatre. "It was so unbearably touching to see this satirist, this hard-boiled Del Close, to see him cry over his friend, who had brought him to . . . his life's work," said Janet Coleman. "It was beyond sentimental. It was true, naked grief . . . and it was palpable." Darden was beloved by those who knew him, but Coleman crystalized his relationship with Del: "Everyone loved Severn. Severn didn't love everyone, but Severn loved Del."

Del lost another friend with whom he had so recently been reunited, when Tiny Tim died in Minnesota on November 30, 1996.

Just over a year later, *Saturday Night Live* and film star Chris Farley died on December 18, 1997. For a time, Del was inconsolable. Farley was the third of his famous students to die prematurely, after John Belushi and John Candy; his first comment to me after Farley's death was announced was "Why does God keep killing all of my fat students?" There was no trace of humor in his voice. Farley had idolized Del, possibly as much as he idolized John Belushi. As much as Del, Halpern, and so many others tried to help Farley curb his self-destructive habits, their efforts proved fruitless. Del's forlorn comment on Farley's death: "I was very fond of that fat boy."

In his final years, Del had become the paterfamilias to a generation of improvisers. (COURTESY OF CHARNA HALPERN)

◆

By the mid-1990s, theaters flew Del out for workshops, and students traveled to Chicago to study with him. He was revered by a whole new generation. One day in Chicago, Del and Halpern ran into a junkie friend from the old days. As Halpern reeled off his many accomplishments, the junkie stared in disbelief, finally gasping, "Close, you've gone sane!"

Del had become much more than a historical figure and a primary source. Del was fresh, contemporary, exciting, and still innovative. Twenty-year-old students quickly found that their gray-bearded instructor, who was three times as old as they were, was three times as hip.

When Del accepted an invitation to the Big Stinkin' Improv Festival in Austin, Texas, the gathering was validated in the eyes of the improvisational community. "They thought that was a real coup," said Mick Napier. "He was such an icon that he probably could have done anything and people would have felt grateful just to be in his presence."

At the festival, Del approached Gary Austin, who had now established himself as a highly respected acting coach, and asked Austin to coach him on a speech from *King Lear*. Austin reported to Del's hotel room to listen. When Austin had acted with him at the Committee, he thought Del was adequate but lacked the performance skills of greats like Hesseman and Bonerz, so his expectations were not high. By the time Del had finished, however, Austin was speechless. "It was so brilliant that I swear it was in the same category as an Olivier or a Gielgud," said Austin. He told him, "Del, I have to apologize to you. I can't help you with this monologue. There's nothing I can say that's going to help you make it better. What you just did is so brilliant, I can't help you. I really feel stupid, I feel inadequate." Del replied "Oh, but you already helped me. I was able to do that because you were sitting here."

Austin felt honored, elated, and even triumphant at the thought that his seeing it allowed Del to elevate his acting to that level. While Del knew of Austin's coaching abilities at the time, it was only at a later festival that he learned Austin had created and directed the Groundlings, L.A.'s celebrated improvisational theater. Del was amazed. He'd had no idea, even though he had seen them many times. "Ah-ha! You've got characters! I love their work. I had no idea you had anything to do with it!"

Perhaps Del's favorite festival memory was a local event that he attempted to view each night in Austin. Gary Austin invited him to the bar at the Four Seasons Hotel, across from the Congress Avenue Bridge, at sundown. Del watched in amazement as a huge black cloud, comprising an estimated one and a half million bats, emerged from beneath the bridge, heading downriver for a full fifteen minutes. Del was fascinated, and would always remember the bats as one of his favorite festival experiences. He loved nothing more than watching the dark mass pulsating through the air, changing shapes, looking for all the world like a blob.

Ironically, by the time the number of improvisational festivals began to proliferate rapidly, Del's health was beginning to decline. It was unfortunate that the festival boom didn't begin until the end of his life, mused Napier, because "he would have been the king of every one of them."

◇

One of his favorite destinations for workshops was Seattle. Roberta Maguire had settled there, and through her, he met Randy Dixon of the Market Theatre of Seattle.

Dixon discovered that they shared a number of mutual interests beyond improvisation and theater, and they struck up a friendship. Both were science fiction fans, and Del enjoyed recommending new books. Dixon had studied mythology and other pagan traditions; they also discussed myth-based improvisational projects.

Del had begun flying to Seattle for workshops beginning in the late 1980s. One in particular held some memorable moments. One of the two dozen students, a girl known as M.J., told Dixon excitedly that she had long wanted to work with Del, because her father had known Del years earlier. During a break, Dixon found Del on the porch standing with M.J. Del was calmly smoking a cigarette, but the girl was as white as a ghost. Neither said a word. When Dixon asked what was going on, Del explained, "Well, I just met M.J. here." Dixon said, "Oh, yeah, she mentioned that her father knew you or something like that." Del revealed, "Well, actually, her father was fucking my ex-wife while we were married." Whether Del's response was true, or simply invented, it served to settle down the agitated young woman.

Eventually, Del learned that the Harold had actually been introduced to that region by Roberta Maguire, and was based on the Harolds performed at the Second City nearly twenty years earlier. "It grew its own little strain here, in this control station in Seattle. . . . It evolved a little bit, but it was basically this unstructured Harold, this idea of 'light the fuse and run.'" The first night Del saw the Seattle group perform a Harold, he excitedly told them, "I haven't seen a Harold like that in fifteen years!" Afterward, he became interested in revisiting the more unstructured approach.

◆

By the late 1990s, film jobs around Chicago were scarce due to lack of tax breaks.

In early November 1995, he was cast in an independent film directed by Chuck Parello and filmed in the Chicago area. Although Del only had two scenes in *Henry: Portrait of a Serial Killer, Part 2*, his character would, as in *The Blob*, be pivotal for *Henry 3*. But *Henry 2* was not even released theatrically. As with *The Blob*, there was not a *Henry 3*. Del proclaimed, "I am the sequel killer!"

His final film role was in another sequel, *Mommy 2: Mommy's Day*, filmed in Iowa in 1996. It was written and directed by Max Allan Collins, acclaimed detective and comic book writer (*The Road to Perdition*), and featured Patty McCormack, Mickey Spillane, and Larry Coven. Collins had met Del in the past, and leaped at the chance when Coven suggested that Del could play a small role.

Del arrived on the set disheveled. His hair was long and unkempt, his beard likewise overgrown and scruffy. One of the makeup girls was afraid that a homeless person had wandered onto the set. Collins was quick to correct her, noting Del's lengthy credentials and informing her that he was deserving of her respect. Del explained that he had been about to get a haircut, but decided to wait so that the hair stylist on the set could trim his hair and beard as much as she deemed necessary for the role.

Ever the bibliophile, Del had brought with him to the film set a huge stack of books. He had learned that Mickey Spillane was going to be there the same day (in fact, he later admitted it was the reason he wanted to do the part so badly), and he had brought them all for autographing. Because neither of the men had large roles that day, Del spent hours talking with Spillane, who happily signed all the books.

In 1997, Del made his final appearance onstage at the Goodman Theatre in the premiere of *All the Rage*, written by Keith Reddin and commissioned by the Goodman. Del realized that his increasing lung problems meant he was no longer physically capable of performing, even in a smaller role. His character had to say the last line of the play, but Del was afraid that he wouldn't be able to deliver it. It was a crucial moment in the show, but it was terribly difficult for him to get the line out.

He was resigned to his fate, but refused to feel sorry for himself. As he put it: "My instrument's all screwed up, and I guess that's the end of my acting." His character was supposed to carry several items across the stage, but he became too short of breath. Del was able to get through it when he was instead given a shopping cart, which his once-rich character ended up pushing across the stage by the end of the play.

A visit to the doctor the next summer informed him that his lung capacity was dwindling. Although he had been able to quit alcohol and cocaine, his tobacco addiction was simply too strong. When the doctor told him that he had a year to live, Del told Halpern he thought that was optimistic.

That year, Falls offered him the opportunity to do one more show for the Goodman. It was a production of *Death of a Salesman*, with Brian Dennehy in the lead as Willy Loman. Del was being offered the role of

Loman's brother, Ben. He didn't have the strength, and was forced to decline the role in the Tony Award–winning production. He was heartbroken. He tried to remain philosophical, and decided to devote his remaining time to his teaching and directing. His acting career was finished.

There was one final disruption of his living situation. The owner of his building on Racine Avenue was going to rehab Del's apartment. He would have to move. Halpern wanted to keep Del nearby, and found him a nearby apartment on Belmont, just around the corner from her own place. It was smaller than his previous dwellings, which forced him to pare down his belongings. But Halpern soon made another grim realization: Del would have to climb a flight of stairs to reach the upstairs flat. He insisted that he was well enough, though he soon had to pause while he climbed, short of breath.

No longer could he could walk the few blocks to the theater. He was always leaning on something during classes. He had trouble walking even a block, and relied on rides from students or cabs. During his final months, Halpern was forced to hire a student to drive him to the grocery store, bank, or bookstore. Nevertheless, even though his movements were increasingly restricted, he continued to stave off boredom. When he wasn't reading, he was teaching, writing, or directing a show at the ImprovOlympic.

Although he balked at getting a computer, he finally bought WebTV so he could surf the Internet using his television. He was delighted with the world that had suddenly opened up for him, and immediately bought one for Halpern as well so they could converse. Pasquesi and I began to get e-mail from him, sharing his thoughts about whatever interested him at that moment, whether it was a book he had just finished, fractal patterns, or conspiracy theorists investigating the former Branch Davidian compound in Waco.

But all was not well. There were times when his brain simply seemed not to be getting enough oxygen. Jamie Swise, who had once again become his neighbor, recalled hearing Del shouting and swearing at the television in a way that would previously have been unthinkable. Other old friends noted that his personality and his stories were unlike those he had told throughout his life, which they attributed to the lack of oxygen.

The worst was, of course, his physical decline. Larry Coven noticed that he could no longer walk a city block without resting several times, and told Halpern. The next time he saw Del, he said, "So you ratted me out, eh?" But he quickly forgave Coven. There was no way he could hide his infirmity any longer.

Perhaps the surest sign that Del realized he was dying was when he finally accepted a boyfriend for Halpern. As he grew weaker, Halpern met Mike Click. At first Del did not like him, and called him another one of Halpern's bimbos. One day, Del came over and met him by accident. Click was fascinated by Del and his experiences with the Pranksters, and asked all sorts of questions. When Del discovered that they liked many of the same authors, he knew it would be difficult to continue his dislike of the young man. Halpern decided to invite both Del and Click for Christmas dinner, and Del bought him a book for Christmas. She couldn't believe Del was finally accepting a boyfriend for her. But Del knew he was not going to be around long, and he didn't want her to be alone.

Yet Halpern remained in a state of denial during Del's final year. "I still didn't believe it," said Halpern. "Maybe it was my ability to get through it by denying it to myself. . . . I just thought, 'No, we'll keep him alive. There's just no reason to think he's going to die.'" But at the same time, they were preparing for the inevitable. Del drew up his will in November 1997. I paid a visit to his new apartment shortly afterward, and he proudly pointed out one provision.

"I'm going to donate my skull to the Goodman Theatre for their productions of *Hamlet*," he told me, cackling with glee. He convinced Robert Falls to agree to accept the gift of the skull, making it legal. The thought of it delighted him. If he was going to die soon, he'd found a way to get one last laugh from beyond the grave.

There is no way to know how or when the idea for the skull first occurred to Del. In the early 1970s, he told his Second City actors that he was going to bequeath it to Kansas State University. But an intriguing possibility has recently surfaced. The fourth issue of *Superman* comics, dated spring 1940, includes a one-page feature similar to *Ripley's Believe It or Not*; one of the facts included the illustration of a skull, captioned "Strange Will . . . An usher, devoted to the stage, left his skull to the management, to be used as the skull of 'Yorick' in the play *Hamlet*." There are no other details. Del's lifelong love of comic books is well documented, and since *Superman* was a highly successful, well-distributed title, Del may have come across the blurb and, finding it interesting, filed it away in the back of his mind.

◇

After the Family left in 1995, Del confined his teaching to classes and workshops, a period interspersed with occasional medical leaves. But some students yearned for him to direct another group of students in a show. Peter Gwinn assembled some of the most talented performers at the theater, and excitedly approached Del about directing them in a new show.

"What sort of a show did you have in mind?" asked Del.

"We don't have a show concept yet, we thought maybe we could work on that with you."

"So let me get this straight. You want to take my ideas, take them so that you can do it in your show."

"In my head, I thought 'When you put it that way, you make it sound like a stupid idea,'" said Gwinn. Instead, Del's classes worked on more variations on the Harold, including the Deconstruction, which he was trying to perfect.

There was no longer one dominant team at the ImprovOlympic, and Del did not rush to fill the gap. Eventually, three teams emerged, with Frank Booth, Faulty Wiring, and Lost Yetis all inspired by different facets of the Family. He worked with a team called Missing Persons that put up a show called *Night of the Mutant Harolds*. A new team called Baby Wants Candy became the singular resident company, improvising musicals at each performance. As undeniably talented as they were, the musical format was, for Del, simply not very interesting.

Del was teaching two upper-level class sessions with the most advanced students. One was the same sort of workshop that he had been conducting for decades. But the second was designed to create a new form of improvisation in one eight-week session. His first new show was with a group called Lindbergh Babies, and he continued his experiments with new shows every eight weeks as his health allowed.

In his final months, Del's mind was as active as ever, but the end was coming. "He was missing classes, but less than you would imagine that close to one's death," noted Gregoropoulos.

Del remained active with the Seattle group. In late 1998, he sent Randy Dixon different outlines for shows centered on myth. One of his last ideas was a show based on the men's movement, whether improvised or scripted, as well as other myth-based scenes. "He had been reading some books on [myth], and we had been discussing this idea of how mythic creatures were sort of manifesting themselves in people," said Dixon.

Del seemed to be experiencing a new burst of creativity. Eight-week sessions would result in a new form of improvisation. "Del was in such a good groove toward the end," recalled Stroth. His goal was to make improvisation more theatrical. He loved the grandness of a subtle gesture delivered well, the creation of a balanced stage picture, even the proper lighting—all reflecting his lifelong love of theater.

During the 1998 holiday season, Stroth began appearing in *The Male Intellect: An Oxymoron*, a one-man show at the Apollo Theater. It was not exactly Del's type of humor, but he came to the Christmastime show. As Stroth thanked the audience for coming, he mentioned that there was a bucket in the lobby for contributions to an AIDS charity. "Immediately—and I knew where he was sitting—I hear 'Boo! Boo!' In my mind, I'm going, 'Del is fucking booing me!' I couldn't believe it!" said Stroth. "I got out of it by saying, 'You're booing a charity? At Christmas? How do you feel about sunshine and laughter?' The audience laughed, but I knew in his mind that he didn't want to have to endure someone's soliciting at the end of a theater piece that he had enjoyed."

Del gave Stroth his Christmas present afterward. It was a carton of cigarettes. Del often borrowed cigarettes from him, and Stroth would make comments like "Happy to put another nail in your coffin, Del! One day this will all be mine!" He had told Del that his own smoker's cough was sometimes a problem while performing, but Del was undeterred. "I only heard you cough twice!" joked Del. "You've got plenty of years of smoking left!"

Del never quit smoking cigarettes or pot, though he did his best to hide it from Halpern. Even while she was telling people, "Oh, Del doesn't smoke," he would be borrowing cigarettes from people when she was out of earshot.

In November 1998, I was in Chicago visiting with Terry Jones of Monty Python when I realized that Del was teaching just a few blocks away. We decided to say hello, and after the class, the three of us had a long, late lunch at the brewpub next to the theater. They compared notes about the Second City's 1962 visit to London and discovered they had several mutual friends. Del was entertaining, funny, talkative; he did not look like a man close to death.

(left to right) Author Howard Johnson, Terry Jones, and Del Close in late 1998. This was the last time I saw Del before he entered the hospital. (AUTHOR'S COLLECTION)

Then we stepped outside. The difference was dramatic. The walk from our table to the front door left him breathless, though he struggled not to let it show. He started to signal for a cab, but I insisted on driving him. Jones and I flanked him as he made it to the car, and drove the remaining blocks to his flat near the northeast corner of Belmont and Racine. We offered to help him upstairs, but he declined. He'd had a delightful time, he assured us, meeting an old friend and a new friend. I assured him that we would see each other soon, and he turned to go, neither of us knowing that the next time we met, he would be in the hospital—for the last time.

24

The Party

Saturday, February 27, 1999, was supposed to be a typical day for Del. He was in the middle of an eight-week session with his most advanced class, working on a brand-new form of improvisation set in a funeral home. He called it the Wake.

But Del would not make it to class that day. He called Halpern to say that he was hallucinating, and it might be best if she drove him to class. She said that if he was hallucinating, he should go to the hospital. "No, no," Del told her. "I don't mind the colors. It's fine. I have a class to teach."

Halpern said that if he was hallucinating, his brain was probably not getting enough oxygen. They argued, but Halpern stood firm: he could either go peacefully or be carried by some of the biggest improvisers in the theater. He finally relented, and Halpern drove him a few blocks south to Illinois Masonic Hospital on Wellington Street.

Del was immediately put on inhalation therapy. Halpern sat as his face was covered with a mask with steam pouring out of it. His color instantly came back. Halpern was asked to leave because Del kept trying to talk to her and the doctor needed him to breathe and be silent. She returned at dinnertime, and Del was thrilled at how good he felt. "Oh, thank you, honey, you saved my life," he told her. She left after dinner and told him she would pick him up in the morning.

Overnight, Del took a turn for the worse. When the nurses could not resuscitate him, they placed a large plastic tube in his throat. When he awoke, he was outraged; while he could breathe, he couldn't speak. He was able to write down Halpern's number for the nurse, however, so when she got the call from the hospital at 5:00 A.M., she rushed to his side, where she witnessed a shocking sight.

"I saw him strapped down to his bed with the tube down his throat," noted Halpern. "The only movement was his hands to the wrist and a slight ability to nod with his head. He was crying." He began opening and closing his hand, clenching it like a claw. The tube felt like a claw inside his body. He stared at her, pleading.

She remembered a long-ago conversation in which he had insisted that he never wanted to be in a situation like that; even if she had to sneak in heroin, he had said, she could not let him die that way. "You want this out now?" she asked, and he nodded his head yes. She ran to the doctor, who told her that she had to have power of attorney to take him off the respirator. She told him she did but had no proof with her; nonetheless, Del was conscious and they could simply ask him.

The doctor went in with her and questioned Del. Do you understood that you will die if you are taken off the ventilator? Del nodded. Do you want that? He nodded again. The doctor said the inhalation therapists who would have to remove the tube would be there in twenty minutes. He told Del and Halpern to say their good-byes.

Halpern cried, kissing Del on the forehead and cheek, and told him how he had changed her life. She asked him to come back and visit her in spirit if he possibly could. He motioned for a pen to write her some final messages.

Del immediately began scrawling notes on whatever scraps of paper they could find. He was ready to die, and knew he had just twenty minutes to say goodbye. He knew they would be his last words, so he was philosophical. He was still angry with the staff for intubating him, but as he awaited death, he relaxed and was cracking jokes as he wrote:

DEATH IS NOT THE ENEMY.
I DONT WANT TO DIE THEIR WAY.
WE DON'T PUT TUBES DOWN OTHERS' THROATS.
CAN I HAVE SOME PAIN MEDICINE

WHERE ARE MY PAGAN CHANTS?
I WAS SO PISSED—BUT I GOT TO SEE YOU AGAIN.
GET ME A BIG STACK OF OUR BOOKS UNSIGNED—PRICE
GOES UP!
I STOPPED BREATHING. THIS WAS A GOOD THING.
POSITIVE IS A GOOD PARTY—I WOULD HAVE LIKED TO PASS
AWAY IN MY SLEEP.
HEY KID—SORRY I DIDNT MAKE IT LONGER. I LOVE YOU.
NOW YOU CAN GET A BOYFRIEND LIKE ME BUT YOUNGER.

Then there was the vague warning TOP RIGHT DRAWER—ROLL
TOP DESK, where he usually kept his pot and other questionable
materials.

Halpern told him that if he could hold out a few more days, he might
still get a birthday party.

I MAY HAVE A COUPLE OF DRINKS, he wrote.

He was still not pleased with being intubated, however, and wrote:
GET ME HOME. MAYBE I WON'T LAST FOR A PARTY.

When the therapists arrived, they were reluctant to act, though
Halpern told them that Del did not want to be on the ventilator.

SHE IS MY CUSTODIAL CARE GIVER, he wrote to the doctor. I
AM NOT BEING TERMINATED.

There was nothing more the doctors could legally do. They had to
comply.

DID THEY TURN OFF THE OXYGEN? wrote Del.

Halpern informed him that they had.

IS THE OXYGEN OFF? he wrote again.

To their astonishment, Del was still breathing. The therapists
quickly took the tube out of his throat. Del began to choke and spit up,
while shouting angrily at the doctor.

"How dare you rob me of my right to die with dignity!" he
shouted.

He demanded his breakfast.

"I felt like a car had run over me," said Halpern, who collapsed in a
chair. "He just wanted to eat. He was as mad as a wet cat."

As weakened as he was, he was determined to die on his own terms,
which included the opportunity to say good-bye to as many friends and
loved ones as possible. On Monday morning, March 1, Halpern began
calling his friends to inform them that Del was dying. When she called

me, I told her I would be up in a couple of days. She implied that it might be too late, so I immediately jumped in my car for the drive to Chicago.

When I arrived, a handful of students were milling around the hospital lobby. As I stepped off the elevator near Del's room, their numbers grew thicker. Most had visited with him briefly and then lingered in the background, not wanting to leave but with little more to say.

In the darkened room, Del was resting. His bed was next to the window, which was closed, with the curtain drawn. One student was apparently standing guard at Halpern's behest, and seemed alarmed when I entered and crossed to his bedside, but Del assured him that he was glad to see me. He was dressed in crisp new red-and-white striped pajamas, in sharp contrast to his usual torn, dirty T-shirts. I had to listen carefully, because his voice was slightly muffled by the oxygen mask that sat in the thick of his full gray beard. I tried to hide my shock at seeing him in such a weakened state, but Del had no time for that.

"Now remember, I've left you a few things in my will."

"I know. Thanks, Del, but I'm not planning on collecting them for a long time."

But as I saw him lying there looking so feeble, we both knew that it wasn't true. Del asked about my wife, Laurie, and I apologized, because she was working and didn't have time to make his favorite dessert, a lemon chess pie. He was in a reflective mood, mellow and forgiving, aware of his own failings and sympathetic to the failings of others.

When David Pasquesi arrived to visit, he was saddened to see Del's strength ebbing, remembering him as a dominant physical force. He shared a few serious moments with Del, discussing fears about dying. "I don't know what's going to happen," Del confessed. But more than that was his urging to "keep this stuff going, remember to keep doing this stuff." He was also in a joking mood for most of the visits. "Every time he'd see me, he'd tell me how they were trying to cut off his balls," recalled Pasquesi. "'Oh, they're trying to take 'em!'"

When Halpern informed Barbara Harris of Del's condition, Harris decided to play nurse, and was soon tinkering and puttering around his room long enough to prove exasperating. Del whispered to Halpern, "Would you get her out of here? All this solicitude is getting me down!" So Halpern turned to Harris and said, "You've been an angel, but I think you're getting tired. You've got to preserve your own health. Let me take you home." So she drove Harris to her home on the Gold Coast, dropped her off, and turned around to face rush-hour traffic. It took her almost two hours to return to the hospital. When she got back to Del's room, Harris was there fidgeting. Harris told her: "I couldn't let my being tired get in the way of where I was supposed to be. I'd feel too guilty." She had gotten on the train and returned to the hospital.

Harris later explained that she hadn't known Del was facing his final days when he entered the hospital: "The doctor was in the hallway, and I asked him 'What are his chances of getting better?' and he said, 'Oh, fifty-fifty,' probably just being vague. But I took it to mean maybe he'd be all right." As a result, she thought he would be coming home. In fact, there was some talk of home hospice care at Halpern's apartment, with Del maintaining that he wanted to die in her living room. It led Halpern and Harris to begin cleaning his apartment. "I washed his bathroom floor in his house; Charna and I washed his clothes; and we were doing all these little girly things. That's where my head was at," explained Harris.

In California, Mina Kolb heard Del was dying, and immediately called him at the hospital. "Oh, yeah, I'm going to die," he told her. "I'm not going to get any better, and I don't like the way I am now." Kolb suggested that he go back home or move in with Harris so she could take care of him. Del protested, "I told Barbara that if the choice was whether to stay with her or die, I'd rather die."

Some students from Texas made a pilgrimage to see him, but Del didn't recognize them. When one of the young people walked in, Del started talking about "Somebody's trying to steal my nuts!" and the student was puzzled. He had a bouquet of flowers in his hand, for which Del criticized him. "I have emphysema—what do I need flowers for? Get 'em out!" And the dazed student wandered away.

Del watched, bemused by the frustration of the nurses who attempted to draw blood but couldn't find an uncollapsed vein. "Sorry! I got there first!" he would tell them with a laugh.

On Tuesday, a hospital representative, Dr. Julie Goldstein, delivered what she called a "reality check" to Del and Halpern. As she questioned him, it was apparent that Del believed he would be dying soon. "All right then, what would you like to do in the next two days?" she asked. Del said that he would like a birthday party. Halpern asked whether she could throw Del a party on his March 9 birthday. Not likely, she was told. The next day, Wednesday, March 3, was chosen. It was not much time to plan a party on the scale that she intended, but she would have help.

Her first call was to Bill Murray, who insisted on picking up the tab. In addition, he hired a saxophone player from the Green Mill, a venerated local jazz institution, who would play that night. Nothing but the best for Uncle Del, he decreed. Halpern began phoning his friends from across the country.

I called Howard Hesseman, who was glad to spread the word to the Committee's alumni. I had likewise asked a mutual friend to inform Robin Williams of Del's condition, and relayed several messages to Del from the star he affectionately referred to as his "grand-student."

Word was spreading that the Guru was fading, and increasing numbers of well-wishers were paying their respects, in person and by telephone. During the day on Tuesday, I helped him field a steady stream of phone calls. Larry Coven, Ed Greenberg, and Randy Dixon had already arrived from L.A. and were constant, morale-lifting presences. The difference in Del's demeanor and energy had changed dramatically in the previous twenty-four hours. With the party, he still had a reason to live: one final audience for one final performance.

That afternoon, I answered a call from Andrew Alexander and quickly passed the phone to Del. They spoke for a couple minutes, and as he gave me the handset to hang up, Del managed a guffaw. "I was right!" bellowed Del, his voice somehow projecting far outside his oxygen mask. "Andrew Alexander said I was right. Improvisation isn't just a tool to develop material. He said it's an art form! He agrees with me!" Del was triumphant. Alexander had settled his dispute with Sahlins. His life's work was vindicated.

On Wednesday, Del seemed to accept that it was his last full day. When Roberta Maguire called in the afternoon and told him she would be flying in the next day, Del suggested that she needn't bother.

That night, March 3, a dining room just off the downstairs cafeteria at Illinois Masonic Hospital was reserved for the private party, though little about it was private. There were jazz musicians, nurses, caterers, pagan priests, reporters, celebrities, novice students, old friends, and even a Comedy Central camera crew sent by the Upright Citizens Brigade.

There was a generous spread of chicken, crabmeat, and other finger foods, with flowers, balloons, and photos decorating the tables, in addition to a chocolate birthday cake with "Happy Birthday, We Love You Del" and numbered candles showing "65." Harold Ramis had flown in, postponing a promotional tour to attend. Bill Murray and Brian Doyle-Murray chatted with friends and waited for the guest of honor to arrive.

At last, under the glare of television lights and with Halpern at his side, Del was wheeled in, attached to an assortment of tubes, still wearing his oxygen mask, and wearing a red-and-yellow striped robe. His wheelchair was rolled to a telephone in one corner, where he spoke to the Upright Citizens Brigade (who were shooting in New York); the camera rolled as Del issued the final instructions to the UCB via telephone.

Del told Matt Besser that they did it: they were spreading improvisation and the love of improvisation, creating Theater of the Heart. Del said he wanted everyone to know the tenets of improvisation, how to listen, and how to work with a group. He knew the world would be a better place when people cherished one another, treating others like poets, like geniuses.

With his UCB obligations discharged, his wheelchair was moved to the center of the room, and, almost reverently, everyone seemed to cue up to spend a few final, personal moments with Del. He was suddenly rejuvenated, pulling off his oxygen mask to speak more clearly to his friends.

Chicago Sun-Times writer Neil Steinberg was amazed by his vigor. He told Halpern, "I thought you said he was gravely ill." She assured him that yes, despite appearances, Del was indeed dying.

Joyce Sloane and Bernie Sahlins each gave him an affectionate hug. Del broke away good-naturedly, and wagged his index finger in the air.

"It *is* an art form!" said Del with an insistent smile.

"Del, for tonight, it is an art form," said Sahlins.

Sloane tapped Sahlins on the arm.

"Bernie," she said, "you're standing on his oxygen line."

Bill Murray inspected both of the saxophone players; Halpern had hired one of her own due to a communication error. "Mine is better," Murray playfully insisted. "Mine has a hat."

A few minutes later, Del addressed the guests. "I guess I'd better die now. Otherwise a lot of people are going to be really disappointed!" He shared with the party guests some final moments of wisdom:

As I leave it, I begin to realize that we haven't done such a bad job as people seem to think. The death of a working man in a big American hospital does not have to be the traumatic agony that people assume that it is. You can have a pretty good life pretty cheap in these States, and I think that's something to be proud of. I didn't know that until I was dying. It's a nice thing to learn on the last day of your life. . . . And if that sounds too sappy or too front-loaded, screw it. So let's hear it for the fucking human race!

Under the somewhat intrusive lights of the TV crew and reporters' eyes, Bill Murray shared a few final moments as they philosophized. Finally, Murray asked whether there was anything else he could get him. "How about that chocolate martini everyone's been talking about?" asked Del with a twinkle in his eye. Murray handed glasses to Del and Halpern. "For me too?" asked the surprised Halpern. "Well, she's the high priestess! And I'm her chosen consort!" quipped Del. They clinked glasses and sipped their drinks as everyone applauded.

A pagan priest in a red robe and a pagan priestess in a black robe stepped forward, and as the crowd formed a semicircle around them, they began to conduct the Ritual of the Four Elements, asking the blessing of the Deity to "prepare Del for his upcoming journey," chanting, "The god blesses you with the strength you already have—the strength of humor. For in the middle of a joke, there is no past, there is no future, there is only the present, and the present never ends. So may you continue to find that strength, especially the strength of irreverent humor."

Larry Coven read a passage from Clark Ashton Smith, and Ed Greenberg followed with a reading by H. P. Lovecraft. Then, after two final blessings, Del addressed the crowd: "In the words of a wise woman from a foreign land who is often misunderstood: Death is not important. Life is important. And life is eternal and life is now. Leni Riefenstahl." Only a few of those gathered picked up on the ironic reference to Hitler's favorite filmmaker. It was his last public joke.

Halpern then led the group in singing "Happy Birthday" to Del, and I stepped forward to read some of the many faxes and e-mails that had been arriving.

Del—Hear you're having a party. Sorry I can't make it. Feel good and have a great time. I'm with you in spirit. Your pal, Peter Boyle.

Oh massuh Del, As the philosopher Taylor Mead observed, "There's no such thing as old age. You just grow up and die." So, maybe you're maturing. Could you send a note with a map to the stash? Luv, Garry Goodrow.

Hey Del, What if Patrick Henry is wrong? Eternity now! See you in Hell, give Severn a hug. Hugh Romney.

I invite everyone at this party to raise your weapons and have at him—because as many times as Del falls, he has to get back up again. My dear Dr. Close: with much love—Bang! Bang! Bang! Now, get back up again! Alan Myerson

There was one final, lengthy passage from Howard Hesseman:

All of us know Del. This means we have often abandoned all common sense, reason, and good manners, in the dogged pursuit of a larger mystery. All of us have felt that eerie rush, that total tingle, that comes with encountering Del. It's like sticking your sense organs in a Mixmaster and hitting blend. When it's over, everything's still there, but it's been radically modified. All the great Masters can make you see with your ears and hear with your eyes and stuff like that, but Del makes you speak with your skin. He takes you into a space—THE Space—where you, all of you, all of your being, your history, your dreams, your neural impulses—can work all at once, without fear of contradiction. And no matter what comes out, no matter how scary it gets, you feel safe. No matter what happens, no matter how confused it feels, no matter how crazy it gets, no matter how wrong it seems, no matter how little sense it makes . . . Relax. Del Close has been there and back, and taught us everything he could. Relax. Follow your impulse. Del will always support you. Thanks, Del.

After a few last good-nights, Del was wheeled off to the elevator; Halpern quietly invited a few people to follow. A few minutes later, after Del had been settled into his bed, we gathered on both sides in the darkened room, representing the stages of his adult life: Barbara Harris, who had been with him in the Second City in 1961; Ed Greenberg, who first met Del during his Committee days in the 1960s; Brian

Doyle-Murray, who attended Committee workshops and then became an enthusiastic advocate when the Second City considered hiring Del as a director; Bill Murray, perhaps his most famous student and one of his most loyal friends; Larry Coven, Second City actor, collaborator, and perhaps his closest living friend; David Pasquesi, who started out as an Improv-Olympic student and became a fellow actor and even director; and me, Kim "Howard" Johnson, another ImprovOlympic pioneer, who became a longtime friend, who helped cowrite *Truth in Comedy*, and, years later, would become his biographer. And there was Charna Halpern, who saved his life, became his partner in business, in art, in family, and in life, who gave him the chance to achieve his life's work and make his dreams come true.

The lights were darkened, and Del was clearly spent. The energy that he had summoned up for the party had clearly left him. We spent a few moments thanking him and saying good-byes. Then he drifted off to sleep, and we drifted into the foggy Chicago evening. We paused at the steps outside the hospital for a few moments. After all the denial, it was clear that Del would be leaving us very soon. He had just said his final good-nights.

◇

The final party has taken on poetic, almost mythic stature in the improvisation world. But as the final night was triumphant, the next day brought painful reality.

Halpern got a call from a frightened Del around 3:00 A.M., and rushed back to the hospital. "I think I'm having delusions, but I wanted to check this out with you," Del told her. "Steven Spielberg is shooting an underground movie that no one is supposed to know about, kind of like *Dune* but underwater. . . . Those cameras at the party were not from Comedy Central; they were really from Spielberg. When you took me back to the room, I found manmade marks all over my body [he referred to his own track marks]. Dean Koontz is involved in this, there are time-traveling Nazis who want to take you and me and Coven back to the '30s, where I, as a fascist dictator, have to order Coven to kill you and dissect you. *But*, I'm not going to let that happen. I'm only going to play the part. What do you think?"

He continued to describe how Roberta Maguire was one of the time-traveling Nazi collaborators out to get him, though she was actually being duped. Halpern finally stopped him and explained to him that it was just the CO_2, and she would talk him down.

Halpern called Coven, who relieved her and sat there through the night, interrupted occasionally by a young Arab-American orderly who asked him about improvisation. Coven answered his questions and more, spreading his teachings even as Del lay dying a few feet away.

In the morning, people started returning, and there was a constant stream of visitors and phone calls. Del would not be alone and forgotten in his final hours. Halpern was clearly in charge; her brother-in-law was a doctor, and he provided support and information. ImprovOlympic students gathered around him, well meaning but obviously uncomfortable. Coven finally told them, "You guys know this isn't your gig anyway. Just take off." Halpern would screen phone calls. In response to one call, when Del snapped, "No! I don't want to talk to that bitch!" Coven reminded him, "Be careful! You never know when it's going to be your last words." People were visiting and calling, even a few of his drug friends. In front of Greenberg, one of them even offered Del something illicit. "It was all there, even the creepy side," said Greenberg. "A lot of people said that Del was really all alone his whole life. I thought to myself 'Who, on their deathbed, has this much love?'"

As the day went on, Del could not get comfortable. On an intravenous drip for his pain, he was "hitting that button like he was trying to get a question on *Jeopardy*," recalled Miles Stroth. Halpern and Dixon each lifted an arm and Coven grabbed his feet to adjust him. As they started to let loose, Del said, "I think touching the patient is appropriate right now."

The pain was becoming too great. Greenberg, Halpern, Coven, and Dixon stayed near his bedside, students wandering in and out. Del was ready for his final exit. He had given the performance of his life the night before as the dying guru. The longer he lived, the more it would detract from that parting public image. Halpern suspected his wish for morphine was simply an overwhelming urge for him to get high one last time, but her concerns may have masked a reluctance to let him go. "Are you sure?" she kept asking, and Del continued to insist "Yes," finally shouting, "I'm ready!" But Halpern was angry, and saw no reason he couldn't hang around and write or talk: "I felt he thought it was more important to get high, even knowing he wouldn't open his eyes again. I was a little pissed off that day. I went through a range of emotions."

Greenberg disagreed with Halpern's theory. He felt it was no longer about getting high, but alleviating suffering. They consulted with Dr. Julie Goldstein, who had helped Halpern plan the party and was in charge of palliative care at the hospital, helping patients live out their remaining time with dignity. Del quickly grew to adore her, and she helped him reach his decision: by midafternoon, he requested the morphine drip that he had been promised to make his last hours more comfortable, and the nurses left to assemble the equipment.

As they waited, Del spoke with his friends. Del felt responsible for getting Coven fired from the Second City many years earlier, and it had obviously preyed on his mind over the years, so he asked Coven to forgive him for not defending him more strongly. He told Greenberg that directing the "Babble" scene was a highlight of his career.

Halpern sat on his bed and held his hand. "Promise me you'll make the skull thing happen. No matter what," he said. "And keep my ashes in the theater where I can affect the work." "I will," Halpern promised. "And tell them all that we succeeded where others have failed. We created Theater of the Heart, a theater where people cherish each other to succeed onstage. Tell the students 'Theater of the Heart.'" Despite his great pain, he concentrated on the importance of their work together. There was no fear in him.

When the morphine arrived, Del was ready. The technician arrived with the doctor and they began the drip into his arm. "Turn it up!" he said in a booming voice. The doctor was surprised, because Del had shown no visible effect after two morphine shots. The doctor turned it up, saying, "We are still within the legal limits." A few seconds later, Del complained. "Come on! I used to be a drug addict. I know what I'm supposed to be feeling. Turn it up!" In disbelief, the doctor increased the dosage, again repeating, "We are still within the legal limits." A few seconds later: "Turn it up!" "Jesus," the doctor said while complying, "he's had enough to put out a horse!" After a few seconds, Del sighed.

"Thank God. I'm tired of being the funniest person in the room."

He clearly intended them as his last words, but after he received the final dose of morphine, the telephone rang. It was Larry Hankin, his former San Francisco roommate. Halpern answered the phone, and Hankin asked for Del. "He's busy now," she said. Ed Greenberg then got on the line, and repeated the message. In the background, Hankin could hear Del ask, "Who is it?" Halpern responded, "Larry Hankin!"

"I once thought very highly of Larry," Del responded, and decided to speak to Hankin. "I can't really talk," he told him. "I'm in the middle of something right now. But thanks for calling." "I just wanted to pay my respects," said Hankin. "I really have to go now, Larry," said Del. Greenberg got back on the line and informed Hankin that what Del was "in the middle of" was dying. "Last night, which was the party, was great," Greenberg told him. "Now it's the next day, and frankly, he just wants to get out of here."

Halpern, Coven, Greenberg, Dixon, Stroth, and a few others tried to help Del become more comfortable. Eventually, he settled in, while sounding a low, guttural "Aarrgh." Coven couldn't resist admonishing his friend, "We're doing the best we can, Del." Without missing a beat, Del retorted, "You could have done better."

They were his final words. The morphine rendered him unconscious. Halpern placed Dixon and Coven in charge, then excused herself, leaving them both to stand vigil.

Coven stepped out for a snack a short time later. Dixon was on the phone with an unnamed friend from Manhattan High School when there was a commotion. Dr. Goldstein rushed into the room, along with the nurse who had been administering the morphine. She looked at Del, peering into his eyes and calling his name a number of times, but getting no response. She spoke to the nurse about taking him off the morphine drip to see whether that would elicit a response, and left the room.

At that point, Dixon and the nurse were alone with the unconscious Del. The agitated nurse began disconnecting the apparatus, saying, "Oh, I'm going to be in trouble." Dixon assured her that she had done nothing wrong, offering to vouch for her. "This is exactly what he wanted," Dixon told her. "He wanted to be relieved of the pain, and he's getting what he wants. You did nothing wrong."

When she left the room, Dixon was alone with his unconscious, dying mentor, and leaned down to whisper in his ear. "Del, if you're going to go, now might be a good time, because they're cutting off the morphine. If you're sticking around for the drugs, you might want to get out of Dodge."

Forty minutes later, just after 6 P.M. on March 4, 1999, it was over. The doctor turned off his monitors and removed his tubes. Halpern returned, and asked Dixon to remove his jewelry while she stood outside the room and talked with the hospital officials. Dixon began taking off his rings and his pentagram necklace, saying, "Thanks Del, thanks for everything. Hopefully you can come back and let us know." As he finished, he reached out and touched his forehead, and realized that his body was starting to get cold. Although they had talked about death, the soul, and the afterlife, this was nothing like what they had discussed, yet it could not have been more deep and meaningful. Del was a teacher to the end.

25

Curtain Call

"I was reading in the newspaper the other day about a sky diver who dived out of the airplane. He did aerial acrobatics for several thousand feet, then he pulls the ripcord, and the main chute did not open. And he pulled the emergency chute cord, and that did not open. And then what did he do? He did flips and acrobatics, head-over-heels at the top of his ability, all the way into the ground. Splat. That's my kind of guy. That's kind of a metaphor for life, isn't it? I mean, we're all going to hit the ground, splat, eventually, aren't we? And what I'm going to do is follow that guy's example and do acrobatics the rest of the way out."[1]

The next day, Halpern felt overwhelmed. In addition to grieving for her partner of more than seventeen years and arranging his cremation, she had to find someone to take off his head and remove the flesh from his skull.

In addition, there was the question of some sort of observance. Although there had already been a wake attended by the guest of honor, I suggested that because so many of Del's friends were not able to make it to the birthday party on such short notice, perhaps a memorial service might be appropriate. Because of the limited seating capacity of the ImprovOlympic, a service was scheduled for March 13 at the Second City.

◇

The next week, Jeffrey Sweet was on his way to teach a course in Ohio. He boarded a train to Pittsburgh that was going on to Chicago. As he sat in the dining car, he began chatting with the person seated opposite him.

"I'm going to Chicago for a memorial for a friend of mine," the other man revealed.

"I looked at him and said 'Del Close?'"

"Yeah! You know Del Close?"

"Yeah, I wrote a book about Second City."

"You're Jeff Sweet."

"Yeah. How do you know Del?"

"I wrote horror comics with him."

"You're John Ostrander!"

◇

The memorial service was held before a full house the afternoon of Saturday, March 13. It began with a video montage of Del's monologues from *My Talk Show*, finishing with a quote from "that inspirational movie *Simon, King of the Witches*: 'Death is only temporary. See ya around.'"

Halpern shared her thoughts:

A long time ago, in his days at the Second City, he was a little envious of Paul Sills, because Paul got to create the theater that he wanted, making sketch comedy. It wasn't Del's dream, but he worried that he might not get the chance to create his dream, until he met me and we worked together at the ImprovOlympic. . . . He did something that was very important, and it was more important than creating the Harold, more important than long-form improvisation, more important than changing the face of improvisational comedy, more important than influencing hundreds and hundreds of talented minds. He created a movement, a movement that you are all part of, and we're just a small part of it.

Del considered us the last bastion of the Counterculture. This movement is what he called Theater of the Heart, a theater where, in order to succeed, the ensemble had to cherish each other on the stage. And folks, if we're not cherishing each other, we're not doing it right. Theater of the Heart. And that's something that will continue on with all of you. You will all pass on his theories, keep them intact, and go on from there. You will tell all the stories—and there are so many—and you will keep the legend alive, that once there was a man who, when he used to walk down the street, people would point and stare and say "There goes Del Close."

Her voice cracked as she finished, and the crowd burst into applause. After another video clip, she introduced a series of speakers. Miles Stroth spoke on behalf of the Family and what he meant to them. After Stroth, I read a note from Alan Myerson, and then read the *Wasteland* story "Subtext Salad." John Ostrander followed, discussing his writing partner and a chance encounter with Jeffrey Sweet, which was, he said, proof that Del was still directing.

Matt Besser spoke for the Upright Citizens Brigade:

"I don't have a funny story or a fond memory to relate, so I really have a challenge. Maybe I shouldn't even have gotten up here," he told the group. "Let's give it up for Del. Not everyone here has given it up for Del. We've got to give credit where credit's due, and I don't think everyone always does that. Everything UCB is came from Del. . . . He's had a lot of people come through who have gone on to do a lot of things, and when I read interviews from them, I don't hear them mention Del. I hear them mention Second City.

"It's kind of ironic that we're doing this at Second City, because if you think about it, what he did was a reaction to Second City. . . . He built ImprovOlympic, and ImprovOlympic's about 100 percent improv, and from what I understand . . . he had arguments with his peers, where they said 'Improv can't be an art form in itself . . . it's a process for writing.' And he said, 'Bullshit, I'm going to make it an art form. I'm going to show you an ensemble can get up there and entertain a crowd with nothing but a suggestion.' It has become a movement."

It was a moment of the sort that Del had always appreciated. As luck would have it, Halpern then introduced Second City's Andrew Alexander, who jokingly asked whether it was for a rebuttal. Alexander discussed the Ozzie Mandias monologues that Del wrote and recorded for

Del as immortalized on the wall of the Old Town Ale House, part of an early 1970s mural of regulars painted by Maureen Munson. (COURTESY OF CHARNA HALPERN)

My Talk Show, then paid a heartfelt tribute as he discussed Del's inspiring final days.

Tim Kazurinsky, referring to remarks by Stroth, quipped, "I think we should get back to the part about Del being a scary prick," then discussed his experiences in Del's classes. "Things became clear. You relived your nightmares onstage, to have people laugh at them, and it was cathartic. . . . It was worth it to have seven shitty classes to have one where that flash of light went through your head! He was not only a genius, he was generous, he gave of himself and the process. He was all about process, and we *are* the process. We are indeed his legacy."

Mick Napier of the Annoyance Theatre took the stage without notes: "When I visited him, it wasn't like any other hospital visit. It was bizarre, because he made no pretense about it: 'I am dying, this is it!' Most of the time, there's a pretense of hope, but Del declared with integrity 'This is it!' As a result of that, it leaves very little room for conversation. There is nothing to say; without hope, there is silence. I stared silently, and, I guess, this is the cool thing he said to me: 'Well, I guess I'm supposed to say something profound right now about you carrying the torch of improvisation on and on, but, just let them play, let them get along.' I thought that was pretty profound."

Roberta Maguire traveled from Seattle to discuss her years with the Second City from 1969 to 1971 with the rest of the Next Generation.

"It's not lost on me that, outside of Charna, I'm the only woman to stand here. . . . Del had that reputation of being a real woman-hater, but he was wonderful," said Maguire, who then read a letter she had written to Del just the day before.

"I understand I was a time-traveling Nazi collaborator out to get you in your final mind-movie," just before he died, she read. "But I was being duped. I'm honored. I raced here from Seattle on Thursday to see you, but you left before I got here, dammit. But that's OK. . . . Despite all the stories and rumors and gossip, I never got anything from you, Delbert, but knowledge and laughter and friendship and love. All the performing and teaching I've done for the last thirty years have been due to you, you big lunk, and I've been teaching in Seattle for twenty years and doing totally improvised shows, and touring all over the Northwest and California and Canada, and really, really carrying on Del's tradition of doing deep and touching and intelligent improvised shows that people will come and pay money to see. I've cocreated several companies there.

"I'm sure whatever quantum reality you're in now, you're making and breaking the rules yourself. I love you, Delbert."

As a closing message, Halpern told the group about Del's late-night phone call after his party. "Del always used to say, 'When you get the message, hang up the phone.' He decided when to go, and as Amy Poehler said, he knew how to edit. So I'll take the cue. Thank you all for coming and sharing today," said Halpern.

◇

Less than a week after Del died, David Pasquesi had an experience that seemed to defy reason.

"I remember him being there in my sleep. Sleep? No. Between awake and asleep," said Pasquesi. "He shook my hand; I remember him shaking my hand; I remember his hand in mine. And I remember seeing a growth—him seeing a growth on my hand, there's a cyst that I have on my hand under the skin, and him saying, 'Oh, I have one of those, too.' And he showed me his. And I remember asking Charna whether he did indeed have one, and she said yeah."

There was no great knowledge passed along, he noted. "It was a handshake—pretty pedestrian. I don't recall any messages or anything like that. It was not as easily dismissible as a dream."

◈

My wife, Laurie Bradach, could not make it to the hospital for a final visit or to say a final good-bye to Del. But a week after his death, she woke up from a dream early in the morning. Del had met her at the edge of a circular blacktopped walkway. "I wanted to get a chance to visit with people I didn't get to visit with," he told her. He led her to a redbrick building with white trim that seemed like a college dormitory; there were plenty of people around, but they paid no attention. Del and Laurie walked up one or two flights of stairs and went to Del's room, a small dormitory room with a desk, small bed, and a window overlooking the walkway. Laurie sat on the wooden chair and Del sat on the edge of the bed and they talked for a while.

At one point, it struck her how absurd the situation was. "But Del," she protested, "you're *dead*!" With a wave of his hand, Del discounted it. "Well, in a manner of speaking . . ." he responded. She mentioned his room, which had nothing personal in it, and he told her it was only temporary. He added that he couldn't stay long because he was going somewhere; he wanted to talk while he could because he wouldn't have a chance later. After that, he walked her back to the spot where they had originally met, and she woke up.

My wife is generally very skeptical of the supernatural and the paranormal, just as I have always tended to be skeptical of dreams, and so I tended to discount what she said as a very vivid dream, filled with distinct and detailed descriptions of the surroundings.

It wasn't until three and a half years later, August 2002, in an e-mail exchange with Halpern, that I happened to mention Laurie's dream about a final visit with Del. Halpern was astonished, and in a flurry of e-mails revealed that she had experienced several communications with Del following his death.

The most incredible was her description of a dream about a conversation with Del about a week after Del had died. He told Halpern that he would be leaving soon, but apparently there was a wait. She reported: "At the end of the conversation he paused and said, 'Charna, I know you know this is me—but I want you to know this is real.' He knew I wanted to know about life after death and I believe that was his way to keep his promise of letting me know."

She said the conversation occurred in a small room in a dormitory in which Del was staying, and described the room, the building, and the surroundings. They were all virtually identical to those experienced by my wife.

◇

His last will and testament stated: "I have one child. . . . I make no provision for him in this will, and it is my intention that he receive no part of my estate." He gave all of his books to Larry Coven, except for his biographies, which were willed to Susan Messing. I was to receive his artwork and toys. John Ostrander was given a page of original art from *Wasteland* depicting the two of them descending a staircase. He left Melanie Blue his snake candleholder. Mike Click was given his choice of Del's 1960s rock posters. To Halpern, he left the clock given to him by Chris Farley, a word ball, magic wand, notebooks, clippings, public-relations items, pictures, his antique pub table and matching chairs, roll-top desk, awards and plaques, and all the money in his savings accounts and CDs, minus $2,000 for Larry Coven to ship the books that were bequeathed to him.

But the provision that he is remembered for is "I give my skull to the Goodman Theatre, for a production of *Hamlet* in which to play Yorick, or for any other purposes the Goodman Theatre deems appropriate."

◇

As part of the Toyota Comedy Festival, held in New York City from June 3 to June 12, 1999, the Upright Citizens Brigade Theatre presented a six-night tribute to Del Close, featuring panel discussions, scenes, and improvisations written and inspired by Del, with guests including Charna Halpern, David Pasquesi, Joel Murray, Garry Goodrow, Mike Gold, John Ostrander, and myself, all culminating in a twenty-four-hour improvisation marathon led by the UCB.

Later that summer, Del was profiled in a segment of *Wild Chicago* on WTTW, Chicago's public television station, written and produced by Will Clinger, and featuring interviews with friends and colleagues. Clinger later expanded it into a thirty-minute *Wild Chronicles* special called "The Legend of Del Close," which aired April 2, 2000.

Another hour-long documentary tribute to Del by filmmakers Cesar Jaime and Jeff Pacocha, called *The Delmonic Interviews*, featuring more clips and interviews, premiered at the ImprovOlympic West. Jeff Griggs wrote a memoir of the months he drove Del on his errands, called *Guru*, published in 2005.

◇

On July 1, 1999, Del starred in yet another performance, this one a press conference at the Del Close Theater at the ImprovOlympic. Newspaper, radio, and television reporters completely filled the theater upstairs.

Originally, Halpern intended to have an actor perform the famous monologue from *Hamlet*, but changed her mind at the last minute. "I came out and gave my little speech, and said, 'I'm the executor of Del's will, and his most profound gift is to go to Bob Falls,'" said Halpern. "Del wants to be remembered in laughter, not sadness. He was an oddity and rarity in this world, and we were glad to have him. Now he just wants to keep working."

The Goodman Theatre artistic director showed up to accept the bequest. Halpern gave him a skull resting on a red velvet cushion inside a Lucite box. Falls quipped that he had recently won a Tony Award for *Death of a Salesman*, and thought nothing could be cooler than that—until today.

"Falls opened the box and picked up the skull," said Halpern. "What happened next brought tears to my eyes and joy to my heart." Falls held out the skull in his right hand and spoke. "Alas, poor Del! I knew him, Horatio: A fellow of infinite jest . . ." He continued with the soliloquy.

"It was just what Del wanted," said Halpern. "I was so glad I didn't have [my actor] there, because that's exactly what I wanted to have happen, and it wouldn't have happened had I had [the actor] do that first. It was so much more powerful that Bob did it himself. And Bob was really the only one who had the right to take that skull out. It's his! It was just beautiful, it really was. It was a lovely ceremony."

◇

In an odd series of events that would have delighted Del, the upper-left-hand corner of the July 21, 2006, *Chicago Tribune*, just below the flag on the newspaper's masthead, was a color photograph of a skull sitting on a piece of red velvet. It accompanied a story that called into question the authenticity of the skull at the Goodman Theatre.

Seven years after his death, Del Close was front-page news.

Tribune reporter Robert K. Elder reported that the skull in Robert Fall's office at the Goodman Theatre was not Del's. There had been rumors ever since his death, and Halpern herself admitted that Del's final request was not an easy one to honor. But Elder interviewed paleopathologist Anne Grauer of Loyola University and Jay Villemarette of Skulls Unlimited International in Oklahoma City, as well as Charles Childs, the president of the Illinois Funeral Directors Association, and Gerald Sullivan, the president of the Cremation Society of Illinois.

Grauer and Villemarette both determined that the skull had been purchased. They cited such evidence as rusty, decades-old screws in the skull, autopsy marks (his death certificate stated that Del did not have an autopsy), and eleven teeth remaining in the back of the mouth.

Halpern continued to defend the authenticity of the skull, though she could not explain the screws and the autopsy marks. She maintained that she couldn't speak about precisely what had happened in order to protect the person or persons who removed and cleaned the skull.

Further clouding the issue was a period of time in which the skull may have gone missing. Former ImprovOlympic actor turned film director Jon Favreau was preparing to shoot the Will Farrell comedy *Elf,* when the idea arose to use Del's skull to help decorate a set. "Scott Armstrong [a former iO guy and uncredited writer on *Elf*] suggested it, and it did indeed appear in the final draft of the shooting script as a piece of set dec in the doctor's office," noted Favreau. "I was told by either the prop dept or producer on the film (I cannot recall whom) that the skull was unavailable as the Goodman was unable to locate it."

Whether the skull was actually lost or stolen was unclear, noted the director, but it did raise yet another possibility. Was Del's skull removed from the Goodman at some point, and then, to cover up the loss, replaced by a skull purchased elsewhere?

Favreau never followed up with the Goodman. "I thought at the time that the theater was saying that to blow me off, or perhaps the call was never made at all and my own team was blowing me off, as it was a big pain in the ass to fly a human skull up to Vancouver for an inside joke between myself and a writer!" noted Favreau. He admitted that his near-experience with the mysterious skull could help illuminate the truth, or could spawn a new urban legend, but "I would guess that Del would be proud to be a part of either."

The skull continued to make Goodman stage appearances, though the theater did not stage a production of *Hamlet* in the intervening years.

Still, questions remained. Did Halpern donate Del's actual skull or a substitute? Or could the real skull have disappeared in the intervening years, replaced by one from a medical supply house?

Halpern finally confessed the truth in the October 9, 2006, issue of *The New Yorker*. After Del died, the hospital personnel laughed at her request to remove the head, but suggested that she contact the Illinois Society of Pathologists. They ultimately refused, apparently afraid of charges of exploitation, which could have affected their funding. After two days, she reluctantly had the body cremated in its entirety. She then went skull shopping at the Anatomical Chart Company in Skokie. She purchased a similarly shaped skull, and she and her sister pulled out as many teeth as they could manage before turning it over to the Goodman.[2]

The truth doesn't seem to matter to most of those who knew him. Robert Falls keeps the skull on his bookshelf, ready to be cast in another upcoming production. (After all, don't many of the most successful actors have doubles?) For so many, what is important is Del's intention, and that is what the skull honors. He taught his students that contradictory truths sometimes exist, that some things are only true at the moment, and that as artists and poets we must learn to discern when contradictory truths may apply.

Most of Del's friends have adopted a simpler attitude: if it wasn't originally Del's skull, it is now.

◇

Each year at the ImprovOlympic (which was eventually forced by the International Olympic Committee to change its name to the iO), fewer teachers and performers remain who were schooled directly by Del, even as his legend grows. New students attempt to learn the Secrets of Improvisation as doled out by the Master, and are often frustrated to learn that those secrets changed as often as the man himself.

If for no other reason, Del would be notable for the longevity of his career in improvisation, beginning in the late 1950s and continuing

Del Close in a rare quiet,
contemplative moment.
(COURTESY OF CHARNA HALPERN)

until his death, long after most of his peers had moved on to other pursuits. More than four decades of improvisation established a body of work like no other. "He is one of the few figures—the only one who comes to mind—who was there at the beginning and stayed with it to the end," said Carl Gottlieb. "I don't think there's anybody else in the form who stayed in it. Del stayed with it."

Del's teachings helped to raise improvisation to a higher level as he shared his firsthand history of the art form. He made it incumbent upon his former students, no matter how successful, to keep doing it, whether creating their own theaters, keeping up their training, or simply by coming home. He taught them to recognize their larger obligations, their commitment to Theater of the Heart. "Del's commitment to teaching and carrying this work forward has become a tradition of his own students," said Janet Coleman. Like any great teacher, there is no way to measure his influence, because it continues to permeate our culture.

His students have spread his teachings across the globe. "I've met people doing long-form from England, Scotland, Ireland, Belgium, Germany, Italy, Austria, Ceylon, New Zealand, Australia," said Noah Gregoropoulos. "I've been all over the world, and wherever there's improv—which is everywhere now—there's hunger for long-form, and people doing it. The Harold has become almost an international term, an umbrella term almost synonymous with long-form improvisation. If there's an afterlife, I imagine that Del can look with some pride on that change that happened during that short part of his lifetime."

When he died, Harold Ramis told the Associated Press, "Del was the single most powerful force in improv comedy in America. He's the intellectual and moral standard that guides us all in our work. He taught everybody the process."[3]

Some go even further in assessing his influence. In the March 7, 1999, *Los Angeles Times*, Second City producer Kelly Leonard pronounced Del "the singular most powerful force in improvisation in the world."[4]

He was drawn to performing through *Hamlet* as a way of addressing the important questions of human existence, but in the end, it was all about the work.

The ImprovOlympic, or iO, goes on without Del, but it carries on his longing for Theater of the Heart. For Halpern, it is his greatest legacy: "When people cherish each other onstage night after night, that can't help but form bonds that turn into lasting friendships. ImprovOlympic has become a giant family that people stay a part of forever."

"He was considered a mad genius and he was entitled to be different. I knew he wasn't mad—he was right. Del left us with the tools to go on without him—to create great works of art, great comedy, and to be a successful business. I, and the performers who studied with him, continue to teach his methods and spread his word."

Del's ashes were placed on a special altar that honors him at the iO in the Del Close Theater—where he can affect the work. The boy who could not finish his toy train, who became the man who could not finish his shows, found that his life's work would never be completed. Because of his teachings, long-form improvisation continues, with no end in sight.

◇

End

Bibliography

Coleman, Janet. *The Compass*. New York: Knopf, 1990.

Halpern, Charna. *Art by Committee: A Guide to Advanced Improvisation*. Colorado Springs: Meriwether, 2006.

Halpern, Charna, Del Close, and Kim "Howard" Johnson. *Truth in Comedy: The Manual of Improvisation*. Colorado Springs: Meriwether, 1994.

Hill, Doug, and Jeff Weingrad. *Saturday Night: A Backstage History of* Saturday Night Live. New York: Vintage, 1987.

Patinkin, Sheldon. *The Second City: Backstage at the World's Greatest Comedy Theater*. Naperville, Ill: Sourcebooks, 2000.

Sweet, Jeffrey. *Something Wonderful Right Away: An Oral History of the Second City and the Compass Players*. New York: Limelight, 1986. First published 1978 by Avon Books.

Notes

Chapter 1

[1] Del Close, interview by Lenny Kleinfeld, *Chicago*, March 1987.

[2] Ibid.

[3] Ibid.

[4] Unpublished notebooks and writings.

[5] Quoted in "The Dinosaur of Improvisation" by Jon Ziomek, *Chicago Tribune Magazine*, November 5, 1978.

[6] Del Close scrapbook (no additional information available).

[7] Quoted in "Curse of the Blob" by Kim "Howard" Johnson, *Starlog*, September 1988.

[8] Ibid.

[9] Del Close scrapbook.

[10] Ibid.

[11] Ibid.

[12] Unpublished notebooks and writings.

[13] Ibid.

Plus interviews, correspondence, and conversations with David Dary, Tal Streeter, Ron Young, James Bascom, Donna Morine Fearing, Laurence Norvell, Carl Englehorn, Bill Johnston, and Dean and Shirley Taylor.

Chapter 2

[1] Quoted in "Comedy and Rage: A Conversation with Del Close and John Guare," *New Theater Review*, Spring 1988.

[2] Quoted in "Focus on Del Close" by Peter B. Gillis, *Focus* 1, no. 1 (Summer 1987).

[3] Interview by Lenny Kleinfeld, *Chicago*, March 1987.

[4] Quoted in "Local Boy Del Close Returns to Home Town as Director of the Committee" by Charlie Eppler, *Manhattan Mercury*, April 13, 1969.

[5] Unpublished notebooks and writings.

[6] Del Close and John Ostrander (writers), and David Lloyd (artist), "Del & Elron," *Wasteland* #9 (August 1988).

[7] Del Close, quoted in *Something Wonderful Right Away* by Jeffrey Sweet (New York: Limelight, 1986). First published 1978 by Avon Books.

[8] Del Close and John Ostrander (writers), and William Messner-Loebs (artist), "Under the Lash," *Wasteland* #5 (April 1988).

[9] Quoted in *Something Wonderful Right Away*.

[10] Quoted in Del Close profile, *Chicago Tribune*, November 4, 1973.

[11] Interview by Kleinfeld.

[12] Quoted in "Comedy and Rage: A Conversation with Del Close and John Guare."

Plus interviews, correspondence, and conversations with Dick Newton, David Dary, John Ostrander, Tal Streeter, Carl Englehorn, Ed Greenberg, Janet Coleman, Hammond Guthrie, and Jack Goldstein.

Chapter 3

[1] Del Close and John Ostrander (writers), and George Freeman (artist), "On the Road," parts 1 and 2, *Wasteland* #6–#7 (May–June 1988).

[2] Del Close, interview by Lenny Kleinfeld, *Chicago*, March 1987.

[3] Quoted in *Something Wonderful Right Away* by Jeffrey Sweet (New York: Limelight, 1986). First published 1978 by Avon Books.

[4] Unpublished notebooks and writings.

[5] Del Close, interview by Kleinfeld.

[6] "New York Has Some Theatre in Odd Places," Tribune Travelers' Guide, *Chicago Tribune*, January 13, 1957.

Plus interviews, correspondence, and conversations with Mitchell Ryan, Tal Streeter, John Ostrander, and Theodore J. Flicker.

Chapter 4

[1] Interview by Lenny Kleinfeld, *Chicago*, March 1987.

[2] Fred Landesman, *Rebel Without Applause* (Sag Harbor, N.Y.: Permanent Press, 1987).

[3] Quoted in *The Compass* by Janet Coleman (New York: Knopf, 1990).

[4] Ibid.

[5] Quoted in "The Dinosaur of Improvisation" by Jon Ziomek, *Chicago Tribune Magazine*, November 5, 1978.

[6] Ted Flicker, "Some Fragments of Memory," *PerformInk* 11, no. 31 (March 12, 1999).

[7] Quoted in *Something Wonderful Right Away* by Jeffrey Sweet (New York: Limelight, 1986). First published 1978 by Avon Books.

[8] Interview by Kleinfeld.

[9] Ibid.

Plus interviews, correspondence, and conversations with Theodore J. Flicker, Janet Coleman, Jeffrey Sweet, and Mike Nichols.

Chapter 5

[1] Quoted in *Something Wonderful Right Away* by Jeffrey Sweet (New York: Limelight, 1986). First published 1978 by Avon Books.

[2] Interview by Lenny Kleinfeld, *Chicago*, March 1987.

[3] Quoted in *Something Wonderful Right Away*.

[4] Peter B. Gillis, "Focus on Del Close," *Focus* 1, no. 1 (Summer 1987).

[5] Ibid.

[6] Interview by Kleinfeld.

[7] Ibid.

[8] Ibid.

[9] Unpublished notebooks and writings.

[10] Interview by Kleinfeld.

[11] Ibid.

[12] Ibid.

[13] Unpublished notebooks and writings.

Plus interviews, correspondence, and conversations with Bobbi Gordon, Theodore J. Flicker, Dave Moon, Tal Streeter, Bernard Sahlins, Paul Sills, Jeffrey Sweet, and Hugh Romney.

Chapter 6

[1] Interview by Lenny Kleinfeld, *Chicago*, March 1987.

[2] Quoted in *Something Wonderful Right Away* by Jeffrey Sweet (New York: Limelight, 1986). First published 1978 by Avon Books.

[3] Ibid.

[4] "The Aardvark Interview," *The Aardvark* 1, no. 4 (Fall 1962).

[5] Ibid.

[6] Quoted in *Something Wonderful Right Away*.

[7] "The Aardvark Interview."

[8] Quoted in *Something Wonderful Right Away*.

[9] Ibid.

[10] Ibid.

[11] Ibid.

[12] Ibid.

[13] "The Aardvark Interview."

[14] Ibid.

Plus interviews, correspondence, and conversations with Barbara Harris, Richard Schaal, Paul Sills, Alan Myerson, Bernard Sahlins, Mina Kolb, Sheldon Patinkin, Dennis Cunningham, and Larry Hankin.

Chapter 7

[1] United Press International, untitled article, October 3, 1962.

[2] Interview by Lenny Kleinfeld, *Chicago*, March 1987.

[3] Quoted in *Something Wonderful Right Away* by Jeffrey Sweet (New York: Limelight, 1986). First published 1978 by Avon Books.

[4] Avery Schreiber, "The Last Shot," *PerformInk* 11, no. 31 (March 12, 1999).

[5] Ibid.

[6] Quoted in *Something Wonderful Right Away*.

[7] Unpublished notebooks and writings.

[8] Ibid.

[9] Interview by Kleinfeld.

[10] Del Close and John Ostrander (writers), and Donald Simpson (artist), "Sewer Rat," *Wasteland* #1 (December 1987).

[11] Quoted in Del Close profile, *Chicago Tribune*, November 4, 1973.

[12] Quoted in *Something Wonderful Right Away*.

[13] Sheldon Patinkin, *The Second City* (Naperville, Ill: Sourcebooks, 2000).

[14] Quoted in *Something Wonderful Right Away*.

Plus interviews, correspondence, and conversations with Mina Kolb, Richard Schaal, Dennis Cunningham, Sheldon Patinkin, Mike Nichols, and Bernard Sahlins.

Chapter 8

[1] Interview by Lenny Kleinfeld, *Chicago*, March 1987.

[2] Ibid.

[3] Ibid.

[4] Ibid.

[5] Quoted in "Friends and Co-conspirators Recall the Crazed Life of an Improv Olympian" by Jack Helbig, *The Reader*, March 12, 1999.

[6] Interview by Kleinfeld

Plus interviews with Hugh Romney and Garry Goodrow.

Chapter 9

[1] Quoted in *Something Wonderful Right Away* by Jeffrey Sweet (New York: Limelight, 1986). First published 1978 by Avon Books.

[2] Interview by Lenny Kleinfeld, *Chicago*, March 1987.

[3] Quoted in "Friends and Co-conspirators Recall the Crazed Life of an Improv Olympian" by Jack Helbig, *The Reader*, March 12, 1999.

[4] Hammond Guthrie, *Aseverwas: Memoirs of a Beat Survivor* (London: SAF, 2002).

[5] Del Close and John Ostrander (writers), and William Messner-Loebs, "Subtext Salad," *Wasteland* #9 (August 1988).

[6] Del Close, interview by Kleinfeld.

Plus interviews, correspondence, and conversations with Alan Myerson, Peter Bonerz, Carl Gottlieb, Larry Hankin, Garry Goodrow, Dan Barrows (aka Beans Morocco), Howard Hesseman, and Hammond Guthrie.

Chapter 10

[1] Quoted in "Friends and Co-conspirators Recall the Crazed Life of an Improv Olympian" by Jack Helbig, *The Reader*, March 12, 1999.

[2] Howard Hesseman to the author, March 3, 1999.

[3] Interview by Lenny Kleinfeld, *Chicago*, March 1987.

[4] Ibid.

Plus interviews, correspondence, and conversations with Carl Gottlieb, Alan Myerson, Ed Greenberg, Garry Goodrow, Peter Bonerz, Janet Coleman, Dan Barrows, and Gary Austin.

Chapter 11

[1] Quoted in *Something Wonderful Right Away* by Jeffrey Sweet (New York: Limelight, 1986). First published 1978 by Avon Books.

[2] Interview by Lenny Kleinfeld, *Chicago*, March 1987.

[3] Ibid.

[4] Ibid.

[5] Quoted in Del Close profile, *Chicago Tribune*, November 4, 1973.

[6] Interview by Kleinfeld.

[7] Quoted in "Curse of the Blob" by Kim "Howard" Johnson, *Starlog*, September 1988.

[8] Del Close and John Ostrander (writers), and Donald Simpson (artist), "The Eye, Like Some Strange Balloon . . ." *Wasteland* #8 (July 1988).

[9] Interview by Kleinfeld.

[10] Quoted in "Slice of Wry" by Ozzie St. George, *St. Paul Pioneer Press*, December 1, 1972.

Plus interviews, correspondence, and conversations with Paul Sills, Alan Myerson, Gerrit Graham, Cordis Heard, Jonathan Abarbanel, Paul Sand, Hugh Romney (aka Wavy Gravy), Roberta Maguire, and Joyce Sloane.

Chapter 12

[1] Quoted in *Something Wonderful Right Away* by Jeffrey Sweet (New York: Limelight, 1986). First published 1978 by Avon Books.

[2] Interview by Lenny Kleinfeld, *Chicago*, March 1987.

[3] Quoted in Del Close profile, *Chicago Tribune*, November 4, 1973.

[4] Quoted in "The Devil's Comic" by Eric Spitznagel, *Chicago*, September 2003.

Plus interviews, correspondence, and conversations with Bernard Sahlins, Roberta Maguire, Tino Insana, Joyce Sloane, and Jonathan Abarbanel.

Chapter 13

[1] Quoted in Del Close profile, *Chicago Tribune*, November 4, 1973.

Interviews, correspondence, and conversations with Tino Insana, Mina Kolb, Fred Kaz, Jamie Swise, Bernard Sahlins, Joyce Sloane, Barbara Harris, Michael Gellman, George Wendt, Larry Coven, Nate Herman, and Danny Breen.

Chapter 14

[1] Quoted in *Something Wonderful Right Away* by Jeffrey Sweet (New York: Limelight, 1986). First published 1978 by Avon Books.
[2] Ibid.
[3] Interview by Lenny Kleinfeld, *Chicago*, March 1987.
[4] Ibid.
[5] "Del's Demons," interview by Ted A. Donner, *The Reader*, March 12, 1999.

Plus interviews, correspondence, and conversations with Jamie Swise, Dennis Cunningham, Sheldon Patinkin, Jeffrey Sweet, Bernard Sahlins, Bernadette Birkett, Tim Kazurinsky, Donna Morine Fearing, Danny Breen, George Wendt, Jim Belushi, Larry Coven, and Charna Halpern.

Chapter 15

[1] Interview by Lenny Kleinfeld, *Chicago*, March 1987.
[2] Ibid.
[3] Ibid.
[4] Ibid.
[5] Bob Woodward, *Wired* (New York: Simon and Shuster, 1984).
[6] Interview by Kleinfeld.

Plus interviews, correspondence, and conversations with Sheldon Patinkin, Jim Belushi, Larry Coven, Jamie Swise, Danny Breen, Gregory Mosher, John Ostrander, George Wendt, and Meagan Fay.

Chapter 16

[1] Interview (unpublished) by Bob Odenkirk, February 1983.
[2] Ibid.
[3] Interview by Lenny Kleinfeld, *Chicago*, March 1987.
[4] Ibid.
[5] Doug Hill and Jeff Weingrad, *Saturday Night: A Backstage History of* Saturday Night Live (New York: Vintage, 1987).
[6] Interview by Odenkirk.
[7] Ibid.
[8] Ibid.
[9] Ibid.
[10] Interview by Kleinfeld.
[11] Interview by Odenkirk.
[12] Interview by Kleinfeld.
[13] Interview by Odenkirk.
[14] Ibid.

[15] Ibid.

[16] Del Close, interview by Kleinfeld.

[17] Ibid.

[18] "The Legend of Del Close," written and produced by Will Clinger, *Wild Chronicles*, WTTW-TV Chicago, April 2, 2000.

[19] Interview by Odenkirk.

[20] Interview by Kleinfeld.

[21] Del Close, interview by Odenkirk.

[22] Ibid.

[23] Ibid.

Plus interviews, correspondence, and conversations with Larry Coven, Jamie Swise, Joel Murray, Nate Herman, Tim Kazurinsky, Joyce Sloane, Jim Belushi, Gregory Mosher, Richard Laible, Jonathan Abarbanel, Charna Halpern, Bernard Sahlins, Roberta Maguire, Danny Breen, Ed Greenberg, and Meagan Fay.

Chapter 17

[1] Interview (unpublished) by Bob Odenkirk, February 1983.

[2] Interview by Lenny Kleinfeld, *Chicago*, March 1987.

[3] Ibid.

[4] Quoted in "Slowdown Takes Improv One Step Beyond" by David Prescott, *Chicago Tribune*, September 28, 1984.

[5] Ibid.

Plus interviews, correspondence, and conversations with Bob Odenkirk, Larry Coven, Charna Halpern, Gregory Mosher, Jim Belushi, Mike Gold, and Jeffrey Sweet.

Chapter 18

[1] Unpublished notebooks and writings.

[2] Linda Winer, "Self-Obsession Carried to Its Logical Absurdity," *Chicago Tribune*, March 8, 1980.

[3] Interview by Lenny Kleinfeld, *Chicago*, March 1987.

[4] Ibid.

[5] Ibid.

[6] Ibid.

Plus interviews, correspondence, and conversations with Jim Belushi, Gregory Mosher, Charna Halpern, and Jeffrey Sweet. *The Steve King Show* was broadcast on WIND-AM, Chicago, on June 6, 1984.

NOTE: Charna Halpern originally provided several of the stories in this and subsequent chapters as we were collaborating on a Del Close screenplay; they have since seen publication in her *Art by Committee* (Colorado Springs: Meriwether, 2006), but are included here as well.

Chapter 19

[1] Quoted in "In His Own Words" by Ted A. Donner, *The Reader*, March 12, 1999.
[2] Interview by Lenny Kleinfeld, *Chicago*, March 1987.

Plus interviews, correspondence, and conversations with Joel Murray, David Pasquesi, William Russell, Charna Halpern, and Steve Burrows.

Chapter 20

[1] Quoted in "Focus on Del Close" by Peter B. Gillis, *Focus* 1, no. 1 (Summer 1987).
[2] Ibid.
[3] Ibid.
[4] Gene Siskel, Siskel's Flicks Picks, *Chicago Tribune*, September 25, 1987.
[5] Roger Ebert, "'Big Town' Hits the Mark," *Chicago Sun-Times*, September 25, 1987.
[6] Lawrence Bommer, "Honor Finnegan Versus the Brain of the Galaxy," *The Reader*, June 18, 1987.

Plus interviews, correspondence, and conversations with Mike Gold, John Ostrander, Richard Laible, and Charna Halpern.

Chapter 21

[1] Quoted in "Curse of the Blob" by Kim "Howard" Johnson, *Starlog*, September 1988.
[2] Ibid.
[3] Unpublished notebooks and writings.
[4] Del Close and John Ostrander (writers), and Rick Magyar (artist), "Crocophagia, or Hamlet in Aegypt," *Wasteland* #15 (Holiday 1988).

Plus interviews, correspondence, and conversations with Gregory Mosher, Mike Gold, Charna Halpern, Chris Farley, Joel Murray, and David Pasquesi.

Chapter 22

[1] Quoted in "Playing the Adventurous Improv Tune" by Rick Kogan, *Chicago Tribune*, June 10, 1990.

Plus interviews, correspondence, and conversations with Charna Halpern, Noah Gregoropoulos, Fred Kaz, Ed Greenberg, Miles Stroth, Ian Roberts, Matt Besser, Peter Gwinn, Danny Breen, David Pasquesi, Richard Laible, Jeffrey Sweet, Howard Hesseman, and John Ostrander. *Moondog's Pop Culture Radio Network* was broadcast on WCBR-FM, Arlington Heights–Chicago, on December 11, 1993.

Chapter 23

Interviews, correspondence, and conversations with Ian Roberts, Matt Besser, Noah Gregoropoulos, Charna Halpern, Miles Stroth, Peter Gwinn, Kelly Leonard, Jamie Swise, David Pasquesi, Janet Goldman, Jeffrey Sweet, Mick Napier, Gary Austin, Roberta Maguire, Randy Dixon, Max Allan Collins, Larry Coven, Janet Coleman, and Terry Jones.

Chapter 24

Interviews, correspondence, and conversations with Charna Halpern, David Pasquesi, Mick Napier, Barbara Harris, Jeffrey Sweet, Mina Kolb, Larry Coven, Ed Greenberg, Randy Dixon, Matt Besser, Joyce Sloane, Bernard Sahlins, Larry Hankin, and Miles Stroth.

Chapter 25

[1] From an Ozzie Mandias monologue written and performed by Del Close for *My Talk Show*, c1990.

[2] Tad Friend, "Skullduggery," *The New Yorker*, October 9, 2006.

[3] Quoted in "Improv Guru Del Close Dies at Age 64" from Associated Press and staff reports, *Manhattan Mercury*, March 11, 1999.

[4] Quoted in "Del Close: Improvisational Comedy Pioneer" by Elaine Woo, *Los Angeles Times*, March 7, 1999.

Plus interviews, correspondence, and conversations with Jeffrey Sweet, John Ostrander, Charna Halpern, Roberta Maguire, George Wendt, Matt Besser, Mick Napier, David Pasquesi, Tim Kazurinsky, Randy Dixon, Laurie Bradach, Robert K. Elder, Jon Favreau, Carl Gottlieb, Janet Coleman, and Noah Gregoropoulos.

Interviews

The following people were interviewed for this book, helping to reconstruct and clarify the sometimes tangled chronology of Del Close. Dates are for the major or initial interviews; in some cases earlier interviews were utilized. There are a mixture of in-person and telephone interviews and e-mail exchanges. Apologies to anyone who was inadvertently omitted. Other sources preferred not to be named. Del and I engaged in countless conversations through the years, and information that is otherwise not identified is often the result of those conversations.

Jonathan Abarbanel	December 5, 2005
Gary Austin	March 15, 2006
Dan Barrows (aka Beans Morocco)	September 16, 2006
James Bascom	November 8, 2005
Jim Belushi	February 20, 2006
Matt Besser	May 9, 2006
Bernadette Birkett	February 15, 2006
Peter Bonerz	June 13, 2006
Laurie Bradach	March 11, 1999
Danny Breen	March 15, 2006
Steve Burrows	November 20, 2006
Janet Coleman	April 2, 2006
Max Allan Collins	November 29, 2006
Larry Coven	January 28, 2006
Dennis Cunningham	August 10, 2006
David Dary	November 15, 2005
Randy Dixon	August 31, 2006
Robert K. Elder	August 23, 2006

Carl Englehorn	January 13, 2007
Chris Farley	June 26, 1992
Jon Favreau	August 9, 2006
Meagan Fay	February 5, 2006
Donna Morine Fearing	November 9, 2005
Theodore J. Flicker	March 14, 2006
Michael Gellman	February 11, 2007
Mike Gold	March 13, 2006
Jack Goldstein	November 28, 2005
Garry Goodrow	October 15, 2002
Bobbi Gordon	April 12, 2007
Carl Gottlieb	April 15, 2006
Gerrit Graham	September 16, 2006
Ed Greenberg	August 10 & 25, 2006
Noah Gregoropoulos	April 20, 2006
Hammond Guthrie	April 18, 2003
Peter Gwinn	May 23, 2006
Charna Halpern	November 21, 2005
Larry Hankin	February 8, 2003
Barbara Harris	August 29, 2006
Cordis Heard	September 26, 2006
Nate Herman	January 23, 2006
Howard Hesseman	March 5, 1994
Tino Insana	December 20, 2005
Bill Johnston	January 14, 2007
Terry Jones	July 6, 2006
Fred Kaz	February 3, 2006
Tim Kazurinsky	June 18, 1992
Mina Kolb	July 18, 2006
Richard Laible	March 15, 2006
Kelly Leonard	August 22, 2006
Roberta Maguire	July 10, 2006
Dave Moon	July 14, 2006
Gregory Mosher	March 1, 2006
Joel Murray	February 3 & March 21, 2006
Alan Myerson	February 8, 2003
Mick Napier	August 26, 2006
Dick Newton	May 28, 2005
Mike Nichols	March 7, 2007
Laurence Norvell	November 28, 2005
Bob Odenkirk	February 14, 2006
John Ostrander	January 24, 2006

David Pasquesi	March 29, 2006
Sheldon Patinkin	February 12, 2006
Ian Roberts	May 1, 2006
Hugh Romney (aka Wavy Gravy)	January 30, 2007
William Russell	March 14, 2006
Mitchell Ryan	March 29, 2006
Bernard Sahlins	April 7, 2006
Richard Schaal	March 16, 2006
Paul Sills	August 9 & 25, 2006
Joyce Sloane	April 2003
Tal Streeter	November 8, 2005
Miles Stroth	May 4, 2006
Jeffrey Sweet	January 23, 2006
Jamie Swise	November 28, 2005
Dean and Shirley Taylor	November 8, 2005
George Wendt	February 15, 2006
Ron Young	November 8, 2005

A few who have been valuable have chosen to remain anonymous, while additional thanks go to:

Chris Barnes
Mark Beltzman
Andrew Duncan
Peter Elbling
Tim Meadows
Rob Reiner
Paul Sand

Acknowledgments

Del once claimed that "junkies know that the way to beat death is to live as many lives as possible." Few people come close to leading as many lives as Del, and very few of them manage to do so for nearly sixty-five years. During that time he touched an astonishing array of people.

Mentioning the name of Del Close in most comedy circles is a bit like a password admitting one to a secret society. Shortly thereafter, stories are being thrown; names are dropped; outrageous behavior is detailed. A few will react with distaste, even anger. But for so many others, he remains a touchstone that unites performers and welcomes them into a fraternity. When researching this book, the message I got from dozens of strangers was "If you knew Del, you must be okay"—but we did not remain strangers for long, as most were eager to see me complete Del's biography. I owe thanks to everyone who was kind enough to speak with me, point me in the right direction, and give me support and encouragement for this daunting project.

First and foremost is Charna Halpern and everyone at the iO (I still have difficulty *not* calling it the ImprovOlympic). Charna turned over Del's scrapbooks, notebooks, and writings to me, and she could not have been more open and forthcoming. Thanks to her and everyone at the iO for keeping Del's dream alive and well.

Thanks also to Kelly Leonard, producer at Second City, for opening up the files at the storied theater and giving me carte blanche to rummage through the cupboards; to Joyce Sloane, who *is* Second City; to archivist Chris Pagnozzi; and to Andrew Alexander.

I first met Tal Streeter through Ian Roberts, and Tal generously served as my tour guide to Del's Manhattan, Kansas, hometown, even organizing a miniature class reunion of several of Del's schoolmates. David Dary has been perceptive, insightful, and encouraging, a constant e-mail presence helping me investigate Del's early years. Thanks also to James Bascom, Kaye Brown (daughter of the late Harold Loy), Carl Englehorn, Donna Morine Fearing, Jack Goldstein, Bill Johnston, Laurence Norvell, Dean and Shirley Taylor, and Ron and Margie Young; and to James and Bonnie Sherow for the delightful accommodations at their bed and breakfast in Manhattan.

And a special thank-you to everyone in Manhattan, Kansas, where I was invited to help accept the award for Del's induction into the Manhattan High School Wall of Fame on January 4, 2008; his fellow inductees included, appropriately, classmates Inger (Stensland) Stevens and Dean Taylor.

For filling in the gaps in Del's early adulthood, thanks to Dick Newton, Mitchell Ryan, Mike Nichols, Theodore J. Flicker, Dave Moon, and Bobbi Gordon.

For helping me patch some holes in Del's tenures at Second City, tremendous thanks to Jim Belushi, Bernadette Birkett, Danny Breen, Larry Coven, Dennis Cunningham, Andrew Duncan, Meagan Fay, Michael Gellman, Barbara Harris, Nate Herman, Tino Insana, Fred Kaz, Mina Kolb, Roberta Maguire, Michael McCarthy, Sheldon Patinkin, Bernie Sahlins, Paul Sand, Richard Schaal, Paul Sills, George Wendt, and especially Tim Kazurinsky, who is as funny as he is supportive—and he has been tremendously supportive.

One of the unexpected delights in writing Del's story has been delving into the history of the Committee, the legendary bastion of West Coast improvisation in the 1960s and early '70s, worthy of a book or three by itself. For taking me back to those days, I am grateful to Gary Austin, Dan Barrows (aka Beans Morocco), Peter Bonerz, Garry Goodrow, Carl Gottlieb, Ed Greenberg, Hammond Guthrie, Larry Hankin, Howard Hesseman, Rob Reiner, and their ringleader, the wise and generous Alan Myerson.

Thanks also to Jonathan Abarbanel, Gerrit Graham, and Cordis Heard for enlightening me with regard to some of Del's more shadowy years.

Another joy of revisiting Del's life was reliving portions of my own, particularly reconnecting with friends from the ImprovOlympic. I owe thanks to fellow Baron's Barracudas Chris Barnes, Mark Beltzman, Steve Burrows, John Judd, Joel Murray, David Pasquesi, and William Russell. It was likewise great to reconnect with other friends from the early days, including Richard Laible, Tim Meadows, Mick Napier, Bob Odenkirk, and Noah Gregoropoulos. My thanks to the Barracudas' successors, including the insightful Matt Besser, James Grace of the iO West, Peter Gwinn, Ian Roberts, and Miles Stroth, along with the late, great Chris Farley. Thanks also to the iO's Mike Balzer and Rachael Mason for the photographic assist, as well as Alex Sidtis of the Upright Citizens Brigade Theatre.

Thanks to Robert K. Elder of the *Chicago Tribune* and the multi-talented Jon Favreau, formerly of the iO, for helping untangle the story of the skull.

I am also indebted to the other scholars and historians of Chicago's improvisational scene—Janet (*The Compass*) Coleman, Sheldon (*The Second City*) Patinkin, and Jeffrey (*Something Wonderful Right Away*) Sweet—for their generosity in sharing their insight and knowledge, and for giving me permission to quote from their works.

Thanks to Meredith Vieira and the staff of *Who Wants to Be a Millionaire*. Without them (and a bit of luck), I would not have been able to subsidize much of the writing of this book—in fact, it might not have existed without them.

And my thanks to all of those others whose lives were touched by Del, and who were generous in their memories and observations, including Max Allan Collins, Randy Dixon, Brian Doyle-Murray, Gregory Mosher, John Ostrander, Hugh Romney (aka Wavy Gravy—an American original), Jamie Swise, my old pal Terry Jones, and Mike Gold, who, in introducing me to Del, is equally culpable for this volume. Thanks as well to Amber Hilgenkamp, Tanya Palmer, and Steve Scott of the Goodman Theatre, and to Joe Quesada, Thomas King, Bob Wayne, Paul Levitz, David Lloyd (for service above and beyond), and everyone at the Chicago History Museum.

The process of writing this book even allowed me to take care of some of Del's unfinished business, including mailing seventeen-year-old letters to John Brent's son, Jeremy, and to Roger Ebert.

Thanks to everyone at Chicago Review Press for the support and encouragement, particularly Devon Freeny, Jerome Pohlen, and Mary Kravenas.

I have met so many new friends and renewed so many old friendships that to single them all out would almost ensure that I forget some, so at this point I will take the expedient way out and issue a blanket thank-you—but not before I thank everyone here on the home front, including my clever and talented wife, Laurie Bradach, who encouraged me as I confronted the daunting prospect of writing this book, my son, Morgan Johnson, who eased up on his demands when necessary, my mother, Margie Johnson, who was there when we needed her, and Comet and Astro.

When I decided to attempt to write the definitive biography of Del Close, I knew it would be challenging. Any measure of success I achieve is due to those who shared memories, opened hearts, and even, in a few cases, vented spleens.

Appendix:
Works of Del Close

FILM, TELEVISION, AND AUDIO PERFORMANCES

Much of Del's earlier work remains lost or undocumented, and while the Second City cast performed on a variety of TV shows, both local and national, during its early years, the records for most of those appearances have vanished as well. As a result, this must remain only a partial listing.

Raid on Beatnik Village, date unknown. Del apparently played a featured role in this dramatic special for television, one of several programs in which he appeared during the days of live TV.

Svengali (title uncertain), date unknown. A poster from what may have been Del's first movie hung in Del's apartment in San Francisco—it featured him as Svengali. The title of the black-and-white film itself was apparently *Svengali* as well; it was likely a low-budget effort that has since been lost.

Diver Dan (title uncertain), c1960. Children's record spun off from the television series. Del reported to friends that he sang a song called "I'm the Toughest Creature in the Sea" as "a fish with a Bela Lugosi accent," filling in for the voice actor who normally portrayed Baron Barracuda.

The Do It Yourself Psychoanalysis Kit, 1960. Written (with some uncredited assistance from Elaine May) and performed by Del, this remains his only solo comedy album.

How to Speak Hip, **1961.** Written, riffed, and improvised with John Brent, Del's second album was a parody of recordings that promised to teach the listener a foreign language with minimal effort. Accompanied by an illustrated instruction manual, along with a "Dictionary of Hip."

The Tonight Show, **week of June 11, 1962.** With Mort Sahl guest-hosting, Del and Bill Alton performed a sketch featuring General Clevis.

Tale of Two Cities, **December 26, 1963.** WLS-TV in Chicago broadcast an hour-long special that chronicled the Second City–Establishment swap of the previous year, following the Establishment players around Chicago and the Second City troupe in London.

Get Smart, **1965.** In this NBC sitcom, Don Adams starred as hapless secret agent Maxwell Smart. Del was featured in the December 11, 1965, episode, "Aboard the Orient Express," an Agatha Christie spoof in which Smart must deliver a briefcase containing the payroll for agents in Eastern Europe.

Goldstein, **1965.** Black-and-white experimental film, shot cinema verité style on location in Chicago. It starred Lou Gilbert and Ellen Madison, with Second City–ites Del, Severn Darden, and Anthony Holland in supporting roles, and also featured Nelson Algren as himself. Written and directed by Philip Kaufman and Benjamin Manaster.

My Mother the Car, **1965–66.** The NBC sitcom starred Jerry Van Dyke as a man whose deceased mother (voiced by Ann Southern) is reincarnated as a 1928 Porter; Avery Schreiber played an evil car collector called Captain Manzini. Del was featured in three episodes: "For Whom the Horn Honks" (December 7, 1965) as Dr. Kadigan, "Many Happy No-Returns" (December 21, 1965) as Cheskin, and "You Can't Get There from Here" (February 1, 1966) as Camp Counselor.

The Double Life of Henry Phyfe, **1966.** The ABC comedy starred Red Buttons as a humble accountant enlisted as a government spy. Del appeared on one episode of the short-lived series, which ran from January 13 to September 1, 1966.

Gold (aka *Jacktail*), **1968.** An "underground" film shot in northern California; there is no evidence that it was ever released theatrically. The low-budget film was apparently reedited in 1989, copyrighted by R. Levis and Flagship Enterprises. Del's character is apparently called Hawk, and Garry Goodrow is Jinks. No writer or director is listed, though Bill Desloge and Bob Lewis are credited as "organizers."

A Session with the Committee (aka *Outrageously Anti-Everything*), **1969.** Del's involvement with this Committee film is unclear; although he was a member of the company and helped develop the material, he apparently does not appear on screen. The cast includes Peter Bonerz, Barbara Bosson, Garry Goodrow, Carl Gottlieb, Howard Hesseman (credited as "Don Sturdy"), Jessica Myerson, J. Christopher Ross, and Melvin Stewart; direction is by Del Jack.

Multiple Choice, **1971.** A low-budget independent film shot in summer 1971 in Chicago, featuring Del and Judy Harris, directed by Don Klugman. An April 2, 1972, *Chicago Sun-Times* article by Gary Houston noted that Del had recently played the lead in a film in which "sometime after editing, the filmmaker's wife, another Second City alumnus, and his production manager ran off with the only available print of the film." The timing of the incident suggests that *Multiple Choice* may be that film.

THX-1138, **1971.** Some filmographies list Del as one of the cast members in the first theatrical feature by an up-and-coming director named George Lucas. It is difficult to confirm Del's participation. He did not speak of this film to friends, which makes it seem unlikely that he was involved. However, Committee contemporaries like Ruth Silveira, Scott Beach, and Bruce Mackey are credited as "announcers"; they supplied voices for the film. If Del was involved, it was likely in the same way, providing a brief, uncredited voiceover.

Son of Blob (aka *Son of the Blob; Beware! The Blob; Beware of the Blob;* **and** *Here Comes the Blob),* **1972.** This ultra low budget film, directed by Larry Hagman under a pseudonym, was cowritten by Jack Woods and Anthony Harris; the cast includes Godfrey Cambridge, Shelley Berman, Burgess Meredith, and Hagman. Del is a tramp who is eaten by the Blob.

American Graffiti, **1973.** Del appears as "Guy at Bar," observing Charles Martin Smith's Terry the Toad vomiting in the gutter. Del may have known Lucas from *THX-1138,* or he may simply have been recommended for the role by his Committee contemporaries. Lucas also cast other Committee members at this early point in his career, here using John Brent ("Car Salesman"), Scott Beach ("Mr. Gordon"), and Ed Greenberg ("Kip Pullman").

Second City, **August 18, 1974.** Local special, 9:30–11:00 P.M. on WBBM-TV Chicago, with Roger Ebert, Bill Kurtis, Walter Jacobson, William Friedkin, and the Second City company. As Second City director during this period, Del undoubtedly helped develop material, though his specific involvement in the TV show is unclear.

A Labor of Love, **c1976.** This X-rated documentary chronicled the making of an explicit film about would-be surrogate parents; Del appeared as a leather-clad male prostitute. Codirected by Robert Flaxman and Daniel Goldman.

The producers eliminated the X-rated footage and released it as an R-rated drama called *Whose Child Am I?*

The Last Affair (aka *Wife, Husband & Friend*), 1976. Little is known about this film, or whether it is connected with *A Labor of Love*. Written and directed by Henri Charr, with a cast including Jack Wallace, Ron Dean, Betty Thomas, William J. Norris, and Del.

Thief, 1981. James Caan stars as a safecracker who agrees to do a job for the mob; Jim Belushi costars. Del appears as "Mechanic #1."

Saturday Night Live, 1981–82. Del was hired as the NBC series' acting coach/ "house metaphysician" during these years, but he apparently did not appear on camera.

First Steps, 1985. TV movie starring Judd Hirsch and Kim Darby. Del appeared as a zoologist in a scene with Hirsch.

No Laughing Matter, March 16, 1985. A one-hour special on teenage alcoholism that aired on WMAQ-TV Chicago, with interview segments and sketches featuring Del, Charna Halpern, Tim Kazurinsky, Lili Taylor, Larry Coven, and Rob Bundy.

One More Saturday Night (aka *Date Night*), 1986. For this film written by Al Franken and Tom Davis, Del played a cranky man. He is not listed in final credits, and it is unclear whether he remains in the final version of the film.

Ferris Bueller's Day Off, 1986. Written and directed by John Hughes, starring Matthew Broderick and Jeffrey Jones. Del appears in a small role as "the world's most boring high school English teacher," as Del described his character, who releases Mia Sara from class when he is wrongly informed that her grandmother has died.

Light of Day, 1986. Directed by Paul Schrader, starring Michael J. Fox and Joan Jett as siblings in a rock band; Del appears in a small role as Dr. Natterson.

The Big Town, 1987. Directed by Ben Bolt, starring Matt Dillon, Diane Lane, Tommy Lee Jones, Bruce Dern, and Tom Skerritt, with Del as Bible-thumping gambler Deacon Daniels.

The Untouchables, 1987. Directed by Brian De Palma, starring Kevin Costner, Andy Garcia, Charles Martin Smith, and Sean Connery; Del appears as Alderman O'Shay.

Sable, 1987. This ABC adventure series starred Lewis Van Bergen as a children's book author and mercenary; Rene Russo costarred. The episode "Serial Killer," which first aired November 28, 1987, featured Del as Middlebury.

The Blob, 1988. Directed by Chuck Russell, starring Kevin Dillon and Shawnee Smith, with Del as Rev. Meeker.

Dream Breakers (aka *In Evil's Grasp*), 1989. TV movie starring Robert Loggia, Hal Linden, and Kyle MacLachlan, with Del as Dr. Stone.

Fat Man and Little Boy, 1989. Starring John Cusack, featuring Del as Dr. Kenneth Whiteside; his part was cut from the final release and appears only in one long shot.

Next of Kin, 1989. Starring Patrick Swayze, featuring Del as Frank.

Opportunity Knocks, 1990. Starring Dana Carvey, featuring Del as Carvey's obnoxious boss, Williamson.

My Talk Show, 1990–91. The syndicated series was presented five days a week and ran for sixty-five episodes beginning in September 1990. It starred Cynthia Stevenson as Jennifer Bass, a Wisconsin housewife who hosts her own talk show from her home. Del made several appearances (mostly separately recorded) to deliver self-penned monologues/rants as neighbor Ozzie Mandias, who jams her broadcast signal.

A League of Their Own, 1992. Directed by Penny Marshall, starring Tom Hanks and Madonna. Del's lines were all cut, and he is only visible in one scene, a meeting with Walter Harvey (played by Garry Marshall).

The Public Eye, 1992. Starring Joe Pesci, featuring Del as H. R. Rineman.

The Untouchables, 1993. The syndicated series was inspired by the success of the De Palma film; it ran from January 1993 through May 1994. Featuring Tom Amandes as Eliot Ness and William Forsythe as Al Capone; Del appeared in one episode as Col. Robert McCormick, legendary publisher of the *Chicago Tribune*.

Henry: Portrait of a Serial Killer, Part 2, 1995. This sequel to *Henry: Portrait of a Serial Killer* was directed by Chuck Parello and starred Neil Giuntoli in the title role. It was filmed in autumn 1995 but apparently never released in theaters. Del had a small role; his character would have been pivotal to a third *Henry*, which was never filmed.

Mommy 2: Mommy's Day, 1997. Directed by Max Allan Collins and featuring Patty McCormack, Mickey Spillane, and Larry Coven, with Del in a small role as the warden.

Upright Citizens Brigade, 1998. Created by and starring Matt Besser, Amy Poehler, Ian Roberts, and Matt Walsh, the Comedy Central series premiered August 19, 1998. Del was asked by his former students to serve as the voice-over announcer.

THEATRICAL PERFORMANCES

Amateur Productions

Cuckoos on the Hearth, Manhattan High School, Manhattan, Kansas, December 2 & 3, 1949. All-school production with Del as Rev. Clarence Underhill.

The Red Velvet Goat and *Gammer Gurton's Needle*, University of Denver Seventh Summer Drama Festival, Studio Theatre, University Park Campus, July 20, 1950. A pair of one-acts with Del in a small role as a villager in the former, and billed fourth as Diccon in the latter (Aneta Corsaut was billed fifth).

Richard III, School of the Theatre of the University of Denver, Little Theatre, July 27 & 28, 1950. College production with Del as the Page, a messenger, and a soldier to Richard.

The Great Big Doorstep, Manhattan High School, Manhattan, Kansas, October 6 & 7, 1950. Junior class play with Del as the Commodore.

The Red Velvet Goat, Manhattan High School, Manhattan, Kansas, January 26, 1951. Language club production presented at a school assembly; Del produced, starred, and directed the cast of eighteen.

Macbeth, Kansas State Players, Kansas State University, February 16 & 17, 1951. Directed by Earl G. Hoover. Del played Young Siward and doubled as a murderer; it marked the first time a high school student had ever been cast by the Kansas State Players.

Balcony Scene, Manhattan High School, District Speech and Drama Festival at Clay County Community High School, March 16, 1951. In this one-act play, Del was top-billed as "Man" (Inger Stensland/Stevens played "Girl" opposite him).

Trial by Jury, Kansas State Players, Kansas State University, spring 1951. Del played a jury member in this Gilbert and Sullivan musical.

The Silver Whistle, Kansas State Players, Kansas State University, July 22, 1951. Directed by Earl G. Hoover; Del played Mr. Beach. The production was scheduled to open on Friday, July 20, 1951, but the Great Kaw River

Flood thwarted those plans. A rehearsal production was staged on July 17 for flood evacuees and other residents, and the show itself was presented on the afternoon of July 22. A 9 P.M. flood curfew necessitated the matinee performance.

Professional Productions

After leaving high school, Del apparently performed in various unrecorded college and summer stock productions before joining the Barter Theatre of Virginia.

***Dial M for Murder, Sabrina Fair,* and *Julius Caesar,* Barter Theatre, Abingdon, Virginia; 1954–56.** Del performed assorted roles, including Brutus, first at the theater in Abingdon and then on tour throughout the Southeast, with a company that included Severn Darden.

***Nine by Six,* Barter Theatre, Abingdon, Virginia, summer 1956–January 1957.** Del played assorted roles in nine pieces that constituted the "history of theater," including scenes from a Restoration comedy and *Julius Caesar,* and a commedia dell'arte piece that required improvisation. The other scenes in the piece included material from the ancient Greeks, an early American play, Chekov, Strindberg, and Arthur Miller. The show opened during the summer at the Abingdon theater, then toured the Southeast. The cast of six included Mitchell Ryan, Jerry Hardin, Richard McKenzie, Marcie Hubert, Annette Hunt, and Del, who left the Barter after their January 1957 performances in New York City.

The St. Louis Compass Players, Crystal Ballroom, St. Louis, April 2, 1957–late 1957. Directed by Theodore J. Flicker and featuring Del, Flicker, Mary Jo Henderson, and Nancy Ponder. Henderson would leave, and Elaine May, Mike Nichols, and Severn Darden would join. Exact closing date is unrecorded.

***The Nervous Set,* Crystal Palace, St. Louis, opened March 10, 1959; Henry Miller's Theatre on Broadway, opened May 12, 1959.** Del played Yogi, a character based on Jack Kerouac. The cast also included Richard Hayes, Tani Seitz, Larry Hagman, Gerald Hiken, Thomas Aldredge, and nine supporting players; directed by Theodore J. Flicker. The Broadway run closed after twenty-one performances.

***New Directions,* Crystal Palace, St. Louis, c1960.** Del starred alongside producer Jay Landesman; exact dates are unknown.

***Lysergic A Go-Go,* AIAA Auditorium, Los Angeles, November 26, 1965.** According to the program, Del was "responsible for the visual effects, using a battery of transparency projectors, UV lamps, a Lissajous wave-pattern generator, and for the 'Retinal circus,' a linear polariscope and a plane inter-ferometer of his own design. He will turn up on stage from time to time as Dwight David Genuine, Azrad the Incombustible, and as himself." The cast also included Hugh "Wavy Gravy" Romney.

The Acid Test, **Valley Unitarian Church, Los Angeles, February 6, 1966.** Fea-tured poetry by Neal Cassady, monologues by Hugh Romney, and a light show by Del.

The Committee, San Francisco and Los Angeles, 1966–69. Del joined in spring 1966 at the original theater at 622 Broadway in San Francisco, and departed in 1969. His role fluctuated, but he primarily served as a director and conducted workshops. During his tenure, the group opened a second theater in San Francisco to present plays, and also performed regularly at the Tiffany Theatre on Sunset Boulevard in Los Angeles. Del was primarily based in San Francisco, but often visited the L.A. company to hold workshops and help direct. Among the Committee's many talents over the years were Carol Androsky, Gary Austin, Scott Beach, Peter Bonerz, John Brent, Everett Cor-nell, Jim Cranna, Nancy Fish, Garry Goodrow, Carl Gottlieb, Ed Greenberg, Larry Hankin, Howard Hesseman, Kathryn Ish, Beans Morocco, Alan Myer-son, Jessica Myerson, Julie Payne, Rob Reiner, Hugh Romney, Chris Ross, Dick Schaal, Avery Schreiber, Ruth Silveira, Dick Stahl, Morgan Upton, and many more.

Freak Out, **Shrine Exhibition Hall, Los Angeles, September 17, 1966.** A hap-pening featuring the Mothers of Invention, the Factory, and the Count Five. Although his participation is unconfirmed, Del apparently furnished a light show.

Double Trip Show, **American Legion Hall (2035 N. Highland), Los Angeles, February 10, 1967.** A "dance-light show and panel on LSD," with the light show by "Del Close the Mad Doctor," according to an advertisement in the *L.A. Free Press*. According to the ad, the show would also feature "Frenz and the New Generation," and the panel discussion on LSD would include Alan Watts.

Story Theatre, Body Politic Theatre, Chicago, opened April 15, 1970; Mark Taper Forum, Los Angeles, December 1970. Del was featured in the Chi-cago run of *The Parson in the Cupboard*, the third Story Theatre production directed by Paul Sills (after *Ovid's Metamorphoses* and *The Master Thief*). The cast was predominantly from Northwestern University, and included Charles Bartlett, Cordis Heard (then Cordis Fejer), Caroline Jones, James Keach (who was replaced by Gerrit Graham), Molly McKasson, Bernadine Redeaux, and Tom Towles. The play opened on Broadway the following fall—but Del and the rest of the original cast were not involved. They were included in a holiday workshop production of Story Theatre that ran briefly in Los Angeles.

The Chicago Extension, Body Politic Theatre, Chicago, summer & fall 1970. Directed by Del, these improvisational performances included Jonathan Abarbanel, Dan Ziskie, Brian Hickey, Bill Noble, Linda Wesley, Jamie Levin, Keith Schwartz, and William McKinney.

The Interstellar Follies (aka *The Voyage of the Light-Ship Mariner*), **Dudley Riggs's Brave New Workshop, Minneapolis, November 1972.** Directed by Del, based on improvisations by the cast, with five actors playing eight roles.

The Night They Shot Harry Lindsey with a 155 MM Howitzer and Blamed It on the Zebras, **Body Politic Theatre, Chicago, opened October 18, 1973.** Directed by Del, written by Dick Cusack, and featuring Byrne Piven, Richard Kurtzman, Mike Nussbaum, Mina Kolb, and David Mamet.

The Play of St. George, **travelling production, Chicago, December 20–31, 1975.** This adaptation of a fifteenth-century English mummers' play opened at a benefit for Mount Sinai Hospital and toured Chicago taverns, including the Ole Town Ale House, the Earl of Old Town, and Somebody Else's Troubles. It featured Del as Father Christmas, Norman Mark as St. George, and Larry Coven as the Doctor.

A Christmas Carol, **Goodman Theatre, Chicago, winter 1978/79–1984/85.** The annual holiday production featured Del as the Ghost of Christmas Present.

Bal (formerly *Baal in the 21st Century*), **Goodman Theatre, Chicago, opened March 1980.** Richard Nelson's adaptation of the Brecht play *Baal*. Directed by Gregory Mosher; featuring Jim Belushi, and Del as Duzack.

Three Brains, No Waiting, **the Post-Rational Players, Crosscurrents, Chicago, 1983.** Revue starring Del, Larry Coven, and Warren Leming.

Hotline, **Goodman Theatre, Chicago, June 3–July 7, 1983.** Written by Elaine May, directed by Art Wolff, and featuring Peter Falk and Del, *Hotline* was part of an evening of three one-acts, along with David Mamet's *Disappearance of the Jews* and Shel Silverstein's *Gorilla* (which featured Del in the small of role a guard).

The Time of Your Life, **Remains Theatre Ensemble, Goodman Theatre, Chicago, opened March 12, 1984.** Written by William Saroyan, directed by Donald Moffet, and featuring William L. Petersen, Amy Morton, Dennis Farina, and Del as Kit Carson.

Hamlet, **Wisdom Bridge, Chicago, opened January 31, 1985.** Directed by Robert Falls; featuring Aidan Quinn as Hamlet and Del as Polonius.

You Can't Take It with You, **Steppenwolf Theatre, Chicago, November 1, 1985–January 31, 1986.** Frank Galati directed the Kaufman and Hart comedy; featuring Jeff Perry, John Mahoney, Amy Morton, Randall Arney, Laurie Metcalf, and Del as Mr. Kirby.

The Tempest, **Goodman Theatre, Chicago, April 17–May 29, 1987.** Directed by Robert Falls; Del played Stephano.

Ron Giovanni, **Lincoln Center, New York, rehearsed November–December 1987.** Written by Tony Hendra and directed by Del, the play was scheduled to open January 1988 but was closed during rehearsals.

Pal Joey, **Goodman Theatre, Chicago, June 3–August 7, 1988.** The Rodgers and Hart musical was directed by Robert Falls; choreography by Ann Reinking, featuring Kevin Anderson in the title role and Del as Ludlow Lowell. The production ran for two months.

The Misanthrope, **La Jolla Playhouse, San Diego, August 15–September 24, 1989; Goodman Theatre, Chicago, September 29–November 4, 1989.** Adapted from Molière by Neil Bartlett and directed by Robert Falls; featuring Del and Kim Cattrall.

Chicago Conspiracy Trial, **Remains Theatre, Chicago, September 22–November 3, 1991.** Adapted by Ron Sossi and Frank Condon from court transcripts of the Chicago Eight (later seven) trial, featuring Bruce Jarchow, David Pasquesi, and Del as David Dellinger.

Harvey, **Steppenwolf Theatre, Chicago, November 1, 1990–February 28, 1991.** Directed by Austin Pendleton, featuring Randall Arney, Sally Murphy, Rondi Reed, and Del.

Del and Dave in Rehearsal for the Apocalypse, **Remains Theatre, Chicago, 1992.** A late-night short-run (ten performances in five weeks) show consisting of prepared monologues by Del and David Pasquesi.

Ghost in the Machine, **Steppenwolf Theatre, Chicago, April 15–May 5, 1993.** Directed by Jim True-Frost, featuring Randall Arney, Martha Lavey, and Del.

Picasso at the Lapin Agile, **Steppenwolf Studio Theatre, Chicago, opened October 23, 1993.** Written by Steve Martin, directed by Randall Arney, and featuring Tracy Letts, Shannon Cochran, Jim Ortlieb, Philip E. Johnson, and Del as Sagot.

The Merchant of Venice, Goodman Theatre, Chicago, September 30–November 5, 1994. Directed by Peter Sellars and featuring Philip Seymour Hoffman, Paul Butler, Elaine Tse, and Del as the Duke of Venice and Old Gobbo. The Chicago production later toured Europe for five weeks, making stops in France and Germany.

All's Well That Ends Well, Goodman Theatre, Chicago, September 22–November 4, 1995. Directed by Mary Zimmerman; Del played Lafeu.

All the Rage, Goodman Theatre, Chicago, May 2–June 7, 1997. Written by Keith Reddin and directed by Michael Maggio, with Del as Norton.

AT SECOND CITY

The Explainers, Playwrights at Second City, opened May 9, 1961. Written by Jules Feiffer, based on his cartoons, directed by Paul Sills; music written by Allaudin (Bill) Mathieu and played by Fred Kaz. The cast included John Brent, Bob (Hamilton) Camp, Paddi Edwards, Tom Erhart, Joan Everett, Charles Lawson, Joan Zell, and Del. (Presented at a newly opened theater next door to Second City at 1846 N. Wells Street.)

Big Deal: An Opera for Politicians, Playwrights at Second City, opened summer 1961. Exact dates unknown. Jazz musical with a scenario by David Shepherd, based on *The Beggar's Opera* and *The Threepenny Opera*, directed by Paul Sills, music written by Allaudin (Bill) Mathieu and played by Fred Kaz. The cast featured Alan Arkin as Macheath, and included Delores Alton, Ann Raim, Dick Schaal, Avery Schreiber, and Del.

Alarums & Excursions, Second City, Chicago, opened October 31, 1961. Revue directed by Alan Myerson, featuring Bill Alton, Bob (Hamilton) Camp, Anthony Holland, Joan Rivers, Avery Schreiber, and Del.

A Knocking Within, Second City, Chicago, opened February 6, 1962. Revue directed by Alan Myerson, featuring Bill Alton, Mina Kolb, Dick Schaal, Avery Schreiber, and Del.

My Friend Art Is Dead, Second City, Chicago, opened June 12, 1962. Revue directed by Paul Sills, featuring Bill Alton, Dennis Cunningham, Severn Darden, Mina Kolb, Dick Schaal, Avery Schreiber, and Del.

The London Show, Establishment Club, London, England, opened October 2, 1962; Second City, Chicago, December 4, 1962. Revue directed by Paul Sills, featuring Bill Alton, Mina Kolb, Dick Schaal, Avery Schreiber, and Del.

To the Water Tower, Second City, Chicago, opened February 1963. Revue directed by Paul Sills, featuring Jack Burns, Dennis Cunningham, Macintyre Dixon, Judy Harris, Richard Libertini, Dick Schaal, and Del.

20,000 Frozen Grenadiers or There's Been a Terrible Accident at the Factory, Second City, Chicago, opened June 1963. Revue directed by Paul Sills and Del; featuring Jack Burns, Dennis Cunningham, Ann Elder, Sally Hart, Dick Schaal, Avery Schreiber, Omar Shapli, and Del.

13 Minotaurs or Slouching Toward Bethlehem, Second City, Chicago, opened September 1963. Revue directed by Sheldon Patinkin with Paul Sills; featuring John Brent, Jack Burns, Ann Elder, Sally Hart, Dick Schaal, Avery Schreiber, Omar Shapli, and Del.

New York City Is Missing, Second City, Chicago, opened January 1964. While Second City records show Del in the cast, and he helped develop material for the show, he was fired during previews and replaced by David Steinberg.

Picasso's Moustache, Second City, Chicago, opened January 7, 1971. Revue directed by Bernie Sahlins; featuring David Blum, Brian Doyle-Murray, Jim Fisher, Joe Flaherty, Roberta Maguire, Judy Morgan, and Dan Ziskie. "Hamlet" scene directed by Del.

43rd Parallel or McCabre & Mrs. Miller, Second City, Chicago, opened March 1972. Revue directed by Del; featuring John Belushi, Jim Fisher, Judy Morgan, Joe Flaherty, Eugenie Ross-Leming, and Harold Ramis.

Phase 46 or Watergate Tomorrow, Comedy Tonight, Second City, Chicago, opened August 15, 1973. Revue directed by Del; featuring John Candy, Tino Insana, Bill Murray, David Rasche, Ann Ryerson, Jim Staahl, and Betty Thomas.

Et Tu Kohoutek or Take 47, Second City, Chicago, opened January 31, 1974. Revue directed by Del Close; featuring John Candy, Cassandra Danz, Tino Insana, Bill Murray, David Rasche, Ann Ryerson, Jim Staahl, and Betty Thomas.

The First 100 Years or So Far, So Good, Second City, Chicago, opened October 10, 1974. Revue directed by Del; featuring Don DePollo, Michael Gellman, Deborah Harmon, Mert Rich, Doug Steckler, and Betty Thomas.

For a Good Time Call DELaware 7-3992, Second City, Chicago, opened February 6, 1975. Revue directed by Del Close; featuring Don DePollo, Michael Gellman, Deborah Harmon, Mert Rich, Doug Steckler, and Betty Thomas.

Once More with Fooling, Second City, Chicago, opened August 7, 1975. Revue directed by Del Close; featuring Don DePollo, Miriam Flynn, Michael Gellman, Mert Rich, Ann Ryerson, and George Wendt.

East of Edens, Second City, Chicago, opened the week of February 22, 1976. Revue directed by Bernie Sahlins; featuring Eric Boardman, Don DePollo, Miriam Flynn, Steven Kampmann, Ann Ryerson, Jim Sherman, and George Wendt. Del's involvement is unclear. The revue's run was interrupted by an exchange program with the Canadian Second City company, which presented a show called *Foreign Exchange* from April 15 to May 2, after which *Edens* resumed its run on May 4.

North by North Wells, Second City, Chicago, opened July 29, 1976. Revue directed by Del; featuring Will Aldis, Eric Boardman, Don DePollo, Miriam Flynn, Steven Kampmann, and Shelley Long.

Wellsapoppin', Second City, Chicago, opened February 17, 1977. Revue directed by Del; featuring Will Aldis, Eric Boardman, Don DePollo, Miriam Flynn, Steven Kampmann, and Shelley Long.

Upstage, Downstage, Second City, Chicago, opened July 27, 1977. Revue directed by Del; featuring Will Aldis, Eric Boardman, Larry Coven, Miriam Flynn, Steven Kampmann, and Shelley Long.

Sexual Perversity Among the Buffalo, Second City, Chicago, opened February 22, 1978. Revue directed by Bernie Sahlins; featuring Will Aldis, Jim Belushi, Larry Coven, Don DePollo, Nate Herman (replaced by Tim Kazurinsky), Audrey Neenan, and Maria Ricossa. Del's involvement is unclear.

Another Fine Pickle, Second City, Chicago, opened October 5, 1978. Revue directed by Del; featuring Will Aldis, Larry Coven, Don DePollo, Tim Kazurinsky, Audrey Neenan, Maria Ricossa, and George Wendt.

Freud Slipped Here, Second City, Chicago, opened April 17, 1979. Revue directed by Del; featuring Danny Breen, Larry Coven, Bruce Jarchow, Tim Kazurinsky, Nancy McCabe-Kelly, Audrey Neenan, and George Wendt.

I Remember Dada or Won't You Come Home, Saul Bellow? Second City, Chicago, opened November 29, 1979. Revue directed by Del and Bernie Sahlins; featuring Danny Breen, Mary Gross, Bruce Jarchow, Tim Kazurinsky, Nancy McCabe-Kelly, and George Wendt.

Well, I'm Off to the 30 Years War or Swing Your Partner to the Right, Second City, Chicago, opened October 8, 1980. Revue directed by Del; featuring Jim Belushi, Danny Breen, Meagan Fay, Mary Gross, Bruce Jarchow, Lance Kinsey, and Rob Riley.

Miro, Miro on the Wall, **Second City, Chicago, opened June 25, 1981.** Revue directed by Del; featuring Jim Belushi, Danny Breen, Susan Bugg, Meagan Fay, John Kapelos, Lance Kinsey, and Rick Thomas.

Glenna Loved It or If You Knew Sushi, **Second City, Chicago, opened February 4, 1982.** Revue directed by Bernie Sahlins; featuring Danny Breen, Meagan Fay, John Kapelos, Lance Kinsey, Nonie Newton, and Rick Thomas. Del's involvement is unclear.

Exit Pursued by a Bear, **Second City, Chicago, opened October 28, 1982.** Revue directed by Bernie Sahlins; featuring Danny Breen, Meagan Fay, John Kapelos, Lance Kinsey, Nonie Newton-Breen, and Rick Thomas. Del's involvement is unclear.

The Gods Must Be Lazy, **Second City, Chicago, opened March 8, 1989.** Revue directed by Del; featuring Chris Farley, Joe Liss, Tim Meadows, Joel Murray, David Pasquesi, Judy Scott, and Holly Wortell.

AT THE IMPROVOLYMPIC (iO)

The ImprovOlympic Presents Harold, **Crosscurrents Cabaret, Chicago, October 1, 1984–December 1984.** Directed by Del.

Honor Finnegan vs. the Brain of the Galaxy, **Crosscurrents Cabaret, Chicago, February–July 1987.** Story and direction by Del; featuring the Baron's Barracudas.

Three Mad Rituals, Dynamite Fun Nest, **and** *The Living Room,* **ImprovOlympic Theatre, Chicago, early–mid 1990s.** Directed by Del; featuring the Family.

Del continued to direct experimental, improvisationally based classes, groups, and shows for the ImprovOlympic (now iO) until his death in 1999.

COMIC BOOK STORIES

Munden's Bar

With John Ostrander, Del wrote a total of eleven Munden's Bar *stories for* Grimjack *and* Munden's Bar Annual, *both published by First Comics.*

"D.T.," *Grimjack* **#3 (October 1984).** Art by Steve Bissette.

"A Quiet Night at the Bar," *Grimjack* **#4 (November 1984).** Art by Hilary Barta.

"**Closing Time,**" *Grimjack* #8 (**March 1985**). Art by Rick Burchett.

"**Dopplegangster,**" *Grimjack* #10 (**May 1985**). Art by Jerry Ordway; credits Del with the "concept" and Ostrander with the actual script.

"**The Clog,**" *Grimjack* #17 (**December 1985**). Art by Barry Crain (who was so inspired that he joined Del's classes at Crosscurrents).

"**Mother's Calling,**" *Grimjack* #22 (**May 1986**). Art by Brian Bolland.

"**Puppy Love in Papua,**" *Grimjack* #25 (**August 1986**). Art by Rick Taylor.

"**A Simple Run of Luck,**" *Grimjack* #28 (**November 1986**). Art by Hilary Barta.

"**Laydeez and Germs**" *Grimjack* #35 (**June 1987**). Art by Jan Duursema; Del co-plotted, and Ostrander wrote the actual script.

"**Closed Set,**" *Grimjack* #42 (**January 1988**). Art by Larry Marder.

"**The Last Vampire,**" *Munden's Bar Annual* #1 (**1988**). Art by Joe Staton and Hilary Barta. *Munden's Bar Annual* #1 also included a reprint of "Mother's Calling."

Munden's Bar (**San Diego, Calif.: IDW Publishing, 2007**). A collection of twelve stories, including five cowritten by Del: "D.T.," "A Quiet Night at the Bar," "Closing Time," "Dopplegangster," and "Mother's Calling."

Wasteland

All Wasteland *stories were cowritten by Del and John Ostrander (unless otherwise noted), edited by Mike Gold, and published by DC Comics.*

"**Foo Goo,**" *Wasteland* #1 (**December 1987**). Art by David Lloyd; scripted by Ostrander from a story co-plotted with Del.

"**R. Ab.,**" *Wasteland* #1. Art by William Messner-Loebs.

"**Sewer Rat,**" *Wasteland* #1. Art by Donald Simpson; written by Del with assistance from Ostrander.

"**That's Entertainment,**" *Wasteland* #2 (**January 1988**). Art by William Messner-Loebs; written by Del with assistance from Ostrander.

"**Ghengis Sings,**" *Wasteland* #2. Art by George Freeman.

"**Warning Signals,**" *Wasteland* #2. Art by David Lloyd.

"American Squalor," *Wasteland* #3 (February 1988). Art by Donald Simpson; written largely by Del with minor assistance from Ostrander. A parody of Harvey Pekar's *American Splendor*, based on a 1961 monologue by Severn Darden and dedicated to the memory of Darden's father.

"Lotus Blossom," *Wasteland* #3. Art by George Freeman; concept by Del and Ostrander, scripted by Ostrander.

"A Safe Place," *Wasteland* #4 (March 1988). Art by William Messner-Loebs.

"Celebrity Rights," *Wasteland* #4. Art by Donald Simpson.

"This Time We Win!" *Wasteland* #5 (April 1988). Art by Donald Simpson.

"Under the Lash," *Wasteland* #5. Art by William Messner-Loebs.

"Big Crossover Issue," *Wasteland* #5. Art by David Lloyd.

"Method Actor," *Wasteland* #6 (May 1988). Art by David Lloyd.

"Paper Hero," *Wasteland* #6. Art by William Messner-Loebs.

"On the Road, Part 1, or . . . How We Changed the Price of Whiskey at the Butterfly Mine #2 in West Virginia," *Wasteland* #6. Art by George Freeman; autobiography by Del, adapted and scripted by Ostrander.

"On the Road, Conclusion, or . . . How We Changed the Price of Whiskey at the Butterfly Mine #2 in West Virginia," *Wasteland* #7, (June 1988). Art by George Freeman; autobiography by Del, adapted and scripted by Ostrander.

"Secret Lords of the DNA," *Wasteland* #7. Art by David Lloyd.

"The St. Louis Electric Giraffe Caper," *Wasteland* #7. Art by Donald Simpson; written by Del Close with assistance from Ostrander.

"The Eye, Like Some Strange Balloon . . ." *Wasteland* #8, (July 1988). Art by Donald Simpson; written by Del with assistance from Ostrander.

"Del & Elron," *Wasteland* #9 (August 1988). Art by David Lloyd; written by Del with assistance from Ostrander.

"Subtext Salad," *Wasteland* #9. Art by William Messner-Loebs.

"The Dreamer in the Darkness," *Wasteland* #10 (September 1988). Art by William Messner-Loebs; written by Del with "script continuity" by Ostrander.

"Life's Illusion" *Wasteland* #10. Art by David Lloyd.

"Revenge of the Swamp Creature," *Wasteland* #11 (October 1988). Art by Donald Simpson.

"Dissecting Mr. Fleming," *Wasteland* #11. Art by Ty Templeton.

"Tipped Toes," *Wasteland* #13 (December 1988). Art by Bill Wray.

"Message from the Star Worm," *Wasteland* #13. Art by Joe Orlando; written by Del with assistance from Ostrander.

"Metamorphfloozie," *Wasteland* #14 (Winter 1988). Art by Bill Wray.

"The Beast," *Wasteland* #14. Art by Michael Davis.

"Crocophagia, or Hamlet in Aegypt," *Wasteland* #15 (Holiday 1988). Art by Rick Magyar; written by Del with assistance from Ostrander.

"Zero Hour," Wasteland #15. Art by Joe Orlando.

"Mother's Withered Hands," Wasteland #15. Art by Donald Simpson.

"All I Want for Christmas Is the Head of Idi Amin," *Wasteland* #16 (February 1989). Art by Donald Simpson.

"The Enemy of Krishna," *Wasteland* #17 (April 1989). Art by Bill Wray; written by Del with "script continuity" by Ostrander.

"86," *Wasteland* #18 (May 1989). Art by Donald Simpson, Bill Wray, and William Messner-Loebs. A book-length tale that incorporated as many story elements from the previous seventeen issues as would fit. Those familiar with Del's work could identify it as, simply, a Harold.

Index